MISSIONARIES
AMONG MINERS,
MIGRANTS & BLACKFOOT

Mary Eggermont-Molenaar
& Paul Callens *Editors*

MISSIONARIES
AMONG MINERS,
MIGRANTS & BLACKFOOT

The Van Tighem Brothers' Diaries
Alberta, 1875–1917

UNIVERSITY OF
CALGARY
PRESS

University of Calgary Press | 2500 University Drive NW | Calgary, Alberta | Canada T2N 1N4
www.uofcpress.com

Library and Archives Canada Cataloguing in Publication

Van Tighem, Leonard, 1851-1917
    Missionaries among Miners, Migrants & Blackfoot: the Van Tighem Brothers' Diaries,
    Alberta, 1875-1917 / Mary Eggermont-Molenaar & Paul Callens, editors.

(Legacies shared 1498-2358; N° 24)
    Includes bibliographical references and index.
    ISBN 978-1-55238-189-2

1. Van Tighem, Leonard, 1851-1917 – Diaries. 2. Van Tighem, Victor, 1845-1940 – Diaries.
3. Frontier and pioneer life – Alberta. 4. Missions, Belgian – Alberta – History.
5. Northwest Territories – History – 1870-1905. 6. Alberta, District of (Alta.) – History.
7. Alberta – History – 1905-1945. 8. Oblates of Mary Immaculate – Missions – Alberta –
History. 9. Siksika Indians – Missions – Alberta – History. 10. Missionaries – Alberta –
Diaries. 11. Missionaries – Belgium – Flanders – Diaries. I. Eggermont-Molenaar, Mary,
1945– II. Callens, Paul, 1954– III. Van Tighem, Victor, 1845-1940 IV. Title. V. Series.

BV2813.A1V35 2007   971.23'020922   C2007-900605-1

The University of Calgary Press acknowledges the support of the *Alberta Foundation
for the Arts* for this published work. We acknowledge the financial support of the
Government of Canada through the *Book Publishing Industry Development Program (BPIDP)* for
our publishing activities. We acknowledge the financial support of the *Canada Council
for the Arts* for our publishing program.
    This book has been published with the help of a grant from the Alberta Historical
Resources Foundation.

Printed and bound in Canada by AGMV Marquis
♾ This book is printed on Silva Enviro paper

Cover design by Melina Cusano
Page design and typesetting by Colin McDonald

To THE COUNTLESS children who died around the turn of the 19th/20th century, among them:

...and to the one who counted so much to so many around the turn of the 20th/21st century:

Amber Star Cross Guns (Many Guns) (Otohkoikakatoosi) Yellow Star

Maria Josephina Van Tieghem

1881–1895
Meulebeke, West-Flanders, Belgium

1988–2005
Siksika Nation, West-Canada, Canada

Table of Contents

90	2004: Forms and shapes at Writing on Stone	Photo: Mary E.M.
90	2004: War deeds engraved at Writing on Stone	Photo: Mary E.M.
105	Nephew Joseph Van Tighem, Father Leonard and friend	Van Tighem Family Archives
112	Little Bear around 1912 on the Blackfeet Reservation, Montana.	Photo Fred Meyer. Sherburne Collection, Mansfield Library, University of Montana, Missoula, Montana
134	Father Leonard's drawing of the proposed box with plants	(drawing in text)
139	1910: Van Tighem Family Tree, drawn by Leonard	Van Tighem Family Archives, Calgary
144	1902: The Flood, Lethbridge	Van Tighem Family Archives, Calgary
144	1902: St. Patrick's Church	Van Tighem Family Archives, Calgary (photo glued in text)
147	Gilruth bells. "These bells came from Germany and were donated by the Gilruth Family. They were given the names of Margaret Theresa, Mary Anna and Hortense Catherine. When the old church was demolished, the bells were transferred to the present church" (The text is from a photo of these bells in the Pincher Creek Museum, 2004)	Photo Mary E.M.
149	2004: Frank Slide	Photo: Mary E.M.
165	Church in Coutts	Van Tighem Family Archives, Calgary (photo glued in text)
168	"Sept. 23, 1906. The Very Reverend Father A. Lavillardiere, O.M.I., Superior General: Nominated and Elected at Rome"	(photo glued in text)
172	2004: Wheat crop in southern Alberta; Sweetgrass Hills America in background	Photo: Mary E.M.
173	1908: St. Patrick's Church and House, Lethbridge	Van Tighem Family Archives, Calgary
173	2004: Father Leonard's house, now De Jourdan Photostudio, Lethbridge	Photo: Mary E.M.
184	2004: Lebel House, built in 1909	Photo: Mary E.M.
190	"Sacred Heart Church, Strathmore, and J. Van Tighem's Residence"	Van Tighem Family Archives, Calgary (photo glued in text)
191	2003: Strathmore Hotel, formerly known as the "Duff Block"	Photo: Mary E.M.

191	January 8, 1910: Ad in the Strathmore and Bow Valley Standard	
192	1910: First church in Strathmore under construction	Van Tighem Family Archives, Calgary
196	"Priest's House and St. Joseph's Church. Langdon, Alta, 1911"	Van Tighem Family Archives, Calgary
196	"In 1938 the old church at Langdon was purchased from the parish of Strathmore by Father Riou, dismantled and moved near a mine about ten miles southeast of Cluny. There it was renovated and on April 7, 1940, was dedicated to St. John the Baptist and opened free of debt, but on land belonging to the Reserve. At the end of the war the mine was worked only intermittently and people began to move away. In July, 1960, Father Poulin, O.M.I., moved the church to a small settlement about five miles south of Cluny, called 'Washington' by the Indians, placed it on a concrete foundation and renovated it again." (Venini Byrne 1973, 51.) Currently, 2005, the chapel at Little Washington is a Full Gospel church.	Photo: Mary E.M.
200	Father Leonard	Van Tighem Family Archives, Calgary
203	War stamps	(photo glued in text)
227	Obituary Father Leonardus Van Tighem	Van Tighem Family Archives, Calgary
236	Reverend Father Van Dale, 1/16–1781	Collection Paul Callens
241	c. 1930: "De Groote Kring:" Motherhouse Brothers Van Dale in Kortrijk (Van Hoonacker 1986, ph. 157)	Courtesy Dr. E. Van Hoonacker.
252	Cover of Victor's diary	Van Dale Congregation, photo Luc Neyt
252	Victor's Diary, page 1	Van Dale Congregation, photo Luc Neyt
256	Father Albert Naessens	Van Tighem Family Archives, Calgary
263	Catechism in Piednoir	Collection Paul Callens
268	2004: Beauvais Lake	Photo: Mary E.M.
268	2004: Lundbreck Falls	Photo: Mary E.M.
269	2004: Turtle Mountains	Photo: Mary E.M.
269	2004: Sulphur pond	Photo: Mary E.M.
269	2004: Brick bath above sulphur pond	Photo: Mary E.M.
279	Chief Crow Eagle	Van Tighem Family Archives, Calgary
285	"One Spot, Blood; Red Crow, Blood; Jean L'Heureux, interpreter; North Axe, Peigan. Mid-1880s"	Glenbow Archives, NA-2968-4

296	Dunbow or St. Joseph's Industrial School, De Winton	Missionary Oblates, Grandin Archives at the Provincial Archives of Alberta. No. A 4703
296	2003: Barns Dunbow School	Photo: Mary E.M.
296	2003: Barns Dunbow School	Photo: Mary E.M.
296	2003: Dunbow School Cemetery	Photo: Mary E.M.
297	2003: Indian offerings at original grave side, High River bank	Photo: Mary E.M.
297	2003: Indian offerings at original grave side, High River bank	Photo: Mary E.M.
297	2003: Remains of St. Paul's Church at Peigan Reserve	Photo: Mary E.M.
297	2003: 1/16th Replica of St. Paul's Church, Brocket, Peigan Reserve	Photo: Mary E.M.
310	Left: St. Jean Berchmans. Stained glass window in St. Joachim's church, Edmonton	Photo: Mary E.M.
314	Brother John Berchmans, Grey Nuns and Indian students	Van Tighem Family Archives, Calgary
315	Brother John Berchmans and Indian Students	Van Tighem Family Archives, Calgary
318	1913: "*Het kerkske dat ik geboudt hebt bij de wilde Sarcee genaamd*" (The little chapel that I built at the savages, called Sarcee)	Courtesy Maria Desseyn-de Witte, Meulebeke
318	"*Eenige van onze wilde katholieken, Sarcee genaamd*" (A few of our savage Catholics, called Sarcee)	Courtesy Maria Desseyn- de Witte
318	2005: Steeple of 1913 church at Sarcee (now Tsuu T'ina) Nation	Photo: Mary E.M.
320	1930: Victor/Brother Joannes Berchmans at the 50th wedding anniversary of his brother Jean and his wife Marie-Mathilde Linclau, Belgium	Van Tighem Family Archives, Calgary
320	1932: Brother Joannes Berchmans' 60th anniversary as Van Dale Brother	Van Tighem Family Archives, Calgary
320	Brother Joannes Berchmans	Van Tighem Family Archives, Calgary
322	c. 1870: Vivenkapelle (Goddeeris 2001, 85)	Courtesy John Goddeeris and Baron E. de Bethune

IN THE FALL of 2000, someone from Belgium sent a series of four books to the President of the Canadian Association for the Advancement of Netherlandic Studies, who was me at the time.[1] One of them, *Amerikaanse Zantingen (American Gleanings)*, contained references to literature regarding the Flemish-Belgian presence in the Americas. My attention was drawn to an entry on page 355. Translated from Dutch, it reads:[2]

> Vantieghem, Victor (1845–1940). *Short Description of My Journey and Adventures in America* (1886–1917).
> Vantieghem, Victor. *Letters to Brother Stanislas, St. Paul's Mission, Macleod, Piegon [sic] Reserve,* (December 12, 1894; May 6, 1896; August 25, 1896; June 4, 1899; March 22, 1904; June 16, 1907).

I asked the sender, Paul Callens, about Victor and the status of the Vantieghem diary. Callens replied that he is related to the Van Tighem family and that in 1996, a certain Brother Lucien had provided him with a copy of Victor's handwritten diary, suggesting that maybe he could do something with it. Since then he, Callens, had been gathering data with regard to Victor's family and diary. Victor had been a Brother who had left for Canada in 1886, where he had lived and worked for forty-three years at the Blackfoot/Peigan reserve in Southern Alberta.[3]

I found out that Victor had had a younger brother, Leonard, who had already left for Canada in 1874. Leonard had also left Belgium as a Brother. Once in Canada he had become an Oblate priest and served as such in the southern Albertan towns of Macleod, Lethbridge, Strathmore, Langdon, and Taber, where he died in 1917.[4] Leonard had also kept a diary, a so-called 'codex historicus,' or 'missionary diary,' that Oblate Fathers had to keep as per the rules and regulations of their congregation.

The Keeper of the Oblate Archives in Ottawa kindly provided me with a copy of Leonard's codex that he started during his temporary stay in Edmonton in 1909.[5] Already on page one Leonard mentions a codex that he had kept, in Lethbridge, from an earlier date.

While tracing Leonard's and Victor's whereabouts in Alberta, I ended up enjoying a pint of beer with a few friends in the Strathmore Hotel in Strathmore.[6] In 1909 Leonard had rented two rooms in this same building, at that time known as the Duff Block, a commercial building with shops on the first floor and rooms for rent on the second floor. Leonard had lived and done his own cooking in one room and used the other one as a chapel.

Paying for the beer I asked the waitress whether she was aware that the premises of the hotel had once been a House of God. She told me that she was unaware of that and informed me about a book, *Strathmore, the Village that Moved*, containing the history of the hotel.

This book also features stories about Strathmore's first inhabitants, among them the story of Joseph Van Tighem, the orphaned nephew who, adopted in 1893 by his uncle Leonard, married and fathered five children. Both Leonard and Victor's diaries mention this nephew.

Calgary's telephone directory helped me to get in touch with the "children." Thanks to the friendly cooperation of Eileen Van Tighem, the widow of Joseph's third child, I was referred to two other siblings, who, to my pleasant surprise, were the faithful keepers of the Van Tighem Family Archives. The Reverend F.P. Van Tighem and his sister Geraldine Van Tighem (1914–2004) provided me with a stack of letters (in Dutch) from Flemish family members to Leonard and Victor; from Victor (in Dutch) to Leonard and fellow Brothers in Belgium and in the 1930's (in English) to the widow of nephew Joseph; and from Bishop Grandin (in French) to Leonard and nephew Joseph.

The keepers of the Van Tighem Family Archives, Leonard C., Geraldine and the Reverend F.P. Van Tighem, granted permission to insert relevant letters, in English translation, between the entries of the diaries.[7] To top off the generous cooperation, nephew Joseph Leon's oldest child, ninety-one-year-old Leonard C. Van Tighem, living in Okotoks, handed me a copy of his grand-uncle's first, handwritten *codex historicus*.[8] Just as the first one, this was written in English as well.

Early on in this quest Callens and I had decided to cooperate. We thought that publication of the diaries, spiced with letters to and from Leonard and Victor and relevant articles from Oblate, Flemish, and Canadian journals retrieved from archives on both sides of the Atlantic Ocean, would provide an unusual blend of miner, migrant, and Blackfoot activities at the turn of the nineteenth century.[9] All of this was set against a background of occasional dramatic family and political affairs unfolding back in Belgium.

This volume, apart from the introductory chapters, comprises Leonard and Victor's diaries. Leonard's first codex deals with his work as a founder, builder, and pastor of a number of southern Albertan parishes, and the circumstances that caused him to adopt his eleven-year-old nephew Joseph in 1893. During the precious years of Joseph's growing pains, we see that Leonard did not find much time for keeping up his codex. Fortunately, this gap could be filled with letters by and about Joseph.

Leonard's second codex starts in 1909. It deals with his endeavours to establish a few more parishes and his dealings with another nephew Joseph, who in 1915 was blinded by a bullet in Belgium. This codex stops as abruptly as Leonard's life, which ended in 1917.

Victor's diary starts to describe his departure from Belgium in 1886 and his journey to his brother Father Leonard in Lethbridge. He follows up by depicting the time he served at the Peigan Reserve in southern Alberta until his 1912 transfer from the Peigan to the Blood reserve in Southern Alberta. From that time on, 1912, we only hear sparsely about and from him. However, that changes after his return in 1929 to his congregation in Belgium where he spent his remaining eleven years. Letters and other documentation provide an endearing impression of Victor's last blissful years.

Appendix A contains the Van Tighem family tree as far as is relevant to this manuscript. Appendix B is a travel account written by Jules Boone, Oblate Brother, once a fellow-villager of the Van Tighem brothers. Boone was with Leonard among the recruits who in 1874 sailed with Bishop Grandin to America and from there, with the bishop and others, went on by train, boats and on foot to St. Albert.

◎·➌ Acknowledgments

HEARTFELT THANKS TO all those who helped out and/or contributed to the preparation of this volume:

In Belgium

Van Dale Congregation Brothers: Lucien (André Iserbijt, 1921–2001), Walter (Georges Gheysens (1924–2006)), Rudolf (Noël Vannoorden), Donatiaan (Geert Naert) [Kortrijk]; Bart Vannieuwenhuyze, Luc Neyt, Lucien Ailliet, Fons Das [Tielt]; Maria Desseyn-De Witte [Meulebeke]; Hilde Vannieuwenhuyze [Pittem]; Henri and Fabienne Desseyn [Kanegem]; Norbert Follens [Sint-Eloois-Vijve]; Lieve Denijs [Roeselare]; Brother Alfons (van den Broucke), Abbey Sint Sixtus [Westvleteren].

In Canada

Jos Eggermont, Marjan Eggermont, Colin McDonald, Nicolas Jekill, Michiel Eggermont, Jenny Eggermont-Reasbeck and Marrit Eggermont, Penelope Waters, Harrie van den Elzen, Haijo and Monique Westra, Ad (1921–2006) en Netty Bezemer, Tuke Rops-Caminada (1932–2006), Glen Campbell, Eileen McParland-Van Tighem, the Reverend F.P. Van Tighem, Geraldine Van Tighem (1914–2004), Arnaud Morena, Marina Siponin, Harry Sanders, Rolande Parel, Jessie Sainsbury, Ayse Tuzlak, Charles Willemen [Calgary]; Douglas McHugh, [De Winton]; Sister Dolores Déry, M.O., Father Camille Piché, O.M.I., Diane Lamoureaux [Edmonton]; Valerie Douglas [Lethbridge]; Leonard C. Van Tighem [Okotoks]; Vera Crowshoe, Brother Leon Jansen, Morris Little Wolf, Reg Crowshoe [Peigan Nation, Alberta]; Anne Jonkers [Purple Springs]; Michiel Horn [Toronto]; Father André Dubois, O.M.I., Cornelius Jaenen [Ottawa]; Rudi Vanvaerenbergh [Waterloo]; Lavina Many Guns, Clyde Cross Guns, Irvine J. Scalplock [Siksika Nation, Alberta].

In the Netherlands

Hugo de Schepper [Nijmegen].

In the USA

Father Karel Denys, CICM [Arlington, Virginia].

In Germany

Andrej Kráľ, [Hamburg].

Heartfelt thanks as well to the staff of the following archives and museums:

Belgium

- Archives Bruges Diocese
- Archives Van Dale Congregation, Kortrijk
- Bibliotheek Vlaamse Vereniging voor Familiekunde (Library Flemish Association for Genealogy), Tielt,
- Municipal Library, Kortrijk
- Municipalities of Meulebeke and Kortrijk

In Canada

- Archives Deschâtelets, Ottawa, Ontario
- Glenbow Museum and Archives, Calgary
- Missionary Oblates, Grandin Archives (c.o. Provincial Archives), Edmonton
- Old Man River Cultural Centre, Brocket, Alberta
- Sir Alexander Galt Museum, Lethbridge, Alberta
- Taber Irrigation Impact Museum
- The Fort, Museum of the North West Mounted Police, Fort Macleod, Alberta
- Van Tighem Family Archives, Calgary, Alberta

In the USA

Catholic Diocese Archives: Helena, Montana

◻ Leonard's Codices • 1875 – 1917

West Flanders

Antwerp

Ghent

Belgium

Paris

The North Sea

The Netherlands

Blankenberge

Oostende

Moerkerke

Brugge

East Flanders

Ghent

Veurne

Torhout

Wingene

Koolskamp

Pittem

Tielt

Leisele

Ardooie

Dentergem

Roeselare

Meulebeke

Westrozebeke

Ingelmunster

Wakken

Ghent

Westvleteren

Oekene

Oostrozebeke

Passendale

Poperinge

Leper

Waregem

Kortrijk

Tiegem

Mesen

Bellegem

France

Paris

Henegouwen

France

Henegouwen

▸ *Map of West Flanders (c. 1874). (Ingelmunster*
– Torhout railway not shown.)
Courtesy Marjan Eggermont

BERNARD VAN TIGHEM (1807–1884) and Angela Kupers (1810–1873), parents of both Leonard and Victor, living in the small village of Meulebeke, north of Kortrijk, Belgium, could look back on a long line of ancestors all of whom had been *Buitenpoorters* of the city of Kortrijk in Meulebeke. The status of *buitenpoorter* – someone living outside the city gate in another town or village – was hereditary, or could be married into, or simply purchased for £3.[10] In the Van Tighem family tree, Jan Frans van Tyghem, Bernard's grandfather, born in 1740, is the last one mentioned being a *'burgher from outside the gates.'*

The 1839 marriage of Jan Frans' grandson, Bernard, with Angela Ghislena Kupers was blessed with nine children, one daughter and eight sons, only one of them stillborn. Two sons, Victor (1845–1940) and Leonard (1851–1917), and several of Bernard's and Angela's grandchildren, went on to live, not in another town, but in another country, on another continent.

For someone from Flanders, crossing the Atlantic Ocean, as Leonard did in 1874, was not entirely novel. At that time, brochures luring Belgium's seasonal labourers to Canada were handed out for free. Many of them did not need much convincing to leave the country and its continuing bad economic situation and prospects. For them, light in that economically dark era could only be imagined on the other side of the ocean.

For centuries, the southern part of the Low Countries had been at the crossroads of warring Spain, France, and Austria. From 1384 to 1555 it was part of the Burgundian Habsburg Netherlands; from 1555 to 1701, as the Spanish Netherlands, it belonged to the Spanish monarchy; from 1701 to 1795, as Austrian Netherlands, it was a part of the Austrian Hapsburg empire, from 1795 to 1815 a part of France. Then, in 1815 by the treaty of Vienna, it was united again with the northern part of the Low Countries as the Kingdom of the Netherlands. However, fifteen years later, after riots in Brussels and a few Wallonian cities, and under pressure of France and England, it was decided, during the 1830 London Conference, that the southern part would separate from the Kingdom of the Netherlands and be constituted as the independent Kingdom of Belgium. The bishops, having been largely appointed by Napoleon, wanted the southern part to be rejoined with France and exercised much pressure as the Catholic clergy in the South never liked having to serve under the authority of the Dutch, Protestant king. The liberal Catholics and the anti-clerical bourgeoisie instead wanted an administrative separation with autonomy in certain areas. Nevertheless, the independent kingdom of Belgium was instituted.

In several regards this was for many people a setback. For example, the Flemish/Dutch language was from then on repressed: French became the official language, and trade opportunities were lost with the Netherlands and her colonies (Smits 1983 I and II passim; Falter 2005, passim).

Four years later another blow was dealt to the new country, this time in the form of the 1836 treaty between Belgium and France that lowered the tariffs for flax imports into France, which was not intended to be a blow to Belgium, but turned out to be one (Musschoot 2002, 11). The treaty somehow caused the French market to be flooded with cheaper and better linen from England, where linen weaving was mechanized. In the Dutch/Flemish-speaking provinces, so-called Flanders, mechanization failed; by 1843 the export of Flemish linen decreased by fifty per cent. In 1844, twenty-four out of every hundred persons received social support with private charities chipping in. One year later the loss of employment was compounded by a loss of the wheat and rapeseed harvests. In 1846 Flanders experienced a severe potato famine. That did not just happen in Ireland, it happened in Flanders as well.

Moreover, in the mid-nineteenth century Flanders' countryside was plagued by failed harvests, and its inhabitants, the Flemish, by contagious diseases such as typhus and cholera. Imports of grain from the United States undermined Flemish agriculture even more: prices of agricultural products decreased while production costs did not (Van de Vijver 1977, 21). It can be rightly concluded, Musschoot argues, that the U.S. imports in Flanders caused the export of Flemish workers to America.

The situation in the Flemish cities was not much different. The famous Flemish author, Louis Paul Boon, dedicated his book, *Pieter Daens*, to the situation during the years 1840–1884 in the industrial town of Aalst. Women, men and children worked twelve to fourteen hours per day, their babies crawled around in the dirt and dust at the workplace, and accidents and mutilations due to lack of safety measures were commonplace. Wages were at an all-time low, food prices increased and families of nine occupied one room in dismal housing; typhus and cholera were endemic and alcoholism was on the rise.

Witte *et al.* (1993) sum it up: the profits from increased industrial productivity ended up in the hands of a very restricted group of capitalists. The number of labourers – isolated and shunned by mainstream society – had increased. People worked twelve to fourteen hours a day for a very minimal wage. Ideology had it that these people did not deserve any better, that their dire circumstances were caused by laziness and stupidity. The church saw the situation as God's will, and charity as an obligation of the better-off. Witte *et al.* argue that both the Catholic Church and the liberal Catholic governments served the interests of the higher classes despite the liberals favouring better education for all. Witte *et al.* go on to describe the emerging labour and freethinkers' movements and the influence of the first International Labour Association established in London in 1864. With all of this, Belgium was eager to let its hungry masses go, even resorted to sending abroad people from its vagrant camps. Around 1870 these camps in Belgium housed about twenty thousand "vagrants" (Musschoot 2002, 45, n. 8.).

Collaboration between labour associations and freethinkers decreased somewhat after the 1871 Parisian revolt, though it was the Freethinkers movement (see below) that kept the organizational structure on its feet. This was the situation when Leonard left Belgium in 1874.

Judging from Leonard's own description of his familial background, which he wrote in English in 1908, transcribed below, it seems that the Van Tighem family was not affected severely by the dire state of affairs in its immediate surroundings.

The Van Tighem Family."
Europa Belgium West-Vlaanderen

Although in the Church Register of Meulebeke our name is written Vantieghem, it should be written without –e–. This I was told by an old cousin: Judocus Van Tighem, of Ghent, who was well learned and surely correctly informed.

It is unknown to us how long the family Van Tighem were residents of Meulebeke because during the centuries of continual wars to which our beautiful provinces were exposed, all books, registers, and documents at home or in Church or in the Communal Buildings have been destroyed. There remains nobody and no documents to tell us the least. The oldest actual record we possess is from the Church Register. In the year 1740 was born at Meulebeke Joannes Franciscus Van Tighem, son of Joseph Van Tighem and Maria Joye.

The Family Van Tighem had a magnificent estate, situated on both sides of the entrance of the Old Ghent Street, now called the Denterghem road. In my time even: latter part of the XIX century, I never, anywhere have seen such wonderful ornamental trees, hedges worked artistically, summer houses, pillars etc., all in rare Spanish evergreens, and they were regularly trimmed and shorn with large clippers just before the great religious Processions took place, the evergreen cuttings serving to cover the street where the Blessed Sacrament was carried and the priests were passing.

Everywhere were found rare trees, shrubs, plants, and flowers. There was first the large orchard covered with immense fruit trees, where the House was situated. This house must have been of large proportions and high, as we could see the remains of old windows in the maçonry of the gables, which remained. Then there was the smaller flower garden just behind the house. It was here that the old ornamental monuments were mostly situated

I have heard my father say that he heard from his ancesters, that for a long time, some big Spanish officers were quartered there, and that our actual dining room was the office of one of them. No doubt that it was through them that all these rarities and Spanish Evergreens were imported.

Then there was what we called the Cows Passage (*Koeiweg*). Then a very large vegetable garden, all surrounded with fine hedge and occupying all the space between the road and the creek called Lapper Beke. Then there was a very large field of high land, called the Kouter, on the opposite side of the road, and extending to the great windmill of Loncke. Then there was a small field called *Her Klein Stukje* [Her Little Lot], and finally another larger one, called the Cat Bush.

I have been told often, by old people that it was well known to their parents, how the Music Band came several times a week to play and practice there; a clear proof of this was the piles of old music sheets on the attic of our house. There was also the well-known piece: Op Tighem's *hof* [At the Van Tighems' farm], which was a favourite to every one.

As I can judge from these traditions, the estate must have been at its best near the end of the XVIII century.

Helas! That this property has not been preserved to our family!!! But I have to record now, what I have seen and observed and witnessed myself. Our grandfather Damianus Van Tighem had four sons and two daughters. All the sons married, but the girls Rosalie and Mary said they would never take husbands and remain single. Clever and far thinking were these virgins; with tears in the eyes they cajoled all their brothers out of the patrimonial domain. Then one after the other, as they married, was coaxed out of the valuable Estate for the poor pittance of a few francs. As we never will marry, said they, the property, after our death, will return to you and to your children.

Did the virgins keep their word?? No! The good daughters broke their promise and, in their last Will and Testament and gave everything to two girls children of a first marriage of Ivo, their brother.

Strange!!! Both these girls became insane. Prudence, the youngest, died at age of about 24, I think in a charitable hospital. The other, Marie, a very good girl and rich, married in Ghent where she had lived with a rich cousin of ours: Judocus Van Tighem.

Helas, she married a clever architect without religion. When she detected that he was a Freemason, she became violently insane, for many, many years, she was kept in an asylum at Ghent; after twenty and more years, on a visit to Belgium, I saw her there, she knew me not. She knew not her own two children.

Our valuable estate was in the hands of lawyers for years. They got the best out of it. It was finaly sold at a public auction. It was 30 years after I left this home, that I returned there, scarcely anything ornamental was left there now, all had dissappered, all disappeared; potatoes, and cabbages, and cows and pigs were, so to say, the Lords of the place and its ornaments.

Father Leonard Van Tighem, O.M.I.
Lethbridge, Alta, Canada, 1908.[12]

Despite describing his parental home as a "valuable, magnificent estate," Leonard, who was sent to Mr. Vianne's boarding school, had to come back home and work in his father's carpenter shop due to the poverty of his parents. By then, in 1874, Mgr. Vital Grandin, Oblate Father, bishop of St. Albert, Canada, came to France, collecting donations and recruiting missionaries for his diocese in western Canada. When the bishop returned to his diocese that same year, Leonard (his fellow-villager and Brother, Jules Boone and his cousin Brother Henri Scheers) were among the bishop's recruits.[13]

Documents do not reveal exactly how the bishop came across the young Meulebeke carpenter and his cousin. One possible explanation is that one of Leonard's cousins, Henri Scheers, who since 1867 had studied and served in the Oblate novitiate in Nancy, might have mentioned his numerous young cousins back in Belgium, during Bishop Grandin's visit to Nancy (Variétés 1874, 132). Cousin Henri Scheers, however, is not the only connection to Leonard's birthplace, Meulebeke, and the Canadian bishop. There is also an older connection.

In 1847 a certain Florent Vandenberghe was seminarist in Bruges. In that same year the founder of the Oblate congregation, Father Eugène de Mazenod, preached at the Bruges seminary. This resulted in Vandenberghe going with de Mazenod to Marseille where he, Vandenberghe, in 1847 entered the French novitiate of Notre-Dame de l'Osier.[14] In 1852 the same Vandenberghe became novitiate master there. In December 1851 Vital Grandin started his novitiate in that same institute, so, Vandenberghe became Grandin's novitiate master. In order to recruit more seminarists, Vandenberghe went in 1856 to Belgium. There, in Meulebeke, his brother, Aloïs Vandenberghe, was from 1862 to 1872 sub-deacon (Meulebeke 1954, 101). From a letter by Victor (January 24, 1886) we learn that Aloïs played a role in the recruiting efforts of his brother Leonard, although in Victor's case, Father Aloïs apparently urged against Victor going anywhere because of his "good late mother." The Vandenberghe connection is also apparent from a line in an undated letter by bishop Grandin, "Father Vandenberghe pressed me to visit the Belgian colleges and seminaries." (Lepage 1954, 286, 294.)

As said before, on May 9, 1874, Henri Scheers, Leonard Van Tighem, Jules Boone and about fifteen other recruits left from Brest, France, and sailed with Bishop Grandin to New York from where they went to Montreal by train.[15] Leonard spent the winter of 1874 at Notre Dame des Anges, the novitiate of the Oblate Fathers in Lachine, Quebec. One year later, on September 5, Mgr. Grandin, noted in his diary: "Brothers Fafard and Van Tighem arrive at last." (Grandin 1989, 15.) Both brothers had walked from Winnipeg to St. Albert. In the company of a caravan of horse and wagons led by Métis and Indians, over a period of three months, they had covered a distance of about 1,360 uneasy, unpaved kilometres.

▶ *Map of Southern Alberta
(c. 1900).* Courtesy
Marjan Eggermont.

LEONARD'S NEW WORLD, the portion of the North-West Territories that in 1905 became the province of Alberta, had been changing rapidly since a Hudson's Bay surveyor, Peter Fidler, noted in his 1792/93 diary: "The Buffalo are still very numerous & the Indians running them on horseback & killed several. They are so plentiful that when the Indians run them they immediately fill up the place like waves in the Sea." (Eggermont-Molenaar Ed. 2000, 47.) Compare the bristling hunter/trader/horse-stealing society Fidler depicted with the 1871 report by Jean L'Heureux, which was only written four years before Leonard appeared on the Albertan scene. L'Heureux (more about him when we deal with Victor's diary), after having elaborated about the geography of the land of the *Chokitapi* [Blackfoot], wrote:[16]

The inhabitants of the country, which we have described in this report are the *Chokita-pix* Indians who are divided into three tribes, the *Sik-sik-kas* or Blackfoot, the *Kan-na-ans* or Bloods and the Piegans, who, with the Sarcees, have been formed into a Nation for almost eighty years. They have a total population of almost twelve hundred tipis and ten thousand souls. They could must[er] a force of four thousand horses, man warriors armed with lances, arrows, pistols and rifles of which the majority are needle guns or Springfield carbines.

Except for the Sarcees who speak the Montagnais dialect of the Beaver Indians, they all speak the same language with a slight change of pronunciation in each tribe. They have a sort of police among themselves which answers well enough to their social needs. The land is possessed in common by the whole nation with territorial divisions for each tribe. The only common obligation of each individual of the nation is to preserve his land from enemies and the encroachment of the invader. Each tribe is subdivided into a certain number of large families each of which have a chief at their head to supervise the police and to negotiate their differences. The chiefs alone have the right to treat together in the great council of the nation on questions of peace or war, treaties or other affairs concerning their common interest.

Their authority is admitted by all and their common decisions become law when once publicly proclaimed by them. The nation has never yet treated collectively with any government and the treaties obtained by American agents have never been sanctioned except by a small number of the Peigan tribe who have no authority from the council of the nation to do this.

Hunting buffalo on horseback constitutes their principal occupation in summer on the plains and in winter by means of Pis-kenou or parks in wooded places. Their principal articles of commerce are robes, dressed skins, animal furs, wood, fat, dried meat and horses. Unfortunately polygamy reigns among them, and it is common for a chief to have seven or eight wives. The punishment of the wife caught in the act with another man is death or mutilation of the nose or ears. The man also has to pay with his life or ransom it by paying in horses. Their religion is the worship of the sun and spirits. They believe in the immortality of the soul but also of animals. On the death of a rich man they kill his best horse. They have the idea that the spirits may be appeased by blood, and in a great emergency they cut off the first phalanges of their fingers and offer them as a sacrifice.

The Catholic missionaries who visit them have almost succeeded in abolishing these horrors. Mgr. Grandin, Roman Catholic Bishop of the Saskatchewan, is charged with the conversion of these Indians to Christianity. The Rev'd Father Imoda and Father Lacombe, missionaries, for ten years have devoted themselves to them and have succeeded in greatly subduing the ferocity of their primitive character. They have become attached to these Indians by their generous devotion. Father Lacombe was in the epidemic of scarlet fever, which killed fifteen hundred and Father Imoda in the terrible scourge of smallpox, which destroyed two thousand. For many years we have been companions in their apostolic labours, and the writer of these lines bears public witness to their courage.

For two years the efforts of the missionaries have been thwarted by the American whisky traders from the Missouri, in spit of the laws of their country and in direct violation of the recent laws of the Manitoba legislature, which they ignore. They have taken the precaution of arming their establishment at Hamilton ville on Belly River with cannon. In the two years that they have been established in this place, twelve thousand gallons of liquor were sold to Indians and twenty-four thousand robes representing a value of more than $150 000 have entered the Montana market instead of that of Manitoba! Without counting the more than six hundred ounces of strychnine distributed to the Indians, more than one hundred and twelve persons have perished in these orgies and horrors. Mothers forgot the maternal instinct under the influence of drunkenness and let their infants fall from their breast for starved dogs to devour under the dulled eyes of these unfortunates. I must give to the public the names of these champions of the demoralization of our Indians for the edification of all honest hearts. These are the firms of Baker and Co., Benton; A.T. & L., Benton; and Healy and Hamilton from Helena, with the multitude of their agents among our Indians.

It is with the hope that the government will certainly want to protect us that I write this report.

(Jean L'Heureux)

Or, compare Fidler's notes with the reports, articles and letters in *Missions des Oblates de Marie Immaculée* (further referred to as *Missions*) corroborating and explicating L'Heureux' observations. *Missions*' articles are written about and by Oblate Fathers who, blissfully unaware of Native spirituality, "with a child-like faith and a single-minded purpose of 'converting' the Heathen" (Venini Byrne 1973, 41) went along with Native hunting expeditions, catechizing children, instructing adults, often witnessing extreme misery due to alcohol and diseases, while enduring hunger, cold, thirst, vermin and heat themselves."

Describing warfare and a hunting party, Father Leduc commented in an 1870 letter, "Life for the savages was harder than that for the buffaloes."[18] One year later, he reported about fights between Cree and Blackfoot; about encountering destitute, hungry and exhausted Blackfoot being robbed of clothes, rifles and other necessities; about people coming back from failed hunting trips; about a woman suffering from the pest; about children dying from smallpox; about a camp decimated in a few days; about children who had to go to an orphanage (Leduc 1873, 194–206).

Fidler's proud hunters of the 1790's appear to have changed into the "poor savages" of the 1870's, who needed help, though they were expected to embrace the faith of their helpers to eventually sustain them, clergymen, in their earthly life, in exchange for the promise of a heavenly afterlife.

The Indians were instructed in the faith of the missionaries, had to trade in the observance of the Sun Dance for the observance of Sunday, and were educated in their schools, in the missionaries' language, first in French, later in English (though it must be said that the Oblate missionaries took many pains to study the Indian languages and compile dictionaries). All this took place amidst a display of as much pomp, bells, flags and banners as possible. Missionaries saw themselves as soldiers: as part of a – festive – army that had to enlarge Christ's kingdom.

All in all, most of these New World features such as diseases, alcoholism, pious pomp, and poverty might not have struck Leonard as something extraordinary. The Indian reserves, established in 1877, might even have reminded him of the vagrant camps back home. The lack of any western infrastructure must have meant for him quite a different story.

At the time of his arrival in St. Albert, a European material infrastructure, one of brick, wood and grown food had yet to be constructed. From Bishop Grandin's notes we learn that Leonard repaired a threshing machine, constructed an outdoor altar, sowed potatoes, and so on. On August 17, 1876, the bishop reported, "Father Blanchet and three other brothers had to pull a cow out of a slough; during this time an awful storm. Father Blanchet and Brother Van Tighem give up. Today Brother van Tighem starts to learn Latin." (Grandin 1989, 44.)[19]

Learning Latin was the start of Leonard's training for priesthood at the old Seminary of St. Albert, then the headquarters of the North-West Territories diocese. He continued to study theology at the Saint Albert Grand Seminary at Lac-la-Nonne and Fort Saskatchewan. In 1882 he started the scholasticate; on March 19, 1883, he was ordained a priest and destined to become pastor for the whites in Macleod (Riou 1902, 160).[20]

Maybe Leonard's assignment to serve the white community had to do with an event that he witnessed in 1879. The story is by Father Leduc (1880, 157–166) wherein he reports that in May 1879 Kakisikutchin, a poor savage of about twenty-five years old, was imprisoned at Fort Saskatchewan under suspicion of having killed and eaten his mother, brother, wife and his six children. His excuse was that his brother, his wife and three of his children had already died of starvation before he ate them. The story proved not to be entirely true and changed a few times: he had killed his wife before he ate her, but his son had died of starvation before he ate him and so on. It ended with Kakisikutchin being sentenced to die by hanging on December 20, 1879.

Before Kakisikutchin was hanged, Father Rémas visited him, instructing him in the faith and converted him. Father Leduc continues his horror story with a detailed description of the blessings of the newly found faith for the convict and then, "On the 20th, accompanied by the Reverend Father Mérer and the scholastic Brothers Dauphin and Van Tighem," Father Leduc went to the fort to assist in the necessary religious preparations for the hanging.[21] He told Kakisikutchin to repeat after him: "*Kije Manito Wekawimisk, ayamihestamawin anotch ka wi nipiyam, Mère de Dieu, prie [sic] pour moi maintenant que je vais mourir* [Mother of God, pray for me now I will die]." The Fathers and the scholastic brothers, Leonard among them, thereafter witnessed, at a temperature of minus 40 degrees, Kakisikutchin fall to his death when a chute of at least six feet was opened under his feet (Leduc 1880, 157–166).

It is just speculating, but perhaps this whole scene also killed any ambition Leonard might have felt to serve on an Indian reserve. Maybe he did not want to be eaten. Or perhaps the prospect of having to learn to pray in an Indian language (Algonquian: Cree or Blackfoot) scared him. Leduc (1888, 168) mentions that Father Lacombe, serving at the Blood Reserve, got two more helpers in 1882, the Fathers Legal and Van Tighem: "But neither the one, nor the other of the two Fathers still know a word of Blackfoot."

On the other hand, it was the bishop who handed out the assignments or 'obediences' that stipulated where people had to go and serve. And it was the bishop who had to adjust his policies to the new developments in his diocese. According to his biographer Jonquet, Bishop Grandin had dark premonitions about the coming of the railroad through his vicariate. It would bring bad doctrines, perfidious journals, firewater and what else?

He had been fighting savagery and now he also had to fight the "barbary of anti-Christianity." (Jonquet 1903, 323.)

Another biographer, Hermant (1948, 104), cites a letter from the bishop who noted:

> Most of the newcomers are Protestants or very lax Catholics and, as many of them surpass even pagans in immorality, I fear for the poor Indians. I have not sufficient Priests to cope with the situation, particularly as the Protestant ministers are now coming in great numbers.

Understanding that the tide of evil to be brought on by the railways was unstoppable, the bishop shifted his priorities. He was convinced that the Indians "had or were doomed to disappear" and still saw it as his duty to bring them to paradise. And though missions were not financially self-supporting, parishes were supposed to be so. Maybe the bishop deemed Leonard too good or not good enough to be the Indians' guide to paradise. Whatever it was, Leonard was destined to consolidate white souls rather than to increase the number of "red" souls in heaven. As such he was to become a pastor in a parish, rather than a missionary among the man-made *misérables*.[22]

LEONARD BEGAN HIS first codex in 1892 with an historical account of the area around Macleod, where he was sent as a pastor and also served as a teacher. In a flashback he describes how he witnessed from a distance the burial of an Indian child, the tears being shed by the bereft, lamenting mother, remarking that, at that very location to which he had wandered from Fort Macleod, the city of Lethbridge would emerge. Leonard provides his readers with a detailed description of the efforts to bring about a western infrastructure: transport, mining and the construction of wooden and later sandstone or brick buildings.[23] The descriptions of his own efforts in this regard, how he doggedly built a church, a house, a convent, a churchyard, and a school, form the backbone of his diary. By the time the infrastructure around him was more or less to his liking, Leonard tried to extend God's Kingdom and his field of activities by building more and more churches. For some reason he never had a Brother assigned to him, but Leonard managed to hire people – maybe that is why, because he constantly proved to be able to do it all on his own, Leonard worked so hard that in the end his superiors decided to call him back to Edmonton. This happened in 1909 after he served for twenty-five years in Lethbridge. One can safely say that Leonard settled with the settlers. In the notes we have summarized the (travelling) careers of nearly all Oblates mentioned in his two codices and in Victor's diary.

The careers of the many visiting Oblates differ blatantly from those of Leonard and Victor. Most Oblates travelled, year in year out, from post to post. *Coureurs des Missions!* Were they not happy at their postings? Was their flock not happy with them? What we know for sure is that Leonard was not at all happy with his 1909 transfer to Edmonton. Still, at the start of his second codex, Leonard admits that he had been killing himself, not so much by building more and more churches, as by distributing Holy Communions, hearing confessions, saying mass and having to deal with a flock of many nationalities that spoke many different languages. This second codex contains a few remarks about his time in Edmonton. Fortunately some letters emerged from the Van Tighem Family Archives, shedding more light on the Edmonton period; also on his enduring compassion for his fellow human beings.

Leonard's first codex often gives the impression that it is written by someone else, as he keeps referring to himself as Father Leonard. Maybe this use of the third person is due to what Choquette (1995, 231) argues: that the regulations of the Oblate seminary, written in 1829, modeled after those of the Sulpicians, tended "to put the priest on a pedestal, underlining his dignity as well as his responsibilities." At the same time, according to Choquette, the Oblates "made more allowance for human weakness, mercy, and kindness" than the traditional Gallican-Jansenist moral theology.

Perhaps the use of the third person (i.e., "Father") in Leonard's first codex may be seen as an attempt to stress his status and/or an attempt to keep the codex a bit impersonal – codices were to remain in the parish and were not to be taken along to whatever new post. When Leonard came to Canada his idea had been to help the bishop out for about ten years as a lay Brother. Still, comparing his codex with the *Missions* articles that often speak of hierarchy, titles, pomp, evil Protestants and poor savages, in general Leonard's writings don't seem to be much affected by the Oblate sense of dignity and self-righteousness. Leonard was also unaffected by the Flemish overzealous piety that we will see in the article about the Van Dale Brothers' expulsion (p. 239–241 this volume).

Leonard seemed to enjoy Protestant ministers attending his church. He hardly ever used derogatory terminology when referring to Protestants or to Indians. Leonard certainly enjoyed tending to the many Slovenians, Slovaks, Poles, Hungarians and Austrians who came to his church, and tried to accommodate them as much as he could with the particulars of their Greek or Roman rites. In that regard he set an exemplary example, even to our days, in accommodating people unfamiliar with their new country.

As for the above-mentioned Oblate "mercy," at least on paper, Leonard did not hesitate to mention the miners' strikes, which he supported. In the year 1896 he agonized about Indians, Big Bear's (in)famous son included, who after a long, unhappy sojourn in the United States were rounded up there and returned to Canada. In 1900 he was agitated about the performance of the Half-Breed Claims Commission and about the treatment of the Métis. In 1909 he took up the case of a black man in prison and by the time he died, in 1917, impoverished as he was, he was helping out a Belgian army chaplain.

In these regards Leonard comes across as a true, "kind," Oblate. Maybe we can attribute as well some influences from his home country. Witte *et al.* (1993) argue that, after the 1848 Parisian revolt, it was the Freemasons who kept up educational structures. The Freemasons were the ones who, in the years prior to Leonard's departure, had shown some sympathy for the causes of the underpaid masses and saw education as a means of lifting people out of poverty. We will see that in the early 1880's Leonard asked his brother Victor to send him a book about Freemasonry; Leonard was certainly open-minded. Apart from the way he expresses himself and the things he seems to care about, Leonard can be seen on the one hand making an Oblate allowance for mercy and kindness and on the other hand thinking as a liberal, free-thinking Catholic. At the same time, as we will see, this last part of his mindset might have influenced his attitude toward his six years older brother Victor, a much more a conservative Catholic and a teacher who did not seem to care much about education.

When his brother Victor arrived at his place in Macleod in 1886, Victor noted that Leonard no longer spoke his mother tongue. Six years later, when a Flemish-Dutch-speaking bishop visited him, Leonard was "happy to converse in that [Flemish] language together." Was speaking French with his brother Victor a way to throw up a barrier between them, to distance himself from him? After all, Victor had spent some time in jail, prior to his arrival in Canada. In 1886, the morning after Victor's arrival, Leonard took off, had to go somewhere. It took Leonard quite a while before he mentioned the presence of his brother Victor in his codex. Was Leonard embarrassed by Victor's presence? Did Victor tell him why he had been arrested and sent to jail back in Belgium? Only after quite some time Leonard mentioned Victor in his codex; favourably, as did all other Oblates who mentioned him in their *Missions* journal.

LEONARD'S SECOND CODEX, which he started in 1909, begins with a flashback as well. This time it dealt with his first twenty-five years of labour in the Lord's vineyard. He also recognizes the reason for his removal from his beloved Lethbridge parish: "I was killing myself."

This second codex differs much in tone from the first one. Leonard writes that he is told to keep a codex. He mentions that he will do so, noting that his first codex was left behind in Lethbridge. He then defiantly continues: "Here we go ... I am the son of ... I am ..." He no longer refers to himself as to "the Father." A sense of humour creeps in even more when he describes how honoured he was when he learned that he had to hear the confessions of the Edmonton nuns, how insulted he was when he learned that he had to visit the prisoners and how, in the end, he preferred to visit the prisoners, as the nuns had nothing to confess. Leonard, quickly bored in Edmonton, was subsequently transferred to Strathmore, where his nephew Joseph had become a successful banker and was about to marry and raise a family. Soon Leonard managed to find himself back in the business of building a church. But already in 1913, when Calgary became a secular diocese, he was replaced by a secular priest and transferred to Langdon where a failed harvest caused his parishioners to move on. Bishop Legal then transferred Leonard to Taber, where he spent the last few years of his life saddened, lonely, disappointed and cash-strapped.

He was saddened, because in distant Calgary, on diocesan/episcopal levels, a struggle was going on caused by the influx of more English-speaking, secular clergy taking over the parishes and the position of the Oblates. In a way he got involved (1915 letter to *The Lethbridge Herald*), but this involvement will not have helped his standing in the secular branches of the diocese of Calgary. Being Flemish was already not the same as being French, and was certainly not the same as being Irish, let alone English. Leonard was lonely, because he did not see many visitors any more and most probably disappointed because his attempt to get his poetry published had failed. He was cash-strapped, because in spite of the good harvests of his few Taber parishioners, the collections on Sundays did not amount to much. Leonard noted that he was kept alive by the charity of his Irish neighbours.

Strange as it may sound, after one of Leonard's nephews at the Belgian front, in 1915, was hit by a bullet and blinded, which will have saddened him as well, Leonard seems to have gained again some focus, some incentive to live, to give, to fight and to write and even to compose some bad poetry. We get the impression that his anger over the ongoing war in Belgium and his concern about his nephew's fate was perhaps fuelled by anxiety about his own and his congregation's precarious position. His 1916 attempt to join the forces fighting in the Great War failed. After three more months, in March 1917, his life ended abruptly through heart failure.

Both codices are written in English, which was not his first language. In this volume we have slightly edited his handwritten script: his spelling of names of places and persons such as "Medecin Hat," "McLeod," and "Mcferland" is standardized into correct spelling, as are some minor spelling mistakes. The names of Oblates standardized as spelled in Carrière (1976, 1977 and 1979). Leonard never succeeded in spelling the word "parishioners" right and in general misspelled prefixes, so often wrote "encrease" instead of "increase" and so on. His use of capitals is brought back to current standard; however, as words father and brother, mother and sister sometimes refer to biological, sometimes to religious persons, capitals are used throughout this volume when religious persons are referred to, also in the family letters. In his time, words such as "Slav," "Slovak" or "Slavonic" were spelled "Szclav" (Kirschbaum 1966, 24), "Slovac" or "Szclavonic"; we have standardized his different spellings of these terms. Most foreign words have been translated and placed between square brackets.

Leonard's syntax is left intact, as is his use of incorrect relative pronouns and prepositions. Punctuation is brought up to current standards. Leonard sometimes created his own English words; these idiosyncrasies are left as they are, as, we think, they add to the flavour of his description of the time and the place wherein he lived. In the letters, interspersed between the texts, names of places have been adjusted to modern spelling.

Abbreviations such as R.P. (Reverend Père) or R.F. (Reverend Father) are also left as they occurred. G.Z.J.C. is an abbreviation of the Dutch greeting: Geloofd Zij Jezus Christus (English: Praise the Lord).

If not indicated otherwise, translations from Flemish-Dutch and French are by Mary Eggermont-Molenaar. Paul Callens helped out greatly to explain the meaning of a number of Flemish expressions and Father Frank Van Tighem kindly helped to proofread the English translation of the family letters.

1▸ *Nicholas Sheran at mine entrance.*
P19640462000. Courtesy Sir
Alexander Galt Museum

2▸ *Nicholas Sheran.* P9738633000.
Courtesy Sir Alexander Galt Museum

Laudetur Jesus Christus
Maria Immaculata Amen

St. Joseph ⎱
St. Patrick ⎰ *Ora Pro Nobis*

Catholic Mission · St. Patrick's church · Lethbridge · Alberta · Canada

COAL BANKS WAS the name of the place where actually stands Lethbridge. This first name was derived, like that of many others in the North West Territories of Canada, from its geological and mineral situation. There was a seam of coal, underlying these immense prairies at the depth of about three hundred feet from its surface, but brought to view by a stream of water, which has its source in the Rocky Mountains. If nature's author had not himself uncovered this treasure of black diamonds, perhaps centuries would have passed before discovering these large coal fields. This stream, which becomes almost a torrent when in June the snow thaws in the mountains, is called the Belly River, or better Big Belly River, "Rivière des Gros Ventres."

Years ago a tribe of Indians, called the Big Bellies, inhabiting these regions had their name given to this river.[24] But, like most of the other streams, the Indians have its name changed before it has run its limpid waters a hundred miles east. After having received the waters of the Bow river, it is called Saskatchewan, which means: Strong or Swift Stream – *Kisiskatchewan*.

This is the south branch of the Saskatchewan and about three hundred miles north of this place the north-branch, taking also its source in the Rocky Mountains, runs eastward and both branches have their confluent not far from a place now called Prince Albert. The first man to handle the pick and shovel, and explore these rich coalfields was Nicholaus Sheran, an Irishman and a Catholic.[25] He came to these then wild regions in the year of our Lord 1870. He built himself a hut on the north side of the river, thus taking possession of the spot. His residence, ever since, has been called the Sheran Mine or the Sheran Estate. Nick Sheran lost his life by drowning in the Old Man River, about fourteen miles from Coal Banks, where he was lending a charitable hand to Colonel MacLeod and family to cross the river at Kipp.[26] His body was never recovered, to the great distress of his sister Mrs. MacFarland, who spared neither time nor money to give her brother a better grave than the wet and sandy bottom of the river.

In the year 1881 application was made to the Dominion Government for the lease of some mining locations in different parts of Alberta. Explorations were made in several localities by M.W. Stafford, sent by Sir A.T. Galt, who with some other gentlemen formed a company.[27] Coal was taken out at Blackfoot Crossing and at Medicine Hat.[28] Specimens of coal were sent for to Edmonton and Red Deer River in the north and from along the Missouri in the south. But the coal taken from Coal Banks was pronounced far superior to all other. The coal is free burning bituminous, excellent for steam producer as well as for domestic purposes. It belongs to the lower cretaceous formation. The vein is about five feet thick.

On the 11th day of December 1882 a mine was opened on the south side of the Belly River, just opposite the Sheran Mine. During the winter a few men were kept busy, as coal was sent for from MacLeod and even from Fort Benton.[29] In this latter place it was sold $22.00 per ton, while at MacLeod it was delivered for about $15.00. The price at Coal Banks was only $3.00. But the intention of the newly formed company was to take the coal to Medicine Hat, where the Canadian Pacific Railway [CPR] was then being constructed. With a capital of £50 000 sterling, the company prepared to build a fleet of barges and a steamer to convey their coal to the CPR by water. Shipbuilders were sent for to Yankton and Pittsburg and a steamer, called *The Baroness*, was launched and floated down to Medicine Hat on the fist day of June 1883.

As the season of navigation on the Belly River proved to be very short, it was decided to build two more steamers and some sixteen new barges, making it altogether three steamboats and twenty-five barges. But, notwithstanding this increase it was observed that this would never be satisfactory, and that some other means of transportation must be thought of.

It was about that time, that the CPR offered the company a contract for a large quantity of coal and for a term of years, if they would build a railway to connect the mines of Coal Banks with the CPR. Accordingly, the company at once applied to the dominion Parliament for a Charter to build a narrow gauge line of railway, which was granted. The Dominion Government gave the Company a railroad-land grant of 3840 acres per mile, at the rate of 10 cts. per acre. In consequence the Company had to increase its capital, and bonds were issued, at once, for £160 000 sterling to build this railway from Coal Banks to Dunmore, a distance of 190 miles.[30]

The contract for this railway was let in April 1885. This is the year of the Halfbreed Rebellion on the north branch of the Saskatchewan.[31] But the Indians of southern Alberta remained peaceful and did not interfere with the construction of this road, which was terminated on August 28th, 1885.

[Jules Boone (1885) wrote, in Dutch, to Leonard:]
St. Albert. August 19, 1885
G.Z.J.C.
Reverend Very dear Father Leonard.

I just came in from the hay field. We took a spot 12 miles north of St. Albert. Brother Boigoutier wants to take the horned animals and sheep there to never them to return to St. Albert. We did our haying there, 450 charges per wagon, we were there only three weeks; the harvest is looking very good. Yesterday I cut the barley and in day or three or four I will start the wheat, which looks like it will yield over a thousand barrels of the best wheat in the world.

It is true that I have been thinking of returning to Belgium, I have sought assurance that I can return here. I asked for your three *sprieten* [parts of a candalabra] but did not yet find them yet. Today it rained, so this morning I asked again for it. Brother Brochard says that he will look for it today.

Dear Father, I did not keep one horse, they are all sold for 1,600 piasters; I will try to buy the first one I see and that would serve you well. I think that Father Leslanc will object. Monsignor left once more for Fort Pitt with Father Rémas. Before August 29th we expect Mother General Superior. Sister Blanchet left for Lac la Biche, and Father Sissier went with Father Gabillon to Peace Hillls. The Sturgeon River mill is not yet finished, a great loss for the mission. The bridge here is made higher: 1500 piasters.

If I didn't have to thresh for strangers, I would go myself to Calgary after finishing our harvest. Maybe I would meet with you somewhere. *Frère* Brochard found the three *sprieten* for your candelabras; the next person to go to Calgary will take them along. He says that your statue will not be finished yet; he has no time to work on it. The two heads have been cut. He says that he only can finish it this winter.

Hoping to be able to embrace you before the winter, I recommend myself in your prayers and remain eternally your very dedicated Jules.

[P.S.] Monsignor has just returned from Fort Pitt with a few old clothes from the people of the murdered missionary Fathers as well as a part of the *Ossensoir*. The crucifix is chipped off and the foot and the rest is wasted.

[Father Leduc's article (1886) was published, in Dutch, in de *Gazette van Thielt,* a Belgian newspaper:]

Something from around the World

The Métis Rebellion in Canada

[Note of the Editor of the *Gazette van Thielt*:] We have written several times about this rebellion, but it is still interesting to learn a few specific particulars about that faction and its leader, Louis Riel. These [particulars] were sent by the Very Reverend Vicar-General Leduc from Saint Albert, Canada, to the *Paris Univers*:

I just returned from a long journey to Calgary, Regina, Winnipeg, Saint-Boniface, Qu'appelle Batoche, Duck Lake and Prince Albert. I left on May 20th, 1886, and returned from a visit to the scene of this unfortunate war on the first of August to Saint Albert.

The Frog Lake Mission is entirely destroyed including the school, presbytery and church. Everything had been set on fire by the rebellious savages (Indians) and the good Fathers Fafard, a Canadian, and Marchand, from the Rennes diocese, have been killed and their bodies scandalously mutilated. Their hearts had been torn from their bodies and undoubtedly devoured! Both fell honourably under the pagan's bullets, who sacrificed them in their blind hatred. They were killed while offering charity and providing help to the victims of those nonbelievers, while trying to calm the Indians' fury. These people, misled by perfidious advice, did not just want to destroy the whites, but the priests also.

In our deep sorrow we still have one big consolation, and it is this; that we have two martyrs, two more protectors of the good God, so that the honour, the outstanding mercy of martyrdom, has been given to the Oblates of the Holy Mary Immaculate in these expansive areas in the northwest, to this dear Saint Albert diocese.

The Lamb Lake mission has also been destroyed and burned down completely; the one at Our Lady of Pontmain was pillaged, the ones at Battleford, Duck Lake, Batoche and Grandin also suffered greatly. The Sisters of Charity at two of our missions fled to the islands on the Lakes Labiche and La Crosse.

The Fathers Vegreville, Fourmont, Touze, Mouton and the five Sisters have for weeks been the prisoners of Riel, the leader of the rebelling Métis.

Mgr. Grandin left some time ago and on the 18th of the following month the rebellion's leader will climb the scaffold (this only took place later), so he might return to the good God and abjure his aberrations. Because this unfortunate fool also wanted to pass as a prophet, a reformer, in one word, as something god-like. He took his foolish fanaticisms so far that he even wanted to establish a new religion and he dragged a few ignorant fools along with him.

[Leonard continues:]
It was the good luck of the company to be able to transfer their fleet of steamers and barges to the Government, which needed them for the immediate conveyance of their troops to different places on both branches of the Saskatchewan, the scene of the rebellion. It was well for the government also, thus saving an immense expense, unavoidable if everything had to be taken over by land; and also gaining much time in moving their troops from place to place as required.

With this new railway Coalbanks became a place of importance. The old name was thought too insignificant; the new name of Lethbridge was proposed, seconded and adopted. Coalbanks became a thing of the past, doomed to the fate of oblivion. Lethbridge was the name of the President of the new railway: the town was baptized.

[Leonard did not mention it, but over the past years he had kept in touch with his six-year-older brother Victor, who signed his letters with his monastic name Joannes, John or Jean Berchmans." By the end of March 1884 Leonard received the following letter from his brother Victor/John Berchmans (1884):]
Kortrijk, March 25, 1884.
Community of Van Dale Brothers.
(G.Z.J.C.) Amen.
Dear beloved brother,

Today in the same mail I am sending you the book: *Le Secret de la Franc-Maçonnery*, by Mgr. Armand-Joseph Java, it is a beautiful volume of about 330 pages. I think that you will like it very much; it cost 4 fr. without postage. Let me know as soon as you have received it, because when I send something I am always afraid, that it will be left behind in the bramble bushes and you will not get it. Also, so far I have not received anything from you, apart from the portraits and drawings which you included with your letters and which I enjoy very much. For a long time I have wanted to get a map from your area, just like the one you sent to Jean."

Dear brother, father is doing much better, although he is old and exhausted. I hope that next summer he will recover completely, so we will beg God for this in our prayers. The brothers, sisters and other family are doing very well.

Brother-Director and all of my fellow-Brothers are in good health. Our schools are flourishing; at Easter one of our students will depart for Turnhout to prepare becoming a missionary. For a long time I have not received any news from Ottawa. I think that Albert Naessens will do quite well and regarding Devriendt, we have not heard from him since he left; we wonder about this."

▸ *Father Leonard Van Tighem.* P1976660221012.
Courtesy Sir Alexander Galt Museum, Lethbridge

Dear brother, the situation in Belgium is even more miserable than it was and persecution is slowly on the increase. We expect much from the coming elections, but not without fear, because many people have neither religion nor morals left. Corruption is widespread; so it might well happen that God will punish our Fatherland even more. Let us pray, dear brother that the unhappy will convert and find courage and strength in the midst of all kinds of persecution. I have not received any more news from Emile Verbrugge, so I don't know where the poor fellow is now.[35] Mr. Van Hollebeke is doing very well in Moerkerke. He generally reads your letters. Does he ever write to you? Mr. Lafontaine, Verougstraete and Aunt Anna's Gustaf will be ordained priests this year. Pray for them.

I haven't received any news either from Brother Jules Boone or from cousin Henri Scheers.[36]

How will these fellows be doing now? Send them my regards if you can.

I end, dear brother, by wishing you much courage in your difficult mission. Yes, if only God would answer the prayers we send to him daily in heaven, He would bless all of your undertakings, help you to save many non-believers and corrupt souls and lead them on the road to salvation. Dear brother, I also assume that you daily think of us in your sacred sacrifice of mass.

Goodbye, your brother in J.C.
Brother Berchmans,

[P.S.] Mr. Jean Goethals died last week in Meulebeke. RIP[37]

According to the new voters' bill; I, and nearly all of my fellow Brothers, have become voters. Mother Vincentia and all her Sisters send their greetings.

[Leonard continues his codex:]

It was in the year 1884 that Holy Mass was for the first time celebrated at Coalbanks. A priest, residing in Macleod, thirty miles west of this place, Father Van Tighem, of the order of the Oblates of Mary Immaculate, was called to administer the last Sacraments to Mr. Sheran, brother of late Nicholaus Sheran.

Being aware of the presence of a priest, some twenty coal miners, employed by the North West Coal and Navigation Comp., Irish Catholics, immediately crossed the river in order to see the Father, to go to their confession and fulfill their Easter duty.

The Father heard their confession during the [illegible] of the midnight hour and early in the morning in a log hut or *chantier* [building under construction] near the bed of the almost dying man, surrounded by his sister the only relative, but by many friends and a crowd of miners. The Holy

Sacrifice of mass was now for the first time celebrated. Holy Communion was distributed as viaticum to the invalid and as Easter Communion to the coal miners. *O Sacrum Convivium in quo Christus Junctus*.

This was on the 17th May, 1884. Half an hour later, while the Father was saying his Rosary on the banks of the Belly River, his attention was suddenly aroused by some lugubrious sighs and lamentations. Turning toward the opposite side of the stream, he saw some creature sitting on the top of an elevated butte. It was an Indian woman (squaw), a mother, lamenting, [who] after the savage fashion buried a child on the spot where now Lethbridge stands. Then, the Father was far from thinking that only a few years later a town would cover that same spot. He was far from thinking that only three years later he would celebrate Holy Mass there in a beautiful little church built of stones taken from the riverbanks, where now he was saying the beads. He was far from thinking that within three years he would have the happiness of coming from MacLeod to this new town for every first Sunday of the month, there to meet a Catholic population really devoted to their God, to their faith, to their church and to their priest.

The Father returned to MacLeod the next day. To the great astonishment of all, Mr. Sheran was much better; the doctor declared him out of danger. The Holy Sacrament of Extreme Unction had had its salutary effects. *Oration Fidei salvabit infirnum et alleviabit eum Dominus.* v. 15.

[A few months later Leonard got another letter from Victor:]
Kortrijk, June 12, 1884.
G.Z.J.C.
Dear beloved brother.

Great news! The day before yesterday the *Geuzen* in Belgium suffered a deadly blow and now are totally crushed.[38] How miraculous is God in his works! We were very anxious and it seemed almost impossible to win, and yet see, of the 30 *Geuzen* to be re-elected, 27 were thrown out and only one in Arlon and one in Virton are re-elected with only a very small majority; both in Virton and in Nivelles there will still be a second round voting. In Brussels the Catholics won with a majority of over 1,500 votes. The whole of West-Flanders, Antwerp, Namen, Leuven, etc., all fine. We are overjoyed. Now we are rid of our freemason ministry and all the *Geuzens'* persecutions. Masses and prayers rise incessantly to heaven out of gratitude. Perhaps the *Geuzen* schools will now be finished and we hope to be able to return to our monastery shortly.[39]

Dear brother, thanks for the beautiful map and the rare book you sent me. Everyone is curious to see them. And then the beautiful little painting! Congratulations! These artifacts, manifesting your progressing artistic skills, are of great value to me. Thanks again!

Brother-Director is doing well. It is at his urging that I am writing now to announce our victory. My fellow-Brothers, apart from Brother

Camiel, are all fine; we think that he will quietly go to heaven. Father carries on; he is old and in poor health, but he even sometimes strolls along the fields. I think that he will not be with us much longer because he is very *caduque* [worn-out]. Pray often for him and write once more to him, he likes it so much to get news from you. Father is at peace with everything God wishes it to be. Brothers and sisters all do well. I don't know much more about the other family members. Aunt Anna's son prepares to be ordained a priest at Christmas. Did he not write to you yet? A few weeks ago he asked me for your address.

With Easter Leo Decaluwe from Roosbeke became a Trappist in Westmalle (Antwerp). That good fellow visited me before his departure and asked me to send his greetings to you and recommends himself for your prayers.

Dear brother. I cannot write anything about Emile Verbrugge, apart that in Meulebeke people speak badly about it and would be glad that if he would leave. It would be good if you could contact his bishop to write to Meulebeke's pastor, because, if he were to become a priest, it would do much harm, even in Meulebeke. Let us pray for the poor misguided fellow. Our two young missionaries do very well in the Ottawa College. Albert Naessens has nearly finished his rhetoric and does not know yet whether he has to stay there for philosophy and theology. He dearly wishes to go to St. Albert. A few months ago he wrote to you and is wondering why he hasn't heard back from you. Try to think about it. One of our students is still studying at the minor seminary at Tornout.

Last Monday, Mgr. Seghers, born in Gent and bishop of Vancouver Island at the other side of the Rocky Mountains, preached here in the church and collected money for the benefit of his missions.[40] Mgr. spoke Flemish and was listened to intently. He stayed the entire week in the town canvassing alms from the well-to-do. He appealed to the young priests, Brothers and Sisters to consider ministering in his poor missions, which I heard are similar to yours in St. Albert. When will you come down to seek recruits and donations?

Dear brother, I will close by assuring you of my daily prayers for your happiness and the prosperity of your missions, hoping that you think of me daily, especially during the H. Sacrifice of Mass.

Pass on my compliments to Brother Jules and suggest that I would be delighted to hear from him. Also I extend my best wishes to Mgr. Grandin and so does Mother Vincentia. She is already 66 years old and still busy as a bee.

Judging by the way the fields and orchards look now, it could be a bumper harvest.

Did the violin arrive yet?

Your dedicated brother,
Brother Jean Berchmans.

[Leonard continues:]

During the year 1885, the year of the Halfbreed Rebellion, Father Van Tighem was kept very busy in MacLeod; consequently no visits were made to Lethbridge. A part of the 9th Battalion of Quebec Volunteers had been sent to MacLeod under command of Lieut. Col. Roy. These, being all Catholics, required the continual presence of the priest.[41]

Though on the 7th day of August the same Michael Sheran received again the last Sacraments from Father Van Tighem and died a few days later.

[In 1885 Leonard, busy in MacLeod, received the following letters from Victor:]

Kortrijk, April 26, 1885.

G.Z.J.C.

Dear beloved and Reverend brother,

This is to let you know that I am in good health, the same as Brother-Director and all of my fellow Brothers and we hope the same for you. Brother Camiel is a bit better. You know, dear brother, over six years ago we bought a big building to turn into a monastery and schools. This building is now at our disposal and in a few days we will start to arrange everything for this summer. It is a big job and big expenses must be made. That is why, dear brother, we hope that Mgr. Grandin, when he resides this summer for a longer time in Europe, will postpone his visit to us until the very last because, since we were chased out of our monastery, we are not in the position to receive His Highness according to his status and there is another reason I will inform you about later.

Dear brother, our old monastery is still being used as a *Geuzen* school. Though we now have a Catholic ministry and a majority in the Chambers of 36 members and 17 in the Senate; one is so careful and concerned about a rebellion of the Liberals and the King who goes along with them, that so far not much change is brought about the sad situation in Belgium, and France as well. To the great regret and indignation of all Catholics, the King laid off M.M. Jacobs and Woeste, two true Catholic ministers, because they were a bit too forceful. God forbid!

Dear brother, I just received a letter from Alida.[42] The family is doing very well, all are in good health and the little ones are growing like cabbages. Alida also wrote to you and added father's memorial card.[43] She was very surprised that you had not received her other letters. I gave her your address again. Gustaf is still alone, but since you wrote to him he has felt braver.[44] He was very happy to receive your letter. Jean and Mathilde and their little ones are also doing well.[45] A few days ago I had a visit from aunt Anna. Gustaf, who has been a priest since Christmas and is now a teacher in Bruges, also wrote twice to you without getting an answer.[46] What might cause this? Victor is still at the station in Dendermonde. Jules is in Bruges; Edmond is headmaster in Oekene and Jean assistant teacher in Veurne. All are doing very well. The family in Pittem is doing quite well too. In particular you should write to your godmother for once, it would please her greatly, she is getting older and often speaks about you. Aunt Siska received your letter; their sadness because of uncle's death is now wearing out a bit. Uncle Louis and Aunt Lucie are also doing well. Eugenie went into a convent in Heule on February 2. Uncle Ivo is doing well, all his children are still at home. Marie in Gent is still the same, quite addled!"

According to their letters, our young missionaries Albert Naessens and Devriendt are doing very well in Canada. They will be looking forward to speak a bit with Mgr. Grandin.

Dear brother, I read in Alida's letter that Jules Boone wrote that the Sunday after Easter he left St. Albert with Mgr. [Grandin] in order to go to Europe and that they will stay there for an entire year. Oh, how happy Father and mother Boone will be and all of us too. How is Brother Scheers doing? He writes so little, do you ever hear from Emile Verbrugge, that poor guy. Have you not got your violin yet? I included 10 fr. for a new bow, strings etc. How is the little organ doing? Did you receive the beautiful little sanctuary lamp and the little cruets? Don't you have any Brothers or Sisters there to help you out? What kind of animals, birds, trees and flowers do you find mostly in the Macleod area? Do you seed wheat there and do you plant potatoes?

Dear brother, I am waiting for some news from you. I request that you include myself and our entire community and our family in your prayers and especially in the H. Sacrifice of the Mass, and promise not to forget you as well.

Your dedicated brother,
Brother Joannes Berchmans.

[P.S.] Is your new building made of stone?

All kinds of news: Emile Boone (Frère Jerome) is still in Tirlemont, he can hardly see anything anymore, the poor guy. Our Lady of Lourdes (Oostakker) still attracts big crowds.⁴⁸ The Jesuit Fathers have a beautiful church there next to the Miraculous Rock. Excellent miracles happen there. Cousin Armand Scheers went last summer with Marez' wife to Lourdes (France); they witnessed a grand miracle. An 8-year-old girl, born mute, suddenly shouted: *"Ave Maria!"* and then could say whatever she wanted to say. We now have about 700 children in school, divided over 10 classrooms with nine Brothers-teachers and monitors. Isn't that a lot? Ms. Cécile Vandenberghe lives since a long time in a convent in Roeselaere. I saw her not long ago, she is doing well.

[Bishop Grandin (1886, 14, 38–40, 43) noted:]

14: In MacLeod, Father van Tighem had also received considerable help for the construction of his house and his chapel. [. . .]

38–40: The 16th [of September] I left for MacLeod in the company of Father Legal. [. . .] In the evening we had the consolation of embracing our Father Van Tighem who, even while he was expecting us, was surprised, because he had wished to have been notified of our arrival.[49] The good Father told us of a serious illness, which even had put his life in danger. It is already sad enough to be sick when there is neither help from a Brother nor from a housekeeper. The good Catholics of MacLeod try to remedy this nasty situation [The bishop goes on how Mrs. MacFarlane helped Father Doucet when he had fallen ill].

This time it was another Catholic, M. Levasseur, who took care of the sick Father Van Tighem.[50] He lives right near the church, but as it was difficult to take care on a regular basis of the sick [Father Van Tighem] at his home, Mr. Levasseur made a room for him in his own house and his young spouse, as well as his sister-in-law, another young lady from the neighbourhood, took turns taking on the role of a nurse. Thanks to this good care, Father Van Tighem soon recovered his health and his strength.[51] He was back home again, but still took his meals at his benefactresses. They did not want him to take again care of his own cooking while I was there. All the time, these two good families and the Girard family cooked our meals. I found that Father Van Tighem was magnificently housed; his whole house breaths good taste, certain elegance, cleanliness without poverty defaulting it. The chapel is especially very convenient. The population is not one that the missionaries should attend to; that is the same with all the inhabitants of our young town. For them their salvation is a minor concern, undoubtedly at some time they will occupy themselves with it, but only when they are well settled or perhaps only when their fortunes are made. These dispositions possibly cause the good Father Van Tighem to be sad and discouraged while the good God in the mean time grants him so many great consolations. At the barracks a good number of new, Catholic soldiers have arrived, which are still totally impregnated with the beliefs and the piety of the family. [. . .]

43: Before leaving Pincher Creek, I had a meeting with the inhabitants in order to advice on the means to build a small church.[52] A Protestant gave the terrain for this purpose and the Catholics will contribute under the direction of Father Van Tighem, who will visit them from time to time. These people would also like to have a house of God. During the duration of our stay at this post, we were lodged at another Mr. Levasseur, a brother of the one in MacLeod. Their wives are sisters.

[Victor to Leonard again, as always in Dutch:]

Kortrijk, October 17, 1885.

G.Z.J.C.

Very dear and Reverend brother.

I have been very busy and that kept me from writing you and as well I did not have much special news. Thank God, my health and the health of Brother Director and all my fellow Brothers, is good. Also, Brother Camiel, who has been sick for so long, recovered. As I already informed you, we have been working on our new buildings the entire summer. Our new monastery and schools are nearly finished, so shortly we will move. The buildings are large and well equipped; it is a pity that construction costs so much, we are over our heads in debts. Fortunately a few charitable souls in Kortrijk will help us out a bit. The two classrooms will easily hold 400 to 500 pupils and on the top floor a drawing class of 150 pupils. For four years we have a second day school of three classes of 200 pupils in the parish of Our Lady. We will keep this school as the government now accepts it. So, at present we have 700 pupils in the day school: 300 youngsters in the Sunday school and 90 to 100 in the drawing class. Two years ago we set up a drawing class, in the winter every evening two hours and the Sunday afternoons. We already have several fine artists who produce beautiful pieces: Baron de Bethune and Mr. Van Ruymbeke of Kortrijk are very involved in these classes and pay all the expenses.

All drawings are done in the Gothic style. Brother Bernardus and a first class artist sculptor from downtown teach the classes. Our other monasteries of Our Lady of Viven and of Sint Pieter op den Dijk [St. Peter on the Dike] also do well. All the Brothers send their greetings; everyone enjoys your letters hearing news about your mission. Send our best wishes to Mgr. Grandin. We ask for his Episcopal blessing and we look forward to his upcoming visit.

Dear brother, now some family news. Gustaf is still alone in his monastery, but I bellef that he still would like to remarry. He does well and does good business in his shop – he keeps himself busy by making furniture.

Jean and Mathilde also do very well, lots of work and sale of cattle. They already have three children, two little guys and a little girl. At home things go well too: Charles and Alida are very confident and work like slaves. Alida has been a bit ill this summer (caused by a little one), but recovered. They are very religious, all three of their children go to school in the convent and two of Jean's make five little Van Tighem children sitting on one bench! Charles' daughter Marie can already read French and Flemish and sing, she is a charming youngster and likes to learn.

Uncle Louis and aunt Lucie also do well, they no longer bake. Uncle L. keeps himself busy on his land. Eugenie in the convent in Heule, she is now called Sister Alberta; certainly one must have been thinking of you, we also have a Brother Albert. Send my compliments to Br. Boone and Br. Scheers if possible. Marie of Gent remains in the situation, remains very simple, and her two children . . . very [illegible].

Uncle Ivo is still sick, it seems that he suffers from peritonitis. He fears not to survive the winter (pray for him). This summer Prudent, the youngest, married the daughter of Devriendt from near the pear tree; he there built him a home.[53] The families of aunt Sophie, aunt Siska, niece Lisa and uncle Charles all do very well too. Uncle Jean's wander a bit around, I think that now they live in Ingelmunster.

Aunt and Gusten died long ago, I am sure you know that. With All Saints Day aunt Anna and uncle will leave Roosbeke and live in Oekene with Edmond who is head master over there. Gustaf is still teacher in the institute for the deaf, mute and blind at Bruges. This holiday he paid us a visit; he is surprised never to have gotten a reply from you on his letter. Alida, she says that she also wrote to you three times to the address I gave her and it seems that you don't receive her letters. Gustaf received your portrait, he is very happy that he is the only one.

The Burneel, Maes' etc., families constantly increase and the little ones grow like cabbages. I also send you best wishes of father and mother Boone, Camille, the sexton's son, and from Odile who married Victor Tieghem and lives in the Casino, from Santens who lives already for about three years in a room of the congregation. Barbara broke her leg two years ago and the maid now hops around with crutches of Depontiens. Send them a little letter and they will for sure prepare some flowers to give along with Mgr. [Grandin]. I will also try to give along something. It will not be much; we have to beg constantly ourselves for our schools etc. Sister Vincentia will also prepare something. Many greetings from her and all the Sisters of Love.[54] We did not get any news from our young missionaries Naessens and Devriendt from Canada, but hope that they do well. They will long to come with Mgr. Grandin and maybe go along with him to St. Albert. Naessens must be almost through his studies.

I transcribe all your letters in a notebook since you have left.

All kinds of news. In the election for the Chambers 14 days ago in France, the Catholics won over 100 seats and tomorrow there will be a runoff election for even more. Everywhere one gets tired of the Liberals! Here in Belgium things happen very quietly, the Catholics are very careful. The run on Our Dear Lady of Lourdes (Oostakker) is still growing; magnificent cures happen! This summer Brother Paulus went to Lourdes (France) with a sick gentleman from Kortrijk. Farmer Hansen's oldest son became a Father at the Récolleten in Thielt. Allardus Delafonteyne recently died. His son Emiel is Coadjutor in Wacken. Also, Delacaluwe now wears the cassock. It was nice for us to receive from you a few rare stones and other artifacts of nature for our collection of natural artifacts, such as the crystal you wrote about in your last letter.

Dear brother, commend me again in your godly prayers and I ask for your priestly blessing.

Your dedicated brother in J.C.,
Brother Joannes Berchmans.

[P.S.] Greet Brother Boone and Brother
Scheers if you find an opportunity.

Marie of Gent is in the same situation. Quite simple, her two children [illegible]. We had a rather bleak summer this year, still the fruit is [illegible]. Many greetings from Brother Director and all the fellow Brothers. Since you left, I transcribe all your letters in a notebook."

1886

[Leonard did not mention it, but right at the start of the new year he received the following letters, in Dutch, from Victor:]

January 24, 1886.

G.Z.J.C.

Very dear and reverend brother,.

Today I have to announce great news and that is that within a few weeks I hope to talk to you personally. Don't be disturbed, dear brother, because God makes miracles in all of his works! You may remember that my dream has always been to go to some far off countries and labour there for the salvation of souls and to help out the poor missionaries with my labour. This was my most ardent wish and it is was because of our good, late mother, [and] upon the urging of my Father Confessor, Mr. Vandenberghe, that I never realized my intention.

Instead I entered the Van Dale congregation where I have spent fifteen happy and peaceful years, caring for the poor who are sick and, especially being involved with the education of the youth. Though happy and content with my situation, I often envied your happiness, dear brother, and upon learning that you need so many Brothers, I have often exclaimed: "Eh! If only it were up to me to go and help them." Now listen how God has answered my prayers. First he wanted to test me like gold in fire. Don't be afraid, dear brother; because it is written, "Blessed are those who are persecuted because of justice."

Not long ago I wrote to you, dear brother, that persecution by the non-believers is widespread in Belgium and that especially the Brothers, Sisters and the Catholic teachers are targeted. Already many have been dragged into the courts and thrown in jail by freemasons or liberal judges. It also happened to me, although everyone was convinced of my innocence. I did not find one person who was against me dear brother, have not been saddened by it and even considered myself fortunate to be somewhat the equal of so many saints and our Godly Saviour who had also been falsely accused and sentenced. Brother Director and all of my fellow Brothers pitied me a lot and went out of their way to help me. Mr. Deacon and the priests in the town often visited me and told me: "We even love you more than we did before." And so those days went by quickly; I hope that they were meritorious. Now everything seems like a dream, and I hardly think about it anymore.

This is the reason they put me in jail: A woman of ill repute, already eight years separated from her husband, at night fried cookies in oil in her house and the servants and maids gathering there were corrupted in the most horrific way. I became aware of it through this woman's child, who told me everything about who went there and what they did. I summoned and reproached all those within my sphere of influence, sent them to confession, even if they had not yet made their First Communion, and I strongly forbade them to enter the house again, which they usually did. But look: about two months later when she had lost her little business, she went with her child to the commissar and accused me of committing the bad deeds that occurred in her house. I was summoned to the tribunal, where I appeared fearlessly and despite my innocence and the testimony of neighbours of this woman and the children who went there, I was sentenced by the freemasons and put in jail. God forgive them; because of their hatred for our holy religion they don't know what they do. Now it is all over and the poor woman is the worst off. She is destitute and can hardly leave her house without being stoned.

Dear brother, after all this I have not lost my honour or reputation in town because I am too well respected. One wanted to receive me in state with music and flowers. In order to avoid this and prevent the ranting and raving, especially the articles written in the godless newspapers, without telling anyone I went one night for a few days to the Trappists in West-Vleteren, where I was given a warm welcome.[56] After a few days I returned to Kortrijk and stayed there several days without going into town.

It has been two months that the Brothers have been in their new monastery and classrooms, there is lots of space and it is beautiful. Brother Director and all my fellow Brothers are doing very well and it saddens them that i will leave them. Without the consent and approval of the bishop of Bruges I would not have been allowed to come to your mission. In order to avoid that the bad ones rant and rave about me or my community and write bad things in their bad newspapers and especially because it has been so long that I desired to go to America, Monsignor supports my request because my brother is there and I am putting myself in the hands of Mgr. Grandin, who has been fully informed of my situation.

Neither Monsignor, Mr. Deacon, nor Brother-Director will release me from my vows and they want me to remain a Van Dale Brother. I am hoping that later more of our Brothers join me and expand our order in America, because here in Belgium we expect worse times ahead.

Dear brother, I would have left already to find Mgr. Grandin in Ottawa from where he last wrote to me, but a young man from Limburg and another one from Leizele near Poperinge would like to accompany me working at Mgr.'s missions as missionaries of the Oblate order and possibly continue their studies for the priesthood. That is why I wrote to Mgr. Grandin and I expect a reply shortly, and if they are accepted and persevere in their wish, we start on our trip as soon as possible.

Dear brother, pray that our endeavours are blessed by God and forgive me for not writing earlier. I did not want to distress you while I was in jail and before I knew the outcome of my wish. Hoping to write to you soon once I am closer by and, who knows, talk to you in person,

I remain as always, longing for you,
Your very dedicated brother in J.C.,
Brother Joannes Berchmans.

P.S. Many good wishes from Brother-Director and all my fellow Brothers. Pray often that their numbers may increase so a few can join me. Many of them fervently wish to do so and would accompany me if they had permission. I visited the entire family and said farewell in Pittem and Oekene. Everywhere everyone is doing very well and many good wishes are sent from our brothers Gustaf, Jean and Charles. Their families, wives and children are doing well and all are happy that I will join you. Gustaf is still alone, but now he feels strong and has lots of money in the bank. I have always advised him to remarry, but he is quite a complainer. Uncle Louis is also doing quite well at aunt Siska's, but Uncle Ivo is sick all the time. I am afraid he will not recover.

Mr. Pastor of Meulebeke sends his best wishes. He also approves of my going to America. The Boone family is doing well. They wrote about the news to Brother Jules and the Scheers family wrote to Brother Henri.

Well dear brother, see you later and pray often for me. Forgive me my bad handwriting, my hands are stiff; it is freezing hard and the snow is a foot deep.

Brother Joannes. West-Vleteren, Trappist Monastery.

[Leonard continues:]
On the 7th day of March 1886, Father Van Tighem came for the first time to the new town of Lethbridge. As there were neither chapel nor mission house, the Father was received by our old and devoted friend Mr. Thomas Curry, the manager of the I.G. Baker's store. The Father, at this first visit, found about sixty Catholics in Lethbridge. He said Holy Mass in a new building, which afterwards became the Royal Hotel and which since has been burnt down. At High Mass, the Father presented him self officially, as being duly sent by his bishop, Mgr. Grandin, to attend to the spiritual wants of the Catholic population of Lethbridge.

[*The Lethbridge Herald* (1935, 96) noted:]
Father Van Tighem, associated with the Roman Catholic Church from the earliest days of the West, was the first priest of that denomination to hold services in the upper town. On March 7, 1886, he held a service in the old Royal Hotel, or Alphonse's hall, later know as Bourgoin's hall, situated where the Arlingon hotel now stands.

[Victor (1886) to Leonard:]
    Montreal, March 15, 1886.
    Very dear brother,

Saturday morning at 9, I arrived safe and sound at the Oblate Fathers in Montréal after a 16-day journey. My reception here is like a son returning home. In the afternoon I had the pleasure to talk for a long time with your holy bishop, Mgr. Grandin. He pressed me against his chest, embraced me, and blessed me, what goodness! As Mgr. is staying here until May or even longer, he still allowed me to continue on my journey to you. Mgr. gave me a good passport and assured me that I should not be shy to ask for anything. He said that you are expecting me.

    Dear brother I impatiently long to be able to talk to you and embrace you. Don't worry about my fate. I will remain a Van Dale Brother, as I used to be. The bishop of Bruges did neither release me from my vows, nor from observing the rules of our congregation, or from anything; he only allows me to work at your missions because I ardently wished to do so and so to avoid the clamour of the godless. I also have most splendid letters of recommendation from my superior with me. More than one of my beloved fellow Brothers would have dearly liked to accompany me, if obedience had allowed them. My superiors and all of us hope that this can occur later, because in Kortrijk we now have established a Normal School especially for training young Brothers in education. If the good God blesses our work, after a short while we will be able to expand our order into the large diocese of St. Albert. This is the full aspiration of Mgr. Grandin, who is already very happy with my arrival. So, dear brother, take courage and be patient! What wonders God makes in his work!!!

    This afternoon I will go with one of your Reverend Fathers to Lachine to visit Mr. Devriendt of Pittem. After a few days I will go to Ottawa to embrace my former pupil Naessens who has now about finished his studies. From there to St. Boniface, then to Calgary and finally, with the grace of God, to Macleod. In anticipation, let us pray for each other.

    Dear brother, best wishes from Brother-Director and all my dear fellow-Brothers. Our separation was sad, but on both sides courageous. Many regards from Gustaf, Jean, Charles, their wives and children, they are all doing fine, as well as from the entire family, friends and acquaintances. I have so much to tell you. I also bring a few things for your chapel.

    Well, dear brother, see you in a few days.

    Farewell

Your dedicated and very happy
Brother Joannes Berchmans

P.S. Uncle Ivo died February 13th. I assisted him for 5 days. How content was he and with him the whole family. Pray for him.

[Victor again:]
Calgary, March 28, 1886.
G.Z.J.C.
My dearest brother,

Right now, at 11 a.m., thank God I have arrived safe and sound in Calgary and have been well-received by Father Lacombe and the other Fathers as well.[57] I am quite tired from the long journey that I just completed in one month, so that is why Father Lacombe wants me to stay here and rest until Monday and eight more days. So dear brother, about ten more days of patience and then, with the grace of God, we will be able to embrace each other and talk together. I have much to tell you and regards are sent from everywhere I have been; in particular from our fellow Flemish, who were very happy with my arrival.

I am glad to learn that you are doing well and that you impatiently await my arrival. I would be happy if you could possibly send me this week a few lines.

In anticipation I remain your very dedicated brother,
Brother Joannes Berchmans.

p.s. I already wrote twice to Meulebeke and Kortrijk. This week I will also announce my arrival to Brother Boone.
Br. J.

[Leonard continues:]
The second visit was made on the 28th of April. The Catholics came to their Easter duties and attended High Mass and vespers in a new building, addition to I.G. Baker's store. From that time, the Father came frequently to Lethbridge. The number of Catholics increasing every day, Holy Mass was usually said in a large hall. But this hall being a part of a restaurant or saloon, it was very inconvenient and the absolute necessity of a little chapel was felt very much.

On the 8th of October 1886, the Father strongly exhorted the Catholics after High Mass, to come to a meeting in the evening, in order to take the first steps towards the erection of a little church. He produced the plans and specifications of a small frame building, thinking that this was all what could be expected for the present. A committee was appointed of which Father Van Tighem was elected President, and after serious discussion a subscription list was circulated amongst the members of the committee, who by themselves alone subscribed the handsome sum of $400.00.

The next day the list was circulated amongst the Catholics and other friends in Lethbridge and when the Father paid his next visit on, Nov. 12th, about one thousand dollars had been subscribed. This, Father Van Tighem announced with joy to His Lordship. When these good tidings arrived in St.

Albert, it so happened that the Bishop (Grandin, O.M.I.) held council with his assistants, deliberating on the situation of our many missions. The news from Lethbridge, and the generosity of the Catholics of that place very much rejoiced the hearts of His Lordship and his assistants. Our good bishop answered the letter at once and very liberally added a cheque of $400.00.

Every year, according to the rules of the Oblate Fathers, the members of that congregation must come together for a spiritual retreat of eight days. This year the mission house of MacLeod had been selected for that purpose, and to the great satisfaction of all Mgr. Grandin was to preside over the exercises of these days of recollection. Oh! The days of salvation, then indeed, the missionary may exclaim: *Ecce quam bonum N. quam secundum habitare Fratres in unum!!* But this happiness is seldom granted to the missionaries. Most of the time he is alone, all alone, for weeks, for months! The vineyard is large, but the labourers are few, too few!!!

Our good bishop, after the retreat, visited Lethbridge and witnessed himself the good dispositions of the Catholic people, their zeal and generosity. It was there and then decided to build during the coming year, and

▶ *"Retreat preached at Ft. Macleod, December 9, 1886: Front row (seated I to r): Rev. Edmond Claude, O.M.I.; Bishop Grandin, O.M.I.; Rev. Leon Doucet, O.M.I. Back row (standing- I to r): Rev. Donat Foisy, O.M.I.; Brother Boone, O.M.I.; Rev. Leonard Van Tighem, O.M.I.;* Brother Jean Berchmans O.M.I. [Van Dale Brother]." Courtesy of the Missionary Oblates, Grandin Archives at the Provincial Archives of Alberta, Photo OB. 3684. "The building is probably that which Father Van Tighem had built in 1884" (Venini Byrne 1973, 211.)

to build not only a frame church, but, as good sandstone had recently been discovered on the river bank, it was decided to erect a stone church.

Great, indeed, was the satisfaction of the Saintly bishop to see the different missions of the southern part of his diocese taking such vigorous roots. Only four years before, we had scarcely any Catholic mission in the south. A few missionary priests had been working amongst the Indians, but they were compelled to live in miserable shacks and tents.

Now, we have a beautiful mission established in MacLeod, a substantial Mission House was lately erected at the Peigan reservation, a neat church was built at Pincher Creek, and now a stone church was to rise up in Lethbridge for Catholic worship. The building was to be 40×25 feet and covered with galvanized iron shingles. Mr. Galt, the manager of the North West Coal and Navigation Comp., presented us with six town lots; this being a piece of land 125×150 feet. The bishop gave a loan of $1000.00 to be repaid in yearly installments of one hundred dollars with the interest of 5%.

The contract for the stonework was given to a certain Mr. Gibbs, the carpenter work and plastering to Mr. G. Cody. The stonework of the church cost $1400.00; the carpenter's work and plasterer's $1150.00. It was decided that St. Patrick was to be the Patron Saint of the new church.

We took the opportunity of the presence of our good bishop to celebrate the Jubilee Year. Most of the Catholics approached the Holy Sacraments on this occasion. Accompanying the bishop were: Rev. Fathers Doucet, Claude and Frère Boone.[58] During the winter months all the necessary sandstones were taken out and transported up the Hill. Early in the spring work was

▶ *2004: St. Michael's Church in Pincher Creek Museum,* originally located across 1909 Lebel House. Photo Mary E.M.

begun. All the windowsills and ornamental stones had been prepared during winter, and everything was ready to lay the corner stone.

The ceremony was to be celebrated with solemnity. The Catholic population of Lethbridge assembled on the site of the future church; an organ had been brought on the spot to accompany the different psalms and to give greater solemnity to the occasion. Father Van Tighem having taken the Holy Vestments, made the introductory prayers, after which he went on to explain the ceremony. A discourse on the Catholic Church, as being the house of God followed. The psalms were sung, the corner stone blessed, the prescribed documents duly enclosed in the cavity of the rock, the stone was moved to its place on the northwest corner of the building. This is a copy of the document enclosed in the stone.

In the year of our Lord MDCCCLXXXVII
Leo XIII being Pope since MXCCCLXXVIII
Vital Justin Grandin Bishop
of St. Albert since MXCCCLVII
Under the reign and in the Jubel Year of
Our Gracious Queen Victoria
Marquis Lansdowne being Governor General
of Canada
Edg, Dewdney, Lieut. Governor of NWT
We Catholic missionary priest and Oblate of Mary Immaculate
having obtained extraordinary permission from His Lordship
the bishop of St. Albert
have blessed and laid the corner stone of the first Catholic
Church in Lethbridge. The building ground being granted
by Sir A. Galt of N.W.C. and N.Co.
Signature L.V.T.

When the stone had been rolled in position and cemented in its place by the Father, he exhorted the assistance to come forward and strike the corner stone as a sign of their willingness to make an offering on the occasion. Some fifty dollars were collected. On the 23rd of April the Father came again to Lethbridge and this time was accompanied by the Superior of this District, the Rev. Father Lacombe. The number of Catholics had increased very rapidly. The hall in which Holy Mass was said could scarcely contain the people and the necessity was more and more felt of a priest to reside in this place to attend to the spiritual wants of the people.

It was with this intention that a delegation came to see the Superior and asked him to give them a priest or, at least, to intercede in their behalf with the bishop of the diocese. This delegation, moreover asked the Rev. Father Superior, the special favour of having Father Van Tighem, who had begun the mission amongst them. Father Lacombe promised that he would do his best to obtain for them what they so ardently desired.

1▸ *1887: St. Patrick's Church, Lethbridge.*
Courtesy Van Tighem Family Archives

2▸ *1887: Interior of St. Patrick's*
church, Father Leonard sitting in aisle.
P19951049004. Courtesy Sir Alexander
Galt Museum, Lethbridge.

Aug. 1887: The stone church was in a rapid course of completion. The carpenters had announced that in a few days everything would be terminated: consequently preparations were made for its blessing. Father Van Tighem invited his Superior from Calgary to come and preside over the ceremony. The church being built of stone, had a right to consecration, but according to the rules of the church the building could not receive the consecration, as there was a debt on it of over one thousand dollars. Father Legal, from the Peigan reservation, had come with Father Van Tighem to Lethbridge, a few days previous in order to arrange an altar and decorate somewhat the interior of the church for the ceremony.

Reverend Fathers Lacombe and Doucet arrived from Calgary and the Blackfoot Reserve. The blessing took place on the 4th of August. A grand ceremony it was! The little church was beautiful. A large congregation attended with great respect. Father Lacombe pronounced an eloquent discourse. The singing was perfect and the Catholic population returned to their homes with joy in their heart, breathing a generous: *Deo Gratias!*

Now we have a church, now we know where to go for divine worship, now we may look with pride upon this little monument: let us go on, let us step forward. We must now have a priest to reside amongst us, and we shall prepare for this, we shall support him. He will guide us and guide our children in the path of virtue and we shall not feel fully happy, neither shall we be at home here before this is realized!!

Such were the reflections, the generous and noble aspirations of the good people of Lethbridge which after the beautiful ceremony they returned to their homes.

It was understood that from this time the Father was to be in Lethbridge for every first Sunday of the month. At the end of this year, while the Father was in Lethbridge, a collection was taken up, and the sum of $142.00 was handed over to our Secretary, Mr. Curry, to pay off some of our debts.

[Father Leduc (1888, 161–64) wrote, in French, to Father L'Hermite:]

161: The Rev. Father Van Tighem actually serves the two towns of MacLeod and Lethbridge, located 30 miles from each other. At present these locations comprise a population of about 1200 souls to whom the good Father Van Tighem dedicates himself with great zeal. He himself has built a house-chapel, which elicits admiration from the Catholics of MacLeod and was visited by the Protestant ministers more than once, so they could see for themselves what a poor Catholic priest can do, alone and without help, while working without a break and without any personal interest in the work entrusted to him. . . .

162–163: Thirty miles to the east of MacLeod one discovered significant coalmines and wealth for the future. A powerful company has acquired it. A railway is projected that will connect the Pacific Canadian to Dunmore over a distance of 109 miles . . . and close to the coalmines another good-

▶ "*Carved wooden polychrome statue of St. Anthony. Made in Quebec in the midnineteenth century, given to the Catholic church in Lethbridge, Alberta, about 1887, and later to the Peigan Indian mission*" (Dempsey c. 1991, 165).

Anonymous, St. Anthony, c. 1900 Collection of the Glenbow Museum Archives, Calgary. Gift of the Oblate Mission, St. Albert [76.5.1]

Was this statue presented to Leonard as St. Anthony was his patron saint?

sized town, named Lethbridge, is being built with extraordinary speed. The numerous Catholics, most of them Irish, ask for a priest to be established among them. Because it is impossible to grant them their rightful wish immediately, and because we don't have anyone available, the Rev. Father Van Tighem promised to visit them from MacLeod on a regular basis. He will spend each month a few days in Lethbridge to provide the good Christians with the opportunity to attend the holy sacrament of mass and approach the sacraments. . . .

Monsignor promised to do what he can to provide them with a missionary as soon as the church is built. A Catholic committee formed right away: the plan to build a nice stone chapel of 40 by 30 feet with a tribune is adopted. Later a sanctuary will be added. . . . When the work is finished, the Catholic committee delivers the church to the diocesan authority and will request again that a priest be sent to Lethbridge. In the meantime the Rev. Father Van Tighem will divide his time up and take turns between MacLeod and Lethbridge. But all this good news is of necessity incomplete because, despite absolute dedication, it is impossible that two important missions, located 30 miles from each other, without a means of communication other than public transport, could be well or even suꭢciently served by one priest alone.

Apart from the two young towns of MacLeod and Lethbridge, the Rev. Father Van Tighem also had to care for a new important village that is recently established 25 miles south of MacLeod, at the foot of the mountains. It is Pincher Creek, a mission dedicated to the archangel St. Michael. The more clement climate, the richness of the soil, the abundance of creeks, timber and fire wood, extensive natural prairies, excellent for raising horses and horned cattle, all these advantages together have drawn the attention of colonists. A good-sized village having a large part, if not a majority, of Catholics, is being established. . . .

164: For almost two years, the Rev. Father Van Tighem has added visits to these Christians onto his regular services in MacLeod and Lethbridge, but this is not really enough at all. He had to reduce his journeys and the colony of Pincher Creek at present usually gets a monthly visit from the Rev. Father Legal. During the feast of the holy apostles Peter and Paul, assisted by Rev. Van Tighem, I also blessed, as solemnly as possible, the new church, dedicated to St. Michael. The entire population attended the ceremony and the chapel was full.

1888

[Leonard continues:]

During the first months of the year 1888, Father Van Tighem prepared at the mission of Macleod a set of Stations of the Cross for this church. He had sent to Montreal for handsome chromas and made the frames himself. When they were terminated he sent them to Lethbridge by some freight teams and on the 3rd of June erected them canonically in the new church. This beautified very much the inside. It was about this time, that the Catholic miners organized a picnic in the bottom near the mines. This festival, the first of that kind in Lethbridge, proved to be a success and the handsome sum of $450.00 was realized. The Father having some sick people in Macleod was not able to assist at the feast.

While his Lordship Bishop Grandin was in the United States with Rev. Father Lacombe, Father Van Tighem wrote to them how badly a bell was wanted for the church of Lethbridge. His Lordship paid a visit to the famous Bell foundry of McShane, and obtained from that gentleman a small bell for this mission. Father Lacombe was kind enough to add a few hundred pounds to the weight of the bell, and on the third of June, Father Van Tighem received the invoice of a splendid bell, weighing, the bell alone, 880 lbs. We read in the register of the Catholic mission of Lethbridge:

Blessing of the Bell

> On the eight day of July, in the year of our Lord, one thousand eight hundred and eighty eight. We, Catholic Priest, undersigned, after having received authorization from His Lordship, Bishop Grandin, have solemnly blessed the bell for the church of Lethbridge, in presence of the Catholic population of Lethbridge.
>
> L. Van Tighem, O.M.I.

The church had never contained such an immense crowd. Many Protestants came to witness the ceremony, which took place in the afternoon. Nearly a hundred people were obliged to remain outside doors. The Father, on this occasion, made a long discourse on the origin of bells, their use and signification. The bell was called Michael Joseph Patrick. Some twenty silk ribbons of all shades and colors attached to the top of the bell were held by as many godfathers and godmothers, who, with holy pride formed a beautiful circle around the estrade [platform] on which the bell rested.

When the ceremony was over, the Father announced that now another ceremony was to begin, that he himself was going to show them what to do and how to do. Then the father walked up in front of the bell, took in hand the nice white silk rope attached to the clapper of the bell and gave a few tremendous pulls, making the sacred edifice almost shake. He then turned to the first sponsors, placed the silk cord in their hands and so the rope, for over one hour, passed from hand to hand, making the silvery tones of the glorious instrument reach the utmost part of the village.

I was told that at this moment people were seen coming from all directions. This being the first church bell in Lethbridge, everyone desired to present it his respect. But the most interesting part for these who had charge of the financial department, was to see that the large silver plate standing under the bell had now disappeared under profuse accumulation of what we generally call green-backs. Yes, it was a grand ceremony, a joyful one, a beneficial one, remarked the treasurer, and one, which will be long remembered, especially by the Catholics of Lethbridge.

The next day, some twenty young men were busily engaged all the evening placing the bell on the top of the stone tower. That very evening the bell for the first time sent far and wide, its angelic voice. *"Deo gratias!"* said again our Catholic people, stepping out doors, to better hear the aerial music. Listen now and hear: there is the voice, which will call us hereafter to divine worship! How beautiful it sounds!! How harmonious!! Many a tear rolled down the cheeks of the pious listeners. Many a joyful event was now suddenly recalled to memory, a solemn baptism, a joyful marriage, and tears rolled on and the sounds of the bell continued.

In some places, however, the tears were not all of joy, for the Bell is not only the universal messenger of happy tidings as it rejoices with the happy and joyous, so by its lugubrious knells and mournful strains, it partakes in the sorrows of the faithful. Oh! Thou! Our faithful friend be welcome amongst us!!!! Today again we feel that we are nearer our homes!!!

As everything in and around the church improved, so also improved and increased the Catholic population. If the population increases we must make room for them. If we expect a priest amongst us, we must provide a shelter for him. Let us make an addition to the church. Let us add to it a sanctuary; let us build a room for the Father.

At the east end of the church a large ogival opening had been left, temporally closed with lumber. A building 24×18 ft. was added to the church; the half of it to be used as a sanctuary, the rest for the residence of the priest. When the outside work of this building was terminated, the Father came himself for several weeks to Lethbridge to finish all the inside work. This frame addition cost about $600.00. The new sanctuary being ready, the Father had some handsome things in store for its ornamentation: a large box had arrived from Belgium, containing beautiful candle sticks, candelabras, artificial flowers, vestments, altar linen etc.

The Father had also purchased two handsome statues of Mary and St. Joseph. A rich carpet covered the floor of the sanctuary and the temporary altar with all its ornamentations looked majestic. Another great acquisition for the church was a reed organ. This instrument purchased from the Bell Organ Co. cost nearly one hundred dollars and added very much to the solemnity of divine services. Almost everything was now provided for. The church, the sanctuary, the Father's rooms, everything was ready and in good shape. The priest only was wanting.

[Brother Jules Boone did not renew his vows. He had returned to Belgium but wanted to come back as an Emigration Agent. He expressed this desire to Father Lestanc who subsequently pleaded his case with Senator Richard Hardisty:]

Honorable Rich. Hardisty: Senator.
Edmonton

Bishop's Palace,
St. Albert. July 21st, 1888.

Dear Sir,

I have the honor to forward you the information in regard to Mr. Jules Boone according to your desire.

Mr. Jules Boone is the son of a rich merchant in Belgium.,

He is 33 or 34 years of age, he is well educated and acquired great experience in farming and stock-raising, during a stay of 13 years in the N.W.T., having all that time been at the head of our farm at St. Albert – he travelled also a good deal and knows Carlon, Battleford, Pitt, Edmonton, Battle and Red Deer Rivers, Calgary, Mcleod, etc.

He speaks fluently Flemish, English and French. He knows all the Indians of the Territories.

Wherever he passed he was greatly esteemed; in fact, he is a favorite here.

He is well posted with the "Geography & Survey" of the N.W.T. In regard to morality and probity, nothing better could be desired.

Now Jules Boone wrote to me lately that he could secure in Belgium numbers of first class immigrants for this country, if he was appointed Emigration Agent by the Canadian Government.

The present emigration agent, speaking only French, has not the same chances of success in Belgium, where most of the people speak only Flemish, as Mr. Boone would have.

Here is his address:

Belgium. Jules Boone, Esqre

I am sure no better man could be found as Emigration Agent, he is a splendid businessman and a true gentleman in every respect. His appointment to such an office would be considered a favor by his Graces Archbishop Taché and by his Lordship, bishop Grandin and by the whole clergy.

With great respect, I have the honor to be
Honorable & Dear Sir,

Your humble servant,
J.J. Lestanc. Obl. P^{tre}.

[A while later Boone wrote to Leonard (1888):]
[Letterhead:] Denrées Coloniales. Farines en tous genres. Pétrole. Jean Boone-De Wulf, Négociant. Meulebeke.

Meulebeke (W. Flanders). July 26, 1888.
Rev. and very dear Father Leonard.

I have the impression that I wrote to you over two months ago and I have not yet received an answer. As there are here several persons who would like to go and to settle in northwest Canada, I am writing to you again to ask you whether anything has changed; whether there is a special place for Belgian colonization. Where is it! And which places would be best? Now M. Watelets, Agent, occupies himself with this expedition, are emigrants assured to get a job? And is there a means to connect with families, as the young people don't know another language than Flemish? As I am convinced that it will be a pleasure for you to provide good advice, good counsel, and to lay out a good route for our brave fellow-compatriots that want to settle there around you or get a job. I will give your address to certain people who deserve to go there. Among others this week there were three men from Marialoop who came to see me: active, intelligent and from good families, one named Vanhollebeke, gardener, Felix Vermeulen, gardener, good carpenter and Bruno Lambrechts, good carpenter, miller.[59] Would they be able to find work around you? They know well how to lead a horse and two are good carpenters, but they don't speak French. Tomorrow they will leave for Detroit in Michigan, but I promised them that I would write to you and that I would let them know what you said about it.

I have written to Rev. Father Lestanc, about organizing a settlement of people around you. Is Macleod still a good area for ranchers?[60] Is ranching still profitable? Does one need money? Are there more [ranchers] than three years ago? I have always wanted to go back. Don't you know a nice old family there or a young rich man with the means to partner with me? Tell me how much money I would need? Maybe you could even find me a good companion among your parishioners, a person with means whom I could marry?[61] In Meulebeke it is always the same, no future, progress is lacking except with knives. Since I am here, stabbings have resulted in four deaths and a good many are maimed and disfigured. Everyday there are public auctions on the farms as many are going bankrupt [due to] a failing harvest, etc., and lack of money to pay their debts. You have never seen such times and I don't see how these poor people can hope for better times.

All of your family is doing fine and I don't know whether Joseph Desmet from de Sterre had died the last time I wrote to you. Since two months he is buried. My father was sick and started to walk around in the garden.

Waiting for the pleasure to hear from you, I ask to be remembered in your prayers and ask you to pass on my affectionate greetings to your brother, Brother Jean Berchmans.

Your very affectionate
Jules.

[Leonard continues:]

This year again, the Oblate Fathers of this district held their spiritual retreat in Macleod. It was after these days of recollection that Father Van Tighem was definitively transferred from Macleod to Lethbridge. Father Lacombe came himself to MacLeod to reside there and to be nearer the Indians for whom he always has felt a special predilection.[62] Then Father Leduc from St. Albert took his place in Calgary and became now the Superior of this district, all this was during September 1888. To describe the satisfaction of the Catholics of Lethbridge would be impossible. Their great wishes were now accomplished – they had the priest permanently in their midst.

Now that the Father had exclusively charge over his flock, he remarked with sorrow the great difficulty of instructing the Catholic children in their religion. Only one hour, on Sunday afternoon, was consecrated to this so important matter. There was a school in the village, our children attended it, but this being a Protestant public school, not a word of religion was ever uttered. If only we had a Catholic school!!

But where could the children be gathered together? Who shall pay for a teacher who necessarily must have a diploma from the government? There is scarcely any property in town belonging to Catholics, hence, no taxes to support the school. To build a schoolhouse would cost about $800.00. Besides, we have no site where to build and town lots are now very highly valued and we have not one dollar in our possession, worse than all, there is some $1200.00 debt on the church.

Our good Bishop Grandin came to our help. His Lordship knowing the great necessity of Catholic schools in Catholic centers bought himself five town lots near the church and furnished the sum of $500.00 to aid us to build a schoolhouse. Bishop bought five lots for school.

The Catholics were called together for the first meeting according to the school laws in our territory. This meeting took place on Monday 31 December 1888. A petition was forwarded to His Honor, J. Royal Lieutenant Governor of NWT.

[Victor to Leonard:]

Peigan Reserve. December 16, 1888.

L.Z.J.C.

Very dear brother,

This week I received a letter from Meulebeke in which they inform me that Alida has still not recovered from her lengthy illness and, to the contrary, is getting worse all the time. Upon her request someone already gave her the Extreme Unction at home. How sad it will be for Charles with his four little children and all his work and what a loss for him if Alida were to die.

Dear brother, let's double our prayers for everything good and wonderful. Gustaf and Jean are doing very well, as well as the other family members. Uncle Ivo's Jules married a daughter from Declerq from Coolscamp and now lives in Denterghem in a mill. Edouard Bruneel married Jean Buyse's sister and now has a daughter after having been married for over thirteen years. Dear brother, I thank you for the good

▸ *1888: The Charles Louis Jules Van Tighem Family: Joseph Leon, Charles Louis, Maria Josephina, Alida Amelia, Elodie, Marie Therese.* Courtesy of Van Tighem Family Archives.

news you communicated in your last letter. Father Legal has not yet left us and is busy building. Mr. Johnson is very happy to join him.

Nobody speaks about Brother Cunningham.[63] Well, after all, our numbers will decrease anyway, that is all I have to say and Father Foisy certainly is of the same opinion. It is mainly because of my health and, again, that big kitchen is killing me and then all those useless expenses!!! Because, without any increases, there are no more than 20 children. They arrive right before noon to have their biscuits and tea; I take the little ones with me into the kitchen and then, if everything goes well, another dozen remain for the schoolmaster who in total, has to teach only 2½ hours. That is how our poor savages are doing. May God improve their lot!

Dear brother, I made an entire second road in order to drive with the wagon up to our house on the hill. Two roads are certainly useful and it was a beautiful job. I also papered the ceiling of our chapel with pale-yellow paper and then with red and blue stars. With the decorations I brought along from Lethbridge and some gold and silver paper I added it really improved the altar. I took up the rest of the carpet from MacLeod to take along to the reserve, but upon leaving I forgot it. Brother Cunningham tells me that someone has sent it to you. In case you need it for your church or house, we can easily do without it, because I made a cloth for our altar out of old stockings and shirts and it looks very good. I made four beautiful chairs from crates for our chapel. Mr. Johnson will try to bring along some yards of flowered fabric from Macleod and I will cover the bare wooden planks next to the altar with it.

Dear brother I would be so pleased if you could send me twenty yards of flowered, but cheap fabric from Lethbridge. I could, I think, cover our entire chapel with it and I also think the Lord would be pleased with it. I prefer reddish fabrics with small flowers. If you still have lace, or other things you don't use, I could certainly use them here. We still lack so many things here and there are so many debts, you know this all too well.

Dear brother, send me a good package to my address; I thank you in advance. Now I am busy carpeting Mr. Johnson's room, the ceiling is clean; I still have no paper for the walls so I wallpapered them with newspapers. I also made a library for my room. I also have a Stations of the Cross here made of little, but beautiful memorial cards. I plan to make fourteen little crosses, glue silver foil on them and then the cards in the centre, I think it will not look too bad in our chapel! Father Foisy is making a splendid tabernacle for Macleod – artsy, but great work. Father Cunningham only studies and smokes a good pipe. Mr. Johnson spends a large part of his time at the Agency. We have Father Lacombe's horse here in order to be broken and also his big dog. Both came from Mr. Macfarland. Today Father Naessens will be ordained sub-deacon by Mgr. Clut.[64]

Dear brother, I wish you a merry Christmas and a healthy and happy New Year.

Your dedicated brother,
Brother John Berchmans.

[P.S.] It is Sunday night. The school inspector arrives here with a voiture of Mr. Stedman. He arrives on the worst day possible, we have no pupils before noon. He looks like a good man and speaks French.

[Leonard continues:]
On the 18th of January 1889 an answer was received that our petition was favorably granted, and the proclamation of erection of a Catholic school district in Lethbridge was announced in the official organ of the N.W. Terr. The contract for erecting a schoolhouse 30×18 ft. was let to Mr. Gay for the sum of $640.00. A teacher Mr. McRae, holding a first class diploma, was engaged and the school was to be opened as soon as the schoolhouse would be ready.

[Father Foisy (1880, 238) about Leonard:]
Father Van Tighem is always in Lethbridge, very encouraged by the Catholic population, many new men have come, full of zeal and good will. Their stone church is the pride of the coal town. It is a real treasure for a country as ours. Since a month two Catholic schools are opened, one in MacLeod organized by Father Lacombe and one in Lethbridge organized by Father Van Tighem. They do already quite well and are the envy of the Protestants of whom several send their children preferably to Protestant schools already established.

[Leonard continues:]
When it became generally known of our efforts of establishing a Catholic school in Lethbridge, the *Lethbridge News*, a small local weekly, very maliciously attacked us. Amongst other things it said:

Hitherto there has been in Lethbridge but the one public school. So far one public school system in the North West has worked well without any clashing between the denominations. In Lethbridge we understand that a vigorous opposition was made by most of the Roman Catholics to a separate school being established. They were however persuaded to consent on the understanding that a convent would be established here. We believe that the possession of such institutions is too high a price to pay for the burden of separate schools, at any event the establishment of one in Lethbridge is certainly at the present time premature, can the assembly not mitigate the evil by providing that no sep. school shall be entitled to Government assistance unless it has at least thirty attendants, the children of resident rate payers?

In the next issue of the *Lethbridge News* Father Van Tighem answered in the following manner:[65]

Febr. 17th, 1889.
To the Editor of the *Lethbridge News*.
Dear Sir,

I have been somewhat astonished by what there appeared in your last issue, against the establishment of a Catholic school in Lethbridge. As I regard your article rather a fanatical utterance than anything else, with sorrow I am compelled to answer it.

You state that, "so far one public school system has worked well, etc., etc." Do you mean to say that until now there were none but protestant public schools in the N.W.T.? If so, you must be very ignorant on historical matters of the past in these Terr. and let me say, that long before you came here, a quarter of a century before you made your appearance in the N.W.T. we had a good number of Catholic schools established.

Dear Sir, you are somewhat too young to try to prevent us going on doing the good works begun by our valiant missionaries. Many will have had a hearty laugh at your statement that: "Public feeling governed on a basis of common sense is strongly opposed to the sep. school system."

Perhaps it may be so for these who are not acquainted with our school laws, or for fanatics without common sense; they may be opposed to Catholics having their schools as well as Protestants.

But it seems, by what you say, that the ratepayers are to be burdened with taxes by the establishment of our school. Now, I am at a loss to see, if any one could be wronged except the Catholic ratepayers who are erecting the school. How then could they take the necessary steps for the establishment of the school? And you have found out how this happened. Saying:

"In Lethbridge a vigorous opposition was made by most of the R. Catholics."

Now, Dear Sir, I regard this assertion as a personal insult; giving the public to understand that I have forced the Catholics to erect a school. That there was a vigorous opposition is untrue, false. There was not the slightest opposition, and let it be known to the public now, that when we held the first and second meetings according to the Ordinance, there was not one to vote against the school. How then can you call this: "the doings of a few malcontents of the religion." By making such false statements you not only insult me, but every Catholic of this place. As to your vain assertion that, "they were persuaded to consent on the understanding that a convent was to be established," all our Catholics can give testimony of what R. Fath. Leduc said to them when he addressed the first meeting that perhaps after two, three years, a Sisterhood could be sent here. But they all asked for the Sisters at once, and Dear Sir, if it had not been for an unfortunate event, viz. the death of the Mother general of the Sisters, last December, we would perhaps have had a convent here this coming summer.

But here again you make some ridiculous assertions, saying, "at any event the establishment of a convent is premature."

Well, Dear Sir, I ask you, what idea will the people abroad form about Lethbridge? What will they think of our town in Calgary, St. Albert, Prince Albert, Brandon and Edmonton, where convents are in such a flourishing state, and for years? What will they think of our poor Lethbridge being obliged, "thoroughly to beat up Southern Alberta to find children for a convent school?"

At least you should not have published in that same issue, all your glorious prospects of railroad for Lethbridge in so near a future.

I repeat your article has astonished me. I rather thought that you would have complemented the Catholics of this place for their energetic enterprise. In one of your last issues you stated that your large school house had become too small; that two teachers could not do the work any longer; and if so, I really thought that you would have thanked us for making your position easier, for, so it must be indeed, as our taxes do not amount to anything, while we take away a fourth or third part of your children.

As to the heavy burden of taxes, our Catholics know well enough that they will not be overtaxed. Having about forty children at school age, we intend to erect a good schoolhouse; it will be built on a block of five lots, which we have already secured. We intend to hire a teacher holding a first class diploma. Now, I hope that we will be able to manage our affairs even without incurring any debenture indebtedness. This perhaps will puzzle you.

The fact is, that whatever Catholics do, fanatics must cry. If we do not erect schools, cries arise that Catholics are enemies of education and progress. So we heard lately with sounding trumpet heralded that in the N.W.T. there were actually 140 protestant schools and only 9 Catholic. Dear Sir, when our friends were erecting their school here, we never uttered a word of disapproval. Never any one has heard me say anything against the school. Would you, please, render us the same charity?

Now Dear Sir, if you be successful in amending the supposed, "radical defects in the school system," if you be successful in preventing the establishment of schools, "unless there are at least 30 attendant children of rate payers," you may begin to mitigate the great evil at home, for, more than the half of the Protestant schools in the N.W.T. do not possess that average attendance. But, I suppose, this amendment, of yours, would regard Catholics only?

I beg pardon from my many Protestant friends. If I have said that much, I have been compelled to it. I know they will forgive me, for they are acquainted with what Catholics have done and still are doing for the progress of our town. Our friends, having common sense, have also their eyes and see and judge for themselves; some of our most respected citizens have been educated in Catholic schools.

In conclusion, Dear Sir, let me say, that whoever is somewhat acquainted with the wide world, will not be shocked at the establishment of a Catholic school here. For, in the whole universe, wherever there is a Catholic church, there is also a school attached to it, a cemetery, if possible, a hospital and a manse. These things are indispensable for Catholics, without them Catholics do not feel at home. I hope that, before long, we will have them also here, except the latter however as I do not intend to erect my mansion just now.

One of your subscribers,
Father Van Tighem, O.M.I.

[Victor (1889) to Leonard:]
Peigan Reserve, February 21, 1889.
L.Z.J.C.
Very dear brother,

Enclosed is the letter I received from Charles. I find it consoling that our brother had the courage to communicate all the circumstances of the illness and death of his beloved wife. Charles has been severely tested and is feeling quite desperate. Let us pray that God will send him courage, strength and blessings. I will send him a letter encouraging him, as much as I can, to be courageous and have trust in the future. Marie is already nine years old and just like I have seen her three years ago, quick and smart. She certainly will offer to help and after two or three years be able to replace the greatly mourned Alida. Joseph will help his father; he is seven years old. Elodie is six and then there is a little angel of seven months.[66] I pray that God and Mary will be their protectors!!!!! Dear brother, send Charles a consoling letter and let him know him about the masses he requested.

Here in the reserve things go quite well, no particular news. How much progress did you make with your school? Is the churchyard finished? Did you frame the beautiful prints of Father Lacombe? Is there no other news about your church? To receive a few words from you is always agreeable to the one who calls himself,

your dedicated brother,
Frère Jean Berchmans

P.S. I received a letter from Frère Scheers. He is doing well. But, there is a lot of misery and poverty over there.[67] I will write him in a few weeks. Would you mind to drop him a line also?

Adieu
Br. J.B.

[The enclosed letter from Karel/Charles, their brother in Belgium:]
[Not dated; must be very early 1889]
Dear brothers,

Already seven weeks went by that in my arms my dearly beloved Alida for the last time said farewell and prayed and she begged that I would take good care of our four dearly beloved children, but that was not yet done when she embraced me [and asked] that I would do everything possible for her five under-age little brothers, who are also without parents. Oh brothers, there is not enough paper to describe what kind of day that Sunday, was. In the afternoon everyone in the room had to cry. She asked everyone to help out in caring for her children. And brothers, it was like a story in a book, it was unheard of and still the Sister encouraged her. But, there was nothing, that could be done to help her, she said, I go to Heaven! And right at four o'clock she collapsed in my arms, and still in complete control of her faculties she spoke until the last minute and then she was gone and neither Alida, nor Karel recognized the moment! You have no idea brothers, what it is to hold in your arms, without knowing it, the dead body of your beloved wife!!! Because you should know brothers, that for the last ten days and ten nights I have not been out of that room for ten hours, and that was to the barn, or it was always: Karel, where are you? But sister Ida, from the Geloof [convent] of Thielt looked after her very well.[68]

She was a good sister, she stayed with me another twelve days after the funeral to wash and sew everything. I had asked the superior whom I had invited to the funeral, if she could stay with me for a few more days to put everything in order, because my house looked like a market place as you can imagine. Alida had been sick in bed, unable to do anything, already for six months. For the entire summer I had two women in my house, and that [illegible] but when she stayed in bed I felt forced, I did not know what was to be done, I ask aunt Siska and she herself said you should have had a nun a long time ago for your own good and thus was said and done. The Sister came with the train of 2:00 and left with the train of 5:30 and Alida was very happy.

Dear brothers, since the death of her mother Alida has never laughed anymore. There was always something going on and everyone always came to Alida. During the time her father was ill, she never had a moment's peace, because brothers, it was always Alida who had to do everything because when Alida was not around, no one came around. As you know perhaps he could not bear to be around Camiel or Elodie; well we will not speak about it, now in the future I will briefly relate this whole story to you.

Well brothers, New Year has passed. I wish both of you a good and blissful New Year, a year of health and happiness in all your undertakings.

But brothers, it was also New Year's morning in Meulebeke. First three children jumped on my bed, shouting "Father, Happy New Year!" In Marie's arms, a fourth one, stretching out his arms, also wanted to wish New Year.[69] Tears streamed down my face, I was not yet dressed and again the door went open, five brothers entered, also extending Karel a good and blissful New Year. I could no longer contain myself when I looked at all of these young people. God works in wonderful, but mysterious ways! In the short period of twenty months a mother, a father and Alida disappeared into eternity. Brothers, I confess that last summer I nearly left too.

One night Alida found me sick in bed. Nobody knew what I suffered from, not even the doctor, but it took only three hours. When last Saturday I told the doctor about my situation he said in six words what I had suffered from to Dewilde, Elodie's husband, who you, Brother Joannes, know. It was colère [fits of anger?] and I should not have worked on and on. I will later tell you, about it, I assure you. Well brother Leonard, Alida asked me three days before her death, if I would have twenty-five masses offered for the repose of her soul. I promised Alida I would. You will certainly do it for a bit less or for 6 frs. as in Meulebeke. Well brother, I request that you say these masses as soon as possible, I will pay whatever it cost. Well brothers, this is all that happened, I have to work harder to make sure I earn about 1200 francs per year. It does not go well and I really don't know what to do. Wherever I show my face, one gives me advice, but when I take all these advises together, without [illegible] to speak. There is always something, sometimes I think, I would like to go to America too. Many of Meulebeke are going to these areas, but when I look at the little one, I know it is not yet possible. Brothers, I request that both of you pray that the Our Lord will give me strength to carry on. I expect a letter from both of you, shortly, straight from your heart, what you think of me or what you require from me.

Karel van Tighem,

[P.S.] Until 14 days.
See brother Joanes, here is one more envelope written by Alida.
Your youngest and sad brother Van Tighem, Karel.

[Bishop Grandin wrote, in French:]

St. Albert, February 20, 1889

LSJC.

Dear Father Van Tighem,

I learned about the death of your sister-in-law and the consequences it has for your poor brother. Tell me what you think I could do despite your poverty. If you know some community where the children can be raised, I could write myself and I think that I could get a discount for half or maybe even full pension just as I obtained for similar cases in France.

Don't let yourself get demoralized, dear Father, write to your brother, tell him that despite your poverty you will do everything to help him, ask him what you could do for him, what his wishes are.

I bless you affectionately, also your dear brother

Your affectionate brother,

†Vital Grandin, bish. of St. Albert, O.M.I.

[Karel/Charles' daughter Marie wrote, in Dutch:]

Meulebeke, March 16, 1889.

Very dear uncle,

I am happy that I may add a few lines to father's letter and tell you that I go daily to church and do my best to learn much and to be of help for my father. I can knit, have already knitted four pairs of stockings and currently I also learn how to sew. If father agrees, I will add a little letter each time he writes to you. I am now in the French school in order to learn there.

Joseph, Elodie and I were happy to receive your praying card.

Please accept, dear Uncle, the best wishes of your little dedicated niece

Marie Van Tighem.

[Karel reflects in his letter again on the death of his wife Alida, assures his brothers that things were not that bad as they assumed and added the following postscript:]

"My help [Marietje] is now going to the Gelove convent in Thielt."

[Leonard continues:]

The Catholic school opened on the 3rd day of April and about thirty-five children were inscribed on the roll. Having a school now of our own, where the Catholic children besides the ordinary branches of science, received daily religious instruction, the Father had something else in view. A few

Catholic children had died and were buried in the open prairie, where their graves were daily desecrated by cattle and other animals.

The different protestant denominations had held several meetings for the purpose of fencing in a piece of land for a graveyard, but they never had come to any understanding. Father Van Tighem, who had carefully examined the location of the burial grounds, went to see Mr. Magrath, who had charge of the company's lands, and asked him for a few acres, just behind the actual graves, but on the eminence of the hill.

After many objections, the principal one being: fear of offending the other denominations by giving us the nicest spot, he consented, saying that they had had time enough to build their fence, that they always were slow, etc., etc. The Father, for fear of *contre* orders, placed at once two men on the spot who begun to dig the post holes for the fence. The next day the Father went around to all the Catholic houses, making a collection, this time to build a cemetery fence. He was well received by all his parishioners, for they all wished to have a blessed ground for their dead and a modest fence to surround it. In two evenings the Father gathered the sum of $140.00 about sufficient to put up the fence. He himself made a large cross of cedar wood and painted it white. After a few weeks everything was finished. The large cross stands on the top of the hill, like on a Calvary, and commands respect. From everywhere it can be seen, miles away.

[From a letter from Karel (1889), it seems that Leonard had suggested that Karel should come to Canada and that Bishop Grandin had offered Karel to take care of his children:]

Meulebeke, April 14, 1889.

Very dear brother Leonard,

I received the letter you sent me on March 10th, but I answered you earlier and you should have the letter I sent you March 17th, in which you will find again the memories of my dearly beloved Alida, because, brother, it is impossible to write you what I have to do from now on and what great loss my children suffer.

Ha brother, what can I do these days? Right now I should be on four or five places at the same time, have to go with the milk, must be at home, people come there the whole day for stuff or plants, should take care of my animals myself, should be on my land and should conduct all my business myself and I should not go to anyone for advice. I have been finding out the hard way the more Karel keeps his mouth shut, less is been said and dear brother, you can image how I am doing in this season, a maid and a servant at home, people at work.

Well, dear brother, there is not much that can be done about it, it is even much better than you [illegible] of me, thank God, I don't lack anything; my businesses do well, people like me and want to be with Karel. You should see me on the market with my help and Marie; it is a pleasure to see how Marie, still so young in years already so skilfully helps out at the market, because brother, without bragging, there are five next to me and I can assure you, when the market is over, in general I have received as much or more money in this season as the other five together, because every year I plant all kinds of seeds and because all people see the plants and see them grow, they all want to have them and I sell gladly.

Dear brother, reading your letter again I could not contain myself anymore and there is not a day that passes I don't cry because you are right, in the entire Meulebeke there are no three children like mine, still so young and going out of their way cheer up their father somewhat. And I say it again, if my dearly beloved Alida had lived I would have been the happiest man of Meulebeke and I would not have wished that the king had been my father.

Dear brother, maybe you made too much out of my letter or maybe I wrote too much because at that time my head was not with it or maybe one of my brothers or a friend wrote this or that, because brother, I don't know myself how I got through the ordeal, but I tell you again, thank God I don't have to be ashamed to anyone, I have no debts, not one cent and can conduct my business openly, what next year will bring I don't know but I do know that our dear Lord never beats twice with a stick and what I wrote about coming to you, that was only a thought, because dear brother, I see every day too many go to America but not those who are too lazy to work and there should also certainly have been [illegible] to leave my place of birth and to wander with my little sheep over the big sea. It is true that I already would have been there, just as you wrote me, what could I do there.

Well brother, let us not talk again about it; I will not give it another thought. I am alone and would bite iron [illegible] to tame our senses in all those businesses, the stones are asking for money and entire days I don't hear anything else than about money, but now I will not talk about it. When everything is over I will explain it extensively to you, the estate of father Smet will be sold on May 9 and then everything will be settled as soon as possible and now some news.

Dewilde, who is married to Elodie, Alida's sister, as Victor knows, now also left with all of their furniture and crossed the big sea to America the good voyage and the [illegible].

Dear brother, thank you and if allowed later, I, or my children will reward you for the masses I asked for and that you said for my dearly beloved Alida.

Dear brother, I have reread the letter one hundred times, if possible, I am stunned when I read the reason that Monsignor Grandin would have wanted to take care of my children, ha, what a great happiness for the little sheep that they don't have [illegible] now there are so many sad orphans and dear brother, thank him on my behalf and from the bottom of my heart and tell him that my children will say a two Paternosters for him. If it can be done, I will try to keep my children with me; what a great sadness it would be if all these little children would be separated from me.

Dear brothers, I don't lack anything, a good prayer from both of you for what is good and blissful for me, because at this time when I start reading one letter, I always fall asleep or one asks for me and I should have three thoughts at the same time.

Dear brothers, our brothers in Meulebeke do very well, they are all healthy and Jean's house is [illegible], they are like a lot of sheep and I will send you soon my portrait and also one of all of the children, there is now a photographer in Meulebeke.

Dear brother Joannes Berchmans, I could not write to you much because of lack of time, I will send you in short some news, that Jules Boone married the widow Debrabander of Belleghem near Kortrijk and has two boys and he lives there and will be a brewer there.

From your brother Karel Van Tighem.

[Leonard continues:]
When his Lordship, our good Bishop Grandin, came to visit Lethbridge again in June of the same year 1889, he blessed our cemetery, and remaining a few days amongst us, His Lordship confirmed 18 persons. On this occasion our saintly bishop received a public reception and three addresses were presented. One by Mr. Thom Curry in English, one by Mr. Noël in French and a Slavonic address by Mr. Lewis Perumko.

His Lordship answered these gentlemen and the whole congregation present, and the Catholics returned to their homes more satisfied than ever. I have mentioned, just now, that there was a Slav or Slavonic address. It may not be out of place to mention here how Lethbridge is a conglomeration of numerous nations of the world.

Lately I counted how many different nationalities I had in my church. I counted fourteen: Irish, English, Scotch, Americans, French, Belgians, Germans, Italians, Slavonic, Hungarians, Spaniards, Canadians, Half-breeds, Indian Blackfoot, besides a Mulatto. But we are alone to have all these different nationalities.

The Protestants have only a few, which is a glaring proof of our title Catholic. *Credo in Ecclesiam Catholicam!* As there were over one hundred of Slavonic Catholics, I thought they should have their own address to our good bishop. They offered His Lordship also one of their old country prayer books, in the Slav language, with wooden covers and iron clasps. It is a specimen of curiosity.

The Slavonic Catholics belong to the Greek United Church and have preserved up to this day, the holy simplicity of our first Christians.[70] They are sincerely attached to their religion and to their priest.[71] They will almost blindly follow his commands and directions. To give only one illustration:

Last spring when we had the church pews publicly rented, an old man came to me the next day, with his grandson, and asked me to rent a pew also for him and his family.

I was aware that the old man was somewhat neglectful and seldom came to church, and before renting the pew I told him my satisfaction and my hopes to see him in church regularly in the future. In fact, said I, you must be there *Lazdy dzem*, which means "every day," while I should have said *Lazdy, Nedzela*, "every Sunday." [72] He rented the pew.

The next morning, while ringing the Angelus, I observed the old man coming across the public square. Taking off his hat and making three times the sign of the cross at the three pulls of the bell. From that day, till late in the fall when the weather became too cold to say mass in church, the good, old father Kranyak, occupied his rented pew every morning.

These Slavonic Catholics make the sign of the cross in the very primitive manner, instead of signing from the left to the right side, as we do, they sign from the right to the left side. When, and where our forefathers have changed this manner of making the sign of the cross, and why they have changed it, my small library has failed to satisfy my researches. [73]

The presence of so many Catholic Slavonians obliged me to prepare for hearing their confessions. Some good young fellows, having been in the United States for several years, could speak fluently the English language. [74] With their assistance, I made immediately a complete interrogatory, as also a few short exhortations, and ever since, I have heard their confessions, baptized, married, and attended to their spiritual wants.

The year 1890 was memorable to Lethbridge, on account of a new railroad from this place to Great Falls in Montana.[75] It was thought that the large smelters of Great Falls would demand a great quantity of our Lethbridge coal. But the two years, which have passed since, have proved the contrary. The company has been to great expenses and derives no benefit from it. Times may change though, especially as the Company has secured the services of a very clever superintendent in the person or Mr. Barclay.

During the summer of 1890 our little church was yet more beautified by six handsome stained glass windows. The summers being very hot here, and the sun letting its burnings rays come down on the sidewalls of the church and through the windows; it was absolutely necessary to think about shading the openings. Besides, the winters being cold, a double window was very much required. This twofold inconvenience was remedied by the placing of stained glass windows on the inside, with small ventilators at the bottom. The different subjects represented are: Sacred Heart of Jesus, Immaculate Conception, St. Patrick, St. John Baptist, St. Peter, St. Paul. De windows were made in Montreal by Castle & Son and cost about $30 each.

▶ *"Tracklayers just finished on Montana Line of Alberta Railway and Coal Co., Lethbridge, Oct. 1, 1890."* P19720115000-GP. Courtesy of Sir Alexander Galt Museum, Lethbridge.

As the year 1890 was nearing its end, a great and happy news was sent to us. It had been finally decided that a Sisterhood was to be sent to Lethbridge. Moreover that three Mothers and one Sister would be here with the beginning of the New Year.

In fact, our school had become too small, there were about 50 children attending, far too many for one teacher. The Father, having continually renewed his instances to obtain a Sisterhood for this place, saw now his hopes realized.

A great news it was; the good Mothers were welcomed many times, long before they arrived. Now, no time was to be lost. We had no buildings to receive the Mothers, and they were to be here in about a month. The Father, at once went to work, made plans and specifications for a building of 40×32 feet; two stories with a mansard roof. The contract for this building was signed on the 22nd of November and work was immediately begun.

When the good Sisters, Faithful Companions of Jesus, arrived on New Years eve, the building was only half terminated.[76] But the addition to the schoolhouse had been converted into a kitchen and the good religious made themselves at home in the large schoolroom, where they remained for over two weeks, that is, during the Christmas holidays. Meanwhile, two rooms were fitted up in the new building, with cotton, flannels, canvas etc., etc. There the Sisters remained till the midsummer holidays, when the building was to be plastered.

[Majeau (1983, 260) about the Sisters' journey:]

Five Sisters from Prince Albert, Edmonton and Calgary met at a small coal trading post called Dunmore, east of Medicine Hat. As early as 1885, Dunmore had a narrow-gauge railway! (No CP or CN train ran into the fort at this time.) Sometimes, at night, a fairly comfortable passenger-coach was attached to the coal trucks but since our nuns were advised by Fr. Van Tighem to travel by day, they used the guard's van at the end of the twenty or so coal cars for this their first, smutty, bumpy, ride of 100 miles to their new mission. Arriving earlier than was expected, the Sisters made their way to the Church where Our Divine Lord was the first to welcome them.

[The Sisters, Faithful Companions of Jesus (1890) reported about their reception. Transcript:]

The good priest, the Rev. Père Leonard Van Tighem, who had been anxiously looking forward to our arrival, gave us a warm reception and had provided everything necessary for us with the greatest kindness and charity. We were conducted to the schoolroom where we found a kitchen stove and good supply of utensils, a tea service, bread meal, fowl, eggs, milk, etc. in fact, all we could wish except beds and bedsteads. Two school desks placed together made, however, a cozy bed and we gathered from our bundles all the clothing we could spare as covering. The new house was not complete so there was no alternative but to give a week's holidays. At the end of this time two rooms only had their doors and windows. These were lathed only as no plastering could be done unless after the frost, one room facing North, the other West, it can easily be imagined what we suffered from the cold. The good Father did his best to make our room habitable and he himself screened the walls as best he could with calicos, sheets, etc.

[Leonard continues:]

Three Sisters were employed in school from nine in the morning till four in the afternoon, though two mistresses only were engaged and drew government salaries. It was hard labor for the good Mothers, and having such poor quarters to retire, they soon experienced the fatal consequences. Rev. Mother Frances, the superior caught first a cold, which soon turned into a severe attack of bronchitis, bringing her almost to the verge of the grave.

For months and months the poor Mother lingered and it was only in the summer time that she temporarily recovered. I say temporarily, for the lungs being affected, a permanent and complete cure is beyond the skill of doctors.

Thus, during the summer of 1891 the convent building was completed, all except the mansard. This building cost $2300.00 besides $130.00 for the outside painting, all of which was furnished by the Catholic mission, with the exception of $500.00, which our good bishop donated for the convent.

How everything changed now in and around the mission! What a great relief to the Father, all the kettles and pots and pans and dishes had now been transferred to the good Sister Helene, good bye, said the Father, and a hearty goodbye it was, goodbye to the cooking department. For eight years he had been his own cook and servant, and now today that heavy burden fled from his conscience.

No longer shall he have to sweep the church himself, nor prepare the vestments, and altar linen. He will be sure now that every Sunday the organist will be there, and the choir will improve, and the angelic voices of the children will mix with the stronger voices of the men and will sweeten them, and all this for the greater glory of God.

Thanks oh! Ye! Angel guardian of Lethbridge mission, thanks, take up to Heaven and place before the throne of the Almighty our prayers and offerings. He has laden us with numerous benefits. He has blessed us. Let His Holy name be praised!! May all the Catholics of Lethbridge acknowledge His gifts and in return faithfully serve Him. *Quid retribuam Domino pro omnibus quid retribuit mihi??* May we all become less unworthy of so many graces and blessings.

The year 1891 was a year of great labors for the priest in Lethbridge. The Catholic population during that year numbered about five hundred. The little church had become far too small and the Father was obliged to say two masses every Sunday: a Low Mass was said at nine o'clock and High Mass at eleven. All the school children assisted at the first mass, during which they sung beautiful hymns. The Father made some familiar and simple instruction at this mass, intended for the children, though a good number of grown up persons assisted. This was often called also the Communion Mass, as the faithful communicated at this rather than at High Mass. So it was the Father's task to make three instructions or sermons for every Sunday. One for the children at nine, at High Mass and again at Vespers in the evening.

Although the mission had been established for almost four years, it had been impossible to fence in the mission property. The convent and school also had no enclosures. It was very inconvenient by times, especially to the good Mothers, to have their dwelling we may say, on the street. The neighbours became more and more numerous, and if up to this moment we had been surrounded by good, quiet people, we might expect different at any moment. Therefore, notwithstanding this year had been an exceptional one for great expenses, the Father endeavored to better our condition by putting up substantial fences around our buildings.

A good occasion soon presented itself and hastened the execution of this necessary improvement. The company offered some lumber for sale, about six dollars per thousand cheaper than at the lumberyard. Also some good strong posts, just what was needed and at reasonable prices. The Father at once bought all the material necessary for both fences around the church and the convent, making an extension of over one thousand feet in length. This material cost over two hundred dollars. Once in possession of the material, the fences arose by little and little as all the work was done by ourselves. Our Slavish Catholics with a few others came to dig the postholes, a few days later, while there was no work in the mines, they again came and planted the posts; and so the work was all done: *Gratis pro Deo*. Thus, before the winter came, all our fences were finished, had their necessary gates and locks and bolts, and we could say again, that a great improvement had been made to the Catholic mission.

The great feast of Christmas was approaching and as during the past summer, the Sisters' Community had increased of one more member and a good musician, preparations were made for a grand High Mass in music. The choir, of late, had been also considerably improved with the arrival of Captain Begin and Mrs. Begin. Peter's celebrated mass was regularly practised in the schoolhouse and when Christmas arrived the choir was prepared to satisfy the desires of the greatest critic.

The weather was bad on Christmas day, strong winds and very stormy, so that most of the ladies could not venture outdoors. The church however was well filled; the singing was beautiful, and something more important, there had been many Communions in the morning.

Up to this date, I have preferred to celebrate no midnight Mass. First, because the church is too small and more than half of the people would be to remain outside. Secondly, for fear of some disturbance, caused by drunken men, as it might happen on such nights. Farther, I am all-alone and my health scarcely would permit me to undertake these nocturnal solemnities, without hindering these of the day.

The year 1891 came to a close, but before saying goodbye, it sent us a most unwelcome visitor, *La Grippe*. Many people had been attacked here by the influenza during the previous years, and now again it made its appearance. The Father, having been spared last winter, when almost everyone was prostrated, received his share this time. For several days he was obliged to remain in bed, unable to speak, as the disease affected principally the throat. After a few days of rest, however, he could resume his ordinary occupations.

I have now given a general record of the principal events and incidents, which have occurred from the foundation of this new mission of Lethbridge, up to this date, January 1892. Having no convenient registers at the beginning, and being encumbered with labors of every description, the Journal of the Mission had been neglected. I hope that hereafter this Record will receive due attention.

L. Van Tighem, P^{tr}. O.M.I.

For several weeks our miners work only two or three days per week. It seems the company cannot find market for their coal.

A new organ has been ordered for the church. As the reverend Father Lacombe is in Montreal, we learned that Mr. Van Horne, President of the CPR, will give a free transportation of the different articles, which the Rev. Father will obtain for the missions."

An organ is needed at the convent for teaching the children hymns, as also to accompany the Calisthenic [sic] movements of the pupils. Therefore we thought it better to purchase a larger one for the church, and hand over the other to the convent.

On the 3rd of February we had rather a celebrated marriage in the church, The nephew of Cardinal Tacherau, Mr. Duchesnay from Quebec, but sergeant of the N.W.M. Police at Lethbridge, was married to Miss Roberge. It was a grand ceremony, assisted and witnessed by all the non-commissioned officers of this post.

Today, February 16th, there was a concert in the Opera House, for the benefit of the convent. Mostly all the performers were Protestants, and this is the best sign that the Mothers are very much respected by the citizens of Lethbridge. Captain Begin was the organizer of this charitable undertaking. The receipts will be over one hundred dollars net.

March 6th: A notice has been published that our coalmines will be closed on the 15th of this month; all the unmarried men will be discharged. This is a very bad blow for our little town, as over three hundred miners will quit Lethbridge.

Today, March 10th: our large organ arrives. It is a very powerful instrument and gives us the greatest satisfaction. It is from the Bell Organ Co. Guelph, Ontario.

Rev. Father Lacombe, now preaching a mission to the Piguis Indians in Manitoba, writes that he will first visit His Lordship at St. Albert, also Calgary, before coming back to Macleod and Pincher Creek.

Today, 15th, our mines are closed and the men receive their wages. We expect many will leave the town tomorrow.

St. Patrick's Day was celebrated with solemnity in our church. The High Mass was assisted by a large congregation; a beautiful mass in music way was rendered by the choir and very ably accompanied by Mrs. Capt. Begin. Father Comiré from Macleod, being on a visit here, was the celebrant.[78] In the sanctuary were Father Van Tighem and Frère Jean, his brother from the Peigan reservation.[79] Father Van Tighem addressed the congregation, taking for his text, "I believe in the communion of the saints – where these words come from? What is their meaning? They prove the Cath. doctrine of praying to the saints of paradise, of praying for the death. Hence our forefathers placed the nations, the towns, the villages, the peoples, and the individuals under the protection of the Saints – why have you the name of Peter, Paul, Joseph, Patrick etc.? Why St. Mary's church, . Peter's, St. Paul's, St. Patrick's cathedral? All this means the communion of the saints."

Our Irish Catholics were very much pleased with the discourse, especially with the eulogy the Father made at the end of the discourse, of the sons of St. Patrick, going the world around to plant the standard of the cross and like St. Patrick to sow the seed of the Word of God.

In the evening our ladies held a grand bazaar at the opera house for the benefit of the convent. At first, we thought it could not be a success on account of the bad times in our mines. But every one was surprised to see a large crowd gathering together in the evening. Very handsome pieces of needlework, paintings had been prepared by the Sisters and some other ladies. Nearly three hundred dollars were made that evening.

Today 20th March: About 60 men left the town for Great Falls.

March 21st: Twenty-one pieces of goods arrive here from Montreal today, for Father Lacombe, mostly all gifts in books and clothing, from friends in the East. A handsome altar and tabernacle are also received from St. Albert, made by Brother Brochard for our church of Lethbridge.[80]

23rd: The new altar and tabernacle are now put up in the church. They will be veiled, however, until Easter Sunday when the altar will be blessed.

28th: At about nine o'clock this evening we had a big fire in town, four houses were destroyed. The worse is that some miserable being must have lighted this fire purposely as it started upstairs in a house unoccupied. We are planting some trees around the church.

April 7th: Father Lacombe, after an absence of over four months, is expected here tomorrow, en route for his mission of Holy Cross, MacLeod, and Pincher Creek. The Reverend Father Lacombe accompanied by Brother

Danis arrived last night, 9th April.[81] The Reverend Father sung High Mass today and will address the congregation this evening. Brother Danis has come to those missions on account of his feeble health. He will continue his theological studies at the Blood Reservation.

Today April 12th: Father Lacombe and Brother Danis take the road of MacLeod. Capt. Dean of the N.W.M.P. kindly offers a fine vehicle and four horses; another team has preceded them with their baggage. During the Holy Week we have the Stations of the Cross on Wednesday, Thursday and Friday evenings followed by an instruction.

Easter Sunday, April 17th: We had beautiful services in the church today, a busy day for the priest in Lethbridge. Early in the morning the Slav women came to church with baskets full of eatables: cakes, meats, eggs, butter, jugs of water even, all this to be solemnly blessed by the priest on Easter Sunday morning, after the manner and custom of their own country.

Confessions, which had been heard till ten o'clock last night, resumed this morning. Holy Communion was distributed at 8 o'clock and at 9 o'clock. High Mass at eleven: grand music and sermon. In the evening at 7 o'clock solemn vespers, sermon and benediction with the Blessed Sacrament and confessions again. A large congregation had gathered for High Mass. The altar was blessed before the service begun, and was most handsomely decorated. As we had some cold rain towards the evening, the attendance at vespers was not so large as at High Mass.

May 2nd: R. Father Lacombe returns to Montreal, tonight. While in the East lately, the Rev. Father obtained from the president of the CPR Mr. Van Horne, a palace car, in order to give an opportunity to several bishops of Canada and other prominent men, to visit our missions in the northwest and also in British Columbia. We have rather bad weather for over two weeks, snow and rain every day and frost at night.

4th: A policeman, a German, was killed here today, his horse falling on him and injuring him gravely interiorly. He only lived a few hours after the accident.

11th: A letter from our beloved bishop announces that our annual retreat will take place in St. Albert, on the thirteenth of June. Rev. Father Royer is to preach this retreat.[82]

14th: This afternoon a telegram arrives from Benton, from His Lordship Bishop Brondel of Helena, stating that he will leave Great Falls on next Tuesday to come to Lethbridge and from here to Dunmore and Med. Hat to meet the illustrious visitors in their journey to the different missions in the northwest and British Columbia.[83] Father Van Tighem starts for Great Falls in order to meet His Lordship there and bring Him to Lethbridge. Arrived in Great Falls on Monday morning, the Father says mass in the church there, where he meets Father Dols, a Hollander.[84] As both the Fathers had the Flemish for their mother tong, they were happy to converse in that language together.[85]

On the next day, Monseignor Brondel arrived in Great Falls, and as he also is from Belgium and from Bruges, they all three could now join in chorus and sing *Vlaandren den Leeuw!!!* [Flanders the Lion!!!].[86] Monsignor Brondel remained in Lethbridge for nearly a week and happy indeed were the days spent together by these two Belgians. On Saturday night 21st May, arrived also in Lethbridge Mgr. McDonnell, bishop of Alexandria, Glengary, Ontario, visiting some of his relatives residing in Lethbridge.

So we had the happiness of possessing two bishops at our Sunday services in the church. Moreover, Father Legal was invited and arrived here with Brother Danis. Father Legal said High Mass. The two bishops assisted in their robes, Brother Danis was master of ceremonies and Father Van Tighem joined the choir for the occasion. Bishop Brondel preached an elaborated sermon at High Mass and a still more effective one in the evening. Several Protestants assisted. A great dinner had been prepared at the convent. On the next day, the party was invited to Mrs. Cody's for Bishop McDonnel is Mrs. Cody's uncle.

On Monday night 23rd the two bishops took the evening train to Dunmore and Father Van Tighem escorted them as far as Medicine Hat. On Tuesday evening, the illustrious visitors arrived at Med. Hat. Arch. Bishop Taché – Archb. Duhamel, Bishop Lorvin, Bishop La Flèche, Bishop Grouard, and many others of the high clergy of Canada.[87] They will pass Ascension Day in Calgary and from there go to St. Albert, return to Calgary, proceed to Kamloops to assist at the meeting of the Indians: thence to New Westmunster, Vancouver and Victoria. Among the visitors was one Redemptorist Father, a Belgian residing in Montreal. He comes to inspect the country and see if some Belgian families could be brought here.

June 1st: Father Van Tighem takes the stage today for MacLeod in order to visit Father Comiré at that place. He had not seen his old mission for over six months.

June 10th: Father Lacombe's great ecclesiastical excursion is over. His Lordship Bishop Brondel arrives in Lethbridge on his way to Great Falls and Helena. His Lordship remains for two days here, and gives us a fine description of the glorious receptions, which the noble party has received all over the North West Terr. and British Columbia. Bishop Brondel is delighted with what he has seen in our different missions.

June 12th: Today a few of our children made their first communion at High Mass. In the afternoon at 4 o'clock they received the Holy Scapular, renewed their baptismal vows, and were consecrated to the Sacred Heart of Jesus and Mary Immaculate.

27th: Father Van Tighem departs tonight from Lethbridge in order to assist at the annual retreat that takes place at St. Albert. When arrived at Gleichen on the CPR a dispatch called the father back to Medicine Hat, where a man is dangerously ill.[88] The Father returned at once, and administered the Last Sacraments to a Slav man suffering from an inflammation in the bowels, returning at once, the father arrived in Calgary at 2 o'clock in the morning to depart again for Edmonton at 8 a.m.

The Reverend Father Royer from Quebec preached the retreat to twenty-nine priests and nineteen lay brothers. The retreat being terminated we, at once, returned to our missions. A secular priest, Mr. Gagnon, accompanied us, and will have charge of the Catholic population of Pincher Creek and MacLeod. We have no rain in Lethbridge for several months. Everything is drying up.

Smallpox are actually in Victoria, over forty cases. This horrible disease has been brought over to Calgary, where five people are infected with it. The good Sisters Grey Nuns are nursing them in their tents, some two miles out of that town.[89] There has been a case of smallpox in MacLeod also. The patients, both in Calgary and Macleod are almost out of danger, and no new cases have occurred since.

July 25th: The good Sisters, Faithful Companions of Jesus, have the happiness of possessing in their midst Rev. Mother Gibson, sent by the Mother General of their order, to visit their different houses of Canada. A new convent is soon to be opened at Rat Portage. As they can give no more subjects to the Lethbridge convent, we shall have no boarders hereafter.

Five cases of smallpox are reported from Gretna, south of Winnipeg, one man has died of this horrible disease.

Aug. 22nd: Father Van Tighem is visiting the different missions West of Lethbridge. Capt. McDonnell kindly offers the Father a place in his rig and in a few hours they arrive at MacLeod. It is the Reverend Mr. Gagnon, a secular priest, who is in charge of this mission for the time being, as the Rev. Father Lacombe has taken permanent charge of St. Michel's Mission, Pincher Creek.

MacLeod, which has now a railway, is menaced of having its town site once more removed or changed; the station of the railway being at three miles distant from the present town site. But the people seem to be resolute not to change for the present, which, perhaps, is wise. Arrived in MacLeod in the afternoon, Father Van Tighem continues his journey with Rev. Mr. Gagnon to the Peigan Reserve, 15 miles distance. This mission has very much improved materially; the house is very comfortable, the surroundings, especially the gardens, are very well cared for. Rev. Father Foisy and

Frère John Berchmans are valiant workers, notwithstanding the difficulties they meet with. For about ten years the missionaries are working in their midst and no conversions have been operated. The Fathers baptize the little children, teach them in their youth, but when arrived at maturity, they follow the example of their heathen parents.

Aug. 23rd: Fathers Foisy and Van Tighem leaving the Peigan mission in the morning, take the direction towards Pincher Creek to visit Rev. Father Lacombe. Rev. Mr. Gagnon returns to Macleod to administer the last Sacraments to an old man dying. About eight miles West of the Peigan Mission, Father Foisy has build another schoolhouse where he teaches himself the little Indians of that camp, while Frère John continues the same tedious work at the previous mission. We pay a visit to this new school, which consists of a small log building, very neatly finished, a stable, etc. All the work has been done by the missionary himself. After a short visit at this place we proceeded to Pincher Creek, where we found Rev. Father Lacombe at work. He is building an addition to the church, which will be used as a residence for some time.

Aug. 27th: Returning to Macleod the next morning, we meet Rev. Father Legal, who resides at the Blood reservation. This Rev. Father is for over ten years in this district and has been most of the time engaged in mission-

▶ *"Tents of Blackfeet"*
Van Tighem Family
Archives.

ary work among the Blackfoot tribes especially those of the Peigans and Bloods.

R. Father Legal took Father Van Tighem with him to the [Blood] reservation where he never had been before, although for about nine years in this district. Father Legal has a fine mission house on the reserve, is assisted by a lay Brother, Br. Bareau, and a teacher, actually, Mr. Burk. There is also a scholastic Brother: Danis, who, under Father Legal, completes his theological studies. The little community lives in perfect harmony, and the rules of our congregation are strictly observed. During his visit to Ottawa, last year, Father Lacombe obtained from the government that a hospital be build on the Blood Reservation.[90]

The work has not been started yet although the Fathers expect daily the plans and specifications of this construction. While at the reserve we paid a visit to the agent, Col. Irvine, who received us very kindly and seems to be full of good dispositions toward the missionary. After a few days passed in this happy little community, Father Van Tighem returned to his mission of Lethbridge. The farm instructor, Mr. Wilson, took the Father back. Rev. Father Thérien of Medicine Hat, who was to take charge of the Lethbridge mission during the absence of Father Van Tighem, could only pay two flying visits, as he had to look after three of four patients in danger at the hospital of Med. Hat.[91] So when Father Van Tighem arrived in Lethbridge, he found the mission without a priest and the good Sisters in great anxiety, as there was presently a person very dangerously ill. Although it was dark when the Father arrived, and after a journey of about forty miles, he, at once, proceeded to visit the dying person; administered her the Last Sacraments and returned home quite fatigued, as he had to walk over two miles, descending and klimming [climbing] up the steep banks of the Belly River.

Aug.31st: The woman patient, who was at agony yesterday, is improved considerably, almost out of danger.

Sept. 6th: Rev. Father Thérien who resides at Med. Hat paid a flying visit to Lethbridge again; as he has to attend several small missions along the Canadian Pacific he never can remain long on one place.

Sept. 13th: Reverend Father Legal arrived here last week with the plans and specifications for a hospital, a small church and a schoolhouse. He advertized for tenders and five or six contractors applied. The government grant toward the hospital is $2500.00 for both buildings and furniture of the hospital. The contractor's estimates amounted to over three thousand dollars for the building alone.

15th: Rev. Father Legal returned to the Blood Reservation.

Oct. 8th: Alarming tidings arrived from France; our Very Reverend Father General of the Oblates is dangerously ill at Royaumont. A second letter announces that our beloved Superior General has received the sacraments of the dying. Special prayers are recommended for this beloved Father to all the members of our congregation.

Oct. 12th: The 400th anniversary of Christopher Columbus discovery of America is celebrated today all over the New World. In Lethbridge we try to have our share of the festivities. A large Canadian flag floats over the schoolhouse. High Mass at October o'clock was celebrated with solemnity. After mass the school children walked back to the schoolhouse where a lottery for handsome prices took place, after which followed a distribution of candies. In the afternoon came the sports: sack races, fast races, three leg races, ring races, boot and shoe races, etc., etc. At four o'clock we had a solemn benediction with the Bl. Sacrament and *Te Deum!* A monster supper was now ready at the convent for all the pupils, and 82 young stomachs attacked the good things set before them. A magnificent show of the *Magic Lantern* by Rev. Father Legal was the crowning of the festival. For over two hours the children gazed with upbraithed silence, to the handsome views appearing as by magic upon the fine white linen sheet.

Before departing another lottery for some agreeable play things took place, and another pail of candies was emptied into their pockets. Never our children had enjoyed such a festival day! Never, they say, the memory of Columbus Day will vanquish out of their memory.

Oct. 31st: Sad news arrives from France: our Very Reverend Father Fabre, Superior-General of the Oblate Fathers, died last week at Royaumont after having been ill for several weeks. RIP. The general administration has sent a large mourning circular to all the houses and missions of our congregation. Every priest of the society will say five masses for the departed soul of our beloved Father General. The Brothers will offer five Holy Communions. May He rest in peace. Amen.

Another fatal message is brought us, also over from France this morning. The Mother-visitor to our convent this spring, having returned to France, send us the painful news, that it has been decided by the Sup. Gen.-in-council to withdraw the Sisters from Lethbridge. The reason why is: because they have no subjects enough for their institutions. And we may ask: why then, has this good Mother Gibson established a new convent at Rat Portage lately? This good Mother-visitor is far from being in odor of sanctity here: now that the mission has been to so great expenses of building a convent, now that the good Sisters after great privations, are so conveniently settled, now that everything is prosperous they must abandon this establishment. However, if it is the will of God, "of which we greatly doubt," we humbly submit, or at least, try to do so.

Nov.: Father Van Tighem received news from Belgium. Some old lady relatives make again the gift of two hundred franks to the missions. This is the fourth time they make such generous gifts. May the Lord reward their kind generosity!

[By November 1892, Leonard must have received the following letter from his cousin Pharailde Lecluyse, addressed to and passed on by Joannes (Victor):]
  Meulebeke, October 10, 1892.
  Brother Joannes,

Since long I have been meaning to write to you, but I had to go to school and did not find the time. When we received your letter, I said that I would now write first to America.

Aunt is in full health, thank God, the entire family does well.

On Vosken's mill things are going well too, Camiel married Francisca Poelvoorde and they live near the Pollevietjes mill in a bakery. Mathilde and Alphons are still at home and do quite well, Jules is also doing quite well.

Eugenie is doing fine too, she is always in full health and enjoys her happy state, she is in Lauwe where she works at the boys' boarding house.[92] Compliments of Rosalie Burgs and of Lefevers; Séraphine has been very sick this summer, one thought that she would not be able to go out anymore, but she fully recovered. Two daughters of aunt Sophie from Pittem married, Euphrasie lives in Wijngene, and Octavie is with her husband and two boys to America. The wife of Jan Demarez is not doing too very well, already four or five months a nun is with her. Jean suffered a great deal, but he has lots of work, he will get through it, they are all healthy. Charles [Karel] also does quite well. They have a son of four months (Adil), and also many compliments of Ms. Henriette and [illegible] Vermeulens.[93] The cassock is from Ms. Henriette, when we got the letter, Aunt got the letter [that was addressed to] to Ms. Henriettekens with the compliments and said that she would read the letter one or another time and she said that she would buy him a new one, she had it [the cassock] made in Kortrijk by the Brothers because they knew the seize, if it had not been freezing so hard, she would have been there two months earlier. Aunt had Léon Boone write quickly that the cassock was being made, and you should have the letter sooner [than the cassock]. Léon says that the letter had not arrived.

Jules Boone does fine too, he has already two sons, both are equally fat, Jules still talks about America. His wife was once a bit sick; they asked him what he would do if she would die, he answered, I would know what to do; I would go with all my belongings to America. He always says that his oldest is one for America. He has lots to do. The Father (Emiel) is also doing fine. He has been at home for fourteen days and he will see how to go on.

From our side we thank you because you read every day for us and to that we attribute our happiness. We also read daily for you in the chapel of Our Lady of Support, for Léonard and for all of your poor savages, so you may convert them.

We speak often of you, when you were here those two months and we walked, day and night, to Boerken, we would be happy if you could come once more for a few months, if it was only 100 hours far, we would once come. Aunt does all kinds of things, reading, cooking and when there is a fair, she bakes pies and during the fair she had to bake about fifty. The potato crop was so big this year that people don't know where to store them.

Many compliments to Leonard. Accept my greetings,
Pharailde Lecluyse.[94]

[Leonard continues:]
Nov. 5th: It seems the hand of God is chastising us: Father Leduc is now prostrated with inflammatory rheumatism at the Calgary Hospital.[95] Beside him, there is at the same charitable institution Father André whose days are now few; he suffers from dropsy and cannot recover.[96]

Dec. 9th: Yesterday we celebrated the festival of the Immaculate Conception. The children sang their own mass and in the afternoon we held the usual procession in church. These devotional ceremonies are liked very much by the children, and make great impression on them.

[Cousin Febronie Tassaert wrote to Victor on the Peigan reserve:][97]
Meulebeke, December 12, 1892.
Dear cousin,

I waited to write to you until Charles, your brother, died. For the last five weeks he has been ill due to his plague, it is not epilepsy ("*diksessen*"), but it looks like it. He got it from commotion and of colère. He had received the last H. Sacraments, he recovered, went to church, visited us, and now, last week he had a relapse and lay five days in his plague without having been able to confess; he only received the Holy Ointment, after which he died this morning at 7:30 a.m.

Wednesday at 9 a.m. he will be buried. Julie, the wife, has a brother who is still young and around 40 years old, Charles himself arranged her brother would look take care of everything, it surely will go well.

The *greffier* and the Goethals ladies received your shoes, we let Leonard know and thank you.[98] Jean received your catechismus, he is doing well despite the burden of all of their children. Gustaf, your brother, has returned to Meulebeke and again lives in the house of Kluizeken, the same one he once left. Jean, your brother is wondering why he hasn't heard from you. Would you mind, cousin, to pass on this news about Charles to Leonard as it might take some time before Julie writes. Anyway, if she does not write, we will write to Leonard and enclose memorial cards. It is good to see that Julie cares much for the three children of the first marriage and likes them; there are now 5 children.

All of the other family is doing well. Please remember us in your prayers, as we remember you in ours, and pass on thousand greetings to Leonard.

We take this opportunity, cousin, to wish both of you good health and blessings in the New Year.

Hoping, cousin, that both of you are in good health, we greet you,

Your dedicated cousin
Febronie Tassaert

Many compliments from the *greffier*, Henriette and all the children, Joseph does quite well in the college. Charles of Smets and Joseph are both in the college in Thielt and do quite well.

[Leonard continues:]
Dec. 20th: The Rev. Father Lacombe is starting tomorrow for Ontario and Quebec in order to find Sisters to take charge of the Indian hospital at the Blood Reserve. The Reverend Father received orders from the bishop to look at the same time after a new community of Sisters to take charge of the schools in Lethbridge, as our sisters could not remain here. But we received good news from France, and the Mother-General of the Faithful Companions of Jesus gives us good hopes. Very likely no such changes will be made.

Doctor Barrett from Winnipeg paid a visit to the mission. He remained for two days with his friend Father Van Tighem. He left this morning to meet Father Lacombe in MacLeod.

The winter is very severe; for over three weeks we have deep snow. Several railroad men were more or less frozen. Mr. Johnson, conductor, is presently at the hospital and part of his left foot shall be amputated in a few days.

Dec. 24th: This man has a large family living at Dunmore.

Dec. 26th: Christmas day was cold and the church was not overcrowded as usual. The first mass was celebrated at 8 o'clock; about fifty persons approached the Holy Table. The church was more beautiful than ever. A set of *tableaux*, six in all, were placed between the windows and filled up that space. They represent the Credo, 'I believe in God, or the Apostles Creed.' Beneath each painting, the explanation is written in four different languages: Latin, English, Slav and French. The Rev. Mother had prepared two very handsome draperies for the bracket altars of St. Mary and Joseph. It is a gold-embossed embroidery on dark, rich, red plush. Mother Elisabeth had made four magnificent white lilies. They look very natural. A new crib, a group of Jesus (infant), Mary, Joseph, oxen and ass, was placed in the center of the sanctuary. This group should be inside of a grotto, but as the church is so small, we have no space to erect one.

Dec. 31st: During the last year there were 34 baptisms in the church, five funerals and four marriages.

Jan. 1st: We have our usual Chinook winds since three days; the snow is disappearing rapidly. There were not many persons in church this morning for the wind was very severe.[99] We will have no evening service in church, and for this reason we had benediction with the Blessed Sacrament after mass.

[Victor (1893) passed on the sad news to Leonard:]

St. Paul's Missions, January 4, 1893.

L.S.J.C.

Very dear brother,

How miraculous is God in His works! Yesterday night aunt Siska's sent us bad news. Our brother Charles, as you know, suffered from a sad plague, which he developed after the loss of his wife Alida and other difficulties. It was not convulsions but something worse. Around All Souls Day Charles suffered again from his plague, so bad that he received the Last Sacrament. After a few days Charles recovered, went to church and worked as he did before. But at the beginning of December the illness returned, so badly that one only could administer him the Holy Ointment and on December 12 at 7:30 a.m. Charles quietly died.

I cry, dear brother, Charles, our youngest brother is no more! He, who was so tall, so sturdy and so healthy! He now lies in a grave. And his poor wife! And these little sheep, his children, five in all, three of whom no longer have a father or a mother! Oh my God, how hard this is! And what can we do being so far away from them! Pray for them and submit to the unrelenting will of God and that is all. Today I will write to his wife Julie.

Your sad brother,

Frère Jean Berchmans.

[Leonard continues:]

Jan. 5th: A very sad news is received this morning by the Father. His brother died in Belgium on the 12th of December. He leaves a widow and five little children; three of them have neither father or mother any more in this world.[100]

The Father has written to Monsignor Grandin, asking his Lordship permission to take the little boy, who is ten years of age, with him on the mission here. The Father is altogether alone for ten years now, and desires very much this little companion.

Jan. 14th: Fatal news tidings continue floating in; today the sad death of our Reverend Father André is announced. This good and zealous father died at the hospital Calgary on the 10th of this month, from dropsy. He had been ill for several months. RIP.

A letter is received from St. Albert, from our good bishop, stating that notwithstanding his sickness, he will proceed to France for the General *Capittel* [meeting] and the election of a Superior-General. His Lordship will receive the skilful treatment of the French doctors and may recover yet. Amen.

Jan. 15th: Another death to record: a few hours only before the Reverend Father André breathed his last at the Calgary hospital, Father Bourgine died at St. Albert.[101] This poor Father was epileptic for many years and was not able to perform any priestly functions, though he said daily Holy Mass. RIP.

[Rosalie Julie Vanhecke, Charles' second wife/widow (1893) to Victor:]

Meulebeke, January 27, 1893.

G.Z.J.C.

Reverend brother-in-law,

Upon receiving your venerable [letter] I hasten to reply; a few days after Charles death I wrote you a long letter about how and what. I don't know whether you received it? Yes dear brother, it is hard and painful, even troublesome to be left with five small children, the youngest only eight months, and already having no father, three having neither father nor mother; but I will take care of them, just as if Charles were still with us. I will try to give them a good education. Pray daily to the Lord that he might help us in our time of tribulations. The year 1892 was for me a year of crosses and sadness. Three times Charles has been so sick that he needed the doctor daily, many days even three times. So you can imagine how much this cost, and then because of the death, expenses followed for the funeral meal, the doctor at home and land rent and, now currently no more good farming years; but dear brother, I trust that God and Our Lady will leave neither me nor my dear children.

Think of us; help me to take care of my dear children, so we can give them what is necessary for body and soul. Marie, the oldest, is now over twelve years. I had to keep her at home to take care of the little one while I attend to my business because there are many things that have to be taken care of now I am by myself. At night Marie helps Joseph and Elody with their studies, she teaches our little Margaretha to pray. She really gives a good example to the others. She attends mass every day and at night she attends lauds when possible. A few weeks before Charles died he spoke to Marie and asked her never to leave me and to be a good example for the others. She promised this to her late father.

Dear brother, this should give you some idea of what is going on; I don't have time to say more, now. Marie will write within a few days. Ms. Loncke acknowledges receipt of your letter and sends greetings from all of them. Aunt Lucie got three rolls of death memorial cards, portraits of the saints from the printer, Camiel Ledure, for you. How should we mail them?

Dear brother, remember Charles, me, and the children in your prayers; we do our best to earn a living and give everyone his due, we daily pray for it in our prayers.

Well, I hope to get a return letter from you when you receive my letters, and some words of consolation, I remain,

your sad sister, Rosalie Julie Vanhecke
Meulebeke.

[Leonard continued:]
Jan. 29th: We have a very severe winter indeed. Today it is very cold and few people assisted at Holy Mass. It is a good time for our miners though as they work now day and night and cannot take out coal enough to satisfy demands.

Febr. 9th: The Reverend Mr. Lemieux, newly ordained by Mgr. Pascal at Regina, passed through Lethbridge today. This young priest had been invited to Butte City, U.S., to marry one of his brothers, residing in that place. The Father here is glad to have company of a brother priest, though it be for a short time only.

[Cousin Febronie to Leonard, in Dutch:]
Meulebeke, February 10, 1893.
Dear Cousin,

Yesterday, we and niece Julie as well, received your venerable letter. Joseph is very eager to join you, we will do everything you ask us for Joseph and you can count on the *greffier* too. He appointed Jean as guardian of the first three children, because he was best suited for it, as soon as we received the letter the *greffier* took it to Jean who fully agreed to have Joseph join you. Moreover, it is rather fortunate because he can go along with Monsignor [Grandin] or with the Fathers. Be assured that Monsignor will be received very well.[102] With regard to Julie, the *greffier* says that she has no reason to complain and the children will be taken much better care of. She has nothing to say about the previous children. It is just Jean who has a say in it. We might be wrong, but we think that she will remarry; it would be better if she didn't.

With regard to Marie, she says, I would be so happy to go to my uncles, but she will go to a convent. The *greffier* has a sister who is Superior in a convent in Berchem; it is a boarding school where also English is being taught. Especially good care will be taken of her and it is the utmost wish of the *greffier* and Jean that she would go there.

As you already know cousin, Adile Smet leaves today for you. We are sending along several items with him, so we don't have to send it by mail: mass book, white alb, altar cloth, four cassocks, four purificators, a long flowered benediction veil, six long stoles, four maniples, many little white finger towels, bobeches for your candelabras, two *écharpes* [cinctures], six pairs of long black stockings. It is too bad, cousin, those stockings have been knitted long ago, we will knit another six pairs and send them with Joseph.

Seeing Adile will be joining you and not knowing whether he confessed at the mission last year, the *greffier* says that he should have his inner being cleansed. I should tell you straightforwardly.

We hope to do the right thing, cousin, using the 50 francs you mentioned, to use to buy things for Joseph. Will you let us know if you had other ideas about it? We think that this is the same, so far she does not many of the family. You can always count on us to do what we can. We do hope that everything will turn out well, would you be so kind to let us know when you have received everything in good order and how Adile is doing? Thank God, the entire family does well; we recommend ourselves in your prayers, we, from our side, will not forget you too.

Best wishes for you as well as for cousin Brother Joannes from us, Henriette and brother Sacrez and especially from mother.[103]

Your dedicated cousin Febronie Tassaert.

P.S., we will keep the relics with us until the arrival of Monsignor or the Fathers, also, we will still have vases that Marie Decroulen donated to Brother Joannes.

[Leonard continues:]
Febr. 13th: The Reverend Father Legal arrives unexpectedly at Lethbridge today. As the Rev. Father Leduc, who has left for Europe, was a member of the Board of Education for the North West Territ.; another was to be appointed to take his place. Therefore the Rev. Father Legal received a dispatch from Regina, announcing his nomination. He will leave for the *Capittel* [meeting] before long.

The news is circulated today that the CPR Company has bought our Galt railroad from Dunmore to Lethbridge, also the chart of extending it to MacLeod and the Crows Nest Pass.

23rd: Coutts. Father Van Tighem arrived from Coutts on the Boundary Line, Montana, having left here on Monday last, to say Holy Mass for the few Catholics of that place. The Father said mass at Mr. H. Tennant's residence.

Returning to Lethbridge, the Father left for a moment the passengers' coach in order to speak to the conductor in the caboose and scarcely he had left the coach, when through the carelessness of a brakes' man, the coach was thrown in the ditch. Fortunately there was only one passenger in the coach, who came out unhurt.

Rev. Father Lacombe writes from Montreal that he shall return to his mission on the 22nd of March next.

March 8th: Today arrived here a young man from Belgium, from Meulebeke, Flanders. He intends to take a cattle ranch somewhere at Pincher Creek, but as he cannot speak the English language he will remain for some time in Lethbridge. He is from the birthplace of the Father here. His name is Adile Desmet.[104]

March 19th: It seems, as there would be no end to the winter. All our railroads are again blockaded and we have no mail from the east for about ten days. Our friend, Captain Begin of the N.W.M.P. is actually making a subscription for the purpose of erecting a house-residence for the priest in Lethbridge. The small apartment, which the Father now occupies, will be employed as a sacristy. Several plans have been prepared, brick and frame, but it has not yet been decided how and where to build. Our Slavonic Catholics are again the most generous in this undertaking. They alone have subscribed nearly five hundred dollars.

April 2nd: Easter Sunday was a well-observed festival by our Catholics. Never before had our little church contained so many people. A fine mass in music was well executed by our few artists. Capt. and Mrs. Begin being the leaders. The church was handsomely decorated.

The Father at High Mass gave an account of the subscription list, which amounted presently to over eight hundred dollars, but said the Father, very likely we will employ this money for the purpose of enlarging the church this summer.

April 4th: Father Lacombe arrived today in MacLeod. He brings a young priest, to reside in Macleod. The Rev. Mr. Gravel is nephew of Bishop Gravel of Nicolet, Canada.

April 6th: Father Lacombe having expressed his desire of meeting the Fathers of our district at Macleod, Father Van Tighem obtains a vehicle from the N.W.M.P. and with a four horse team starts for MacLeod in company of Serqt. Major McDonnell.

Father Lacombe brought us the good news that finally he had found Sisters for his hospital at the Blood reserve. As soon [as] the building will be terminated, four or five Sisters, Grey Nuns will come from the Nicolet branch of Grey Nuns.

Father Van Tighem has begun again the arduous task of saying two masses every Sunday, as the church has become far too small. The first mass is said at nine o'clock, at which the schoolchildren assist, as also those who have to stay home during High Mass.

Our school also is daily progressing. There are now over eighty children attending, of which a dozen are Protestant. Thus has the so-called separate school become more public than the public school.

April 14th: The large stables of Sam Davis, as also a house, were destroyed by fire this week. Several horses and carriages were inside the stable and nothing was saved. The fire and chemical engines did their work well and saved the adjoining buildings. The cause of the fire is altogether a mystery, as no one was supposed to be in the building at the time of the fire about midnight.

Good news from France!! Our good bishop has undergone a painful operation. Three stones were growing for years in the bladder and the doctors have crushed and extracted them. This operation must have been horrible and surely, if our illustrious patient had not been the strongest of constitutions, he never could have endured it. His Lordship is improving fast. The operation has been a real success.

May 11th: The General Chapter of our congregation meets today. The new Superior-General will be elected this evening.

May 22nd: We learn from the newspapers, that the reverend Father Soullier is our new Superior-General. It was generally expected that it would be him, as certainly he is the most able to fill this so important position. This very Reverend Father has visited all our houses in the five parts of the world. The only regret expressed by everybody is that this Very Reverend Father is so advanced in years – over fifty. May God preserve him for another half century!!!

June 4th: As we are approaching the vacation holidays, and as we are obliged to enlarge our schoolrooms during the absence of the children, we held two meetings lately to deliberate and find out, if the people would be consenting that the money, subscribed for the priest's residence or church, should be employed for enlargement of the convent schools. Most of the Catholics objected to this and said that the money collected for the church must be employed for the church.

As it was impossible to come to any understanding and as no one could suggest the means of obtaining the money necessary to enlarge the schools. The Father resolved that he should take a loan of five hundred dollars, that the trustees of the school should ask for three hundred dollars from the church money for one year and that this amount should be paid up by farther subscriptions next fall. As to the loan of $500.00, the Father would pay it up by early installments, as he paid off the late church debt.

June 12th: Father Van Tighem gave the contract today to Mr. Oliver for placing a stone foundation under the convent building and at the same time to lay the foundation for the new schoolrooms. This addition is to be 40×26 feet, part of which shall be two stories high, to be used as a chapel for the Sisters. These stone foundations cost $95.00. We have a very favorable year: abundant rains have frequently fallen.

June 29th: Two lay Brothers Oblates of Mary Immaculate have arrived at Lethbridge from the north, for the purpose of erecting the new schoolrooms and interior chapel at the convent. They are our famous Brother Bowes, who, for thirty-nine years is devoting himself to the missions.[105] God alone knows the immense services he has rendered in these as yet not long ago savage regions. The other is Brother Brochard, a German, who is possessed with extra-ordinary talent for carvings and sculpture. His works will be for many years admired.

July 3rd: Today, work has begun on the court and customhouse just behind our church. Mr. Oliver from Lethbridge has secured the contract. The building is to be of brick and stone.

We learn that Father Lacombe is to be in MacLeod for tomorrow, with the Sisters Grey Nuns from Nicolet, for the Blood Reserve hospital. Father Legal, the missionary from the Blood Reserve, was here last Sunday and told us that the buildings, hospital, dwelling house and chapel for the Sisters, are almost completed.

July 10th: This evening, about five o'clock, a cloud burst above our town and never before have we witnessed such a downpour of rain. All the low places became lakes in a few minutes and the coulees were changed in torrents. A woman was ascending the hill in one of these coulees with her baby in a carriage; the roaring torrent came down upon her. Her carriage was carried away and after having held her child in her arms for some time she fainted. The baby, about a year old, rolled down with the steam and was picked up far below. It was first thought the child was dead, but it revived after a while and is still alive. The mother is also out of danger.

July 12-July 20th: Coutts. Father Van Tighem just arrives from Coutts and the Boundary Line where he has been to visit the few Catholics of that place. Capt. Begin, who is in charge of the different detachments along the line, took the father as far as Writing on Stone, on the Milk River. The banks of this river, a soft sandstone, are cut and carved and sculptured in all imaginable forms and shapes, the most picturesque views can be seen there. The heavy winds, and rains and storms have, in the course of time, modeled

1▶ *2004: Forms and shapes at Writing on Stone.* Photo Mary E.M.

2▶ *2004: War deeds engraved at Writing on Stone.* Photo Mary E.M.

villages and towns with domes and towers and columns and monuments, worth to be seen.

The Indians of ancient times seem to have admired these strange formations. They must have passed considerable time among these natural fortresses, for their exploits and *haut-faits d'armes* [brave war deeds] are cut in the bases of these huge rocks and monuments. It is to be deplored that time is destroying fast the ancient hieroglyphic signs.

25th July: News is received from Calgary today that two young Fathers have arrived there. One is destined for Mackenzie River, the other, Father Lefevre, shall be sent to the High River Industrial School, there to be the assistant of Father Naessens, principal.[106] These two Fathers brought with them, Father Van Tighem's little nephew, a lad of eleven years and an orphan. Father Van Tighem started with this afternoon train for Calgary, in order to bring the little boy over to Lethbridge, where he is to reside, for the future with the Father. Our new school buildings are progressing and will be terminated for the reopening of the school year.

Aug.12th: Father Lacombe has opened the Indian hospital at the Blood Reserve. Mr. Daly, Minister of the Interior, Mr. White, Mr. Davis, M.P., and many others were there for the inauguration. The St. Joseph's Industrial School-Band had been invited and gave excellent music on the occasion. The good Sisters had prepared a banquet and the numerous visitors were their welcomed guests. May God bless this new undertaking.

19th: The small belfry on the convent is almost completed. It has changed wonderfully the general appearance of the convent.

As the classrooms were not completely finished we had to postpone the opening of the school for a week.

Sept. 2nd: Today our good Superior the Rev. Father Lestanc arrived in Lethbridge. It is his first visit. The Rev. Father comes from Calgary and has been to MacLeod, Pincher Creek, the Peigan and Blood Reserves. As he arrived here with Father Legal's team, the two Brothers Bowes and Brochard who have worked at our convent schools for about two months, will go to the Blood Reserve for about two weeks.

Our convent school has now one hundred and six children on the roll. Two boarders were sent here from Montana, a son and daughter of Mr. Toole, rancher and custom officer at Sweet Grass. The boy lodges at the Father's.

Sept. 5th: Our good Father Lestanc only stayed two days in Lethbridge; he left this morning by the stage to MacLeod.

Sept. 18th: The Rev. Father Legal arrives in Lethbridge with two Sisters, Grey Nuns, from the Blood Reserve Hospital. They come for the purpose of purchasing linens, cottons, flannels, etc., etc., for the use of the hospital.

The Reverend Father Thérien from Med. Hat has arrived also and will remain for next Sunday.

Sept. 20th: We have some snow today and the weather is rather cold. The news has arrived that Sir Alex. Galt from Montreal has died yesterday.

Sept. 25th: Today two young men, Thomas and Laurence Morkin, leave for the novitiate of the Holy Angels, Lachine.[107] May God bless them, may they make a solid novitiate, and may they, at the end of the year of probation, return to us, armed with the cross of the Oblates!!!

Oct. 21st: Father Van Tighem leaves his mission of Lethbridge for about ten days, in order to assist the annual retreat, which takes place at Calgary this year. Being absent for two Sundays, the service on Sunday morning will be presided by Mr. Lowell, who will recite the Holy Rosary, read the Epistle and Gospel of the day, while the Sisters with their pupils will sing hymns and cantatas.

Nov. 1st: When leaving Lethbridge the weather was beautiful but during the night the wind changed north and a few inches of snow covered the ground. After a day or two, it cleared up however, but on returning to Lethbridge, it became again cold and frosty. The Rev. Father Lacombe preached the retreat to the Fathers of the district. Were present at the retreat R.R. Fathers: Lestanc, Lacombe, Doucet, Legal, Van Tighem, Foisy, Naessens, Thérien *et Comiré, ansi que les Frères Converts*: Bowes, Brochard, Barrassé et Petit Demarche. *Notre Frère Scholastique Danis y assistait aussi.*

Nov. 6th: Our school has been closed for over two weeks on account of the measles; almost all the children are prostrated, and the small ones are seriously in danger. We have benediction of the Blessed Sacrament and the H. Rosary prayers every night, for the departed souls in purgatory. These devotions will continue during the Octave of All Souls, and take place at 4 p.m. at the convent chapel.

Nov. 15th: Grassy Lake. Father Van Tighem went up last Monday to Grassy Lake where a Catholic family, Mr. Devine, is living.[108] These people, having no opportunity to come to town were deprived for many months from all religious services. Therefore the Father went up and said mass for them, heard their confession and gave Holy Communion. The weather is beautiful, but our heavy winds are very inconvenient.

Nov. 17th: Today a Lethbridge boy, Johnny Murray, departs for a College in Quebec. Last year the Reverend Father Lacombe obtained from the different directors of the Canadian colleges the privilege of sending one boy to their institution respectively; these boys, there to be educated for the holy priesthood. About eight boys have already been sent. John Murray is about fourteen years of age.

Nov. 20th: A man, father of six children, was run over, last night near the shaft. He died a few hours after. We have snowstorms, succeeding one another too frequently.

Nov. 29th: The weather is very cold for several days, and the thermometer is frequently below [zero]. Our school opened again last Monday, after having been closed by order of the doctor, on account of the measles, which have been spread all over town. Several little children have succumbed from the disease.

Dec. 3rd: A strong Chinook-wind has made the snow disappear fast. There was a large congregation at mass; but very few people in the evening, the roads being very muddy. A concert, in favor of the Cath. Mission is to take place on Wednesday next. Mr. Lowell, Mrs. Tennant and Ms. Tucker are the organizers.

Dec. 8th: The concert was a great success. The net receipts were about one hundred dollars. The feast of the Immaculate Conception was better observed than any time before; a large congregation assembled at mass. We had our usual procession at 3 o'clock in the afternoon; about two dozens of little girls were dressed in white.

Dec. 17th: After a few cold days, we have again our mild Chinook winds blowing. Imagine that on December 17th. We open our doors and windows from early till later. My little canary bird hangs outside and sings the praises of the Lord. No fire in church today and although very windy, there was a large crowd of people attending at High Mass.

[Rosalie Julie Van Hecke (1893), Karel's widow, wrote to Leonard:]
Meulebeke, December 20, 1893.
Dear brother-in-law,

Since a long time we have not received any letter from you. Now, near the start of the year, we hasten to wish you a happy New Year. Thank God we are all in good health and by doing our best and God's help we manage through life. The three oldest girls, Marie, Elodie and Margaretha go to school every day while little Adiel is at home with me playing mischievously. He is such a busy boy; he would like to hang around the cows, pigs and rabbits for the entire day. He is just like a farmer, just like his father and his brother Joseph. It is a pity that they are separated such distance from each other! So be it, it is God's will. How is Joseph doing? Does he behave? Obey? Does he study hard? Does he learn well? Does he sometimes speak of us? Does he take time to pray for his deceased father and mother? On December 11th we had a High Mass celebrated for the two of them, for the benefit of their souls. Oh! how quickly time passes. It is now over a year that Karel died but it seems that it was just yesterday.

Dear brother-in-law, time does not permit a longer letter. Pass on our New Year's wishes to Joseph. He was asking about his parents and when he was born. Joseph Van Tighem is born on October 7, 1882.

I also have to tell you that Mathilde, the wife of your brother Jean, is often not well. Oh, that household with seven small children has so many problems. Gustaf and his wife are doing well. Tell Joseph that Mr. Jos Bossuit, age of 22 years, was buried on the 18th of December. Would you please send us a few stamps, the little Robert Bossuit, Joseph's friend from school, asked for it.

Well, hoping to receive some news from you, I am calling myself

Your humble sister-in-law,
Julie and children.

[In the same letter:]
Meulebeke, le 13 Décembre 1893.
Cher et digne Oncle,

Je suis heureux de pouvoir vous offrir, avec l'hommage de mon profound respect, l'expression des voeux sinceres, que je forme pur votre bonheur. Oui, cher Oncle, soyez heureux ici-bas, et que l'Immortel vous introduire, après une longue carrière, dans son saint paradis pur y rècompenser les efforts dus à vos nobles travaux.

Daignez agréer, cher et digne Oncle, les voeux de

Votre respectueuze niece,
Elodie Vantighem.

[Leonard continues:]
Dec. 25th: Yesterday, Sunday and today Christmas day there has been a very large congregation attending the church services, both morning and night. Last night confessions were heard till after midnight. It is the first time that so many approach the Sacrament on a festival day. Our mild weather continues. We scarcely need any fire in church.

Dec. 26th: Last night our children had their Christmas tree in the new schoolrooms. About one hundred and fifty children with their parents attended. Young Mr. Tennant, Henri, was St. Nicholas and was a good one indeed.

Dec. 30th: A concert was given last night, by the school children, to their parents and friends. It was the first time that strangers were invited and a large crowd had assembled in the school. Our young actors and actresses did very well, far better than we all expected.

Jan. 1st: Last night we song the *Miserere* and the *Te Deum* at the Benediction for it was the last day of the year. Being Sunday, many assisted. Today, after mass, the Blessed Sacrament was exposed immediately after mass, and the *Veni Creator* chanted. We held no evening service, as parents and friends generally meet on such evenings.

Jan. 10th: Last night our Slavonians met at the convent schoolrooms for the organization of a Catholic beneficial Society. This is exclusively for the Slavonic Roman and Greek Catholics. There are already over one hundred branches in the United States, with about five thousand members.[109] Matthew Petras was chosen President. About seventy have made application to join.

For two days we have the most terrible winds, almost impossible to sleep at night, so great is the noise.

[Marie Van Tighem (1894) to Leonard. Transcript:]
Meulebeke, nouvel an, 1894.
Digne Oncle,

A vous mes souhaits les plus ardents, mes voeux les plus sincère. Oui en ce premier jour de l'an, je me souviendrai de vous d'une manière tout spéciale, quoique je puisse vous dire en toute sincérité, que tous les jours ma prière monte vers le Seigneur et implore pour vous des grâces sante et répondre à tous vos bienfaits par ma bonne conduite en mon application constante à l'étude.

Daignez, digne Oncle, agréer cette faible expression de mes sentiments avec l'assurance de mon profond respect,

Votre niece,
Marie Vantieghem.

[Leonard continues:]
Febr.: As usual candles were blessed on the Sunday following the feast of the Purification. On that occasion were brought a great quantity of candles by the faithful to be used on the altar during the year.

20th: Our mines are closed for several days. The new superintendent, Simpson, tries to cut the wages of the poor miners, but these, most justly, refuse to go to work, so the miners are on strike. Many are leaving the place. Last week a man named Purcel was sentenced to three years only prison life for having shot dead a neighbor in a quarrel, D. Akers.

Father Lacombe is at Ottawa again to battle against the unjust school laws of the North West Territories.

March 5th: Work has not resumed in our mines. The company proposes a rebate of 17%, which the miners say they could not accept. So everything is in a *status quo* for several weeks. The greatest order prevails in town and around the mines. Notwithstanding about four hundred persons have left the town, our little church remains, as yet, by far too small. It is consoling indeed, to see the Catholics so well attend the divine services.

15th: About one hundred miners have signed their names yesterday and almost as many again today showing their intention to return to work and accept the considerable rebate of 17%. Of course this we may call a forced action, as many have no money, nor means to leave the town.

24th: The news arrives today that our good bishop has arrived at Montreal from France on the 13th of March. His Lordship will remain for some time there. Another great, and extraordinary news is the future visit to Canada and the northwest of our Very Reverend Father Superior-General accompanied by Rev. Father Antoine, Asst. Gen., and a secretary. This will rejoice the hearts of all the Oblates on this side of the ocean.

25th: Easter Sunday was celebrated with extraordinary splendor in Lethbridge. The Father said two masses on that day, which were very largely attended. At High Mass about twenty persons had to remain outside doors and some even walked away. The music at High Mass was grand. Three brass instruments accompanied the organ during mass; the N.W.M.P. band played three fine pieces before and after mass. The church is beautifully decorated as usual.

April 2nd: Father Van Tighem set out on a journey today to Pincher Creek, with two four horse teams, kindly furnished by Cap. Dean from the N.W.M. Police. The Sergt. Major McDonnell accompanies the Father. The father goes after a load of small pine trees to be planted around the church in Lethbridge. Mr. Beauvais, an old friend of the missionary, residing near the Rocky Mountains, receives the Father with great courtesy and accompanies him to the foothills. On the 6th the Father returns to Lethbridge and immediately plants the little evergreen trees.

News from our good bishop! His Lordship will be in Calgary on the 10th of this month. All the Fathers are invited to go and meet Monsignor at Calgary. In consequence father Van Tighem leaves Lethbridge again, and proceeds to Calgary by Macleod. There were fourteen Fathers to meet His Lordship, whose health is very much improved. Monsignor will go to St. Albert at once, and our missions in this district will be visited by Him, in June only.

On the 14th of April Father Van Tighem returns to MacLeod and on the same day accompanies Father Foisy to the Peigan Reserve to visit his brother, *Frère* Jean, whom he has not met for almost a year.

April 15th: Father Van Tighem says High Mass at the Peigan mission assisted by three little Indians only and one lady. This young lady is a Protestant by name but Catholic in her heart, and every Sunday attends Holy Mass at the Catholic Church although there is a Minister and a Ministress, and some Sisters even, of the Anglican Church at the reserve. She will be received in the church before long.

The Father returns on the same day to MacLeod with his little nephew Joseph, and there conducts the evening service and addresses the congregation.

16th: The next day, Capt. McDonnell kindly offers the Father his fine team and in a few hours arrives home again. During the Father's absence from Lethbridge, Father Bourveau from Brandon remained at this mission. Almost all our Slovak Catholics have departed from Lethbridge.[10] Most of them had no work and the others, although they had work would not remain on account of the low salary.

May 21st: Our children, twenty-two in number, did their first communion yesterday. Trinity Sunday. Among them were two Belgians.

May 28th: A dispatch from Calgary announces that His Lordship, Bishop Grandin, will visit Lethbridge on the 29th and administer the Sacrament of Confirmation on the first day of June.

June 2nd: His Lordship administered Confirmation to 32 people, and only remained two days in Lethbridge. Our Very Reverend Father General Soullier has arrived at Calgary, accompanied by Rev. Father Antoine, Assistant-General. All the Fathers of the district are called together and Father Antoine preaches them a retreat of three days. Father Van Tighem goeth again to Calgary to assist at the retreat and to meet the Superior-General.

On the 9th of June, the father returns to MacLeod. The General will visit the Blood reservation only. So Lethbridge and the other missions are left out.

[Father Lestanc (1894, 388–89) reported:]

Father Antoine gave a sermon during the retreat: thirteen Fathers, two scholastic students, five Fathers-converts-assistants attended. . . .

At the Blood Indians: The retreat had barely ended on June 9, at 7:30 p.m., and Father General Antoine, the Fathers Lacombe, Legal, Van Tighem and Foisy and Father Barbeau took the train to MacLeod. Despite the rivers being high and quite dangerous, F. General insisted on visiting the savages' missions. We were not without fear about the subject of this journey. Thanks to the police we could visit Father Legal's mission at the Blood. . . . The Blood haughtily conceded that they wanted to keep their superstitions and did not want to become Christians.

[Leonard continues:]
18th: An advertisement for tenders is posted out today by the Father for an addition to the church of 25×45 ft. with two side chapels of 12×12 ft. and a vestry of 10×16 ft. The old addition will be removed to the south side of the church to be used as a mission house and residence for the priest.

We have a magnificent springtime: fine rains about every week, never our prairies were greener and more beautiful. The trees around the church are growing well and every one admires them.

26th: The contract for moving the old church-addition, which is to serve as a mission house and to be enlarged with a brick front addition of 22×14 ft. inside – also the building of an addition to the church, brick veneer 45×25 ft. with a hexagonal addition of 8 ft. These contracts have been let to Mr. Cody, the first for the sum of $750.00, the second $1380.00. So we have to look forward to gather in the round sum of $2130.00.

The great and very sad news of the death of our beloved archbishop Monsignor Taché reaches us today. After long sufferings indeed, torments of many years, his Grace has been finally released and gone to his reward. A large stone of two inches long was found in the bladder, and many smaller ones had been crushed by a previous operation. The remains of His Grace will be laid besides these of his predecessor, Mgr. Provencher, first bishop of St. Boniface. RIP.

July 14th: Work on our new church and presbytery was begun last week. The old addition was removed and placed in Southwest corner of the lots.

20th: Our very Reverend Father-General having visited our missions in British Columbia these last weeks, has gone north to visit St. Albert, and we learn today that several changes have been made in the personnel of the diocese. Father Lacombe will henceforth reside in Edmonton, having for assistant Father Dauphin from Onion Lake.

Father Thérien takes Father Dauphin's place at Onion Lake and Father Fouquet, who resided in Edmonton, has been transferred to Calgary."

Aug. 2nd: The works on the church and presbytery are progressing slowly although the weather is very fine. Our contractor gives very little satisfaction; it will be a great relief when all is terminated. Father Deroches has gone to New Westminster.

5th: We had not a drop of rain for about two months; everything is drying up.

Sept. 30th: During this month of September the work has progressed very slowly. Although there are three carpenters constantly working, the contractor Cody being absent most of the time, nothing advances. It becomes evident that the contractor has bad intentions.

The Rev. Father Legal arrives from the Blood Reserve and will remain a few days in Lethbridge. It is decided between the Fathers to invite Mr. Curry and Mr. Tennant and to summon Cody in their presence to force him to give a statement of affairs; for it is now a month after time and the work is only half done.

It is at this meeting that the contractor reveals his inability to fulfill the contract. He has moreover the impudence to ask for nearly five hundred dollars extra. This man has taken revenge, because a small contract in the convent was let to Mr. Oliver. In his anger he threatened the Father, and said, that he would be sorry for having given this work to another contractor. The Fathers, together with Mr. Curry and Mr. Tennant decide to order Cody away, at once. So the Father will now engage a few carpenters and will him self oversee the work.

Oct. 20th: The Reverend Father Lestanc, Superior of this district and residing in Calgary, arrives at Lethbridge and will remain for about two weeks. During this time Father Van Tighem goes to work himself in order to complete the church. Four carpenters have been engaged and the work is progressing rapidly. Instead of the iron metallic shingles, it has been decided to put on cedar, which is much cheaper and it may be, as durable.

Nov. 1st: Rev. Father Lestanc has returned to his mission. It was a real comfort for the priest here to have a companion for a few days; so much the more so, that this companion is the ancient protector and great Benefactor of the Father. They know one another for about twenty years now.

Nov. 20th: Last week we took out the forest of scaffolding from the inside of the church. The vault being finished, painted blue with a thousand of golden stars to decorate. The new pews have also arrived and will be put together next week.

We have mild fall weather up to this time and all the work is terminated outside. During the month of November mass was said every day for the souls of Purgatory. These masses were to the intention, mostly of our school children, who made a little collection among themselves for this purpose. Many parishioners also have ordered masses for the souls during this month.

Dec. 26th: We had midnight mass in Lethbridge, for the first time. On previous years the church being too small, it was impossible to celebrate this solemn night service. The church although spacious now, was well filled up, many of our separate brethren attending. The church looked beautiful and the many lights on the high altar showed all the richness of the handsome gold bouquets decorating the sanctuary. The singing was very good. The N.W.M. Police Band attended and gave some fine pieces of music, especially before and after the service. We had also, for the first time, ten altar boys in red robes and white surplices attending in the sanctuary.

Anno Domini 1895

Jan. 2nd: The New Year stepped in very quietly in Lethbridge. We had the *Miserere* and *Te Deum* at the convent chapel and many confessions followed. Although we had almost a general communion at midnight mass, many of our Catholics approached the sacraments again at the opening of the New Year. The winter so far has been very mild.

Rev. Father Gravel, the young parish priest of MacLeod, paid a visit to Lethbridge. We are always glad to see this reverend gentleman.

We learned today, by the voice of our newspapers that the Reverend Father Langevin of St. Mary's church, Winnipeg, has been elected at Rome, as the successor of our lamented archbishop Taché![112] This Reverend Father is an Oblate of Mary Immaculate, a French Canadian, and not yet forty years of age. It is universally stated that it is the best choice there could have been made: young, energetic, healthy, learned and a renowned pulpit orator. *Dominus Conservabum!!!* etc.

Jan. 28th: Today we have the pleasing visit of Rev. Father Doucet, the Blackfoot missionary. A young son of Mr. Leonard from Medicine Hat accompanied the Father and is to remain at the mission of Lethbridge, in order to frequent the convent school.

A monster petition is circulated all over Canada and all adult Catholics are asked to sign their names to it, this petition is addressed to the Governor General in Council, asking for redress and interference in the unjust school laws of Manitoba and the N.W. Territoria. For, the Imperial Privy Council, has decided in favor of the Catholics, and declared that the Government of the Dominion can force the (Bigots of) Manitoba Provincial Gov. to change their unjust laws.[113]

Febr. 1st: By order of our good bishop every priest in the diocese shall say daily at mass the prayer *De Spiritu Sanctu*, in stead of the usual one, *Pro Propagatione Fidei*, for the archbishop of St. Boniface, Dr. Langevin, from the day forward till the consecration of the Elect.

3rd: We also have signed the petition, together with most of the parishioners of Lethbridge. If the weather had not been so extraordinarily stormy and cold, and if we had had more time to circulate the petition, we could have had much more signatures; but the petitions must be presented on the 15th of this month.

March 17th: This morning, Sunday, we had a solemn mass, on account of the feast of St. Patrick, the patron saint of our church. The congregation was a large one. Young Leonard played on the violin and did very well. St. Patrick's banner was exposed and decorated.

Prayers were again asked from the congregation for a certain sick man at the hospital here. He was brought here from Great Falls and is in great danger, but he has refused the assistance of the church. He says: it is of no use to play the hypocrite now, after having left everything for 22 years. Nothing could move him, but asked to be left alone. For three times I have visited him, all in vain.

After tomorrow takes place the consecration of the new archbishop of St. Boniface, R. Father Langevin. Several bishops from the east have arrived at Winnipeg and are now celebrating St. Patrick's Day in good shape.

March 18th: We also have had our St. Patrick's Day. It was the feast of our church and we had fine music. Master Leonard played the violin both morning and night, which was something new for Lethbridge.

April 12th: It was announced last Sunday that we would have the services of the Holy Week, the church being large enough now. A fine *repositoir* has been prepared in one of the lateral chapels and now the people are in adoration before the altar of our Lord. The watches will be kept all the night, and two men at the time will remain there for one hour. During the day the Mothers have the schoolchildren continually with Jesus.

The church was well filled, every Wednesday and Friday evening during Lent at the Stations of the Cross. The weather is fine, but we have our old heavy winds, continually blowing.

April 14th: Easter has come and gone. Beautiful services took place in the church during the Holy Week and Easter Sunday was the crowning of all.

April 15th: A large congregation assembled in church both morning and evening. The singing was grand, and the music of the organ, flute and violin combined was something new and very pleasing. It was Mr. Tennant, custom-officer at Coutts, who played the flute.

May 1st: The Reverend Father Lacombe, after an absence of about three years, paid a flying visit to Lethbridge, arriving yesterday with a four-horse-team. He departed this morning. This visit, short as it was, pleased very much, the Father and Sisters of Lethbridge. Were would Father Lacombe not be welcomed? We began our May devotions yesterday: hymns, rosary, and Benediction every afternoon at 4 o'clock.

13th: Father Van Tighem takes the train south this morning and goes as far as Pandora, "better Pend'Oreille," Montana for the purpose of visiting a Catholic family and makes them fulfill their Eastern duties."[14] Of course the Father had no jurisdiction there, but these good people wrote to Bishop Brondel of Helena and asked jurisdiction for the father, which was easily and promptly obtained, His Lordship being a friend of the Father.

28th: Last night, a snowstorm set in and all this day the blizzard continues. As we had no rain this spring, this storm will benefit the grass.

June 20th: The weather has been cold up to this day and we have had good rains, the grass is green now.

24th: Our Slavish Catholics, belonging to the society celebrated the patron saint of their association; all approached the sacraments, came to their confession and received H. Communion at High Mass in a body. The banner for their society, made in Germany and costing $40.00 has arrived. It is not as handsome as we expected it would be for that money. The banner will be blessed on Sunday next.

July 2nd: Yesterday, while the bell was calling the faithful to mass, the Miners Band, escorting the members of the Society of St. John the Baptist, marched from the town and proceeded to the church. Banner in front. The church was crowded with people and after mass the banner was solemnly blessed. The ceremony was touching; the president of the society held the banner and stood on the first step of the sanctuary, while the sponsors, Mr. Thomas Curry and Mrs. Barclay held the tassels; then two lines were formed by the members of the society, encircling the priest and altar boys. The Father made a short allocution and congratulated the Slavonians on their spirit of charity and union.

The Reverend Father Fouquet, an old missionary of the Oblate Order, shall be here for next Sunday. He cometh for the purpose of preaching the yearly retreat to the Mothers and Sisters, Faithful Companions of Jesus.

Yesterday two adults, Hungarians, and a child of about five years, were received in the Catholic faith and baptized *sub condition*. They previously belonged to the Calvinistic church. These conversions are the good result of the Slavish Society of St. John the Baptist.

[On July 27, 1895, Marie Van Tighem, Joseph's one-year-older sister, died.]

Aug. 11th: Another Hungarian, a young man of about twenty-one years, was received in the bosom of the Catholic Church this morning. *Deo Gratias!*

Aug. 22nd: His Lordship Bishop Grandin has arrived in Lethbridge, accompanied by the Rev. Father Lestanc, Superior of the Calgary Mission, Rev. Fathers Fouquet, Lecoq and Cunningham.[115]

Rev. Father Legal will arrive on Saturday with three Sisters, Grey Nuns, to assist also at the first consecration of a Catholic Church in the North West Territories. R. Father Doucet from the Blackfoot Reserve will arrive tomorrow.

AUG. 26TH: The great ceremony is passed!!! The prayers of the consecration began at eight o'clock yesterday and terminated at one o'clock only. Everybody, especially His Lordship, was very tired. The High Mass began at half passed eleven only. The music was the best we ever had in Lethbridge: two brass instruments, two violins, one sub base, together with the grand organ, filled the church with their melodious strains. The North West Review giveth the following report of the festivity.[116]

On Sunday, August 25th, 1895, the right Reverend Bishop Grandin, assisted by the Reverend Fathers Lestanc, Fouquet, Legal, Lecoq, Cunningham, Doucet and the Reverend pastor Father Van Tighem, solemnly consecrated the church of St. Patrick in Lethbridge. It is the fourth church consecrated in this country – St. Boniface, Cathedral, St. Mary's Winnipeg, and St. Norbert's church having been consecrated in 1889 – according to the prescriptions of the Canon Law and with all the beautiful ceremonies of the Pontifical. The building is of stone and brick and is free from all debt.[117] It has been erected from the generous donations of the poor Slavonians, Irish, Hungarians, English, Scotch, Flemish, French and Italians. The congregation is a wonderful proof of the Catholicity of the church. In no part of this great northwest can a more cosmopolitan congregation be found than in Lethbridge.

▸ *Nephew Joseph, Father Leonard and friend.*
Courtesy Van Tighem Family Archives.

The Venerable consecrator of St. Patrick's church gave a very substantial aid in its construction and we are sure that dear St. Patrick must have blessed the efforts of the zealous Pastor, who deserves more than the usual amount of credit due to zealous and industrious priests for, with his own hands he has worked long and hard in its construction, every part of which received his skilled attention. The finishing, ornamenting and decorating can testify to his constant and persevering labor. Father Van Tighem is a Flemish artist of no mean ability, as a visit to this church will bear high testimony. The church can seat from three to four hundred persons, has a tidy, substantial unpretentious appearance and is built in the old monastic Gothic style. Altars, pews, in fact everything is tasteful and bright.

[Variétés (1895, 506–07) quoted 'le Manitoba' about the consecration:]
Singing was quit excellent, thanks to the dedication and the musical talent of the Rev. Father van Tighem, O.M.I., Flemish of origin.

Praise for the Rev. Father van Tighem. His Highness already spoke during the ceremony about his approval about everything this small church has cost in efforts and work by the zeal and the dedication of the missionary of Lethbridge. He worked with his own hands on all the parts of the church and worked on some more than on others: the roof, the woodwork and all of the ornaments are partly or in total owed to him. This Father is carpenter and sculptor. I saw him cut easily through marble and paint as an artist. Unfortunately his health is damaged by this excessive work.

[Leonard continues:]
SATURDAY 24TH OF AUGUST was a feastday in Lethbridge. The bishop and seven priests in the evening recited the Office of the Martyrs before the relics exposed according to the prescription of the Pontifical. On Sunday the consecration ceremonies began at 8 o'clock a.m. and were concluded at 1 p.m. These ceremonies are most beautiful; Faith, Hope, Charity, Piety and all religious virtues, prayers and sentiments are expressed in a most vivid manner.

The Society of St. John Baptist among the Slavonians is a great credit to the Catholic parish. All its members came in a body and assisted in uniform at the ceremonies. High Mass, with assisting priest, deacon and sub deacon and other clerics, was sung by the consecrating bishop. The choir, under the direction of the Faithful Companions of Jesus, ably assisted by Sergt. Davis of the N.W.M.P., was by far the best ever heard here.

His Lordship, the bishop, gave a short address in the morning and the venerable and holy missionary and learned professor of divinity, Rev. Father Fouquet, O.M.I., preached an able and most instructive sermon in the evening. The Sisters, Faithful Companions of Jesus, gave a dinner to the bishop, the clergy and principal, representatives of the different Catholic nationalities about thirty in number. Mr. J. Kenny and Mr. Curry, U.S. Consul, made happy speeches to which His Lordship gave equally happy replies.

On Monday the school children, who numbered one hundred, presented His Lordship with a beautiful illuminated address, the style of which corresponded with the beauty and value of the designs. His Lordship found it rather heavy and on close examination discovered several gold buttons artistically fitted in clusters and flower branches. The discovery seemed to please the little ones immensely.

This closed one of the brightest and happiest days every known to the Catholics of the town. They have reason to be proud of being the first congregation in the North West Territories, who have made it possible by their devout generosity to have their church solemnly consecrated. How deeply it must have touched the saintly heart of the Venerable Bishop Grandin to consecrate this church to the honor and glory of God under the patronage of the glorious apostle of Ireland. We heartily congratulate the Reverend pastor and his people on making such a festal day possible for Lethbridge.

SEPT. 14TH: The Rev. Father Fouquet will remain for about two weeks more in Lethbridge, while Father Van Tighem visits some stray Catholics along the south line and in Montana.

OCT. 1ST: This morning at one o'clock the Reverend Father Fouquet, who had passed over a month in Lethbridge, returned to Calgary, via Medicine Hat. The Fathers have been busily engaged during this sojourn in this mission, visiting the people in their homes, preaching, instructing, advising, in a word, leading the life of a true apostle. Joseph van Tighem, the nephew of Father Van Tighem left also this morning for Montreal, where he enters in the College of the Sulpiciens.[118]

OCT. 28TH: Early this morning arrived here from their different missions the Reverend Fathers Legal and Naessens, also Brother Morkin. These two last named come from the Industrial School, High River, where R. Father Naessens is principal and Brother Morkin, farm-instructor. They will make together their annual retreat in Lethbridge and on All Saints Day. Brother Morkin will pronounce his vows for five years in the Congregation of the Oblates of Mary Immaculate.

NOV. 2ND: Yesterday took place at the convent chapel a nice and touching ceremony, when Brother Morkin, at the Communion of the mass and before receiving the H. Host, pronounced vows for five years. The other Oblates present renewed their perpetual vows, while the good Mothers sang some very pious hymns.

Today, our three visitors departed and the father is alone again, with a few boys, who lodge at the mission. A new boy arrived here today from Coutts, his name is Howard Porter, colored about ten years of age, a little infidel as yet.

[The Sisters Faithful Companions (1895) reported:]

On **December 8th** took place the usual procession for the children, after which they all received little souvenirs of the Priest, from the Rev. Father Van Tighem. This year, owing to an epidemic of measles among the children, we had not the usual Christmas tree for them. For the same reason we were deprived of the privilege of Midnight Mass, the authorities having forbidden all public assemblies for fear of spreading the disease, which was of a far more dangerous kind than usual.

[Leonard continues:]

DEC. 10TH: The Rev. Father Doucet arrived here yesterday but remains only for a few hours; he has to visit some Catholic families east of Med. Hat.

DEC. 21ST: Yesterday a letter was brought to the mission by the town clerk, a letter asking the Father to close the church on account of there being a few cases of measles in town. The letter came directly from the mayor, our lumber merchant. Who has ever heard of such a thing? Closing churches on account of a few children being laid up with measles? The same request was made to the different Protestant ministers. This strange letter was far from being welcomed by the Father who presently is not at the best of terms with that glorious kind of mayor, for, together with his councillors he has deprived our convent school from their just share of school taxes. The finest piece of bigotry ever enacted as yet in our town. They robbed us of six hundred dollars."[19]

Therefore the Father made an immediate answer to the mayor, refusing to close the church, saying that it never was heard of before: to close a Catholic church, even in the worst cases of epidemic; that if ever people needed help and assistance from heaven, it was, most certainly at such times as these, etc. For several Sundays all the churches were indeed closed with the exception of the Catholic Church. Strange, there was not a fatal case in town and not one child died of the disease. The whole town ridiculed this stupid action of the mayor.

The feast of Christmas was celebrated with great solemnity. The weather was fine and many approached the Sacraments.

There were during the past year:

Baptisms:	36
Marriages:	2
Confirmations:	9
Burials:	2
Conversions:	4

Laudetur Jesus Christus Maria Immaculata Amen!!!
Father Van Tighem, O.M.I.

1896

Jan. 12th: Last Friday at half past five in the evening, they called by telephone for the priest. A man, a Frenchman, had fallen from a coal wagon and had been badly crushed under the wheels. The Father was on the spot no longer than five minutes after the call, but came too late, the poor man had breathed his last a few minutes before. His name was Paul Beaufils. He was unconscious from the moment he fell and gave no sign of life. The Father learned that this man was in town for over five years, that he never set a foot in church and never approached the sacraments.

In fact, his name was not to be found on any of the lists in the presbytery. What to do with him? After mature reflection the Father decided that under no circumstances this man could be buried in the Catholic graveyard. So, when the superintendent sent for inquiries, the Father answered that he could do nothing for the poor man. On Sunday afternoon his body was taken to the Presbyterian Church and from there to the protestant burying grounds.

This was a terrible example for many parishioners who were neglecting their Christian duties. It had its good effect, for several careless men have attended church regularly since. May the Lord have mercy on the soul of that unfortunate man and have inspired him with feelings of contrition at the last moment.

This man was an old French soldier who had taken part in the Prussian War. Some Protestants who knew him, said, that he was an infidel.

Febr. 2/th: Our mines will work only three or four days. The weather being so mild very little coal is needed. Several miners have left already for Montana.

March 14th: Father Van Tighem has been suffering for these three last weeks from rheumatism, and the Rev. Father Fouquet has arrived last night, from Calgary to remain in Lethbridge until Easter.

News from St. Albert and Edmonton, announces that our good bishop is ill also, while Father Leduc has a bad attack of inflammatory rheumatism.

29th: Today, Palm Sunday, we were unfortunate enough of being deprived from the blessing of palms for the simple reason that we had none. Living in a desert where there is not a green branch for sixty miles around, it is rather sad. Two weeks ago, palms or evergreens were asked for from Pincher Creek, an answer was received that we would have them, but nothing arrived. There was a large congregation this morning at both masses.

Our choir is preparing some fine music for Easter; three Protestant gentlemen have offered their services and talents for the occasion. It is Easter Sunday and never before has our church contained more people than at High

Mass this morning. It so happened that the Anglican Church was closed last week, the minister having left for British Columbia. Consequently most of the Anglicans came to the Catholic Church. The people in town had learned that an excellent program of music had been prepared; three violins and two brass instruments were added to the music of our powerful organ, so that it formed a kind orchestra worth hearing. Hence the great affluence. The Rev. Father Fouquet sung the High Mass while Father Van Tighem aided the choir and preached the sermon.

A surprise to all was the Slavonian band, conducting the members of Slavonian Union to church. These enterprising men about twelve in number, bought themselves new instruments, engaged a teacher and practised twice a week. This is only since a few months and to our great surprise they came through the town, walking to the church and playing joyous tunes. All praise to them. The collection in church today amounted to $19.75.

APRIL 5TH: A dispatch arrived here yesterday bringing the sad news that the Rev. Father Leduc has received the last sacraments.

15TH: The weather remains cold.

MAY 9TH: Last night we opened the May devotions, and every day at four o'clock in the afternoon we will say the H. Rosary; hymns, the Litany followed by the benediction of the Bl. Sacrament.

MAY 15TH: Yesterday, Ascension Day, took place in the church, the First Communion of ten of our schoolchildren. Immediately before High Mass another ceremony took place. It was the solemn baptism of our little Negro boy Howard Porter from Great Falls. This boy is about 12 years old and desired very much to be baptized and received in the Catholic Church. He wrote to his parents and even, obtained a pass on the railway, from Mr. Barclay, to go and see his parents in the Falls, for the sole purpose of asking them this favor. Of course we knew not that this was the object of his long journey and how glad he was, when he returned to announce the good news. His father sent us a fine letter afterwards, thanking us for the interest we took in his son and confessing that he was very proud to see him a Catholic. Both father and mother of the child are Baptist Protestant.

The High Mass took place at 10 o'clock. Mr. Barclay, a prominent Protestant of the town, superintendent of the Coal Company, was present, for his only daughter, Mamiry, did her first communion. The ceremony was very imposing. The Rev. Father Doucet celebrated the High Mass having arrived the day before. Father Van Tighem who had been instructing the children for 40 days, this is: since Easter Sunday, preached at High Mass from the text – unless you eat the flesh of the son of man – this plain and simple instruction seemed to have penetrated to the soul of the hearers, especially of those who were not of the flock.

In the afternoon took place the renewal of the baptismal vows, the consecration of the children to Mary the Mother of God. The children were also enrolled in the H. Scapular of Mount Carmel.

JUNE: The general election is to take place of the 23rd of this month. Sir Charles Tupper is the premier of the Conservative, and Mr. Wilfried Laurier the Premier of the Liberal party. The Manitoba school question is again thrown into politics and great excitement prevails everywhere. It is to be hoped that the Conservative party will be returned as they are in favor of remedial legislation for our brethren of Manitoba, who are now unjustly deprived of their schools for six years.

A pastoral has been issued by the archbishop and bishops of Canada, re: the election and the duty of Catholics in this regard. Special prayers have been recommended by our bishop to this intention. The two candidates for Alberta, or better the three for a third one has lately appeared, are I.J. Clare from Calgary; T.B.H. Cochrane also from Calgary and F. Oliver from Edmonton, this last is the Liberal candidate.

About fifty Slavonian-Hungarian and Italian Catholics have been naturalized and will vote on this occasion. Father Van Tighem, who until now had remained a Belgian, has also become a British subject.

JUNE 19TH: Over one hundred Cris [Cree] Indians have arrived here from the United States.[120] They are forbidden to stay there any longer and are turned over to the Canadian government. These Indians have left Canada at the time of the rebellion in 1885. They will be located somewhere on the North Saskatchewan.

JUNE 21ST: Another train brings over again a large band of Cris Indians from the States. The weather is very dry, we have had no rain whatever during this month of June.

29TH: A message is brought over from the police barracks, saying that an Indian prisoner asked to see the priest. In fact it is said that this Indian is no other than the son of the great chief Big Bear, who at the time of North-West Rebellion, caused so much trouble and anxiety in the environs of Fort Pitt and Frog Lake.[121]

The Father takes with him a Half-breed as interpreter and finds this prince, a handsome specimen of humanity, a man in the bloom and force of live, imprisoned together with a very old man on the border of the grave. It appears that they took a too warm part in that unfortunate rebellion and that they are connected with the horrible Frog Lake massacre, where our good Fathers Fafard and Marchand lost their lives in the performance of their sacred duties.[122]

With the greatest affection this Indian seizes the Father's hand, and after the preliminary ceremonies, never to be omitted according to the Indian

▶ *Little Bear around 1912 on the Blackfeet Reservation, Montana.*
Photo Fred Meyer. Sherburne Collection, Mansfield
Library, University of Montana, Missoula, Montana.

ritual, especially when a prince beginneth his speech, Big Bear's son sayth he has had a revelation or inspiration from the Great Spirit. While sitting in attentive recollection, his hands over his eyes, all at once a voice spoke to him inwardly:

Send for the man of prayer, the black robe, give yourself over to him, that is, to God, to the Great Spirit whom he represents: you, your wife, your children and all the souls of the camps. The black robe will speak for you; show you the trail you must follow. Therefore, Father, I have sent for you. We are shut up here, we don't know why. At the time of the rebellion my father, Big Bear, the chief of the north, said to me and my followers: 'Depart my son, flee to the south at once, across the line there shall be liberty for you; here you could enjoy it no longer, we are surrounded. Depart.' For ten years we have lived in the country across the line; today we are turned on, they have forced us back to these regions. We have led good lives, why have they taken me a prisoner??? Why have they closed up this old man? He has only a few moons to live now???

Man of prayer, speak for us, but especially baptize us, baptize us at once, me, my wife, my children, the young men of my camp. I had a paper, they have taken it away from my tent now. This paper came from Washington; this paper sayeth that liberty, pardon, amnesty has been granted to all, why then are we shut up. Father, get that paper back for me, I will need it, speak for us, that they let us return to our own regions, where we will lead good and industrious lives,

Etc., etc., this speech was delivered with great solemnity, it lasted nearly two hours.

[*The Lethbridge News* of June 29, 1896, reported:]

Not in jeopardy

The Great Falls Leader has the following in reference to the arrest of Little Bear and Lucky Man

From an official source it is learned today that the Canadian Government, through its agent, had advised the American government that the lives of Little Bear and Lucky Man, the two Cree Indians arrested for the Mission murder as soon as they arrived on Canadian soil, are not in jeopardy. According to the explanation given by the Canadian government, while nothing was said to either Indian regarding the outcome of their arrest, it was their intention to impress upon Little Bear and his sub-chief the fact that the old indictment had not been forgotten and that its quashing lay in their future conduct toward good order and morals.

It is the intention of the government to keep them in prison a sufficient length of time to impress this upon them and their people and after that elapse they will be sent to their tribe on the banks of the Saskatchewan.

Both Indians are being held at Regina in the mounted police barracks and are subject to release when it suits Indian Commissioner Forget.

[Leonard continues:]

JUNE 30TH: When the son of Big Bear had terminated his discourse, I answered and said that I was glad of his excellent disposition towards embracing our Holy Religion, that I would gladly baptize him and his wife, but that grown up persons must be first instructed in their religion, that however I was ready at any moment to baptize his children, that I would do all I could to help him.

All right, he said, tomorrow I shall send my wife with my children to the mission, ask the chief of these soldiers to let me go and witness the ceremony; I desire very much to see it. They can send an escort and conduct me back here.

What was my astonishment when the next morning I learned that my prisoners had been transported to Regina last night. A dispatch had arrived late last night, ordering to send both prisoners east at once.[123]

However, I went to the camp and interviewed the wife and parents of the young chief. They were glad to hear the words of Little Bear and they would stand by them, they were too be send North in two days and would go to the mission at Onion Lake and do according to the words of their husband and parents.[124]

Today a young priest, the Rev. Bigaouette, arrives here from MacLeod, were he has taken the place of Rev. Father Lebret who has gone North for two months to preach several retreats.[125]

This young priest can talk well the Italian and will remain a few days in Lethbridge for the sake of our Italian Catholics. A sermon will be preached to them tonight and tomorrow at 8 o'clock. They are invited to Holy Mass. It is to be hoped that they will perform their Easter duties on this favorable occasion.

Last Sunday, the solemnity of St. John the Baptist, our Slavonians' society, came in a body to the church with their band. Early in the morning they had already visited the church for their general Communion on the feast of the Patron Saint of the society. Their banner had been placed in a conspicuous place and was surrounded with beautiful natural flowers. The High Mass was celebrated with solemnity and the singing was very good.

The general elections are over, and to the great astonishment of many, the Liberals are now in power with a good majority. We will see now what Mr. Laurier's intentions are with regard to the school question.[126]

JULY 12TH: Tonight a dozen Italians went to the river to bath and one of them venturing too far in the current disappeared, all efforts were needless to recover him as the river runs very swift at the spot were [he] went down.

The summer is advancing and no rain yet. Everything is dried up.

27TH: Yesterday, while a few Slavonians were down the river about four miles, they discovered the body of Frank Bonini, the Italian, who disappeared in the river while bathing near the pump house at Lethbridge. The police was notified and today the body, being already in a state of decomposition, was brought to town. We learn that this unfortunate man was only about two months in Lethbridge. We know him not. We have not seen him in church. He did not come while Father Bigaouette was here, for the special benefit of the Italians. He did not come to his confession and communion on that occasion as many others did. But charity makes us suppose that he was more faithful before he came here, so we buried him in the Cath. graveyard. RIP.

AUG. 4TH: Rain has at last appeared. Last night it begun and it continues today. It is a great pity it did not come a month sooner, but better late than never.

The Rev. Father Doucet spent a day in Lethbridge but departed again this morning.

AUG. 14TH: About two hundred Cris Indians have been brought over again from the United States. They are camped at the boundary line near Milk River and as the measles have appeared among the children, they are in quarantine now. Father Van Tighem has written to the Rev. Father Leslanc of Calgary, asking him, if possible, to come down and visit these poor Indians at their camp, as many children are in danger, and likely not baptized.

17TH: The Rev. Father Lestanc, superior of Calgary, has arrived here this morning and will proceed to the Cris' Indian camp at Milk River tonight. Mr. Barclay, superintendent of the Great Falls and Canada Railway, has kindly granted a pass to the Rev. Father.

20TH: We had an abjuration this morning at the convent chapel, when a young man, Henri Taylor, interpreter for the North West Mounted Police of this place, renounced Protestantism, embraced the Holy Catholic Faith, was baptized sub condition and did his first communion. Previously he belonged to the Anglican Church.

AUG. 30TH: The newspapers bring us the sad news that our good bishop is very ill at Montreal. Public prayers have been requested for him.

Sept. 1st: Father Van Tighem takes the MacLeod stage this morning, en route, for Calgary to take part in the annual retreat on the third day of September. It is the Rev. Father Lebret, O.M.I., who will preach this retreat.

The Archbishop of St. Boniface, Mgr. Langevin, is actually in Rome, paying his visit *Ad Limina*. We understand that His Grace took up with him six names as candidates for the coadjutor bishops of St. Albert and British Columbia respectively. Both bishops Grandin and Durieu are old and infirm and require help in their difficult and most important functions.[127]

Sept. 10th: Father Van Tighem, O.M.I., was called back to Lethbridge immediately after the retreat; a daughter of Mr. Callaghan has been taken suddenly ill and died. Happily the child was not seven years of age yet.

Sept. 12th: Rain continues falling for several days. Last night a south train departed from Lethbridge; arriving at the first section, a brakeman, McAdams, had to uncouple some carts. The night was very dark and unfortunately the man fell under the wheels, being crushed and instantly killed. He leaves a young wife, but no children. He will be buried tomorrow by the Methodist minister.

Oct. 12th: Our beloved bishop has returned from Montreal and is now at St. Albert. His Lordship had not to undergo any operation, but his health is far from what we would like it to be. We know not, as yet, the name of the coadjutor who has been appointed to our good bishop. The Rev. Father Doucet pays a short visit to Lethbridge; arrived on Monday morning, he departed the following night; he was at Maple Creek for last Sunday. We have the regular October devotions, as prescribed by the Holy Father, to our Lady of the Most Holy Rosary. These devotions take place in church, every day at 4 o'clock except Saturdays when they are postponed till 7 o'clock in the evening. We have a most beautiful (fall) autumn.

Oct. 17th: At eight o'clock this morning a man came rushing towards the house praying the priest to be ready at once, that a rig would be at the door in a moment and convey him to the bridge bottom, where Mrs. MacFarland was actually dying.

Indeed a son of Mr. Stafford was seen approaching already, so down the hills we went flying. Alas, too late, Mrs. McFarland was no more! She came down from MacLeod, with her husband a week or so ago. On her way, she contracted a cold, which turned to pneumonia and pleurisy. Although the illness was dangerous, she would not, so they say, send for the priest, as she thought she would be well in a short time and visit herself the mission, where she was well-known and loved. She was improving a little and on Monday, when leaving late in the night, the doctor had great hopes. On Tuesday morning she felt better – ate a little and desired to change some linen as she had been transpiring much during the night, while changing she helped herself, spoke and seemed to be well when all at a sudden she gasped heavily for breath, fainted, so they thought, but it was death. She passed away without a word or a sign. RIP.

Mrs. MacFarland was one of the first white women in this part of the world, coming to Coal Banks in 1878 to keep house for her brother Nicholas Sheran who had taken possession of the coal mines across the river here. In 1880 she married Mr. Jos MacFarland, a rancher from MacLeod, and moved to that place about two miles east of the settlement. She lived there ever since. This lady had a well-known and well-deserved reputation of being very charitable and consequently was loved by all. The first missionary will remember long what she did for them; she received them at her home and was rather a mother than a friend to them. Mr. MacFarland had just renovated his residence at Macleod, it appears they were just to take again possession of their palatial mansion and see: the Lord hath ordained differently. The body of this good lady was transported to Macleod on Wednesday, to be buried there by the side of her brother Michael, on the 29th of October. RIP.

Oct. 29th: A boy of about ten years of age, son of Archie McLean, was trying to steal a ride, the boy was crushed between an iron water tank and a loaded car of rails, he lived for two days, but was unconscious. He was buried today, from some Protestant church. Another warning to lads who try to ascend wagons and engines.

Nov. 25th: The month of November is extremely cold. The snow has fallen two feet deep and the cattle must be suffering much. During this month the people have recommended many masses for the Holy souls.

Dec. 6th: This month has begun with warmer days than during November. The Chinook winds have cleared away nearly all the snow.

28th. We have had a really beautiful Christmas time. The weather has continued warm, so that [we] scarcely needed any fire in the church. We had Midnight Mass. The church was filled up with people from all denominations. The service was very solemn and the singing beautiful. The altar looked magnificent, ablaze with lighted tapers. It was two o'clock before the thanksgivings mass, which followed immediately the midnight mass, was over. There was almost a general communion. Confessions were heard from 3½ o'clock in the afternoon until midnight. I am told that the Methodist minister was present.

Jan. 1st: L.J.C. and M.Im.

The first day of the year has nearly passed away. We have no evening service tonight. There was not very many people at mass and the reason, I suppose is that too many have been feasting last night.

This is the rather sad news I received today from the North:

- Rev. Father Leduc is worse, going slowly
- Rev. Father Rémas can go no farther[128]
- His Lordship, Bishop Grandin, continually suffering
- Rev. Father Perrault succumbs from weak chest and goes to the hospital.

Who shall take all their places?? We have as yet no news of the Coadjutor who was to be appointed since long to help our invalid bishop. The Archbishop is dying at Montreal, Mr. Faber.

Febr. 6th: We shall have the blessing of candles tomorrow. Many have already brought packages of tapers to the church. In the afternoon we shall have the usual procession with the statue of the infant Jesus in church. Then, also, the children are blessed and all the mothers bring their babies to church. After the ceremony the children all go to the schoolrooms where a little lottery takes place and the customary distribution of candies. It is the children's feast!

7th: There were a good number of children present in church today and the little Jesus' feast was well celebrated.

March 18th: ...

April 17th: Holy Saturday today. We had all the ceremonies performed in the church during the Holy Week. Our Slavonians kept the watches in presence of the Blessed Sacrament between Holy Thursday and Friday. Confessions and Communions are going on all this week.

19th: Yesterday, Easter Sunday, all was nice in church, fine decorations, good singing, many people!!! The Slavonian band came to church and played before and after mass in front of the church. Serg. Major Spicer had come from MacLeod to sing the base part of Peter's mass. Our schools are closed on account of sickness in town of scarlet fever, diphtheria and chicken pox.

28th: Father Van Tighem bought four brass musical instruments from the N.W.M.P. today: a bass, alto baritone and tenor horn, for the sum of $32.00.

Corporal Calla[g]han is going to add two cornets and probably we start a little band with the schoolboys.

MAY 2ND: We have begun the May devotions, instead of having the rosary and benediction at 4 o'clock in the afternoon; we have these May month exercises at 7½ in the evening.

MAY 10TH: Great news arrives us today!! Our coadjutor bishop is nominated and Rev. Father Legal is now our help-bishop. For a long time we awaited this nomination and were almost sure of the appointment, so that the news was not a surprise but rather a happy relief of our long suspense. Monsignor Legal is quite young, enjoys good health, is a man of good learning and has been in the diocese for about sixteen years, Ad multos annos!!!

Father Van Tighem goes to Montana tonight for the fulfillment of Easter duties of some persons along our south road.

Our school reopened today after having been closed for over a month on account of sickness in town.

28TH: Brother John Berchmans came to visit his brother to Lethbridge. A young Indian Blackfoot was his companion. He is one of the few who have resolved to lead a Christian life; he has done his first communion lately.[129] The Rev. Father Doucet came also to celebrate the feast of the Ascension in Lethbridge. They all departed last night to the Peigan Reserve.

News has arrived from St. Albert, that Mgr. Legal will be consecrated on Corpus Christi, 17th June, in the cathedral of St. Albert. Our annual retreat is to precede this great ceremony and therefore the Father will be absent from Lethbridge for two or three weeks. He will leave on Monday the 7th of June.

JUNE 4TH: A dispatch arrives today announcing that the new railway from Lethbridge through the Crowsnest Pass is to be built at once.

JUNE 20TH. There were present at the consecration of Mgr. Legal: one Archbishop, Mgr. Langevin; four bishops, Durieu, Clut, Legal, and the conse-crating Prelate Mgr. Grandin. There were about forty priests, many Brothers and Sisters from different convents and missions. It rained the whole day of the consecration and consequently there were not so many visitors as it was expected, though the cathedral was well filled. Archbishop Langevin made an eloquent sermon at mass.

The very day of the consecration many Fathers left St. Albert in the evening in order to take the train early in the morning from Edmonton to Calgary, but arrived at Red Deer River news arrived from the south that many bridges had been carried away by the flood. It was late in the evening of the 18th when we left Red Deer and we passed the night about three miles from Calgary.[130] We walked in to town partly then, a handcar took us somewhat farther and finally an engine with caboose brought us to the station. It was nearly noon before we reached the mission. Among the unfortunate voyageurs were the Archbishop Mgr. Durieu, and six Fathers. R. Mother Green was there also.[131] On Sunday the 20th the Archbishop preached a most eloquent sermon in the church at Calgary. This being the Jubilee Sunday of Queen Victoria, the sermon was for the occasion. Several Protestant ministers were in church as also some distinguished visitors who were detained at Calgary on account of the flood. It was a great surprise indeed to all, who, for the first time heard Mgr. Langevin. We may very well be proud to have such an able man at the head of our ecclesiastical province.

JULY 13TH: Yesterday were let the different contracts for the grading of the Crows Nest Pass R.R. There arrived in Lethbridge two special trains loaded with men, horses and tools to start the work immediately.

The Rev. Father Lacombe is coming to Lethbridge at the end of the week, for the purpose of preaching the retreat to the Sisters. Father Van Tighem must go to Calgary to replace R.F. Lacombe during his absence.

JULY 22ND: After a week absence in Calgary Father Van Tighem returns here, and R.P. Lacombe takes to road to Macleod and his own mission Calgary. There are very few Catholics in that place and the grand church presents a melancholic aspect with all its empty pews on Sundays and Holy days.

JULY 30TH: Last Wednesday there arrived a Slavonian or Greek priest in Lethbridge. He has celebrated mass in the Slavonian language according to ritual of that country. Our Slavonians were glad to see him and answered his calls to church. Most of them came to confession and received communion under both the elements of bread and wine. The priest Nicolaus Seregelly from Streator, Illinois, returns home tonight. A collection was made among the Slavonians for him.

AUG. 10TH: Our mines are closed since a few days, the strike is on, the miners ask for an increase of wages and many grievances must be removed before they will return to their labors.

AUG. 30TH: The miners are resuming their work in the mines, no advance in wages was granted by the company, but mostly all the grievances complained of shall be removed in the future. The strike lasted nearly a month.

AUG. 31ST: We had no rain for about two months. It is really discouraging; it is no use to plant trees or make gardens unless we have a system of waterworks, and when shall this be?

Sept. 6th: Many people are daily arriving to work on the new railway, the Crows Nest Pass. Many of these laborers unfortunately take to drink, so that our little town is not as quiet as usual. The priest just returned now from a call, I don't know how I should call it, a sick call or a dead call. One [of] the parishioners called about half an hour ago, saying that a man was dying at the Queens and there was suspicion of poison. In haste the priest went there and found the man, a certain Flanagan, it appears, in the last pangs of agony. With haste the priest administered the extreme unction; for although the man was unknown to the Father, he learned that he had been at church and, of course, the name would have been sufficient. Just as I administered the Last Unction the unfortunate man breathed his last. I learned that the man had been drinking for several days. How terrible to appear in that state before the throne of God.

Oct.: His Lordship, our Coadjutor Mgr. Legal, has announced that he would come to Lethbridge for the 7th of next month.

16th: Scarlet fever is again in town; one of [the] boys was removed to the terrace where two Sisters are nursing him. We expect the mother of the boy in a few days.

16th: Today, Saturday, the news came from France that our Very Reverend Father General, Louis Soullier, was seriously ill. Certain prayers were ordered to be said by all the members of communities all over the world. But when, after having read the circular, I opened a Winnipeg daily newspaper; what was my astonishment and affliction to read that at St. Boniface the flags were all at half-mast. For a telegram announcing the death the Father-General of the Oblates, had just arrived there. What a loss for our congregation. RIP.

19th: A solemn funeral service was celebrated this morning for the repose of the soul of our Father-General. There was quite a good attendance at church to pray for him.

Nov. 8th: His Lordship Émile Legal, our coadjutor bishop, arrived in Lethbridge last Friday afternoon, Nov. 5th, coming from MacLeod.

On Saturday evening at 8 o'clock addresses were presented to His Lordship, in church, by the members of the societies, the C.M.B.A. and the St. John Baptist of the Slavonians. His Lordship replied to the congregation in general, and to the members of the associations in particular. There was a good gathering in church for the occasion. A solemn benediction with the Blessed Sacrament followed and terminated the reception.

Yesterday, Sunday, His Lordship said H. Mass at 8 o'clock. If there had been any other priest, we would have had High Mass by the bishop. A large number came to communion at this first mass. After High-Mass, the bishop addressed a few words on the H. Sacrament of Confirmation, and confirmed nineteen of our parishioners, most of them children who have made their fist communion, this or last year.

His Lordship gave a fine sermon at the evening service, speaking for nearly an hour on the persecutions of the church of Christ. A great snowstorm was raging all the day, but notwithstanding the church was full in the morning.

DEC. 28TH: Christmas time with all its beautiful ceremonies in the Cath. Church has come and gone. This year again we had very solemn services in the church. The midnight mass was celebrated in the presence of a large congregation, many of whom were Protestants. The Anglican minister occupied one of the front pews. The church was as usual on such occasions beautifully decorated. A new carpet, Brussels, had been presented to the church the week previous; it covers the entire sanctuary and costs $1.60 per yard. Mrs. Barclay together with some kind friends are the donators of this handsome gift.

The singing was very good this year; a certain Mr. Lamb, a surveyor on the Crows Nest Pass, gave us some fine solo.

Our hospital for several months is crowded with patients from the construction of our new railway. Inflammatory rheumatism and mountain or typhoid fever are the most prominent cases. There are also a few frozen limbs. Hence the priest must frequently visit these patients as many of them are Catholics. Thus far none have died.

The sad news arrives us from Calgary that the Reverend Father Lacombe, our veteran missionary, is suffering very much from an attack of lumbago. It seems the Rev. Father is prostrated for over two weeks and entirely helpless. Being seventy-one years of age and having never been sick in his life, the Rev. Father feels it sadly. He has been transported to the Holy Cross Hospital, conducted by the Grey Nuns of Montreal, where he shall receive good attendance.

We have very fine weather ever since November.

Anno Domini 1898

JAN. 3RD: When Christmas and consequently New Year day cometh on a Saturday, it is rather a trying time for the priest who is all-alone in a mission. This is the case this year and I feel rather tired after all these festivals. However, when all passes quietly away, when the religious services were well attended, when many faithful approached the Holy Sacraments, when no abuses are to be recorded, the missionary is well repaid for his fatigues. Therefore we breathe a grateful *Deo Gratias!!!*

But now Father Van Tighem prepared for a long journey to St. Albert. He has been nominated the delegate for the district of Calgary, to the Vicarial Chapter, which is to take place at the bishop's palace on the 12th day of January. For, news has arrived from France, that the general chapter and the election of a new Superior General for the Oblate Order, is to take place at Paris on the 19th of May, being Ascension Day.

The Father was to leave for Medicine Hat in order to conduct the religious services there on the Sunday previous to the twelfth, but a letter from the bishop called him at once to Calgary for that Sunday as there was no priest to say mass there. On the following day the Father took the train to Edmonton and from thence to St. Albert. The election took place in the parlor of the palace after the Conventual Mass celebrated by His Lordship, Bishop Legal. Present: our saintly Bishop Grandin, Bishop Legal, Rev. Fathers: Lestanc, Leduc, Doucet, Mérer, Van Tighem, Thérien, Grandin and Lizée.[132] The Rev. Father Mérer, actually Superior of the house of St. Albert, was nominated the delegate for the General Chapter.

Father Van Tighem, being unable to reach his mission for the following Sunday, returned by Medicine Hat and held the religious services there in our little church, both morning and evening; arriving home again on the following day, Monday, January 17th.

JAN. 17TH: The Rev. Father Lacombe is slowly recovering from his illness and being [able] to walk a little in his room.

MAY 16TH: Father Van Tighem was called to Pincher Creek last week there to meet the other R. Fathers of this southern district for the monthly retreat; also to hold council with the Rev. Fathers Lacombe and Lebret, especially for the situation and future erection of a church in Macleod.

During the absence of the Father, a German Catholic, Mr. Younger, aged about sixty, felt sick and was brought to the hospital. He asked several times for the priest and after a few days his mind becoming greatly disturbed, he was to be removed to the guardroom in the barrack. It was there that during the night, [in] a moment of mental aberration he took his own life by hanging himself. Very sad news for the priest when returning and this showeth once more how very dangerous it is to leave a mission without a priest.

21ST: We have been saying the *Veni Creator* for weeks, to ask the Light of the Holy Spirit for the General Chapter of the Oblate fathers in Paris, France, and for the election of the new general Superior-General. Our bishop, Mgr. Legal, and the R. Father Mérer, the delegate for this diocese, are in Paris now and assisting at this great and holy meeting. We learn by telegraphic dispatches that the Reverend Father Augier-Cassien has been elected Superior-General on May the 19th, being Ascension Day. *Ad Multos Annos!!!*

JUNE 6TH: Yesterday, Trinity Sunday, was a red-letter day for the Cath. Church in Lethbridge. It was the first Sunday of June, the month of the Sacred Heart and we organized the league of the Sacred Heart in this parish. This took place at the evening service and really it surpassed all our expectations. About one hundred joined the League and I am sure that quite a few regret not to be members today. It will be for the next enrolling. We expect great results from this Union or Apostleship of Prayer.

Brother John Morkin from the Industrial School of St. Joseph, Dunbow is actually at the mission here and, is making his retreat in preparation for the pronouncing of his Holy Vows for five years. This will take place on next Thursday: *Corpus Christi!*

JUNE 13TH: Brother Morkin, John, returned this morning to St. Joseph Industrial School, via Macleod. This good Brother was all piety and recollection during these days of retreat. May the Lord grant us many such good Brothers as Br. John and Thomas Morkin.

17TH: The Rev. Fathers Lacombe and Lebret paid a short visit to this mission and remained for two nights and one day. The R.F. Lacombe is daily recovering from his great illness last winter.

AUG. 16TH: Father Van Tighem, having been appointed to preach the annual retreat to the Sisters, Faithful Companions of Jesus, opened this retreat on Wednesday, the third day of August, at the convent of Calgary. Passes on the CPR had been kindly granted to fourteen Sisters of Edmonton and eight from Lethbridge.

The Rev. Father Lacombe had arrived at Lethbridge during the absence of the Father, but illness compelled him to leave almost immediately. Dispatches were sent to Calgary recalling the Father immediately after the retreat. Arriving at Lethbridge on Friday evening the 12th, the Father was telephoned up at midnight to the hospital where a young man was dying. This man was buried on Sunday afternoon, Aug. 14th.

Aug. 20th: It has been decided to place a hot-air furnace in the church or better under the church; for this purpose the contract for making the necessary excavations was given to three Slavonians for $30.00 dollars. They have terminated their work. The Father has written to Winnipeg inquiring the cost of such a furnace. One thousand bricks have also been purchased to make a chimney of about twenty-eight feet high.

Aug. 30th: The contract for placing the furnace under the church has been given to Mr. Kirkman of Lethbridge for the sum of two hundred dollars.

Nov. 14th: The Rev. Father Lebret, being ill at MacLeod, has requested Father Van Tighem to visit the ranchers of the Porcupine Hills; consequently the father left Lethbridge on the seventh of November with the morning train to MacLeod. Mr. William Lyndon awaited him there with a rig and the father started with him. He remained for thee days on the Lyndon Ranch, where three first communions of adults took place. From there the Father visited the Glengary Ranch, where Mr. McDonald is in charge. He remained there till Sunday afternoon. Holy Mass was celebrated there on Sunday 13th Nov. Sacred hymns were sung before and after the mass, accompanied by Mrs. McDonald at the organ.

In the afternoon the Father came to Mr. Sharples, the son-in-law of Mr. McDonald, where he said H. Mass on Monday morning. All the Catholics where the Father visited approached the Sacraments There were no exceptions. Mr. MacDonald brought the Father back to Macleod the same day, where he took the train of seven o'clock in the evening and arrived at Lethbridge at 9:30 p.m.

Nov. 19th: A telegram called the Father to MacLeod again on the 17th. Our good and saintly bishop, Mgr. Grandin had just arrived in MacLeod and His Lordship wished to see the fathers. Therefore Father Van Tighem took the train on Friday morning to return the same night. Mgr. Grandin seems to be in good health. R. Father Lebret is also improving, but the doctors order a complete rest for two or three months. In consequence the R. Father will visit his brethren in Manitoba and take the well-earned repose.

Lately we had two conversions and baptisms of adults; a certain Miss Carman for a long time assisted at the services of the church; having to undergo a dangerous operation on account of the now common disease of appendicitis, she came and begged to be received in the church, as the Father was to be absent for over a week. Although she was not sufficiently prepared, we would not refuse her just request and we baptized her under condition. The same day Miss Ragglen from Montana, aged about sixteen, was also baptized. Her father professes no religion whatever, but her mother was a Catholic. I heard rumors of two more who wish to enter the true fold of the good Shepherd.

Nov. 21ST: The operation on Miss Carman has been very successful and she [is] doing well.

[The Sisters, Faithful Companions of Jesus (1898) stated in their annual report:]

It is a great consolation for us to receive so many souls belonging to the true faith or desirous of embracing it. The devotion to the Holy Souls is a favourite in the parish. The children, by their savings, were able to have Masses said during the month. One little girl, on being reminded by the mistress to bring her five cents for the Poor Souls, answered: "My mother says we have no one dead in our family."

We close our usuals this year with the festival of the Immaculate Conception.[33] As this is also the feast of the Rev. Father Van Tighem, O.M.I. we had a little reception for him in the schoolroom. The children read an address, recited a beautiful poem on the Immaculate Conception. They presented the Father with three handsome chairs for the Sanctuary & a credence table: for ten years the Father has during the services sat upon a box covered with red calico.

[Leonard continues:]
Dec. 26th: Christmas has come and passed. It was celebrated as usual with all due solemnity. But a horrible windstorm prevented many, especially ladies, from coming to church both at midnight and at High mass during the day. However, the church was well filled.

["Rapport du vicariat de Saint-Albert" (1898, 228–29):]

228: The Rev. Father Van Tighem, who has worked, for the future of Lethbridge as well, with energy and perseverance, and thanks to his knowledge, he could, without making debts, give his parish complete buildings that are perfectly furnished. The church, built in two instances, is partly of stone, partly of bricks. The interior is very well decorated and large enough for the population. It gloriously beats the three Protestant churches at that location. In 1895 this church was consecrated by Mgr. Grandin. It is the only consecrated church of the diocese.

229: The Catholic population of Lethbridge amounts to about 550 on 1600 inhabitants. These Catholics mainly belong to the poor classes. For the most part they are miners who make their living during the day, but who prove to be generous enough to maintain their pastor.

Apart from Slavonians, there are a whole lot of other nationalities: Germans, Hungarians, Flemish, Italians, Scottish, Irish, Métis and Blackfoot. The Rev. Father hears confessions in six different languages: for three of these languages he uses a dictionary.

1899

[Leonard continues:]

Jan. 20th: The annual retreat for the Oblate Fathers has taken place at St. Albert. It was the Reverend Father Lestanc, who preached this retreat. The Coadjutor Bishop Legal had just returned from France and from Rome. The Father of Lethbridge also went to the retreat so that he was absent for over three weeks. However, the Rev. Father Lepine, O.M.I., came on one of these Sundays and celebrated mass in Lethbridge.

On his return from the retreat Father Van Tighem was sent to Med. Hat where the Blessed Sacrament had been left in the church; the priest, Mr. Pufas, being sick and gone to the Calgary hospital. Things are going far from smoothly in that place; the priest will not be able to remain there.

Febr. 6th: Our coadjutor-bishop, Mgr. Legal, came and surprised us last week. Having been called to Medicine Hat on account of the existing difficulties between the priest and the parishioners of that place. His Lordship arrived here at 5 o'clock in the morning, all alone, and on his way to visit the Indian reservations of the Peigans and Blood, Mgr. remained here only two days and confirmed a few persons, who would likely not be here next summer at the appointed time for confirmation.

March 10th: During the Holy Time of Lent we have the Stations of the Cross every Wednesday and Friday, but these pious exercises are not as well attended as in previous years. The weather has been very cold and stormy, and this is one of the reasons. Another is the removal of most of our Slavonians to the shaft called No. 3, which is about a mile from church. We could not expect these poor miners to come so far through cold and stormy weather after their fatiguing work of the day. When this people lived in town, the church was well-filled during Lenten exercises.

May: We have the daily exercises of the month of Mary at seven o'clock every evening.

May 20th: Coutts. During the May month Father Van Tighem went twice to Montana to visit certain Catholics and make them fulfill their Easter duties. The spring is very late; cold and snow even in this month.

June 13th: His Lordship, Bishop Legal, O.M.I., came to Lethbridge on last Friday night and confirmed nineteen of our children on last Sunday after High Mass. The Rev. Father Lebret of MacLeod accompanied his Lordship and helped us in the ceremonies. The bishop addressed the congregation twice. In the afternoon a reception took place at the Convent School, when the children, with songs and recitations welcomed their first pastor, they also presented His Lordship with a small basket of blossoms, which basket the bishop found rather heavy, but after examination it was found that the bottom of the famous basket was covered with silver dollars beautifully shining under the flowers. This bishop returned early on Monday morning to MacLeod. We have almost continual rains, which makes the country beautiful.

JULY 3RD: The pupils of the Convent School gave a fine concert in the Opera Hall, for the closing of the school. It was really wonderful how the little ones performed. Master Adjustor Begin and his eldest sister, Lydia, deserve special mention.

JULY 17TH: The Rev. Father Leduc is here to preach the retreat to the Sisters. The new building at the convent, the contract of which was let to Mr. McGuire from MacLeod, has been pushed forward; the foundations are laid, but the lumber has not all arrived. It is actually very hot, but our continual rains have kept the prairie green.

["Un temoin" (1899, 381) about Father Lacombe's golden jubilee on the 25th of September that year:]

Father Van Tighem, O.M.I., was charged with the ceremonies, Mgr. the archbishop [Mgr. Langevin of St. Boniface] was seated on the throne and Mgr. Grandin assisted with the choir.

1900

MARCH 18TH: A Greek Cath. priest, Johan Ardan from Olyphant, Pennsylvania, visited our Slovak Catholics and remained here for three days. Having wired to the bishop for jurisdiction for him, the answer came in the affirmative and he heard the confession of sixty-three Slavonians and gave them H. Communion according to their rites.

We have fine spring weather; the blue bird arrived two weeks ago, which is a sign of early spring. Our Rev. Father Lacombe left for Europe and may be absent for about a year.

MAY 10TH: A Polish priest residing at the bishop's palace, and in charge of the Galicians around Edmonton arrived in Lethbridge visiting the Slavonians of this place. As it was only a short time since Rev. Ardan had been here, there was little to do for him.

JUNE 4TH: Our coadjutor-bishop, Mgr. Legal, arrived in Lethbridge on Friday night, and gave Confirmation to nineteen persons yesterday, Sunday, in the church. Fourteen of them had received their First Communion in the morning from the hands of the bishop. His Lordship will go to Med. Hat this evening, from thence to the reserve at Blackfoot Crossing, Calgary and MacLeod, where on next Sunday the new church is to be blessed. Father Van Tighem has been invited to preach on this occasion. A concert was given last week in aid of the church, which realized $47.00 only.

The Rev. Father Blanchet, O.M.I., from Pincher Creek accompanied His Lordship in his visit to Lethbridge.

JUNE 11TH: Yesterday, Trinity Sunday, took place in MacLeod the blessing of the new church by the right Rev. Emile Legal, O.M.I., Coadjutor of Mgr. Grandin. The Fathers present were: Father Van Tighem, Le Vern, Danis, and Brothers Barrau and [blank space].[134]

The new church was well filled; a good number of Protestants attending. The church is quite spacious, strongly built with a handsome little spire.

JULY 6TH: The Rev. Father Lebret after having preached the annual retreat to the Sisters returned to MacLeod.

Coutts: Father Van Tighem leaves the R. Father in charge at Lethbridge and goeth along the south line to visit some people and restore peace in some families where it had unfortunately been disturbed. Strange it is that both the families where the Father was invited were Protestant. The Father goeth as far as Great Falls, where he visits the priest who is a Belgian, Rev. Father Allaeys from Ypres.[135] The Rev. Father Doucet paid us a visit also at Lethbridge.

JULY 16TH: The Half-Breed Commission charged to settle the claims of these people were to be here on June the 19th.[136] About one hundred Half-Breeds from the United States arrived here and were obliged to return, the date for the meeting being postponed till the 10th of July. Again these poor people were here for this date. It is already the 16th of July today, and they have not arrived as yet. Many Half-Breeds are destitute and we have wired to Ottawa for assistance.

The Rev. Father Thérien, O.M.I., arrived here yesterday en route to Lewistown, Montana, to preach a mission to the Half-Breeds there.

19TH: It appears they number 400. Ottawa will do nothing for the Half-Breeds. The commission has not arrived yet.

27TH: The gentlemen of the commission came on Monday morning and started work at once. After three days work they went to MacLeod. It is unfortunate that the conditions for right to scripts were not given out in time. Many poor Half-Breeds came here and, though they had been born in the North West Terr., were refused their claim because their parents had been in the United States previously. Others are refused because they had no permanent home but were roving here and there. Thus an old widow was refused although she had three of her children born in the Territory. Many women could not come and sent their parents or relatives to collect for them, but the commission would not accept power of attorney. If all this had been published in time, the people would have known what to do, I myself knew these and other conditions only in the evening of the departure of the commission from Lethbridge. Never was a commission so badly organized.[137] May this be the end of it!!! The worse is that this mission spent over two hundred dollars in assisting the destitute Halfbreeds, in fact, more than three hundred dollars was lent to this unfortunate people, but some have returned the money, others have promised to do so, but a good number having obtained no scripts will be unable to repay. It is to be hoped that the Department of the Interior will repay the mission.

Rev. Father Thérien after an absence of about three weeks has returned from his voyage in Montana; he is well satisfied with the mission he gave at Lewistown.

Our dear Father Perreault, in the last stage of consumption, arrived here from Texas, where he had been sent for his health.[138] He is very weak indeed and can scarcely move; he goeth to the Calgary Hospital.

AUG. 4TH:

AUG. 27TH: Our annual retreat is to take place in Calgary at the beginning of next month. Rev. Father Allard from Manitoba is to preach it. Many teams are at work in our streets, leveling and making ditches for the irrigation. The water is expected here soon. The Governor-General, Lord Minto, will visit our town and pronounce the irr. canal opened in the beginning of September.

SEPT. 14TH: Having been absent for nearly two weeks in Calgary, there was no mass in Lethbridge last Sunday. Two new fathers arrived in Calgary while we were there and will remain in the diocese. It was announced that our good and saintly bishop, Mgr. Grandin, would once more come south, and visit all the missions of his diocese in these parts. This visit was to take place just before the coming of the Apostolic Delegate, Mgr. Falconia, to this diocese. His Lordship was already in Calgary and MacLeod, when a telegram called Him to meet the delegate at once. So that to our great sorrow we are deprived of this great and most desired visit of our first pastor.

[Leonard did not have an entry in his journal for September 1900, but from a letter he wrote to the mayor and council of the City of Lethbridge, we get an impression of his occupations. Transcript:]

To his Worship the Mayor and the Gentlemen of the Council.
Lethbridge, Sept. 29, 1900.
Dear Sirs,

Last spring it was decided in the Council that lights should be placed at several points of the town; among which was one at the Corner of the Catholic Church. I have remarked that with the exception of this last one all the others have been placed in position for months.

Now that the ditches are in our streets, this Corner of the Catholic Church has become a dangerous place in dark evenings; and before long we may have to deplore some sad accident.

Hoping, Dear Sirs, that You Will be able to remedy this
I remain

Your Obt. Servant
Father Van Tighem.

[Leonard continues:]
OCT. 10TH: The Rev. Father Doucet passed a day in Lethbridge and reports all well at the Peigan reserve.

OCT. 13TH: The Rev. Father Danis from Blackfoot Crossing came in on this morning train and will remain with us for a day or two.

DEC. 8TH: The Rev. Father Lacombe has returned from Europe and is actually in Montreal, but will come home next week.

DEC. 9TH: Yesterday took place in the church a ceremony, which never before had been witnessed in Lethbridge: a Brother Oblate made his perpetual vows. Both the Brothers Morkin arrived here over a week ago and made their annual retreat; Brother Thomas consecrated himself for life to God in the congregation of the Oblates of Mary Immaculate. The Brothers will return to the Industrial School, on next Monday night.

[The Sisters, Faithful Companions of Jesus (1900) transcript:]
The feast of the Immaculate Conception was ushered in by a little entertainment, given by the children to the Rev. L. Van Tighem on the occasion of his patronal feast, consisting of religious & secular recitations, vocal & instrumental music. They presented him with 51 ft. of matting for the main aisle of the Church, thus adding to the silence & adornment of the house of God. The Rev. Father was very pleased with their progress & their generous offering. The next day, the glorious Feast of Our Immaculate Mother was celebrated with all possible pomp.

[Leonard continues:]
DEC. 10TH: We learn today, that our saintly Father Perrault went to heaven on the feast of Mary Imm. at 2:30 in the morning. What a beautiful day to die on!!!!!.

DEC. 26TH: Christmas is celebrated with the usual solemnities. The English-speaking people present a purse to the Priest with $55.00. The Austrian Catholics every month present about $20.00.

MAY 16TH: Our winter is not severe. We had some small-pocks in town. Our Holy Week is passed; we had the ceremonies customary. Today, Ascension day, we had our First Communions, and next Sunday His Lordship, Bishop Legal, will administer a few confirmations.

MAY 19TH: Bishop Legal, R. Father Lacombe and Lacase, also Brother John arrived by last night's train, we had solemn High Mass, the bishop preached and confirmed after mass. The Rev. Father Lacase addressed the congregation at the evening service. It rained all the day along and very few were at church.

[Leonard, in Dutch, to his nephew Joseph:]
    Lethbridge, June 4, 1901.
    Dear Joseph,

No news from Father Lacombe. We still expect him this week in Macleod. I wrote to him asking him to send you the pass himself as soon as he has it, so that is done. Look for Father Lebret and try to put the little statues in your suitcase as well as the twelve small lamps and my *capote*. Father Lebret knows all about it. The statues are Carli's, my coat from the Sisters of N.D. de Lourdes'. Tell them to send the bills to me. If you have still more room in your suitcase, ask the bursar for candles just as last year. Wax is there 20 ct. or 25 ct. per pound cheaper, the more the better. As you offer me to ask for flowers, yes I would quite like to get some plants. Check with the gardener to see if he can supply the following:

Camelia = Palms, different kinds
Azalia = Magnolia = Acasia
Aroucaria or Norfolk Pine
Sanseveria = Pleroma
Dwarf Justitia = Hibiscus chinese
Brugmansia = Jasmin.

If you could get any of these, or different ones, I would be very happy. To reduce the weight, you could replant them in a flat box and take them along [letter continues in English] in a small box about 4 inch high, without pots.

If you need money for the journey write to me immediately. Do you have enough clothes? Buy in Montreal all you need and shoes. If there is no time, [letter goes on in French] ask Rev. Father Lebret for the money – I will re-imburse him everything, buy all you would need.

Yours, L. Van Tighem, O.M.I.

[Leonard continues:]

JUNE 11TH: The Rev. Father Leduc arrived last night and will stay for a day.

JUNE 16TH: Joseph Van Tighem arrived from Montreal College this morning. He is to remain in the northwest for a year to recuperate his health.

JUNE 22ND: Last night the pupils of the convent school gave their annual entertainment. An address was read and a presentation of a purse made to Father Van Tighem on the occasion of his 50th birthday.

25TH: The Father left this morning for MacLeod and Calgary and from there shall proceed, in company with R. Father Lacombe, to St. Paul, Minnesota, to be present at the Jubilee, the 50th anniversary of the arrival there of the first bishop, Mgr. Cretin. Monsignor Ravoux and Father Lacombe were the only priests who were there at that time and are still living.

Indien gy er zulke Krygen Kondet of andere Van deze Soorten, zou ik zeer blyde zyn... Gy zoudt ze Kunnen in eene plate Box planten en by u nemen. a Small Box about 4 inch. high, and without pots, so that it be lighter... —

Schryf my onmiddelyk indien gy geld noodig hebt voor de reis.... hebt gy Kleeren genoeg Koopt ze tot Montreal, alles gy noodig hebt... en schoen... indien er geen tyd ware, Demandez de l'argent au R. P. Lebret — Je lui rendrai tout — achetez tout ce dont vous auriez besoin — Jou — L Van Tighem ui.

▸ *Father Leonard's drawing of the proposed*
box with plants – drawing in text

[While Leonard was in Minnesota, *The Lethbridge News*, June 27, 1901, reported:]

Convent Concert

A Very Amusing Programme Capitally Rendered. Presentation to Rev. Father Van Tighem.

The concert and presentation which took place at the Convent School on Friday last was a happy conception, and the excellent manner in which the long programme was carried through reflected great credit on those in charge of the arrangement and at the same time bore testimony to possession and considerable historic ability on the part of the young performers. A pleasing feature on the evening entertainment was the presentation of an address and purse to the Rev. Father Van Tighem by the pupils of the school to celebrate his 50th birthday.

The programme opened with a prologue by Misses Delay and Kelly, which was delivered in a highly creditable manner. The "Welcome Chorus" by a large number of girl pupils and solo part taken by Miss Clyne was a very pleasing item. Miss Gateau following with a well rendered piano solo. Next came the Belgian Soldier's Drill. About 16 boys took part in this and acquitted themselves very creditably indeed. They were dressed to resemble Belgian soldiers and each carried two flags. They [illegible] Needham piano, Rushaski (cornet), and M. Petras (mandolin), gave a number of selections, which were much enjoyed.

The Address

Rev. and Beloved Father. Few words suffice to convey to you our heartfelt congratulations on the joyful occasion of your "Golden Jubilee." Your happy children are honored in meeting you here, in order to give expression to their esteem to you, and their gratitude for your interest in their welfare.

Looking back on the fifty years, which have silently developed your career, we can understand that sacrifices and consolations, griefs and joys, labors and success, have each in their turn contributed to the attaining of the sole end of your life, namely the spreading of the knowledge and love of God in this vast country. Are not St. Patrick's church, St. Aloysius Convent, our schools and their surroundings a sufficient proof of your compliance with the wish of your divine Master, who said: "Suffer the little children to come unto me, and forbid them not, but for them is the kingdom of heaven."

Our earnest prayer is that when you, Reverend Father, shall arrive at your true home in heaven, we may be as so many jewels in your crown for all eternity. Accept then Reverend and Beloved Father, our respectful homage and this small offering of esteem from the pupils of St. Aloysius' convent School, Lethbridge, June 13th, 1901.

Rev. Father Van Tighem addressed a few words in reply to the pupils, thanking them for their kind words, and expressing pleasure for himself and people that their efforts had been crowned with success. He referred to the coming examinations and holiday and hoped they would prove not only clever, but good and virtuous.

On Sunday the Rev. Father was also made a very handsome present by the sisters of the Convent, whose offering took the form of a beautifully illuminated text nicely framed and a handworked surplice.

[The Sisters, Faithful Companions of Jesus (1901, 108–109). Transcript:]
108: A telegram was communicated to us by telephone about passing away of our Noble Queen. The Rev. Father Van Tighem ringing out the solemn death knell and thus was the 1st indication of the sad news to the public.

109: Our annual concert this year took the form of a Jubilee celebration in honour of our devoted Pastor, the Rev. Father Van Tighem. The programme was exceedingly well rendered by the pupils. The Rev. Father being a native of Belgium, the decorations, flags, drills etc. all served to remind him of his country so nobly sacrificed for the Salvation of Souls in his adopted country. The proceeds of this concert, consisting of 50 dollars in gold were presented to the Father besides several minor souvenirs.

[Leonard continues:]
JUNE 7TH [SHOULD BE JULY 7TH]: The Father returned from St. Paul last night. Having left via CPR and Soo Line, he returned by the great Northern and Shelby junction. It was a glorious celebration in St. Paul. A dozen bishops and four hundred priests were there. Mass was celebrated in the open air, on the seminary ground. Four thousand people assisted. Archbishop Ireland preached the sermon, which was very eloquent. In the afternoon the corner stone of the seminary chapel was laid and the sermon preached by Bishop O. Gorman, who is a very powerful speaker. R.F. Lacombe has remained a few days longer in St. Paul to interview the archbishop. We received free passes at J.J. Hills offices to return home. R. Father Le Vern said mass here once, and Father Thérien arrived here also for the second Sunday, but the Father had returned himself in time, to announce to his people that the Jubilee mission is to begin on Wednesday night.

JUNE [JULY] 10TH: Rev. Father Sinnet arrived here yesterday, will open the Jubilee retreat tonight. We shall have mass followed by an instruction every morning at 8 o'clock, and in the evening also at 8, sermon followed by benediction.

[JULY] 13TH: All our children came to confession yesterday afternoon, and those above their First Communion came to communion this morning. Last night the Rev. Father gave a magnificent sermon on death.

Tomorrow is the last day of the little retreat; our Slavonian Catholics come to their confession tonight. News arrives from St. Albert that R. Père Rémas has died. RIP. Amen!!!

Yesterday, one of our young Catholics, instead of coming to the sermon went to play football on the square. When his mother returned home from church, she found her boy with his collarbone broken at her door, where two of his companions had brought him. May the admonition be fruitful to him!

[JULY] 16TH: Last night the R.F. Sinnett gave his lecture on the South African War in Oliver's Hall. It was a great success, the Father in his soldier garb spoke for over two hours; the audience was indeed well pleased. Mr. McKillop proposed a vote of thanks to the Rev. lecturer, seconded by lawyer Atkinson, and at the motion of the chairman all stood up in a body tendering their vote of thanks to Father Sinnett. Immediately after were given some 150 fine views of the war and South Africa. The light "Electric carbon" was perfect. It was after midnight when God Save the King was entoned. It was a great success. I know not yet, what is the financial result. Rev. Father Sinnet went to MacLeod this morning and shall lecture there tomorrow night and the day after in Pincher Creek.

JUNE [JULY] 18TH: The superior of the seminary of St. Albert arrived here for a visit. He will remain for Sunday and address the congregation on the necessity in this country of a diocesan clergy. May parents and children hear his appeal!!! May he succeed in obtaining children with a vocation to the Holy Priesthood!!!

AUG. 5TH: Last Saturday arrived in Lethbridge by the evening train from the west two illustrious visitors: Rev. Father Tatin, assistant to the Superior General of the Oblates, from Paris; and the Rev. Father Constantineau, rector of the University of Ottawa. They remained here for Sunday and the Father being indisposed, they conducted all the services in church. Rev. Father Constantineau, who is a very eloquent preacher, gave both sermons in the morning and evening. They left here last night for Winnipeg.

AUG. 10TH: Both the R. Fathers Lapointe, secular priest, of Med. Hat, and Danis, O.M.I., from the Peigan Reservation, paid a short visit to Lethbridge.

AUG. 13TH: Father Van Tighem left this morning for MacLeod, where he will remain till next Friday night, 16th, in order to preach the retreat for the Jubilee there to the people.

AUG. 19TH: Returned from MacLeod where the Father had been last week, he reports that the little retreat was very poorly attended, the attendance not reaching twenty. About eighteen persons only made their Jubilee.

[Leonard, in Dutch, to Belgian family member:]
Lethbridge, Sept. 26, 1901.
To Mr. Boeckard, Meulebeke.
Beloved Cousin,

Would you allow me to ask you to do me and my relatives here a big favour???
As several of our family members are now in Canada and because probably others will follow, it could happen, as the years fly by, that the later generations of the family will later not know from where they come and from whom they have descended.
As you are in the town hall, where all old registries are kept, would it be possible to look up our Van Tighem family?
It would be greatly appreciated, as I cannot get any further than to my grandfather, Damianus Van Tighem.
If am asking too much, perhaps you could get one of my friends to assist you an hour or two.
And, how are you and your family doing?? I still have fond memories of my visit with all of you some three years ago.
If I could be of service to you in some way, write to me.

Your dedicated Cousin,
Father L. van Tighem, O.M.I.
Lethbridge, Alta, Canada.

[On the back of this letter is written:]
This is all I can remember: Leo Boeckard can not find any more, than that he filled in hereunder, after having researched everything. Of this side he does not know what else you would like to know, so he does not understand it. If he could give more information, he would like to do it.

[Half-filled-out chart of family tree back to 1740. In 1910 Leonard drew a family tree:]

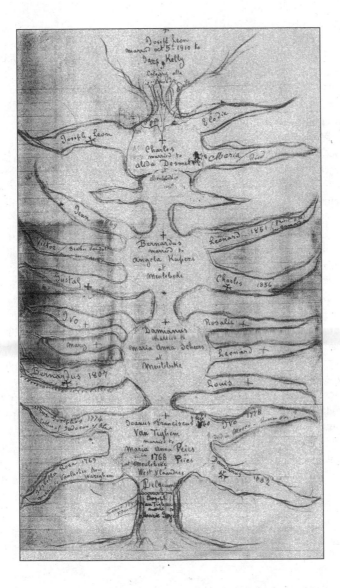

▸ 1910: *Van Tighem Family Tree drawn by Leonard*, Courtesy Van Tighem Family Archives

[Joseph Van Tighem, in French, to Mgr. Grandin:]
Lethbridge, November 5, 1901.
L.J.C. & M.I.
Monsignor,

Upon your request I haste myself to write you a few words so you can arrange everything during your stay in the east.

Monsignor, since a few years I have a desire to enter the novitiate and certainly I would have loved to have come back directly after the rhetoric, but I fear that my health was not good enough.

Monsignor, please believe me that I am ready to go when you want me.

I finish asking for your benediction

Your child,
Jos. Van Tighem.

[Leonard (1901), in French, to Mgr. Legal:]
Lethbridge, November 14, 1901.
L.J.C. M.I.
Monsignor and very dear Father,

I am sending you Mgr. Grandin's letter. He believes that Joseph has already returned to Lachine. I would have liked it if His Highness would have communicated his fears, so I could have acted right away. Also, I did not get any answer from you Monsignor [Legal]. I hope that you got a pass for him. I don't think that Mr. Kerr would have refused it. I myself would like to see Joseph in the novitiate. I think that he certainly will come back to the diocese; I have not the least doubt about it. The young Bégin is sent to Brandon with the fools; he was 19 years, too old for the Brothers of Charity.

Monsignor, here everything goes well. I hope to have your p. answer and the pass tomorrow.

Monsignor, please bless me

Your affectionate son
L. Van Tighem.

[Leonard (1901a), in French, to Mgr. Legal:]
Lethbridge, November 20, 1901.
Monsignor and dear Father.

Today Joseph received the pass and will, I think, leave tomorrow. Monsignor, as I see it, don't tell him that I wrote to you about the topic of his departure because I made him understand that it was your wish and the one of Mgr. Grandin that he would start his novitiate. That could cause him pain. I fear to see him here much longer without having anything to do. He is in good health, but always coughs a bit.

It is well decided that he will go to the novitiate and I hope that he will persevere. Monsignor, everything here goes well. Tomorrow I will bury a Frenchman, who was killed in the mine. Wasile Spartk, 24 years old. Crushed by a piece of coal. The Rev. Father Lebret is very weak and hardly eats anything. He cannot go far. He has a lot of chagrin in Macleod.

We have here a splendid time.

Monsignor, would you please bless us.

Your affectionate son,
L. Van Tighem, O.M.I.

[Bishop Grandin, in French, to Joseph Van Tighem:][139]
Saint Albert. November 28, 1901.
M. Joseph Van Tighem.
My very dear child.

Your letter of the 22nd surprised me even more since I believed that you were already in the novitiate. Your letters have in fact been received in good order and from them I have concluded, I admit, that you are tarrying a bit at St. Albert. Certainly, dear child, being an Oblate means that one has to be a good and true Oblate or to give up on it and by the fact of your dedication you will be absolutely under the authority of the Most Reverend Father Gé.

You will absolutely have to be prepared to go where you will be sent. But one thing you can and should do in a case like this is to make known the ties of affection, gratitude and justice that attach you to St. Albert.

You will remember the circumstances from which I took you from Meulebeke and brought you to Paris, since, you crossed the sea with P. Leduc. You went on to find your worthy uncle and at his place just as in St. Sulpice while you were taking your breaks from the juniorat, you have always been a charge of the diocese of St. Albert or the Vicariate. I have to add that I never had second thoughts because you always responded to our dedication by your good conduct for which I congratulate you.

There are also other persons to whom you owe gratitude, that are the gentlemen of St. Sulpice who on my request and for the good of the diocese of St. Albert have consented in receiving you and make you do your classes for the love of God. I hope that you went to see them, and if you did not, go there as soon as you can. See at least Mr. Lelontan; thank him in your and my name for what the institution has done for you.

Sending me a photograph of you was a great idea. Thank you very much. Certainly I no longer recognize the little Joseph from Meulebeke, not even the one who, a few years ago, came to see me at the Notre Dame

Hospitium. Father Leduc did recognize you and told me that you are as tall as he is. I am not at all surprised that you would be sick. That is often the result of growing too fast.

For the same reason I too had the greatest difficulties in the world in finishing my studies. I was unable to prepare for the exams without spitting blood. And, once I had become a priest, and even when I was bishop, until 1867, at all the missions that I preached, I would cough after having become unusually exhausted and somewhat feverish; I would cough blood for two or three days, after which I would resume my ordinary daily routine. You should nevertheless protect yourself from unnecessary risks without being soft and too meticulous. That would be a way to be sick all the time.

I, my poor child, I arrive at the end of my career after tomorrow I will celebrate the 42nd anniversary of my consecration as bishop. In a few days it will be 44 years that I was counted among the bishops of Rome. All this means that I have more than the age to die and especially that I have a frightening account to render to God. I hope that you will pray to the Sovereign judge by the mediation of the Holy Virgin that he does not judge me according to the rigor's of strict justice but according to the width of his pity.

I ask the same charity from the Rev. Father Maître and of my religious Brothers in Notre Dame des Anges and even from my young, budding Brothers of whom you are perhaps already a member. I pray to God to make you bear courageously the pains of the novitiate and grant you perseverance. I embrace you and bless you and we will meet as soon as possible in Paradise. Don't come there too soon; only come after long labour, and after having sent up many prayers.

Your dedicated in J.C. and M.I.
† Vital G. Bishop of St. Albert, O.M.I.

1902

[Leonard started the New Year by writing a letter, in English, to Father Lacombe. Transcript:]

Lethbridge, January 1, 1902.

LJC et MI.

Reverend Father Lacombe,

Reverend and Very Dear Father,

Your very kind letter arrived this morning: New Years morn. Many thanks for it and for what it contains. I shall go to the depot tomorrow and inquire if the baggage has arrived. I wish you, with all my heart, Dear Father, a holy New Year, replenished with God's richest Blessings. May He keep you long in that perfect trim, which enables you to do so much for our poor missions. I hear that your enterprise is blessed with success, notwithstanding the vexing efforts of some mean class of people, of course, we know what they are working for: politics is their hobby.

All goeth well here, Dear Father; Lethbridge is increasing every day, and increasing fast; I find myself in [a] bad fix: my church is too small again; I don't know really what to do. I shall be obliged to say two masses on Sundays and thus go on for a year or two and then what? Build an entirely new church, and employ the present buildings for a Boys' school or College. I must begin by gathering all my nickels and five-cent pieces.

Today is our first winter day; we have snow. Up till now we had summer weather, a most extraordinary year indeed.

I am so glad all the feast days are nearly passed. I am played-out. It is too much for one on such days.

Our old Sister Marguerite is not worse; the old soul may linger for months yet. I buried a little german boy, last night, who died with scarlet fever. Two other children died of it last week, all imported from Winnipeg.

I am sure, you know that we all went to Pincher Creek for the blessing of the church. It was a great success. All was well organized. Mye!!! They have a fine organ!!!

A lady, Mrs. McCartine, is here from McLeod and says: that on Christmas day there was a young priest but that Father Lebret looked very very bad. Poor old Father, he ought to be at some hospital. But it appears he prefers to remain in McLeod. It is really sad. I shall go soon and see him and persuade him, if possible; for I know that he has been offered to go either to Calgary or Edmonton or St. Albert.

Goodbye, Dear Father, I am glad for what you tell me about Joseph. I always found him a good and willing boy. May he persevere.

Please, ask a blessing for me of Mgr. Legal.

Your affectionate brother

L. Van Tighem, O.M.I.

1▶

2▶

1▶ 1902: *The flood, Lethbridge.*
Courtesy Van Tighem Family Archives

2▶ 1902: *St. Patrick's Church,*
photo glued in text

[Leonard continues:]

JUNE 5TH: The sad news has arrived that our beloved bishop, Grandin, has died. For 30 years he was the head of the church of St. Albert. For 45 years he has worked as a bishop in the N.W. Territories. Great is the loss!!! The Father goeth to the funeral and will be absent for about a week.

JUNE: Our saintly Bishop Grandin was buried under the Sanctuary of the old wooden cathedral. There was an immense concourse of people, though the weather was very bad. The roads are unpracticable. Never was there so heavy a rainfall in Alberta as we have this spring. Our river here in Lethbridge rose 23 feet above its low water mark. Our heavy bridge was partly carried away and many houses have been destroyed in the river bottoms. Great is the loss of property.

MARCH 12TH: Rev. Mother McCormack went to the hospital, two days ago, there to undergo a very dangerous operation. She has been suffering very much ever since.

MARCH 13TH: The Rev. Mother is very low, hemorrhaging of the bowels has set in and we fear very much. This is the critical moment.

APRIL: The R. Mother is out of all danger. *Deo gratias.*

AUG. 15TH: All the Mothers and Sisters are in Calgary for their annual retreat. Bennie Larson returned to school yesterday and brought his little brother, about seven years of age. The Father also has been to Calgary to the retreat, preached by Bishop Legal. It began on the 23rd and terminated the 30th July.

Mr. John Kenny has been appointed Custom Collector of the port of Lethbridge, instead of Mr. Fr. Champness who died lately. The widow of Mr. Champness is erecting a frame two-story residence near our church here. The lots were given free to her. The house will cost about 1,700 dollars.

26TH: The Rev. Father Doucet pays a short visit to Lethbridge and reports all well at the Peigan reserve, where he resides with Frère Jean Berchmans, since the desertion of our unfortunate Father Danis, who is actually in Willow City, N.D.[140] The weather is very hot now and favorable for the harvest. The Sisters are building actually a little hospital in the lane (closed now) to be used in case of contagious diseases.

AUG. 31ST: ...

SEPT. 2ND: The Reverend Father Lepine of the Industrial School of High River passed a day in Lethbridge; arriving yesterday morning, he returned this morning by MacLeod, taking a basket full of plants for his new conservatory. The weather continues very favorable.

SEPT. 15TH: Father Van Tighem, on the invitation of R.P. Lebret, went to Macleod on Saturday night in order to preach at High Mass an occasional sermon. For a new High Altar had been purchased in Montreal and was to be blessed before High Mass. It was also the patronal feast of the Mission, Holy Cross, and in the evening, after the solemn Station of the Cross, the Father preached again. The assistance was good, but nothing extra. The R.P. Lebret received H. Communion at 3 o'clock a.m. as he is unable to celebrate now. He, however, assisted at the High Mass and blessed himself the altar.

SEPT. 23RD: R. Père Doucet visits Lethbridge and reports that all goeth well at the Peigan Reserve Mission, Brother John Berchmans also enjoys better health.

OCT. 15TH: Father Van Tighem left last Sunday night for Pincher Creek, there to meet His Lordship, Bishop Legal. A great ceremony had taken place that day at St. Michael's church of Pincher: three fine bells, the gift of Mr. Gilruth, had arrived from France, and were blessed by Monseignor.[141] R.P. Lestanc had preached the sermon, and the Fathers from the Indian reserves were present: Doucet and Le Vern. The bells are a fine set, quite large, as the biggest weights nearly 900 lbs.

R.P. Lebret went under an operation last week, at his residence in Macleod, he is very much exhausted now and with his old age and infirmities may not recover. R.P. Danis, who had suddenly left that mission some time ago, has returned, and so R.P. LeGoff returns north.[142] We have beautiful weather.

16TH: Mr. Costello, Inspector of Weights and Measures, is actually in Lethbridge on an official visit; a good Catholic, and a warm friend of the mission. Mr. Costello is always welcome!

22ND: Black Eye, a Peigan Indian, brought down two Sisters, Grey Nuns, from that reservation to see the dentist here.[143] They return home this morning. We have glorious weather, but it looks as if it were going to rain. Tonight begins the bazar in aid of the convent, in Oliver's hall. A post card just received from Macleod announces that R.P. Lebret refuses all food and medicines and that the end cannot be far off.

NOV. 14TH: But, R.P. Lebret is alive yet, and is better: R.P. Danis who has lately returned to Macleod is now taking care of him, and is assisted by two Grey Nuns from the Blood reserve. R.P. Doucet came here last week and remained two days. Also the Rev. Mr. Janotte, the curate of Medicine Hat made his first visit to Lethbridge.

There are actually two Sisters of Mercy from Winnipeg in town. One of them is Sister Piché, the daughter of our esteemed octogenarian. She is the sister of our good butcher of Piché and Miron, and of course, aunt of his children, for in that blessed home there are actually three generations in full bloom. After a few days of cold weather, it has turned quite warm again.

DEC. 6TH: We have 20 below o this morning, but it is nice and calm. We hear that R.P. Lacombe has returned from his begging expedition in Eastern Canada. R. Father Lebret remains about the same.

26TH: Christmas has passed with the customary solemnities. Midnight mass and High Mass were both well attended; many confessions and holy Communions.

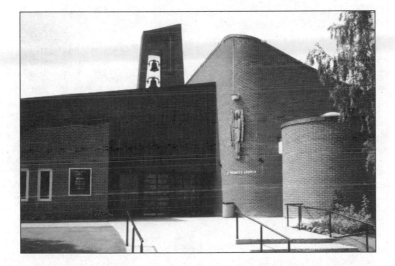

▶ 2004: Gilruth bells. "These bells came from Germany and were donated by the Gilruth Family. They were given the names of Margaret Theresa, Mary Anna and Hortense Catherine. When the old church was demolished, the bells were transferred to the present church" (text is from a photo of these bells in the Pincher Creek Museum). Photo Mary E.M.

Anno Domini 1903

The first day of the year has already disappeared; we have beautiful weather. The masses today were well attended. Brother John Morkin has arrived here from the Industrial School. His health is far from good, and he comes here for a good rest and to consult our eminent Doctor Mewburn.[144]

Brother Lalican, an old and very devoted Brother Oblate has been called to his reward.[145] Almighty God knows better than anyone of us the good this faithful servant of God has performed in our missions. May his soul rest in peace!!! Amen.

Epiphany; magnificent weather, some are working in their gardens. Mr. W. Lyndon is visiting here. Brother John Morkin is much improved. The stomach pump and the doctor's medicine have almost cured him entirely. He will return to the school in about two weeks.

JAN. 10TH: We have a nice snowfall today, and it looks quite wintery today. We have received the sad news of the death of R.P. Lebret, the priest in charge of the Macleod mission. After many months of patient sufferings he died on the 5th of this month at the Holy Cross hospital of Calgary where he had gone since a few weeks. May God reward his many years of hard labor in the vineyard of His church!

FEBR. 18TH: Father Van Tighem went to MacLeod for the feast of the 17th Feb. Were there the Reverend Fathers Lestanc, Doucet, Danis, Riou, Lepine, Le Vern, Salaün, and Brother Bareau.[146] No Father Lacombe. Rev. Mr. Jeanotte visited Lethbridge last week.[147]

MAY 8TH: The news of the death of Mr. Lyndon at Calgary arrives here. The Father goeth to Macleod for the funeral.

10TH: Another death is announced, one of our boys, Dan Delay, has been crushed between two cars at Ferney, and died a few days after. He will be buried here tomorrow.

22ND: A Basilian monk from Edmonton has visited our Slovaks, remaining for three days. A collection was made for him, a little over $39.00. He heard about 30 confessions and baptized and confirmed two children. Two Sisters from Blackfoot Crossing were also collecting here in town and made about $90.00.

29TH: We had the visit of the reknown Father Drummond S.J. and he gave a lecture here on the reasonableness of faith. He is a fine speaker and his lecture was very well received. The proceeds of the lecture amounted to $64.00 and were handed over to the Public Hospital fund.

April: Easter was celebrated with great solemnity. The church was well filled at the first mass, a hundred communions, no standing place sufficient at the High Mass. The blessing of eatables took place after the first mass as usual. Last week was received in the church, Mrs. Johnstone, the wife of our lawyer. Over 300 persons have already performed their Easter duties.

17th: R.P. Doucet came here for two days this week.

May: The small mining town of Frank, on the east slope of the Rockies has almost been buried beneath a huge mountain of limestone, which fell on part of the village at 4 a.m. on the 29th of April. Millions of tons of rock lay now in the canyon. Nearly a hundred people have been crushed and killed, and some lay buried till the day of the general resurrection. It will take months before the Crows Nest R.R. [rail road] will be able to resume her operations of traffic. It is all very sad and terrible!

May 17th: It is Sunday, the 5th after Easter, the 17th day of the May month and we are visited with a blinding snowstorm. Only half a dozen people ventured through the blizzard to the first mass. At High Mass there were not a hundred persons present. The storm rages more and more; there is over six inches of snow, and snow banks three, four, five feet deep. A little child was to be buried this afternoon, but the weather is too bad.

May 23rd: The snow still covers the ground. It freezes hard every night, no fruit this year, our little apple trees were blooming for the first time.

▸ *2004: Frank Slide.*
Photo Mary E.M.

MAY 24TH: Today after High Mass, when the people of No. 3 just reached their homes, a covered wagon was seen approaching the village, and came and stopped in front of Mrs. Jos. Garrick's house. She, with her youngest children was living in the Stafford village, while her husband since about two years had taken a homestead ranch on Chin coulee, some 30 miles east of Lethbridge.[148] This man had been here about three weeks ago and returning to the ranch had taken with him his two oldest boys, Jos. and George, 13 and 10 years old respectively. The two boys were out with some sheep and lambs, camping in a tent about a mile from the house. When the storm set in, their tent being blown over, their father, toward evening, went over with the wagon and loaded-up the lambs and a smaller boy and requested Jos. and George also to go in the wagon, but these preferred to stay with the sheep till the father would return for them all. Unfortunately the rain changed soon into heavy flakes of snow, a real blinding blizzard, and when the father came to the old camp, it was empty, no one there. He shouted, went around and around, went home, went out again on a horseback and so the whole night was spent in a desperate search after his sons. All the next day this continued without success as the storm continued raging also. The third day a stranger turned up there, asking for shelter and he also aided in the search. Then the oldest boy was found quite near the house, of course, cold and dead. There being no neighbours to send for help and taking the body of his oldest boy home to the mother, and of course, expecting every moment to find the youngest lad, they continued their search for the whole week and it was only on the next Sunday morning that the body was found through the instinct of a dog, under a snow bank. At once the poor father, who had not slept, scarcely eaten or drank this whole week, started out with his covered wagon for home in Lethbridge, arriving there just after High Mass. Who could describe the scene that followed there at that house!! May the Almighty console these people, and may the souls of the young lads rest in peace. Amen!!!

25TH: They were buried here the following day in the same grave. RIP.

31ST: Pentecost and first Communion of 19 of our children today. It was a most beautiful ceremony. The church was filled to the utmost and the children showed by their great piety and modesty that they were well-knowing Who came to them. All this took place at the High Mass, at 11 o.c. and none of the children were at all fatigued. In the evening, they renewed their baptismal vows, were consecrated to the Sacred Heart, to the Bl. Virgin and received the Holy Scapular of Mount Carmel. This was one of the happiest days of my life, and yet I was limping with my old rheumatisme. This attack of rheum. was caused by a long walk, some four, five miles, two days previous, when called out in the middle of the night to administer the Last Sacraments to a young lad, Jos. Kovatch, sick with pneumonia. I made him do his First Communion the next day. All this tired me out very much, as I was much occupied with our children, then in retreat, for their First Communion. The boy, Kovatch is better today. The weather is very hot now.

June 1st: A case of mild scarlet fever at the convent: Carrey Hughs of Montana.

June 15th: After a long spell of dry weather we had a fine little rain yesterday as it happened just in the morning. There were few persons at mass. This was our first rain this year. Of course we had our grand snowstorm at the end of May. Mosquitoes have been a torment here for the last two weeks. We seldom see them on other years.

July 4th: Rev. Father Fitzpatrick, parish priest of Calgary, arrived here this morning, to preach the annual retreat to the Sisters, Faithful Companions of Jesus.[149]

July 5th: R.F. Fitz ... preached twice today in church. Father Van Tighem went to No. 3 after mass today and made a house-to-house collection among the miners for the bishop's cathedral in course of erection at St. Albert.

8th: Two Sisters, exiled from France, are here on their way to Lewistown, Montana, with prospects of a foundation there. We have heavy rains and the weather is rather cold. His Lordship, Bishop Legal, O.M.I., will arrive here next Saturday and administer confirmation next Sunday. As this is his first visit as bishop of St. Albert, several addresses are being prepared, one in English, French, Slovak, Hungarian and Italian. The subscription for the cathedral is reaching three hundred dollars, $300.00.

14th: Our beloved bishop arrived here from the West by the night train this morning, in company of R. Father Doucet of the Peigan Reserve and Blanchet from Pincher. Two rigs, kindly offered by Mr. Harry Taylor, met His Lordship and the Fathers at the station. Confirmation was administered on Sunday 12th to nineteen candidates. The ceremony took place immediately after High Mass. The bishop himself gave the sermon.

What was the most striking spectacle on Sunday morning was the marching of the different societies to the church accompanied by the brass band and preceded by their magnificent banners. It was grand indeed, to see these young men, adorned with the regalia of their different societies, with admirable order and military comportment marching from the town to the church. Then, forming, so to say, in three different battalions, they paraded in front of the presbytery while the band executed several pieces.

The High Mass was a grand affair, the bishop officiating, with deacon and sub-deacon. The church could not contain the people and many had to remain out off the sacred edifice. In the evening the societies, "All Austrians," again came to church, and before the service commenced, several addresses, in different languages, read by the different nationalities, were presented to the bishop. These addresses of welcome were in English, French, Slovak, Hungarian and Italian. The bishop replied to the addresses and thanked the Catholic population of Lethbridge for their kindness and generosity. He praised the admirable union and concord, which reigns in the community, composed of so many nationalities. The glorious day was closed with solemn blessing of the Holy Sacrament; the altar was ablaze with colored lights.

JULY 14: Prayers have been ordered for the restoration to health of the Holy Father Leo XIII. The whole world lamented over the illness of the Holy Pontiff. The Protestants papers especially exalt the successor of Peter, not a discordant voice is heard, all praise and exalt the illustrious pope, now in His 94th year. May God restore him soon! *Oremus pro Pontificus Nostrum Leo.*

His Lordship, Bishop Legal, O.M.I., accompanied by R. Father Blanchet went this morning, by train, to Medicine Hat. R.P. Doucet went west to Pincher Creek to visit Father Lacombe, O.M.I., at the Hermitage.[150] Pope Leo XIII very ill, had undergone two operations extracting the serum of the pleuric gatherings, cannot live much longer.

JULY 20TH: Our bishop has ordered special prayers for His Holiness who now is nearing the end of illustrious career. At eleven this morning, the telegraph brought us the sad news that our glorious Pope Leo XIII had died. RIP. Immediately we ring the knells in mourning. The Holy Father died on Monday, 20th July at four minutes after four in the afternoon. So we knew it here five hours before, according to our time.

25TH: The R.F. Lacombe arrived in Lethbridge this morning. It was now over two years since the old missionary had visited this mission, no need to say that he was welcomed among his friends.

26TH: High Mass was celebrated by Father Lacombe. He also preached, morning and night, to an eager and most interesting congregation. At the evening service especially, we, very much, enjoyed this: reminiscences, visits to Rome, to the Pope, to Austria, to the Emperor, etc., etc.[151]

29TH: R. Père Lacombe left here this early morning for Medicine Hat. We had a solemn funeral service for the soul of Leo XIII on Monday morning. The bishop ordered also: three Our fathers and three Hail Mary's, Eternal Rest grant after every *Mass L'Oraison De Spiritu Sancto* up to the nomination of the new pope, then *Pro Papa* for the rest of the year. Since the Pope's death we ring 21 knells in mourning. The flag at half-mast till the burial day. Also *Veni Creator* at Benedictisus.

Who shall be the new pope??

Some say Rampolla, some Ghotti, some Origlia, some Vanutelli. Ghotti would be my choice. But if there were any possibility, Card. Gibbons would be my special favor.

AUG. 4TH: Rev. Mother Provincial Green from Calgary is expected here to-morrow. On Tuesday afternoon, the fourth day of Aug. at five-thirty the following telegram arrived here: "Cardinal Sarto has been elected Pope, and has chosen the name of Pius X. He is one of the greatest preachers in the church. He belonged to the Ecclesiastical Congregations of Bishops and Regulars, Sacred Rites, Indulgences and Sacred Relics. He gained great popularity in his diocese and was honored by all for his purity, strict uprightness of his life and for liberalities. He is a modest agreeable man, highly cultivated, very kindhearted, and still strong and robust in spite of his sixty eight years. London 4th."

The election of Cardinal Sarto as Pope Leo's successor is well received in Great Britain, Germany and France. *Deo Gratias!!! Vivat Pius X!!! Ad Multos Annos!!!*

11TH: R.F. Le Vern, O.M.I., from the Blood Reserve arrived here last night. Today is a town holiday and many people have arrived for the occasion.

23RD: R.F. Salaün, O.M.I., from the Peigan Reserve was in Lethbridge for two days.

SEPT. 8TH: Today were purchased from Mr. Lord, Banker, Great Falls, two town lots, in front of the church for two hundred and fifty dollars, $250.00.

25TH: Have just returned from the annual retreat at Calgary, preached by our able Father Jonquet, O.M.I., who has come here for the purpose of taking all necessary information on the life and virtues of our regretted Lord, Bishop Grandin, and writing the life of this saintly and noble man.[152] During the absence of the priest (Coutts) there were two funerals and the priest from Medicine Hat was called here twice.

[Nephew Joseph received the following letter, in French, from Bishop Legal:]
September 25, 1903.
Brother Jos. Van Tighem, O.M.I., Scholasticate
My dear Brother, Diocese of Saint Albert.

Your letter of the 12 September caused me some disappointment and some sadness; actually I had counted that one day you would become a good missionary of the St. Albert diocese; but now that this no longer appeals to you you, and now your Director of Conscience judges that such is not your vocation, nothing rest me than to subject to it. That would be the greatest and even the most regrettable mistake to push you, as one should be called to the priesthood by the voice of God. The Christian education you received will still be useful; you always guard the good principles that are inculcated; you will be a good fervent Christian in the world.

Your uncle, who I saw the other day in Calgary, will send you a ticket to return to the northwest. I bless you always well, offer *tucusement* and believe me

Your wholly dedicated in J.C. and M.I.
†Emile J. O.M.I., Bishop of St. Albert.

[Leonard continues:]
OCT. 23RD: Father Van Tighem went to Coutts last Tuesday, said mass at Mr. Tennant's homestead on the 21st, went to Mr. Thom Farrell on the Milk River and said mass there on the 22nd. Returning to Lethbridge the same night.

OCT. 26TH: Joseph Van Tighem, the nephew of the Father, who has been at college for years in eastern Canada, returned here yesterday and will go to work.

NOV. 10TH: R. Father Blanchet of Pincher met with an accident when on a sick call during night; the horses running in a wire fence. Father Van Tighem went up to see him and returned the same day. Brother Ryan who stays with Father Blanchet was bitten by a dog, in the arm, and went to the hospital.[153] Father Blanchet had his ankle badly sprained, but is doing well. Father Van Tighem a few days ago went to Stirling and said mass at the station.[154]

NOV. 30TH: Rev. Father Lestanc who has been to the Frank, Blairmore and Lille coalmines, arrived here this morning. It is most beautiful weather. But it has been very windy of late. Great calm this morning and we may soon expect a change.

DEC. 4TH: Coutts. Father Van Tighem visited the Catholics of Coutts on the first, second and third of December and said H. Mass at Mr. Tennant's house. Mr. FitzPatrick and family drove in 14 miles and there were ten persons who approached the sacraments. No definite steps were as yet taken for the building of a little church at Coutts, but it may be that a couple of men will canvas the country soon for that purpose.

[Leonard, in French, to Father Lacombe:]
Lethbridge, December 8, 1903.
LJC et M.I.
Reverend and Very Dear Father,

Thanks in advance, for you kindly agreeing to be here at Christmas. It is the feast I fear most every year. It is the most beautiful, so to say, because of its nightly solemnity, but such heavy task when being alone. Yes, that will help me a lot. Could you tell me which mass you prefer to celebrate? For me, it makes absolutely no difference, so please choose. I ask you this so I can prepare things and announce that it will be the Rev. Father Lacombe who will sing and preach the mass of the ?? Now we can also share the job.

It is in fact very sad that you have all these sick people. You will have to leave Brother Ryan at the hospital.

Here, Joseph helps me with work and singing, but he might leave any moment, because I got him a place in the Union Bank of Canada. I still don't know where they will send him! Maybe near you, in Pincher Creek, if they need someone who can speak French.

Yes, that fire was terrible. I remember what you said previously: a reproach you made to the superior in Ottawa – not to have a guard at night continuously – now too late – what a loss!!!

I wrote you these lines the other day, thinking that you would go to the funeral of Mr. Piché, so I did not mail it yet.

Your notes, calling us to McLeod in March, arrived this morning. We will go to the roll call.

Here everything goes well, my Rev. Father. See you soon,

Your affectionate son,
L. Van Tighem.

[Leonard continues:]
DEC. 15TH: There was held a reunion of the Oblate Fathers for the district of Calgary at MacLeod, for the purpose of choosing a delegate to the Vicarial Chapter at St. Albert. The Chapter General of the congregation is to be at Liege, Belgium, in September 1904. Rev. Father Lacombe has promised to come to Lethbridge and help Father Van Tighem for the feast of Christmas.

26th: The Holy Feast of Christmas is passed and well passed! We had fine services in the church. R.P. Lacombe celebrated the Midnight Mass. There were very many communions. Two low masses followed.

Joseph Van Tighem, the Father's nephew went to Okotoks, there to take a position in the Union Bank of Canada, on the 24th inst.

We have beautiful weather; the ferryboat crosses the river. R.P. Lacombe left for Regina this morning, we had a horrible wind gale, for about two hours last night. The coll. in church: $36.00.

We had, during the past year:

59 Baptisms	17 Sepultures
9 Marriages	18 Confirmations

1904

JAN. 7TH: Ever since Christmas the weather is fine, but we have sometimes very heavy winds.

16TH: Rev. Father Coccola came to Lethbridge from his actual mission Ferny, B.C.[155] It was his first visit here, but he remained only till evening, so he left last night. R.P. Schulte came also for two hours last night and immediately returned to Med. Hat where he actually resided for a time.[156] The weather continues beautiful.

After having made application to the Dept. of the Interior, for 40 acres of land at Coutts, there to build a church, Father Van Tighem was twice refused, the first time, they answered and said that this land was on quarantine Reserve, and this having proved untrue, then they told the father the land was not available, as a Rail Road Comp. had the first choice. The father, on learning this, at once wrote to Sir Wilfred Laurier, the premier, and told him that if the government refused land for a church at Coutts on the Canadian side, we were resolved to build the church across the International Line, on American ground, in Montana. Two three days after, the answer came that the land was available and we could get it.[157] The entree was made accordingly, and the ten dollar fee was paid for the legal subdivision 1 S. 5 Town 1 Range 15 – west of 4th meridian; on the 20th day December 1903.

JAN. 19TH: Cold weather started in on last Sunday, yesterday morning it went to 17/0 and today 12/0 only.

FEBR. 6TH: After some two weeks of fine weather, we enjoy a few cold days, we had so few this year. We had 18 below [zero] last night. R.P. Schulte, who actually resides at Med. Hat passed the day at Lethbridge yesterday and returned last night. He is there only for a short time

MARCH 2ND: Yesterday we had the pleasing visit of the curate of Nelson B.C., the Rev. Mr. Althoff. He is a Hollander from Amsterdam. He is a very fine man, a gentleman in fact, and above all, a good priest. Had we many like him!!! The R. Father Cocola, from Fernie, accompanied him and we spent a day in good company. The weather was too cold to visit in and around town. We had a very bad month of February; one night we had 30 below [zero].

7TH: Another surprise was the visit of R.P. Le Vern, who, visiting the east part of the Blood reserve, where he is Superior of the mission, came to see us and passed the Sunday here. We officiated at High Mass and consequently we were not obliged, for once, to say two masses. The Reverend

Father returned Monday morning early, as he had to see some more Indian villages on his way home, which [are] about 50 miles from Lethbridge.

14TH: The Basilian, Father Stroski, from near Edmonton, arrived here yesterday morning and celebrated High Mass in the old Slavonic Rite. Most of Slavonians will perform their Easter duties while the Father is here.

APRIL 5TH: Easter Sunday was a most beautiful day, nice, calm weather. The Holy Week passed as usual; the services were well attended. The night watches were kept as usual by the Slavonians. There were one hundred and thirty communions on Easter morning. The Slovaks as in previous years, brought nice things to the church for blessing after the first mass. The church was full from early morning. But some fifty had to remain outside during High Mass.

24TH: Two Belgians from Tielt arrived here this week, having bought a team of horses, wagons, etc., etc.[158] They go tomorrow to the Milk River district.

An independent Slavonian preacher has arrived in town, and collects money to build a church at No. 3 or 4, some Slavonians have been duped by him already, and given him money for his new church. Ignorance, of course, excuses these people.

MAY 30TH: We had the May devotions at 4 o' clock p.m. every day during this month.

JUNE 4TH: For about five days we have abundant rains, everything looks beautiful in the nature.

13TH: Six Belgians arrived here two days ago and intend to settle here. Two more from Meulebeke came this morning. They go to work in the ditch of the waterworks.

21ST: His Lordship, Bishop Legal, arrived here Friday night 17th and administered the H. Sacrament of Confirmation to fourteen children and men. The ceremony took place on Sunday night. The church could not contain the people. R. Father Salaün accompanied his Lordship from MacLeod and returned home to the Blood Reserve last night while His Lordship went to Med. Hat. Yesterday the schoolchildren offered the bishop $50.00 in gold for his cathedral, this being the proceeds of a concert given by them.

JULY 2ND: The Rev. Father J. Frigon arrived here this morning and begins to preach the Jubilee Mission tomorrow at High Mass.[159]

JULY 1904: Father Van Tighem is called to Europe to the General Chapter of the congregation.

[*Variétés* (1905, 85) about Leonard's trip:]
Several of our missionaries had the equal opportunity to participate in this unforgettable feast: The R.F. de Chambeuil, and R.F. Van Tighem, went there; the first one from Athabasca, the second one from St. Albert to assist at the General Chapter of 1904 and they have not yet returned to their missions.

[Leonard, in English, to Joseph. Transcript:]
Liège, [Belgium], August 16, 1904.
Dear Joseph, (Union Bank, Okotoks, Alberta, Canada).

Last week, I went home to Meulebeke. They knew not I was coming, but they recognized me at once, even before I spoke. What a scene it was!!! What a fine family is Jean's. I saw your sister. She is exactly like you, just the same; and also your little half-sister and brother, of Tighem's hof. They are all very well and contented. All inquired after you and I had to answer a thousand questions. The Chapter has began; I know not how long it will last. They all say that I will not return to Canada. I cannot believe it. It would be a terrible cross for me. Write me the news. Respects to R.P. Lestanc and Naessens. Write to Meulebeke.

Your uncle
L.V.T., O.M.I.

[Leonard, in English, to Victor. Transcript:]
Houthem, October 2, '04.
LJC et M.Im.
Dear Brother,

I am actually here in the Land of Waas. Yesterday I was at Furne at the college where cousin Bruneel and l'abbé Kesteloot are professors. It is again kermesse [fair] in the villages here. This is the third one since I came to Belgium: first at Grimbergen at the Premontré Abbey, than Meulebeke, now Houthem. I have been twice to Torhout where cousin D'Hertoghe is head teacher of the schools. There I found Mr. Em. Delafontaine, who is Vicar of the church. Never a man was more glad to see me. He was the first to give me something for my church. 20 frs. I tell you there [is] nothing to get in this country, and I wish I could return next week to my dear Mission. Don't tell this to the Fathers, they would laugh at me; but it is so.

Mgr. wishes me to go to Rome with him; I am glad to go, but I would prefer to return, in order not to have these great expenses.

Cousin Gustave is well here; they have a large church, far too big for the parish. I wish I had a piece of it. This afternoon I go to Alverighem, to visit my old friend and companion Mr. Van Hollebeke, who is curate.

If possible, I will go from there to Winghene to see the family of Virginie De Craemer. Their son is now in his second year of the Divinity-classes in the great Seminary at Bruge. I saw him there in the beginning of the week. I slept one night at Jules D'Hertoghe at Bruge. One of his daughters married a few months ago with a gardener, a good young man who came to see me there. They may come to the Canadian West.

I must be home, at Meulebeke for next Wednesday, because I have been invited at the chateau for next Thursday. Shall I receive something good there??? I know not.

It is finally decided that *Frère* Henri, the son of Jean, will accompany us to St. Albert.[160] We have asked for him and the Sup. General has consented. He is 19 years of age, and must take out his conscription number this coming spring. Jean, our brother, is quite undecided what to do. The whole family desires to go to the West Canada; Jean alone hesitates. I have not said a word to them, they must do as they please.

You will see that in a few years, hundreds of Flemish will go to our country with their priest. There is a great movement on hand now, but, it is so far.

I shall remain in Flanders till the end of this month. Then the bishop will write to me, to meet him in France, we shall go to Rome, where His Lordship will arrange His affairs with the sacred congregations. Then, I shall remain with the bishop in his voyages till the Imm. Conception feasts in Rome, and after we shall return immediately to our Dear Missions.

I have to see many people of our family yet, Gent, Grammene, Oekene, Wijnghene, etc., etc. If possible, I shall go also to La Trappe to see Leo Decaluwe.

It would have been more pleasing to me to tell you that I had obtained many nice things and some money, but, I repeat, I receive very little, about enough to pay the expenses of my travels here. I have not spoken any English for two or more months now, so I thought I would write you in that tongue, not to forget it all together.

I have sent 20 masses at 2 frs. each to Fathers Doucet and Le Vern, again today I send the same number (20).

Many compliments from couzijn Gustav.

[no signature]

[Leonard (1904) wrote an account, in English, of his meeting with Pope Pius X:]

In Audience with the Pope, Nov. 23, 1904.
Bishop Legal, O.M.I., after a private audience presented me to His Holiness saying that for more than 30 years I was engaged in Mission-work in St. Albert, Canada.

Immediately Pius X turned towards me prostrated at His feet: 30 years, 30 years, repeated several times the Holy Father:

- Most beloved and most happy son, exclaimed He,
- May the Almighty God bless you! May he render your Ministry in the far land, fruitful, consoling, happy, abundant!
- May He grant you a long life and health and strenght to continue the great work you have undertaken.
- Return to your good people and tell them that the Pope blesses them all.
- Encourage them – guide them in the path of virtue.
- Console them in their afflictions.
- Be ye to them a father a true pastor.

"Amen," I exclaimed, while I eagerly grasped His Hand extended in blessing, and while I laid it upon a box full with beady crosses and medals and pictures, twice I kissed the ring of the H. Father, and while leaving I kissed His foot.

L. Van Tighem. O.M.I., Ptre
Lethbridge, Alta, Canada.

[At the back of a photo of Pope Pius X, Leonard wrote, in Dutch:]
In Memoriam. Nov. 23rd. 1904.

- Audience at the Pope.
- Pope Pius X addressed some very consoling words to me, being kneeled down.
- He blessed me twice.
- Twice he offered me to kiss His ring.
- The Pope also blessed all my relatives and friends; he then blessed the sacred medals and death memorial cards while touching them with His hands.

L. Van Tighem, Priest, O.M.I.
Lethbridge, Alberta, Canada.

1905

[Leonard continues:]

MARCH 1ST: Almost eight months have passed since Father Van Tighem received a message from the Superior General of the Oblates of Mary Imm., of which order the Father is a member, that he should go to Europe to take part in the General Chapter, to begin in Liege, Belgium, in August. This invitation was quite unexpected. For thirty years the Father had been quietly working in the missions and he thought here to end his life without every seeing again the old fatherland. The news was received with joy, and a few days later the long journey began.

After seven months of absence during which the Father visited his old relatives and friends, went to Rome, saw and was received in audience by the Holy Father Pius X, assisted at the glorious feasts of the Jubilee of the Immaculate Conception and the canonisation of two new Saints. After this long vacation he returned to Lethbridge during the first days of February 1905 and now, as this journal has been ever interrupted since our departure, we shall begin again this day being the first of St. Joseph's month.

A whole block, 22 town lots, was purchased today from Mr. Bowman, real estate agent, for the sum of five thousand dollars. It is block 10 in the legal map of the town site of Lethbridge. It is on this block that we intend to erect our new church.

[While Leonard was already back in Canada, his nephew Joseph received a letter from his sister Elodie:]

Etterbeek, March 12, 1905.

Dear brother Joseph,

I was very happy to receive such long letter from you and to hear that you also are doing well.

Since March 6th I am alone at home. I have had a four week long holiday, I never longed more to go to Meulebeke with New Year, but Madam unfortunately postponed it until the very last of the New Year and that is why I did not see again Uncle Leonard and Henri. Joseph, did you already see Uncle Leonard and Henri? They surely must have told how Meulebeke had changed and that, if you had to return to Meulebeke, you would not recognize it anymore, but they don't expect me to see you again in Belgium.

Well, in the four weeks I spend in Meulebeke I eagerly learned some handicraft at the French nuns, uncle and Henri know them; the sessions run from 9:00 a.m. to noon and from 1:30 until 4:00 p.m.

Madam was very pleased with it; I liked to go there. While I was at home, uncle Joseph was enriched with a little daughter. Now they have already four, two sons and two daughters. The Desmet family is increasing and uncle Aloïs, who lives in Lens, [town south of Lille, France] also has a son, named Camille, and uncle Joseph of Thielt was to be godfather. I also visited the Tieghem farmer, and Alfons told me that you will have smoked a pipe from the tobacco he had sent along with Uncle Leonard.

Now, from the hof.[161] When I was at home, Marguerite was sick. The doctor came twice a day, but she recovered, she grew a lot and Adiel looks like you did at the time you left. Well, things are much better when I was there. He works a lot more and it is now quite good with little Marguerite and Adielsken; they were quite happy, it could not be better, Adiel has a wagon and a dog that can pull it and now they were building a stable for horses and a kitchen behind the house. They say that he is a strong farmer and always on the road selling milk. Marguerite was selling milk for the first time again since after I had left. I am happy because things are now much better; sometimes I shed some tears about it.

Joseph, do you sometimes write to uncle pastor in Thielt? At Easter we can go home again for two or three weeks, it does not sound like much, but it compensates a little for our separation.

Joseph, for the moment no special news. Yes, I am now in a pension plan. I have to pay annually 24 fr. until I am 55 years and when I am lucky, my pension will start. In Meulebeke, so many are in it, I was recommended to join it [the pension plan].

Greetings from all here in Meulebeke. They are too many to mention.

I am in good health, thank God, and hope you are too and let us pray for each other Joseph.

Your dedicated sister,
Elodie Van Tighem.
No, 18 Avenue des Nerviens / Etterbeek.
Joseph, thanks a lot for the stamp.
My best wishes to uncle Leonard and uncle Victor and to Henri.

[Leonard continues:]
17TH: Coutts. Father Van Tighem went to Coutts last Tuesday and remained for three days at Mr. Tennant's residence. Most of the Catholics came to assist at H. Mass and performed their Easter duties. The Father seeing the good dispositions of the people and profitting of the presence, near Coutts, of a good carpenter, gave the contract for a little church, to be built immediately on the 40 acres plot, which the government granted us last year. The building to be 40×24 ft. with a porch of 6×6 ft.; all finished in and outside with two coats of paint, such for the sum of $600.00. The contractor is Mr. Paul Audet, a French Canadian.

21ST: R.P. Naessens stayed one day with us. Last week R.P. Kulawy was here for two days.[162]

April 25th: Easter has passed again; we again held all the services of the Holy Week. R.P. Lepine of Blairmore came to help a little on Holy Thurs- and Friday.

On May the first we paid the balance for the block we have lately purchased, we have received the transfer and the patent.

May 4th: The Rev. Father Leduc has arrived here, to consult our eminent physician. An abscess has formed under the tongue and must absolutely be removed. The Rev. Father Lacombe will arrive tonight in order to go to Montreal with the patient if needed.

6th: Rev. Father Leduc has been operated today and so far, the results are bright and cheerful and so is the Rev. patient who can find a joke even now in his precarious state.

July: We expect our beloved bishop for the 9th of this month. His Lordship will administer the Sacrament of Confirmation. There are very few children, as our first communicants were almost all Slavonians belonging to the Greek United church and have been confirmed by their priest at their baptism.

15th: Coutts: We had again fine ceremonies in church on the occasion of the bishop's presence. R.F. Blanchet, O.M.I., of Pincher Creek accompanied His Lordship. Confirmation was administered at the evening service to fifteen candidates.

11th: On the eleventh of this month of July, His Lordship, Mgr. Legal, O.M.I., bishop of St. Albert, went to Coutts, on the boundary line to the south, there to bless a new little church, just erected and completed. Two priests, two Sisters, three altar boys and a few singers went with His Lordship. Father Van Tighem had left the day previous in order to prepare things; in fact the Father had been there several days, every week, for a long time.

The train leaving Lethbridge at 7:30 arrived at Coutts at 11 a.m. Some vehicles arrived at the depot and soon all were at the new chapel. The ceremony began at once, the church being blessed outside, the procession entered the chapel singing the Litany of the Saints. The High Mass was celebrated by Father Van Tighem, O.M.I. His Lordship gave the sermon after the gospel and it was nearly two o'clock before all was terminated. Several rigs were waiting for the party and soon were on their way to Mr. Tennant's ranch, three miles distance, where a sumptuous dinner awaited us. Such ceremonies are very affecting, so primitive is everything, that one thinks himself to be at the first ages of Christianity. Many a European would give money to witness such a ceremony in the prairies of the Wild West. The little church, built of wood, is 40×25 feet, neatly finished. It is dedicated to the Holy Angels. The priest from Lethbridge will go to Coutts every second Tuesday of each month and remain two or three days.

21ST: Father Van Tighem went to the retreat at St. Albert and has returned. It was the Rev. Father Lacoste O.M.I., vice-rector of the Ottawa University, who preached the retreat to over 40 Oblates. There is actually an illustrious visitor in the Vicariate of St. Albert. One of the Assistant-Generals, the Rev. Father Dozois, O.M.I., has been sent from Europe to visit our different missions in the northwest.[163]

25TH: Many people come to see our fine apple trees, loaded with apples, five trees bearing fruit; three crabs and two large sized. The Hon. Minister of Agriculture came also today in company with Mr. MacGrath, Major Begin, and some other gentlemen. They were astonished when they came in the garden to see such fine fruit, apples and plums. These trees were planted in the spring of 1900.

We have a new agent at the CPR station here, Mr. McRae, who is a good Catholic gentleman of Ontario, but who has resided a few years in the West.

OCT. 10TH: News arrives from St. Albert that our beloved bishop is no longer vicar of the Oblate Fathers in this diocese, notwithstanding the vigorous protestations of almost all the Fathers and Brothers. His Lordship has insisted that another vicar should be appointed. Therefore, it is officially announced that Rev. Father Henri Grandin, nephew of our late and saintly bishop, is nominated to that important position.[164] R.P. Mérer is now first

▸ *Church in Coutts*: Photo glued in text.
Courtesy Van Tighem Family Archives

consultor with R.P. Jan, second consultor, R.P. Leduc and Naessens.[165] The retiring authorities are the R.F. Lacombe and Lestanc.

12TH: The contract for our new depot is being given; it is to be started at once. Brick and stone over one hundred feet long by thirty.

13TH: Father Van Tighem just returned from Coutts, where he remained for three days and there baptized the first child in the new church.

20TH: Rev. Father Thérien, O.M.I., passed yesterday through Lethbridge and remained a few hours. These three last days were rather cold for the time of the year.

30TH: The Reverend Father Dozois, assistant-general of the congregation of the Oblate Fathers and visiteur to this vicariate of St. Albert, arrived here yesterday morning and will remain a few days.

Nov. 15TH: A good young man, Mick Kelly, this morning fell from his wagon and was crushed under its wheels. He only lived a few hours, received absolution in *articulo mortis* and the Extreme Unction. The Father was with him, immediately after his accident and left him only when he had breathed his last. Just a few months ago, the very same accident arrived to his brother, who did not live an hour after, and this Mick went home to Ontario with the body. Today, two of his friends go down with his body. Mick was certainly one of the best young men in town, beloved and respected by all, without exception. RIP.

23RD: Father Van Tighem went to Pincher Creek yesterday; it being the feast day of R.F. Lacombe, St. Albert. Besides Father Lacombe and Father Blanchet, the resident priest, there were the Rev. M. De Wilde from Frank, R.P. Lepine from the Peigan Reserve.[166]

We have very fine weather up to now, but today it starts snowing. This will stop the work on our New Depot, just opposite our church, which was begun two weeks ago.

1906

MAY 28TH: This record was lent to the Sisters of our convent some months ago and consequently no entrees were made.

The new station or CPR Union Depot is completed and soon will be occupied. We have a continued rainfall for over two weeks, a blessing to the country.

In March a little nephew, Ferdinand Van Tighem, of the Father arrived here with the Heytens family; the boy is about 11 years of age and will remain with the father.[167]

Our ladies held a sort of sale of fancy needlework, about a month ago and realized about $160.00 for the church.

A small piece of ground, in front of the new depot, was sold by the Oblate Father to Mr. Heytens, the tailor, 25×15 feet on the lane.

Our miners are on strike for several months, and, no semblance of a settlement in view. These are very bad times for our town. But, I should say city now, for Lethbridge, since a few weeks, has acquired that title: The City of Lethbridge!!

28TH: Rev. Mr. De Wilde of Coleman arrived here on a visit this morning. He bought a Louvain bell from Father Van Tighem for $50.00 and one hundred intentions of masses. The Father received the bell from cousin Scheers of Meulebeke for 200 intentions of masses.

JUNE 18TH: The Priest from Med. Hat is here for a day.

21ST: Frère Jean from the Peigan Reserve is here for a few days on a visit. It is raining almost every day.

AUG. 2ND: The second retreat for the Oblate Fathers, preached by the Rev. Father Lejeune D.D., O.M.I. from Ottawa, terminated yesterday in Calgary.[168] There were about twenty Fathers and Brothers attending. Father Van Tighem went also and during his absence, a Premontré, Father Van Wetten, preached the retreat for the Sisters in Lethbridge.[169]

Our strike in the coal mines lasts, it is now five months.

AUG. 4TH: Our new station is completed for several weeks but the new track is not in position yet. A cut nine feet deep is to be made; over 20 teams are at work. We have fine weather, warm and good rains from time to time. No apples in our garden this year, no plums, no cherries, only currants and strawberries.

OCT. 7TH: Today, Oct. 7th, while a funeral was taking place at 10:30 a telegram from Taber was delivered, "come at once, Mother very ill."[170] On the road to the cemetery a rig met us and halted: Father come at once to Staffordville, a child is dying and is not baptized."' With haste the funeral was terminated, half an hour later the baby was christened, a livery team was ordered and, en route to Tabor, the new town and coal mining place between Lethbridge and Medicine Hat. Four hours later the viaticum was given and the Extreme Unction administered to Mrs. Jos Filgas. It was half past one in the night before we reached home, a drive (and a fine one) of about eighty miles.

Oct. 13th: Coutts: Just returned from Coutts, there was a good attendance at mass there yesterday. Some young ladies from Lethbridge are there helping their friends in Coutts for a social in benefit of the church, which [is] in debt for about $150.00. This social held at the depot in a new building, which was offered free of cost to the church for the occasion, was a success and brought up close to one hundred dollars.

Nov. 10th: Our strike in the mines continues, it is now eight months. We have a fine fall, scarcely any frost.

Dec. 2nd: Thank God, our strike is over, and most of the miners will return to work tomorrow. It was now nine months, and every one was getting tired of it, there is an increase of wages in favor of the miners."²

Dec. 8th: It is 28 below o this morning and on this account we will have no feast nor procession in the church this afternoon, too cold for the children to come to church.

28th: No midnight mass this year.

▶ "Nominated and Elected at Rome: Sept. 23rd, 1906. The Very Reverend Father A. Lavillardiere, O.M.I., Superior General."
Photo glued in text

JAN. 3RD: Rev. Father Le Vern was visiting the Indian camps of (his) the Blood Reserve, when at about 22 miles from Lethbridge, his horse, having no shoes, slipped and fell and he, having no time to extricate his foot from the stirrup, had the anklebone broken. He rode as quickly as he could to Lethbridge. Dr. Mewburn was called in; the bone is cracked. After two days the dr. put it in plaster of paris as the little Father wants to go home as soon as possible. He may take the train to Macleod tomorrow and from there drive to the mission.

There was a fire in the Begin building in the city today; it ruined the old frame building.

11TH, Coutts: Just returned from Coutts, very cold and stormy, deep snow, no person could come from the ranches to church, 28 below [zero].

14TH: This is the coldest spell I ever have seen in these parts, last night the thermometer went down to 45 below [zero] and this morning at 8:30 it is actually 43 yet. Notwithstanding a good fire in the furnace there was frost in the house. Cattle are dying by the hundreds in the prairie.

24TH: The cold weather continues; last Sunday, at 8 a.m. it was 46 below, the coldest I ever knew in the south of Alberta.

FEBR. 11TH: The Chinook has arrived and the snow is disappearing fast. It was greatly time, the winter has been very severe.

23RD: Fine warm weather. Dr. Mewburn has his hand and arm poisoned by a scratch during an operation, hope it will not be serious. What a loss it would be for us all.

MAY 12TH: After a most severe winter, our May month starts in cold and dry, on the twelfth of this month we have had no warm weather.

His Lordship, Bishop Legal, will be here for Pentecost the 19th of May confirmation.

20TH: Monsignor Legal administered the Holy Sacrament of Confirmation to 24 persons of this parish. His Lordship celebrated himself the High Mass and the Rev. Father Leduc preached. There were present for the occasion: Reverend Fathers Henri Grandin, our Vicar, Leduc, Lacombe, Culerier, Le Chevallier, Turbiaux from Med. Hat.[13] The Reverend Fathers had come especially to Lethbridge for the celebration of the Jubilee of 25 years of priesthood of Father Van Tighem.

June 26th: Warner. Some Catholics having arrived at Warner (formerly Brunton) on our southern railway, about 45 miles south of Lethbridge a new town.[174] These wrote to Lethbridge asking if the priest could go and say mass there for them. So the Father went yesterday and said H. Mass there immediately after the train arrived about ten o.c. a.m. It was at Mr. Mangin's residence that the first mass was celebrated; that is upstairs, about the hardware store, there were Mr. and Mrs. Mangin, child, Mr. Egau from the hotel, also Mr. Kaspar, Mr. Joyce and Mr. Henri Tennant. The Father returned the same day.

July 12th: Coutts. The Rev. Father Emard, O.M.I., was here for a week, preaching the retreat to our Sisters.[175] The Rev. Father was kind enough to give two sermons in the church also last Sunday. Father Van Tighem went to Coutts this week also, it was decided there to make a small addition to the church, two small rooms for the priest.

[Coutts Parishioners' Notes, quoted in Venini Byrne (1973, 246):]

> Both Father Van Tighem and Father Bidault visited the people of the parish on horseback and with buggies. Mass was said occasionally in the Sexton Creek School house, 8 miles east of Coutts and also at the Leonard Stelton home, and at the Grain School which was 30 miles east of Coutts. The seating conditions in the early church were quite primitive as the pioneers sat on planks supported by kegs, and knelt on the floor.

[Leonard continues:]

July: We have rain nearly every day, the country looks most beautiful, for many years the grass has not been so plentiful. Our land office is filled everyday by people making homestead entrees; no one ever thought of seeing such an influx of people to the northwest.

15th: There will, perhaps, be a half-dozen apples on our trees. The currents are plentiful, also a good crop of strawberries.

Dec. 15th: Bad news arrives from Europe; our very Reverend Superior-General is dying, in fact has already received the last Sacraments. It appears there is no hope of recovery, except of course by a miracle of God.

26th: We had midnight mass and all was very quiet and pious; many could not get in the little church.

31st: Rev. Father Lanfer will stay a short time at Lethbridge waiting the moment he shall preach some retreat in the United States.

1908

JAN. 2ND: We had our Christmas tree, yesterday, New Years Day, at 3 o'clock p.m. Over 200 children were there. The collection at High Mass yesterday was for the H. Father, an offering for his Golden Jubilee Mass $16.00.

We have had no winter yet so far. A few days ago a young girl who was an Anglican by faith before was received in the church and baptized *sub condition*.

7TH: Mr. Charles Wood, a convert, was married this morning to the eldest daughter of J.K. Barrett from Winnipeg in our convent chapel. A parishioner, who for over thirty years had not been to confession, came to his duties, confessed and will receive H. Communion next Sunday, with his wife who is overjoyed.

About two weeks ago, another man made hundreds of miles to come to confession and Communion. It was exactly thirty one years, since he had received these sacraments. Before returning home, he asked me for a certificate, that he may show it to his wife and large family, and, said he: "There shall be joy for the one sheep returned."

12TH: And now, don't be overjoyed for these returns to God. Defection has entered the flock!!! A young girl, Adriene Vanhecke, who came from Belgium less than two years ago, was married in the Protestant temple, two days ago, to a Protestant and the same night another daughter of the same family left her home and says she is going to do the same. May God forgive these unfortunate girls and may not the tears of their aged parents cry for vengeance to heaven.

Two young married men, three in fact, who were received lately in the church, one in Winnipeg, a second in Med. Hat, the third in Great Falls, are now under instruction and preparing for their First Communion. They all came to Lethbridge to live.

JAN. 14TH: This is the 14th of January and no sign of winter yet and today, the 25th of January, we have summer weather.

Sad, very sad news! A telegram announces that our Very Reverend Father Lavillardière has died yesterday. May his soul repose in Peace!!! Amen.

Elected in Rome September 23rd, 1906.
Died in Lyon France, the 28th January 1908
Aged 64 years: 41 years an Oblate
RIP. Amen

And who shall be our new Superior-General???

MARCH 31ST: We had no winter, but our spring is late. The weather keeps cold and we have a snow storm almost every week.

R.P. Emard, O.M.I., is actually preaching a mission in Great Falls cathedral; he will return this way in the beginning of next week.

JULY 16TH: We returned from our annual retreat, which took place at Edmonton, this year; there were about fifty Oblate Fathers participating. The Rev. Father Lacombe took the Father's place in Lethbridge during the retreat.

His Lordship, Bishop Legal, is expected here for next Sunday to administer Confirmation. The R. Father Lacombe has returned again and will help us tomorrow.

18TH: His Lordship has administered the H. Sacrament of Confirmation and has departed for Medicine Hat, visiting on his way the new posts of Taber and Grassy Lake and Bow Island.[76]

OCT. 20TH: We have a slight snowstorm; after a fine summer abundant wheat crop etc. Our garden was most beautiful this summer, plenty of large strawberries, red and white currents, a wagonload. Ten trees bearing apples, seven with large apples and three crabs, one tree had as many as four hundred good-sized apples.

Mgr. Dontenwill, O.M.I., Archbishop of Victoria of New Westminster, has been elected Superior-General of the Oblates. *Ad multos annos!!!*[77]

The work has increased so rapidly here, that it has been impossible to note down our mission work.

1▶ *2004: Wheat crop in southern Alberta.*
American Sweetgrass Hills in background.
Photo Mary E.M.

2▶ R.C. CHURCH, LETHBRIDGE, ALTA.   in summer

1908

2▶ *1908: St. Patrick's Church
and House, Lethbridge, Alta.*
Van Tighem Family Archives,
Calgary

3▶ *2004: St. Patrick's Church house, now De
Jourdan photostudio, Lethbridge. Father Frank
Van Tighem, nephew Joseph youngest son, in door
opening.* Photo Mary E.M.

[1909]

JUNE 1, 1909: On the 17th of last May, Father Van Tighem celebrated Holy Mass here twenty-five years ago, on the river bottom, at the Sheran Mine. News arrived that he will no longer have charge of the Lethbridge parish, so after 25 years of labor and toil, goodbye!!!

We shall not write in this book any longer.

[Father Lestanc continued the Lethbridge Codex Historicus, until now written by Leonard, and dedicates his first pages to him:]

JUNE 26TH: On the 11th of June Rev. Father Lestanc was appointed Superior of the St. Patrick's with R.P. Rosenthal, for nearly four years assistant at St. Joachim's church, Edmonton, and R.P. Meyer, since his arrival in Canada last November stationed in Calgary, as assistants.[178] R.P. Rosenthal arrived here on the 12th inst., R.P. Meyer on the 15th inst. He will be in special charge of the missions in the outlying districts, Coutts, Milk River, Warner.

Rev. Father Van Tighem has left on the 17th inst. to the greatest regret of all Catholics and Non-Catholics, for Edmonton, where he has been appointed chaplain of the Penitentiary. *The Lethbridge Herald* seized the occasion to pay the following editorial tribute to the Rev. Father:

[The title of this newspaper article is left out in Father's Lestanc's rendering, but is *Father Van Tighem's Removal*.]

Every citizen who has enjoyed the acquaintance of Father Van Tighem will learn with much regret that he is to leave the city. As the shepherd of his flock Father Van Tighem has been faithful in his ministrations. Day in and day out he has been at the service of his people and as a result he has built up a loyal congregation of men, women and children, who will part with the Reverend Father reluctantly. As a citizen Father Van Tighem has moved among us in a gentle, kindly way. Tolerant in spirit and friendly in his manner he won the admiration and respect of all classes and his removal will be more sincerely regretted than the modest Father may imagine. Father Van Tighem, it must not be forgotten, has been a good advertiser for his city. His garden producing various kinds of fruits and the beautiful trees surrounding the church have convinced the doubting Thomasses that Lethbridge can raise small and large fruits and become set in a forest instead of on the bald prairie. *The Herald* trusts that Father Van Tighem will find the surroundings in his new field of labor pleasant and agreeable. He can always rest assured that in the hearts of the people of Lethbridge there abides a sincere feeling of regard.

The new Superieur, R. Father Lestanc, O.M.I., arrived here from Calgary on the 23rd inst.

[AFTER HIS ARRIVAL in Edmonton, and before starting his second codex, Leonard (1909) wrote to Willie English, a family friend.[180] Transcript:]

Edmonton, Alta., June 23rd, 1909.

St. Joachim's Church.

L.J.C. et M.I.

Dear Willie,

I thank you for your kind words; it was the first message from my old home. I hope the people understood well enough my act of leaving so suddenly. I cannot stand these separations. Just think, after twenty and more years in that little spot, no. I could not say goodbye without making a fool of myself.

Here I am, at the principal church doing nothing so far, awaiting my appointment, as Chaplain of the Provincial Penitentiary, nice, isn't it?? Wit[h] a government salary of Eight Hundred dollars per annum and, if I should go and live at that institution, it would be one thousand and rooms and board. What do you think of that? Shall I go and live there???

Well, Willie, it is not myself to decide that question. Our Father Provincial lives here, in the same convent, and he decides everything. For how long shall I be here??

I don't know, according to our rules, we should ask for nothing and refuse nothing. But, to tell you the truth, I am just like a fish out [of] the water, for the present. I just wish to be in some little parish, with my people like in the old days of Lethbridge

I don't know, something tells me that it will all be short with me now. The blues?? Well yes, a little bit.

Goodbye, dear Willie, a little prayer for me please, for old times sake.

Best regards and excuses to all.

Your friend

L. Van Tighem, O.M.I.

Thank Mr. Cuthbert for his kind remembrance, please. LVT.

[Leonard started his second codex a few months later:]
Laudatur Jesus Christus et Maria Immaculata

EDMONTON, AUG. 17TH – 1909: We just finished our annual retreat, which, terminating, the R. Father Will. Charlebois, the preacher, said to us: "Reverend Fathers, you don't write enough. The annals of our congregations are neglected, etc., etc."[181] Reflecting on the subject, who could say that this is not true??

We are the pioneers of the west. We witnessed the origin of every city and town or village in these northwestern regions 30 to 40 years ago, how many white people were there, west of Winnipeg? How easily they were counted! Winnipeg itself was only a small borough having less than a thousand inhabitants. It could not boast of a railway as yet. Who would imagined this rapid growth?

Fifty years from now, they will blame us for our silence. Besides the members of our congregation, the people everywhere will ask: Who began this parish, village or town? Who said first mass here for the people, and who were these people? And lo!! Few there will be to answer the questions.

At my arrival in St. Albert in 1875 and during my sojourn there, I remarked that the records were well kept at the mission. The saintly Bishop Grandin saw to it. He himself kept always his private diary besides.[182]

When in 1883, I was placed in charge of the Fort Macleod Mission, I started a Codex Historicus at once and I asked the Rev. Father (now bishop) Legal, O.M.I., to write the introductory chapter, as he was there about a year before me, residing among the Blackfoot Indians, the Bloods and Peigans.[183]

When in 1888 I was transferred from Macleod to Lethbridge, I kept the record there also, and continued to do so for more than twenty years; giving a detailed narration of its origin. In both the records of MacLeod and Lethbridge, which of course I left there, will be found at least a compendium of my missionary labors.

And now, (Aug 17th, 1909) as, at any moment I may be assigned to some new mission field, a short recapitulation of certain dates, deeds and facts, may not be out of place, it may serve as a preface to my new Codex Historicus, although I loathe to say or write: I am a so and so. I did this here and that there.

This is the only excuse I can bring forth for my silence in the annals of our congregation of the Oblates of Mary Imm. I may mention, however, that the Codex Historicus of Lethbridge has been published for the greater part in England, in the famous monthly *Magazyne* of the Abbey of the Benedictine Fathers.[184]

It happened in this way: The bishop of Port Maurice, the Right Reverend O'Neil, a Benedictine, wrote to his sister, Mother Anna, a Sister in the convent at Lethbridge, for some information, with regard to the Oblate missions of the far west of Canada. I gave permission to Mother Anna to take some notes from the record, but she copied it *mot à mot*. When it was published, they sent me a copy and this I transmitted to Bishop Legal, O.M.I.

Yesterday, Aug. 16th, 1909, at the Coulpe the R.R. Henri Grandin, O.M.I., our vicar, told us to note down our name, place of birth and date, name of parents, where we studied, where and when ordained etc., etc. So here we go:

Leonard van Tighem was born at Meulebeke, West Vlaanderen, Belgium, on St. Antony's Day, 13th June, 1851. My father was Bernard Van Tighem, my mother Angela Kupers. My first education I received at the communal school and pensionate of the same town. For several years, I remained home, and worked with my uncle and elder brothers, who were contractors.

I was the youngest, but one of five sons. At the age of twenty-three, I left my native town and fatherland, in order to give ten years of my life to God and to the Venerable Bishop Grandin of St. Albert to help the missionary in their arduous work in Canadian missions. It was a kind of trial: for I had never left the paternal roof before, and I thought, the religious life may not be my vocation; perhaps I will not be able to stand all their hardships, and better, not venture too far. I left home in 1874. I arrived at Notre Dame des Anges, Lachine, at the novitiate of the Oblate Fathers in the summer of that year, 1874.[185]

I passed the winter there, awaiting the spring weather to continue the journey to the west. Père Boisramó, the saintly novice master, kept me pretty busy during that winter, making pews and pulpit and some fancy painting in the little chapel of N.D. des Anges.

In company with Brothers, Grandin Henri and Fafard etc., I took boat in Montreal, by Lachine on the St. Laurent River, over all the big lakes and through the Red River till we arrived at Saint Boniface in the middle of June 1875. From Winnipeg we positively walked through the immense prairies of the west, following a large caravan of some eighty Red River carts conducted by Halfbreeds and Indians. It took us nearly three months.

We arrived, Brother Lafard and myself, at St. Albert, in the beginning of September 1875. The next day after my arrival, I was on the top of the roof of a new stable, then in course of construction there. One of my first labours also, was to demolish the Catholic chapel, which stood in the centre of all the buildings of the old Ford L'Auguste Edmonton.[186] I may as well mention here how this came to pass, as at this moment I am at our motherhouse here in Edmonton, and within a stone cast almost of the very spot where the chapel once stood.

It must be remembered that up to my arrival in the west, 1875, there was no militia nor police protection in these regions. The fact is that the Catholic priest was generally the guardian of the peace, the magistrate and soldier. All came for protection to him. Hence it was that the famous Hudson's Bay Company was glad to avail itself of this efficatious security;

so that the priest was always welcome at the home and at the table of the *bourgois de la company.*[187]

The Catholic chapel in Edmonton fort stood in the centre. Around it the great stores, office buildings, residence and warehouses; and, encircling all, a high fence of planted tree trunks with a strong bastion at each corner where the cannons were kept loaded. But in 1874 the Canadian government resolved to establish that famous body of valiant men, called the North West Mounted Police.

The first contingent arrived in 1875 and see the moment they were there, the H.B. Company had no use, any longer for the Catholic priest. He was simply told to go: "Break down your chapel and decamp."[188]

How well I remember the chagrin and the mortification of our humble bishop, Mgr. Grandin! How he tried to obtain a small piece of land near the Fort, to rebuild the chapel. No, he was cruelly refused, the honourable? Company claimed all the land for two miles.

A Protestant gentlemen, Mr. Groat, when he heard of this, was indignated, he came to His Lordship and offered him a few acres of his own homestead, some two miles away.[189] The bishop accepted the kind offer. So, I repeat, one of my first tasks was to break down the first chapel ever built in Edmonton.

Not long after my arrival at St. Albert my spiritual director, the Rev. Père Lestanc, O.M.I., remarked that I had a sacerdotal vocation, and after a consultation with the bishop, they offered me to continue my studies, which I accepted with all my heart; still continuing to help the missions with my manual labours. My mornings were employed with my books. The afternoon was passed in the carpenter shop.

The Rev. Father Henri Grandin was my professor. At the end of my classics, I passed nearly a year at Lake la Nonne near the Pembina River, building a new mission house there.[190] For my philosophy, I was sent, in company with Brother Dauphin to Fort Saskatchewan. The good and patient Father Mérer, O.M.I., was our professor.

I think we were all lonesome there. It seemed so very unphilosophical and dry there, up on the shore of the majestic Saskatchewan. I say no more.

[Leonard says no more, but Bishop Grandin (1881, 189) did:]

May 20, 1880: The bad weather continued, we arrived only late at the Notre Dame of Lourdes, a small, new mission founded at the left shore of the Saskatchewan River. At that same shore a few Canadian families have settled, at the other shore a prison and colony dwellings for several denominations and origins have been constructed. Actually, Father Mérer will leave this mission and, as the parishioners aren't yet big in number and several don't help out the priests much, it is also Father Mérer to whom I have entrusted my Grand Seminary for the time being, or, to put it better, my scholasticate. It is there that Father Dauphin, young Oblate and Frère Tighem, juniorist and postulant study philosophy. The etablissement consists of a chapel etc. It is a very small apartment. It could better be called an alcove of 5 or 6 feet by 3 or 4.

[Leonard continues:]
We returned to St. Albert after a little over a year, and passed our examination. Then we began our theology. The Rev. Father Leduc was our teacher and, I tell you, we had to work. Father Mérer was rather too good. Father Leduc was rather too…? Many a time I worked and studied till midnight, in order to get my lessons and thesis ready for the morning.

And now, when I think of it, I must record this: every night, at exactly ten o'clock, I heard our holy Bishop Grandin leave his little room down stairs and come to the chapel, there to make the Stations of the Cross. Not a single night passed.

Many a time, the moment he had retired I myself hastened to the chapel, while the perfumes of these saintly prayers were as yet fresh, and permeated, so to say, the atmosphere of that primitive sanctuary.

Oh! The Holy Hour!!!

Oh! The sweet remembrance!!!

This he did again in the early morning.

The end of our theological studies came. All our examinations were over. In the old and modest wooded cathedral of St. Albert, I received all the orders, from the hands of His Lordship, Vital Justin Grandin, O.M.I., bishop of St. Albert, who had been ordained and consecrated by our venerable founder, Monsignor Charles Eugène de Mazenod, bishop of Marseille, France.

La tonsure I received on the 16th of April, 1881. Minor orders all on the same day.

Sub-deacon on October 23rd, 1881.

Deacon on October 30th, 1881.

Ordained priest on the 19th of March, 1882.

I began my novitiate on the 18th March, 1882. Bishop Grandin was my novice master. Perpetual vows, March 19th, 1884. Deo Gratias!!!!!

For some time I was economist at St. Albert. In the summer of 1883, I was sent to the south of our diocese. The Canadian government was erecting an Industrial School for Indian children near the junction of the High River and the Bow. I was destined to take charge of the school, but as the buildings were only half completed at the time, I was sent to the old Fort MacLeod, the only place in the south where there were any white people. There I lived all alone, in a miserable log shack. It was a wretched dwelling, but it was just as good as all the other residences of that picturesque and primitive burg.

My time there was well employed: in the forenoon I was schoolteacher to our Catholic children.[191] In the afternoon I was again in the carpenter shop, making doors and windows, preparing doors etc., for a new mission house and provisory church. My evenings were taken up with my spiritual exercises, not a minute was lost.

[Leonard (1884, 198–200) about his ordeal to Father Leduc:]
MacLeod, November 11, 1883.
Dear Reverend Father Leduc,

You will forgive me, I hope, my lengthy silence, because, so to say, I can hardly breathe after all these endless travels. Finally I am where one wants me to be, at least for some time. I am here in a *local* that belongs to the Sisters; it is a hut, less comfortable than an animal shelter and surrounded by dwellings of the same kind. To all of this one will give in some time the name *Town of MacLeod*.

Yes, my Reverend and very dear Father, I am now over three hundred miles from St. Albert, in the far south of the diocese, at the feet of the Rocky Mountains, and not far from the boundary, among people who are near heathens, who work on Sunday as they do during the week, when they don't drink and don't play pool. I don't know if they know that there is a God. But yes, they should know, for that sacred name of God is often on their lips, but in what way! If they know God, it is only in blasphemies, because for them, blasphemies illustrate and embellish the conversation. What an unfortunate change for me! Eight years ago I left Catholic Flanders and my parents who raised me in piety and peace. This peace, this quiet life, I also found in the homes that I had the luck to visit and look at me, suddenly being thrown in the other extreme. No more communes, no more fellow brothers, no more joyful recreations; not even a small garden or a tree to sit or to find shelter under. Yes, I repeat: what a change for me! In the meantime one matter, the main matter is left: I have the very Holy Sacrament with me. Meaning to say: this treasure should be enough for me, but the change is so sudden, that it does not make me feel any better. Don't think in the meantime, dear Father, that I am bored. That is not so, at least, not at present. I would be a poor missionary who would complain a lot, if that were the case. On the contrary. I congratulate myself to finally be able, so me too, to work in the vineyard of the Lord, despite being sadly stricken by my sudden beginning here.

I have made a list of my Catholics. All together I count about sixty, children included. But what kind of Catholics? This number should be reduced as I hardly found twenty real ones. This is a field asking for another kind of missionary than I am. I will be pleased to provide you with the details. Since last Tuesday I have opened a school in my house. I have only ten students, meaning children of our Catholics. Not one Protestant has come and asked to be admitted. Doctor Girard, a very good Catholic, is leaving for Calgary.[192] He is also having some difficulties with he government about his payments. This departure obliges me to read

Low Mass on Sunday, because Père Legal is not coming because he has no singers. I have invited several, but nobody came yet for practice. This is how it goes in general, but it won't extinguish the zeal!

I think that some of our few good Catholics will ask for Sisters for a school. They say that they will pay for all the costs. With regard to these Sisters, dear Reverend Father, we have to travel a bit to find out the good these holy daughters do. People everywhere talk about them with admiration; they are raising and educating over fifty orphans.

But Calgary certainly has a need for Sisters, a school and a hospital. They are injured there continuously! I have seen them several times, and when I told them that St. Albert has a hospital and Sisters to take care of the sick, these poor patients, more Protestants than Catholics, they cried and wish the same good thing for themselves. And they are already well taken care of in the *Police-Hospital*.

Our Catholic religious people are not missing out.

Please accept my . . . etc.

L. Van Tighem, O.M.I.

[Leonard continues:]
When, in the spring of 1884 the Industrial School buildings were ready, the people of Fort Macleod would not let me go. So, another priest was appointed principal of the school, and I remained in charge of the Macleod mission.[93] We built the new mission house, in the new town site, about one-mile west of the old Fort, in the spring of 1884. I say "we," for the Reverend Father (now bishop) Legal, who at that time was the missionary of both the Blood and the Peigan Reserves, came to help me for several weeks. We did the work nearly all ourselves.

As we both were very little acquainted with the English language, and whereas we had to address an English-speaking congregation every Sunday, it was rather hard work. But we divided the job so that each of us had a sermon to prepare and preach every other Sunday only. But we had to learn it by heart, and *mot à mot, s'il vous plait*.

[Leonard's efforts did not go unnoticed. *The Manitoba Journal* of July 30, 1884, quoted in *Missions* (1884, 489–99) recorded:]
Last Sunday there was a feast at the Calgary mission. A beautiful organ harmonium, which arrived without accidents from Montreal, was inaugurated. The good Brother Foisy played with ease the excellent instrument in our new chapel. Father Van Tighem sung mass and gave an excellent sermon in English. It is good to know that this dear little Belgian Father, since his arrival among us, has given his whole heart to the study of the English language, which is crowned with success.

[Leonard continues:]

When most of the work was done at the new MacLeod mission, I began a small log church at Pincher Creek, 30 miles west of MacLeod, on the top of the hill overlooking the village. I said Holy Mass there many a time before, in the village hotel at Mr. Cyr's, or at Mr. Beauvais, about seven miles south west of the town.[194] Mr. Lebel had always a room ready for the priest.[195] That was our home for years.

At that time, 1885, I had three missions to attend. Once a month I visited Lethbridge, once Pincher Creek and the balance of my time was spent at MacLeod. At one of my visits to Lethbridge in 1886 we resolved to build a church there also. Constructed of sandstone, it was finished in the summer of 1887. About one year after, in the summer of 1888, when the Catholic population of Lethbridge outnumbered that of Macleod, I was transferred to Lethbridge permanently. The Rev. Father Lacombe took my place at Macleod for a while. I felt rather lonesome in the beginning at Lethbridge; having left a fine mission house at Macleod, I had not even a semblance of a shelter at Lethbridge, not a stone to rest my head on, so to say.

For some time, I had to sleep and study in the organ loft of the church. But before long we accommodated ourselves. We built a sanctuary to the small stone church, and two rooms behind the altar. Then we built a modest schoolhouse and engaged a teacher for our Catholic children. Then our cemetery, then in 1890, we erected the convent buildings. And the greatest requisition was, most certainly, the little community of four Sisters, of the Faithful Companions of Jesus.

▶ 2004: *Lebel House, built in 1909.*
Photo: Mary E.M.

Up to that date, and for about eight years, I had been my own cook. Now, the good Sisters were kind enough to give me something to eat when I felt hungry. Every year, we made some improvements at the mission. In 1894 we enlarged our church by more than half; and this our venerable Bishop Grandin consecrated. It was the first and only one His Lordship consecrated in all his life. And so the years passed by!!!

In 1904, I was called to the General Chapter of our congregation, taking place in Liege, Belgium. Ever since 1874, I had never revisited my fatherland, [that I left] exactly thirty years ago. In fact, I had never left the diocese. It was a great satisfaction to me. Through the kindness of our good Bishop Legal I was enabled to visit Rome. See and speak to the Holy Father Pius X and visit, for about a month all these marvels of holiness, antiquity and wonder; the very cradle of Christianity, the eternal city. I was absent from my missions for about seven months.

On my return to Lethbridge, I bought a whole block of land in the city to build our new church for five thousand dollars. The country was now settling fast. I built a small frame church at Coutts on the international boundary line, on the forty acres of land granted us by the Canadian government. I was going there once a month, for a long time before, and I said mass in the large dining room of Mr. Tennant's residence, some three miles west of Coutts.

I was fast going to build another one at Warner. I had obtained six town lots free for the purpose, when I received notification of my removal from Lethbridge. The work in that parish was increasing so rapidly the last years that it became absolutely impossible to do it alone any longer. For fifteen years or more I was saying two masses every Sunday, preaching three times etc. The work was simply ruining me.

For instance: early on Sundays, I was up and around in order to distribute Holy Communion at the convent chapel at seven, again H. Communion at the church, for those, who had been to confession on Saturday night. Then sit in the confessional for an hour and a half: confessions in English, French, Flemish, Polish, Hungarian and Italian, as the different nations present themselves. The first mass at eight-thirty, principally for the children of the parish, and sermons. The High Mass at eleven and sermon again.

Almost every Sunday one or two baptisms after High Mass; so that it was always one o'clock before I could get a cup of coffee with a piece of toast. Catechism for an hour, from 3 to 4 vespers or rosary and benediction at 7:30 and a third sermon. This was my task for every Sunday. I scarcely ever slept between Sunday and Monday; my nerves were that strained. I could find no rest. In winter it was still worse, when I had to attend to two large furnaces.

I did all the work myself. I could have hired people to do this work but I wished to save all the money I could to build the new church, which was so necessary in Lethbridge. What made the work more arduous yet, was the accumulation of all these different nationalities. I had some five hundred

Slavonians from Austria, a good number of Hungarians, Tirolians, etc. These Slovaks, almost exclusively belong to the Rhutenian Rite. So I had to act with the greatest prudence and tact, especially in the beginning. But they are a good people, faithful Catholics.

They were my best parishioners, simple in their ways, with the faith of the first ages of Christianity: generous towards the church, always ready to render service and really attached to their priest. Some of these I married, when I first came to Lethbridge. I baptized their children. I married these children and before I left the parish, I had the happiness to baptize the children of these children.

Really, I could sing now: *Nunc Dimitis, Sacrum tuum Domine!!!*

It was now twenty-five years that I labored all alone in that heart of the Lord's vineyard. I could do it no longer. So I wrote to my superiors, telling them that there was work in and around Lethbridge for five priests, a real community. That they should send some right away, but I wrote also, that I could not be the superior of this new community. And doing so, I think, I made the greatest blunder in my life. In my simplicity I seemed to imagine that because I had been so long in Lethbridge, in charge of the parish, that I was entitled to that superiority.

What a presumption on my part!! To write to my superiors that I could not become the superior. They never had told me that I was to be the superior; they never had made even the suggestion. I wrote to them that, after having been all alone for a quarter of a century, I was not fit to be at the head of a community.

And they thought the same!!!

Immediately they appointed the most Reverend of our missionary, the Rev. Father Lestanc, O.M.I., two young priests were at once sent down with him; and two more are to follow shortly.

Goodbye, dear old Lethbridge!

Goodbye my dear parishioners!

Perhaps we will never meet again.

I was called to our Motherhouse in Edmonton.

I left Lethbridge June 17th, 1909.

I arrived in Edmonton on the 19th June.

I had made a blunder.

My presumption was to be punished. In consequence I was sent to the penitentiary, with the convicts of all ages, and races, and tribes, having committed all the crimes under the sun. This was my dose of medicine. But an anti-dose was added. I am also the appointed Father Confessor of three religious communities of Sisters in the city of Edmonton. Extremes touch!!! In Flemish, my mother tong, we have a proverb, which I cannot appropriately translate in English: *Soorte zoekt soorte.* The meaning is: that everyone likes to associate with his own kind. Well, I must say it: I prefer the dose to the anti-dose.

[From the motherhouse in Edmonton, Leonard (1909a) wrote again to Willie English, "The Teller of the Union Bank, Lethbridge." Transcript:]

Edmonton, Alta., Sept. 20, 1909.
St. Joachim's Church. L.J.C. et M.I.
William English. Esq. Lethbridge
My Dear Willie.

I thank you for your kind letter and all the news it brought me. So you are a caged bird?? Well, I congratulate you. It is a pretty fast promotion, and I doubt not but you will do that work just as well as a man who stood there for years already.

Do you know that there is not much difference between your cage and these occupied here by my winged birds? I mean winged from their liberty. It is about the same, and therefore I think you have the hardest job of the bank. You get all the money, of course, and that is something.

The Misses Roy and Burns called the very next day after their arrival, and of course, gave me a lot of news. We may get some more of Lethbridge teachers soon in these parts.

Well, Willie, I am still at the Pen., and I tell you, it is pretty interesting by times.

Last Sunday, I heard the confession of a poor fellow, who for 30 years [was] kept away from the H. Sacraments. I am going to baptise a baby of 23 years, there also, in a few days. I have two niggers [sic], 2 Indians, some half-breeds, a Mexican, a Japanese, a french Seminarian, some Canadians, Junkers half a dozen, the balance are English, Scots and Irish and Germans and Italians. No Belgians of course.

The Seminarian is my sacristain and mass servant. One of my niggers is condemned for life, and is here for two years already, and mind, I sincerely believe, the fellow is innocent.

I am writing to the Minister of the Justice for him, trying to get him out. While working in the office, my Seminarian converted his fellow prisoner, a fine young English lad, with a good education, and he is free actually and comes for instruction to the mission. I am going to teach him french also. You must know, that the government is very very strict with regard to religion. One could never change in here, and they must strictly follow their religion Catholic or Protestant. Last Sunday, a Protestant boy asked to see me. I don't know yet why. I am going to see him privately this afternoon. He told the warden, he wanted to find out something about his parents through me. If he had said, it had anything to do with religion; he could never never have spoken to me. I tell you them fellows like me, and when I pass in front of their cages, they just spring up and would stand for hours talking if they might. The Protestant Minister seldom goes near them, he holds his service and that's about all. I am sorry I am so far from the Penn. Two miles and more, but I have a fine horse and rig, but if I were near, I would be with my lads every day, as it is, I go twice on Sunday Mass and Vespers or Rosary just as I did in the Lethbridge Church. I go on Thursday, also for choir practice, then I can see any one privately, if he so desires, for instruction or confession or information and they are there, you bet; poor fellows!!

Bad?? Well Willie, there are many running our streets worse than them, Yee, a hundred times worse; and I know it. It is the only thing that interests me in Edmonton and I would be dead lonesome, were it not for my convict chums. But I expect to be changed before long and very likely shall be sent to Strathmore and vicinity, where 4 new parishes are to be started, but actually there is nothing there, no church or chapel or house, not a shack even for the priest

Goodbye, Dear Willie, offer my respects and best wishes to all, please. May almighty God help you and bless you.

Your friend,
L. Van Tighem, O.M.I.

[Leonard continues:]
OCTOBER 19TH, 1909: Two months have passed since I wrote the above introductory pages. Two months, which I have found rather long, after a quarter of a century in active service in our missions of the south, I found the most necessary rest quite oppressive. Although 58 summers (and winters) have passed over my head, which is bleaching rapidly now, my heart is still young, and, as yet, I feel it impossible to sit down, quietly looking around when there is so much work to be done in the field of the Lord. No, I could not remain inactive. I would pine away, languish and wither before my time. So I told my superiors.

It was the intention of our beloved bishop at my arrival here, to send me to Strathmore to the Holland's colony and other new settlements immediately east of Calgary. But our provincial thought it atrocious and wanton, after such long service in the missions, to send me now, to new fields, where there were no churches nor chapels, not even a shack for the priest to live in.

I had no objection to go and start these new parishes, but I thought I had to tell the bishop that is was almost impossible for me, after 35 years absence from my fatherland to speak and preach to the Hollanders in the old Flemish language.

Therefore things remained in abeyance. Meanwhile, all our superiors were called to Quebec to the General Council of the church. And I, quietly continued swallowing my doses and anti doses systematically.

Twice, every week, I went to the penitentiary, on Tuesday for catechism. There being several who never had done their First Communion. Some even never confessed; one was not baptized at 22 years and others had not made their confessions for thirty years and more. Poor lost sheep.

On Thursday we held our practice for the hymns to be sung the follow-ing Sunday. Sometimes on Saturday, I went to hear their confessions. And then on Sunday, I went there both morning and night, giving a sermon both at mass and at the rosary service. As I said it before, these medicine doses were more suitable to my taste, so I mention them first. I liked the poor convict lads.

My work at the hospital also became rather interesting after a few days. I remarked the eagerness with which the patients were awaiting my com ing each day; by so far, that if the hour was a bit retarded, they seemed to be disappointed. So I passed many an hour with them in their wards, cheering them up, and so the time began to pass more rapidly.

But the anti-dose "annoyed" me. The confessions of the nuns of three different communities were a *gauchemar* [nightmare] for me, and yet, these Holy Women, God bless them!!! (most of them would never need any confes-sion) were to be heard. Well, all will be over soon.

A few days ago, our provincial, the Rev. Father Grandin, O.M.I., who first objected to my going to the new missions, wrote to me from Quebec:

St. Souveur, Quebec.
Dear Father,

On our way coming here, Mgr. Legal again told me of his desire of you going to Strathmore and surrounding places on the CPR Tell me of It would please you to go and start these new missions or if you prefer to keep your parishioners of the penitentiary? I would like to give satisfac-tion to Mgr. Legal, and yet, I would not impose on you a task, which might be too heavy etc., etc.

My answer was: *Ecce ego*, and the sooner the better. I had to tell him now, how I had had a serious nervous attack for three weeks; and how I thought that this inactive, indolent life was the cause of it and detrimental to my health. I wrote to the bishop also, asking His Lordship to determine the limits of my new mission field – also what name His Lordship would give in the building of all their new churches. The answer came soon:

His Lordship wrote:

Quebec, Oct. 13. [1909]

I am glad that you may be sent to Strathmore. I understand this position will be better suited to your activity. You will have to organize several new centers and build in several places, I am sure you will be able to understand, and speak to the Hollanders.

With regard to the limits: you could take charge of the stations be-tween Calgary and Gleichen. Visit along the new R.R. line and from

Langdon, north. If it were too much, Calgary could keep Shepherd Station.

Likewise you could make arrangements with R.P. Simonin, as to the new places between Strathmore and Gleichen. He might keep Stobart and Namaka.[196]

To help in the construction of the new chapel, I would give about $50 – unless I would have to purchase the ground, which would be more already.

When arrived there, please, send me a detailed report of the conditions of the different missions, also of the doing of Mr. Van Aaken.

I arrived in Strathmore a few days before All Saints 1909 and found there were about eighty Catholic souls in the village. Then there was the Dutch colony with about 90; also the Polish settlement in the south. These however, were leaving their purchased, so-called irrigated lands, and were moving to homesteads in the north.

At Langdon I found over a hundred Catholics, nearly all French Canadians coming from the United States.[197] At Shepard there were about forty, and at Cheadle about twenty-five Catholics in all.[198]

I rented two large rooms at Strathmore, in the Duff-Block upstairs, one for a chapel, the other for myself.[199] I did my own cooking in my room.

However we soon started collecting for a chapel building. A few town lots were purchased by the bishop. I tried to obtain a free site for the church from the CPR, which owned all the land in these parts. But a certain Mr. Demonis, who was in charge at that time in Calgary, absolutely refused me.

1▶

1▶ *"Sacred Heart Church, Strathmore, and J. Van Tighem's Residence"* (photo glued in text) Van Tighem Family Archives

Our subscription amounted to about five hundred dollars. Then we got a loan, from the Church Extention Society of five hundred and so we started our cement foundation.[200]

During the winter of 1909–1910 the bishop wrote to me that, besides all the places above named, I was to visit Medicine Hat at least once a month as there was no priest there actually. So I was kept very busy and always on the move.

[Mgr. H. Grandin, *vicaire des missions* (1909, 141):]

The most urgent care of the vicariates seems to be the creation of a minor seminary that will prepare for the vocations we so badly need. In the meantime, we have to rely on the older and more advanced provinces. . . . Right now we have one Polish Oblate short and one who can

2▶ 2004: *Strathmore Hotel, formerly known as the Duff Block.* Photo Mary E.M.

3▶ *Jan. 8, 1910: Ad in* The Strathmore and Bow Valley Standard

THE CHURCHES.

CATHOLIC CHURCH.

STRATHMORE DISTRICT—
Father Van Tighem, O.M.I., has rented two large rooms in the James Duff Block, where he will reside when not visiting the surrounding places.

HOLY MASS will be celebrated :

FIRST SUNDAY of the month ;
Strathmore at 8.30 a.m.
Akenstad at 10.30 a.m.

SECOND SUNDAY :
Shepherd at 10.30 a.m.

THIRD SUNDAY :
Akenstad at 8.30 a.m.
Strathmore at 10.30 a.m.

FOURTH SUNDAY :
Langdon at 10.30 a.m.

At Mr M'Donald's farm, south of Strathmore, in the Polish Colony, every first Wednesday of the month, also when there are five Sundays in the month at 10.30 a.m.

On week days, Holy Mass every morning at 7.30

The Father is at his rooms in the Duff Block upstairs, at the service of his people.

speak Slav. We only have two Polish Fathers for the two dioceses that form the vicariate and it is absolutely impossible for them to provide the desired instructions to their Catholics dispersed throughout the extended Vicariate. We don't have one Oblate who speaks the Slav language and in the meantime we have numerous Catholics with that language working in the mines and even as the Rev. Father Van Tighem can hear the confessions of his Slav parishioners, he can't give them the desired care and can't occupy himself with those in the Rocky Mountains, working in mines or at the railways.

[Leonard continues:]
Our new church in Strathmore was begun in the summer of 1910. It was 26 × 48 ft. with a sanctuary of 18 × 24 ft., containing two rooms for the priest.

▸ 1910: First church in Strathmore under construction.
Van Tighem Family Archives.

The material for these buildings cost about nine hundred dollars. The labor was all done by our selves. The men of the parish came by turn giving a week each. Mr. Tom McRae, a young Ontarian, and Mr. Armrod, a young Englishman, both expert carpenters, lent a good hand and some of the parishioners were generous, especially my nephew, Joseph van Tighem, and Mr. Carufel.

But, like in all other places, there were some who refused to do anything. Their names should be written down for their own shame, but then, what good would it do?? These, instead of helping, they did all they could to counteract; especially by their vile tongue.

Before we started the church however, I had moved out of the Duff-Block because my nephew, having built a large residence just near the church-site, let me have it for church purposes. This being near the site of the proposed church, was very convenient. So we held services in the cottage and I resided there during the summer months, while we were erecting the church. When this building was finished on the outside we could not think of terminating it on the inside, no money!!

[Leonard (1910) to Father Lacombe, transcript:]
Strathcona, April 11, 1910.
My Reverend Father

R.F. Leduc has just bought 4 lots here for the church – and in a few weeks I will begin my new church. The Church Extension lend us $500 – my people here gave me $9 – a few days ago, to purchase a ciborium and a turible (encensoir).

I have written to Desmarais, but got no answer. Up till now I could not preserve the Bl. Sacrament, having no ciborium. Perhaps you could obtain these things cheaper than I could – or you may find some old things, which would do for here. If not, please, purchase them for me, and send me the Bill.

I learn that the Church Extension received many old things from the churches in Canada. These they repair, and send them to the missions.

Well, Dear Father, you will see our great Benefactor Rev. Dr. Burke of Toronto and, please tell him I am building here three new churches and forming three new parishes: Strathmore, Langdon and Shepard; and there is absolutely nothing to put in these churches. All I have is one portative chapel box, which the Delegate Apostolic gave to the bishop, last fall.

[letter continues in French] What I would like to get right now, Dear Father, and what I ask you to send me, are the following things: a ciborium, an incensoir, a little box: Viaticum Cabinet of $5.00. This last item is ordered by a benefactor, who will pay for it. If you can send these objects as luggage, I will be very grateful to you.

[letter continues in English] So, Dear Father I am doing exactly the work, which I began over 25 years ago, when you sent me to old Fort Macleod. Even then I was better off than now. For you had built a log shack for me, and we had a little chapel. Here, I am in a room, for which I must pay $10.- per month. I do my own cooking like at McLeod in a heating stove.

But, there is no Jos. Carr here, to furnish me with meat, as there was in McLeod, and so, since I came here in November, I have not paid a nickel for meat of any kind. Thank God, my health is perfect, far better than in Lethbridge, where I was simply killing myself.

Goodbye, Dear Father,

Your old friend,
L. Van Tighem, O.M.I.

[Leonard continues:]
I was looking toward Langdon; there was my largest congregation and no church. For several years a priest had come from Calgary, now and then, and held service at the residence of Mr. Joseph Besse, who always was kind and generous, and who deserves the most grateful thanks we ever could offer him. May God bless him and his good family!!!

But this could not last forever. So one day, on my visit to these people, I told them it was time to build a church. Mr. Besse offered an acre of his land, close to the Langdon village and CPR depot; and as the people had no means of subscribing themselves, they started collecting among their friends and acquaintances; so that after a short time, nearly one thousand dollars was promised. This was well done indeed. It was about what we needed for the material of the church.

[On October 5, 1910, nephew Joseph married to Jane Kelly. Leonard does not mention it, but some newspaper did, transcript:][201]

Van Tighem-Kelly
On Wednesday morning, Oct 5, St. Mary's church, Calgary, was the scene of a very pretty wedding, when Miss. J. Kelly, eldest daughter of Mr. and Mrs. P.M. Kelly of De Winton was married to Mr. J. Van Tighem, manager of the Union Bank at Strathmore. Rev. Father Van Tighem, assisted by Fathers Dubois and Rioux, performed the ceremony.[202]

The bride, who was given away by her father, wore a beautiful gown of ivory duc[h]esse satin, made entraine, with a graceful veil, and carried a shower bouquet of roses and maidenhair fern. She was assisted by Miss Margaret Kelly, who wore an attractive costume of pale blue Russell cord, with trimmings of gold lace. She wore a large black picture hat and carried a bouquet of pink roses. Mr. Shimnoski, assistant manager of the Union Bank in Calgary, performed the duties of groomsman.

The groom's gift to the bride was a very handsome pendant of pearls. To the bridesmaid a pearl sunburst, and to the groomsman a pearl cravat pin.

After the ceremony the bridal party drove to the home of the bride's parents where a dainty wedding breakfast was served, at which a number of friends of the contracting parties were present. The bride received a great many beautiful presents, mostly cut glass and silver. Mr. and Mrs. Van Tighem left on the midnight train for the coast. They purpose spending some time in Vancouver, Victoria, Seattle and other cities. The bride wore a travelling suit of brown cloth, with mink furs and hat to correspond. Mr. and Mrs. Van Tighem will be at home to their friends after Nov. 9, at Strathmore.

[Leonard continues:]
So here we started again, in the early spring 1911. It was freezing, yet when we made concrete foundations, the men all came to lend a hand. Some days I had as many as fourteen and sixteen men working with the best will of the world. So that in a short time the church was up, a building of 28×48 ft. with a handsome, good shaped, though very simple little tower.

It looks grand from the passing cars of the main line of the Canadian Pacific.

Of course, here also we could not finish the church on the inside. But this was all I wanted; a place of worship, an altar where to celebrate mass, a real chapel of our own. But now I had so many places to attend; the new north branch of the CPR called me to come to Acme and Irricana.[203] I could do no justice to all these places so I wrote to the bishop, telling His Lordship the necessity of another priest. The Langdon people having heard of this immediately wrote to Bishop Legal asking him that I might be sent to them, and reside permanently at Langdon.

There was, at that time, a young priest who was to be removed from the teaching staff of the seminary of St. Albert on account of ill health. So His Lordship wrote to me, that I was free to choose between Strathmore and Langdon but, I would not make the choice myself. So the bishop sent Rev. Father Rock to Strathmore and told me to reside at Langdon. When this news reached the people of Langdon they were glad, and we began to deliberate how to build a residence or presbytery.

It was decided to take a loan of four hundred dollars, which was offered at six per cent to be repaid in one year. Just money enough to purchase the material of a cottage 24×30 ft. Again the people came to do all the labor our selves, and I resided in it before it was finished: four rooms and a large hall to be used as a winter chapel.

Unfortunately the *hagel* [hail] destroyed the crops that year and the people could not repay the loan the following spring. It was difficult to make both ends meet. No dues were paid, not a nickel. There was practically no revenue whatever. Some of our Catholic families left, and we had

1▶ *"Priest's House and St. Joseph's Church. Langdon, Alta, 1911 ±"* Van Tighem Family Archives

2▶ *"In 1938 the old church at Langdon was purchased from the parish of Strathmore by Father Riou, dismantled and moved near a mine about ten miles southeast of Cluny. There it was renovated and on April 7, 1940, was dedicated to St. John the Baptist and opened free of debt, but on land belonging to the Reserve. At the end of the war the mine was worked only intermittently and people began to move away. In July, 1960, Father Poulin, O.M.I., moved the church to a small settlement about five miles south of Cluny, called 'Washington' by the Indians, place it on a concrete foundation and renovated it again."* (Venini Byrne 1973, 51.) Currently, 2005, the chapel at Little Washington is a Full Gospel church. Photo Mary E.M.

hard times. The Sunday collections were all I got and this amounted, here at Langdon, to one or two dollars per Sunday, generally.

I received a trifle more at Shepard and at Acme when I visited there.. Fortunately, I was·called to Bassano once a month for about [a] year, and the collection was better there."[204]

1911–1912

Our farmers had a good crop during the summer of 1912. So, in the fall of that year I made a great effort to have the $400.00 loan paid. I knew the people could do it. So, I told them that for three and a half years I had received no dues and that I wanted them to pay this debt. Some came forward at once. Mr. Jos. Besse was the first again, to give the example, God bless him! But I must acknowledge again of the bad sprit of others, who absolutely refused to do their share. By so far were they rebellious that I refused absolution to some, according to orders received from our bishop. I have a good mind to put their names down here – for they are the very ones who could pay best. One of them had thousands of dollars in the bank and was unmarried, the other had a large grown up, money making family.

We are in the spring of 1913. We have our diocese of St. Albert divided.[205] Bishop Legal, my old companion of the south is now archbishop of Edmonton, and Right Reverend Dr. McNally has been nominated bishop of Calgary.

The flock increases. More shepherds and pastors are needed. But lo!! These pastors decrease. Rev. P. Lafar, who was in charge of Strathmore since the departure of R.F. Rock, was called to eastern Canada, where the Benedictines open a house. So there is no priest in Strathmore and I have to take charge there and visit regularly. Well, I am rather glad, here in Langdon several families have left. Some other have taken homesteads and will be away half of the time. Then, there is no revenue in Langdon, not five dollars a month to live on. Yes, I am glad to go to Strathmore twice a month. But, alas, I have to neglect all the other small missions, the parishes Shepard, Acme, Irricana, Cheadle, etc. These places I have to visit during the week. But, of course, this cannot continue. A priest is needed permanently at Strathmore. So I have written to our provincial, that he better send Rev. P. Deman to Strathmore and my request has been answered and I myself, have been notified that I would be removed from Langdon after our annual retreat.[206]

There being no Oblates Fathers any longer at Calgary in St. Mary's, we have to go to Edmonton for the retreat and, there I was told to go to Taber, 32 miles east of Lethbridge, a new parish, which never had a residence priest, and was only visited once a month from Lethbridge. Rev. F. Meyers, a young German Oblate, has built a small church in Taber, but there is no residence for the priest.

I arrived in Taber on the 16th Sept. 1913 and I was called north about 30 miles that very night for a funeral; a young woman had died almost suddenly, an automobile took me there I celebrated Requiem Mass there at Retlaw; then returned to Taber and it was four in the afternoon before I broke my fast.[207]

The first Sunday I celebrated mass in Taber, the church was filled. I don't know the exact number of Catholics yet.[208] I am told there are some three thousand souls in Taber. I have rented a small house for $10 per month. But we will build soon a small addition to the *sacristie*. The people here have just paid up the debt of the church and cannot actually build a residence for the priest.

I will be here three Sundays per month and go to Grassy Lake one Sunday. Then visit Purple Springs and Chin during the week, also Coal City and Coaldale.[209]

Well, I have been here over two weeks now, and I cannot say that I like Taber very much yet. The fact is that there is more life in a Trappist monastery than there is here where I am. Our little church is built south of the CPR line and depot and the town is on the north side. There is not a soul to be seen all day and from Monday till Saturday. I am little acquainted as yet, and I have no visitors. I suppose every one is busy during the day and need rest after their labors.

There are a very few at mass in the morning and the October devotions of the rosary are not much attended. Let us hope for the better!!!

▶ *Father Van Tighem*. Van Tighem Family Archives

The year 1914 has passed and a terrible year it has been, ever since the beginning of August, almost the entire European states have been at war.

[On August 30, 1914, Leonard wrote to Bishop McNally. This letter is completely quoted in Venini Byrne (1973, 269):]

> In the general depression of business and now on account of the war, they offer us six lots for $450.00; previously the price was $150.00 a lot. Were there any possibility of raising the money I would not hesitate to purchase them; but half the Catholic population has left the town and there is absolutely no revenue.

[Leonard continues:]

Our good Catholic little Belgium has fallen in the hands of the murderous Germans who invaded the small land and invaded it without reason whatever, thinking that they could sweep through the little land and reach Paris in a week or two. But the Belgians have defended their neutrality and have died by the thousands for the defense of the freedom of their nation.

History has never recorded the crimes committed by the hordes of Germans in Belgium. They are branded forever as the worst of barbarians. May God put an end to all this!!!

On account of these cruel wars, business is now at stand still everywhere. We had no crops this year in southern Alberta, too dry. So that half of the farmers have left and these who remain, are supported by the government. Besides, our coalmines are idle so that the little town of Taber is in bad conditions. About half of its population has also left.

During the year we have made some improvements. We have built two rooms on the south side of the church where the priest lives now. These will make the *sacristie* later on. We have broken down the brick chimney badly built inside the church. We have placed a furnace under the church and also have made a fence around the church property. All this has cost money: the rooms cost over $300.00, the furnace about $80.00 and the fence over $100.00.

We have been able more over to pay part of the debt of the church; so that we begin the New Year with a debt less than two hundred dollars. But we have been unable to make any improvements inside the church. There is no bell as yet, nor a single statue in the church. The church is not even painted inside. No altar, no Stations of the Cross, although we have the loan of some fine painting (stations) which belong to the Oblates, and were in our mother house in Paris. I brought them with me, ten yeas ago, when I was to our General Chapter.

As there were few Catholics left at Grassy Lake, I do not give them a Sunday service now but I remain in Taber for every Sunday, as the congregation is too large to be left without mass. I cannot complain with the attendance with the exception of some foreigners, the Catholics hear mass regularly.

There are more over, half a dozen daily communions. The Sunday school has much improved; there are over 50 present at catechism every Sunday. But the revenue is almost nil.

June 1st, 1915. Month after month has passed and the war continues as fierce as ever. Italy has joined the Allies now, and declared war on Austria.

The Germans, they are called Huns, now, continue their murderous tactics; they abuse every law of humanity, break any treaty or convention. Lately they torpedoed and sunk a large passenger boat and over a thousand were drowned, innocent non-combatants: men, women and children.[210] As there were over a hundred Americans among the victims, the United States may soon declare war on Germany now.

The whole world today, curses this nation. For some time past they employed poisonous gasses to suffocate their opponents in the war, which is against all rules and conventions and forbidden by The Hague Tribunal.

May God put an end to all their murderous and barbarian tactics of the German *Kultur*! May their nefarious militarism be crushed out of the world!! May they be so humiliated over their deeds of shame (which cannot be written down) that they don't dare to show their heads for centuries to come!!!

The thought of what is going on in our poor little Belgium is very trying. Day and night we think of those near and dear to us. What they must undergo and suffer under the domination of the cruel Germans.

of the german Kultur!

May their nefarious Militarism be crushed out of the World!! May they be so humiliated over their deeds of shame, (which cannot be written down) that they dont dare to show their heads for Centuries to Come.!!!

and May God forgive them their crimes!

The thought of what is going on in our poor little Belgium is Very trying. Day and night we think of those, Near and Dear to us. What they must undergo and suffer under th. domination of th. Cruel Germans.

▸ *War stamps*, glued in page 32 of Leonard's codex.

[Leonard continues with poetry in Dutch:]

Aan de soldaten van West-Vlaanderen
Ons Vaderland is wreedlijk neergeslagen.
Door een snodaard kwaadaardig aangerand.
O! Belgenvolk. Dit zijn ak'lige dagen
waar kerk en school en huizen zijn verbrand.
Vooruit, Vooruit. Wij moeten roem behalen
zoo zingen wij, en harhalen wij nog
Vooruit, Vooruit, mij moeten zege pralen
Over Valsheid, en over Duitsch bedrog.
Over —
Over —

Kom Engeland, ter hulp der arme Belgen
Ter hulp Vrankrijk en gij ook Russland
Kom Canada, en met dat Irlansch helden,
Verplettren wij den helschen Kulturband.
Vooruit —

Zie hoe uw Vorst het voorbeeld heeft gegeven
als Vrome Belg, met ware leeuwenhart
Zeg, is uw naam het leger ingeschreven
of zoudt gij met kanker zijn besmart.
Vooruit —

Luister gij ook, o brave Vlaamsche Vrouwen
Neemt acht of uw Edle Koningin;
Ziet waar Zij is, vol moed en vol betrouwen
Met Echtgenoot en gansch haar huisgezin.
Voorruit —

Jong doch ik ben, en thans maar 14 Jaren
Zoo sprak den Prins den Adel Koningzoon.
Ik ben gereed, met krachten zonder sparen
Voor Vader's land, en voor de Zegekroon.
Voorruit —

God schonke rust, aan onze Vrome helden,
Die vochten voor, hunnen vrijdom en recht:
Zulk ed'len moed, de wereld zal vermelden
Waren zij niet, als leeuwen in 't gevecht??
Vooruit, Vooruit.
July 30' 1915

[Translation by Mary E.M.:]

To West-Flanders' Soldiers
Our Fatherland is cruelly defeated
By a villain viciously attacked.
Oh! Belgians. These are awful days, with
churches, schools and houses burning down.
Forward, Forward. We sing about
achieving victory and we repeat once more
Forward. Forward. We should flaunt glory
Over Falsity and German gory
Over —
Over —

Come England, help the poor Belgians,
France and Russia you should help too
Come Canada and alongside Irish heroes,
We will crush the hellish Kultur Band.
Forward —

See how as pious Belgian your Sovereign
with genuine lion heart gave an example
Say, is your name registered in the army
or do you suffer from some cancer.
Forward —

You good Flemish Women, you listen too
Look at your noble Queen;
Look at where she is, full of courage and trust
With her spouse and all of her family.
Forward —

Young as I am, and only 14 years of age
Thus spoke the Prince, the king's noble son.
I am ready and won't spare my powers
For Father's land and for the Laurel Crown.
Forward —

That God gave rest to our Pious heroes,
Which fought for freedom and for rights:
The world will mention such noble courage
Weren't they as lions in their fights??
Forward, Forward.
July 30' 1915

Brabançonne

O Belgenland, wat is er voorgevallen?
Wat is d'oorzaak, dezer rampzaligheid?
tranen zie ik, in d'oogen van u allen.
Wie heeft verward, uw rust en veiligheid?
Ik dacht dat gy, door al te groote Machten
Een vrije land, met verbond, wierdt verklaard;
Dit Staatsverbond, wie was er te verachten?
Wie is de schel, en wie is de valsehaard?
Wie —
Wie —

Ons Vaderland is wreedlijk neergeslagen.
Door een snodaard kwaadaardig aangerand.
O! Belgenvolk. Dit zijn ak'lige dagen
waar kerk en school en huizen zijn verbrandt
'T was een gebuur, die wij onz' vriend bedachten,
Zelfs bloedverwant van onz' edel Vorstin,
Die eer en recht, in zijn hart deed versmachten.

Bavaria — Wat hebt gij in den zin?
Bavaria
Bavaria
Beschouw God, de gruwelijke heuveldaden
Door Duitschen Keiz'r en soldaten verricht.
Veracht zijn zij, en met schande beladen
'T was moord en brand, en erger nog gesticht.
Zij broken open, onze kloosterdeuren,
Waar Zusters rein, leefden in veiligheid,
Daar spreiden zij, hun vuige beeste geuren
'Lijk helsche gespuis, de vuile pest verspreid.
Lijk —
Lijk —

Onz' Bisschoppenen geestelijke heern
Wierden versmaad, rampzalig aangerand.
Zelfs Cardinal moest Duitse lessen leeren,
Wierd Vreemdeling, in zijn goed Belgenland.
Zij hielden op, apostelijke Brieven
In zijn paleis, sloten zij hem op.
Het waren 'lijk een ware bende dieven
En wie verweerde, schoot men door de kop,
En —
En —

Brabançonne

O Belgium, whatever happened?
What caused this disastrous situation?
I see tears in the eyes of all of you.
Who disturbed your peace and your security?
I thought that you, by too great Powers
were declared a free country with a treaty;
This Treaty of Nations: who had to be despised?
Who is the culprit who the viper?
Who —
Who —

Our Fatherland cruelly beaten down
By a villain viciously attacked.
Oh! Belgians. These are awful days
churches, schools and houses being burnt down.
It was a neighbour we thought to be a friend,
even a relative of our noble Queen,
Who, in his heart, denied honor and rights.

Bavaria — What do you have in mind?
Bavaria
Bavaria
Consider God, the gruesome evil deeds
Performed by German emp'ror and soldiers
They are despised, loaded with shame
It was murder and arson and even worse
They broke and entered our convent doors,
Where pure Sisters lived in security,
There they spread their beastly vapours
Like hellish rabble spread the dirty pest.
Like —
Like —

Our Bishops, spiritual leaders
were scorned, disastrously attacked.
Even the Cardinal had to take German lessons,
Became a foreigner is his good Belgian country.
They withheld apostolic Letters
In his Palace they locked him up.
They were like a band of thieves
And who defended himself was shot through the head.
And —
And —

God schenke rust aan onze vrome Helden,
die vochten voor hunnen vrijdom en recht.
Zulk ed'len moed, de wereld zal vermelden,
Waren zij niet, als leeuwen in 't gevecht?
Bij duizenden zijn roemrijk neergevallen
Stortend hun bloed, voor God, recht en 't Vaderland.
Nu hebben zij, de zegekroon behalen,
Zoo zullen wij, o God! met zwaard in d'hand
Zoo zullen —
Zoo zullen —

Taber
August 3rd. 1915. L.V.T., O.M.I.

I have sent a copy of this soldier-song to the son of our glorious king, Albert the Great, as they call him now.²" The boy is only fourteen and is doing hard work in the army. He enlisted as private in the Belgian army in Flanders.

It is strange how the mother tong can be thus remembered after more than forty years absence from the fatherland. It must be deep imprinted in de cells of the brain, indeed.

God give rest to our pious Heroes,
Who fought for their freedom and their rights.
Such noble courage, the world will mention,
Weren't they as lions in the fights?
Fallen down gloriously by the thousands
Spilling their blood for God, justice and the Fatherland.
Now they have obtained a crown of laurels,
Thus we will, Oh God! with sword in hand
Thus we —
Thus we —

Taber
August 3rd. 1915. L.V.T., O.M.I

□

Sept. 1915

God has blessed our North West Territories with a splendid crop. We had copious rains all spring and summer, and now the fall has arrived and our farmers are busy threshing and delivering their grains. I hear that wheat is sold [for] about 70 cents at the moment. Last year it went up to $1.50. But even at 70 cents our farmers can make a good profit.

And the European war remains the same. The Russians have been driven back by the German and Austrian armies. In Flanders and France, no advance is made, and very likely the soldiers will have to winter out again in their trenches. Slow progress is made in the Dardanelles and the Italians also, have their hands full.

No peace in view as yet, in fact, peace is impossible just now. For it would be only of short duration. In order to obtain a permanent peace the German *Kultur* and militarism must be crushed out of the world. And Taber, our parish, is very, very much at peace, these days. All the people have left for the harvest. There is scarcely a soul to be seen on the streets. Let us hope that after the harvest, times will be better.

OCTOBER: Bulgary has joined the Germans and Austrians and this complicates much the Dardanelles business. Dardanelles has been abandoned.

[Leonard (1915) wrote to *The Lethbridge Herald,* transcript:]
Taber, Nov. 25. 1915.
Editor of *The Lethbridge Herald*:

Complaint of an old missionary
Sir: It is now over forty years, when a young lad, I left my home in Belgium and came to the wilds of Western Canada, and I have labored here in the territory, now called Alberta, without ever leaving it, not even for a day, only once, when in 1904 I was called to Europe to the General Chapter of the Oblate fathers, when also I was favored with an introduction to His Holiness Pope Pius X of blessed memory. Never have I left the diocese of St. Albert – no holiday, vacations, but work, work, with my hands as well in the Holy Ministry, building church and chapels, and mission houses and schools and altars.

In 1875, after three months on foot through the then virgin prairies, from Fort Garry (Winnipeg) to Fort L'Auguste (Edmonton), I arrived in St. Albert, and the next day I was on top of the roof of a large shed they were building there at the Mission to shelter the few cows which furnished milk and butter to over a hundred people at the Mission. In fact, there were close to a hundred orphans, outcasts of the world, poor Indian children, abandoned by their parents or relatives, most of them misformed in flesh and bones, and brought to the Mission by the small band of

Black robed Voyageurs from some forest camps of the north, or from our ocean like prairies, of the south of our immense diocese. When we speak of olden days, people imagine that the life of the missionary must have been almost unbearable in those days, without bread for years, except a small galette on feast days, only pemmican, dried meat or fish and not always fresh. No my friends, those were the truly happy days of the primitive missionary.

Never shall I forget our recreative amusements and childlike frolics, our concerts and entertainments in the old Mission log house of St. Albert on the occasion for instance of the return of our Saintly Bishop Grandin, O.M.I., from some far away part of his immense diocese after an absence of many months. Never shall I forget the serenades we gave the holy man on such occasions, for he, like the rest of the priests and brothers, had his little corner in the long log house of St. Albert, a true charivary, with poker on cans or pans. Anything to welcome home the holiest of men who ever trod this territory.

Yes, these were our happy days, and it brings me to my subject. They are gone these days, and with them our true happiness and innocent amusements also. We are no longer surrounded by the poor docile Indian or the roving half-breed, we have now the so-called civilized surroundings. These territories were prepared by the early missionary. The fertility of the soil was communicated by the missionary to the nations of the world, for the Mission had its little field and garden, and lo, do the newcomers appreciate the work done by these valiant pioneers? Will they give thanks to those who prepared the way for them? Many of them are rich now; they have made fortunes in a few years. Alas no. Listen, a few days ago I heard all kinds of rumors with regard to the missionary who had taken my place in Lethbridge when I left five years ago. Unfortunately they are Germans, poor priests, they cannot change their flesh and blood, either can they very well abandon their nationality, they can not but feel for their country. They may have made imprudent remarks, but I understand the house searching brought little or no evidence of any wrongdoing. Well, they have been removed from Lethbridge, and I think it is best during these dark days. But here is what pained me and made my heart bleed when yesterday I arrived in Lethbridge on a short business visit. I was told there that some of the Catholic population had sent a petition to the bishop of Calgary, asking that secular priests be sent to Lethbridge, and consequently the chasing away from Lethbridge of the Oblate Fathers who were there when Lethbridge was Coalbanks and before there was even a fence post planted or a shack erected where now Lethbridge stands. I myself am an Oblate, and for over twenty-five years I have labored there. No boasting is needed, there are old timers enough to tell the tale of the beginning of the burg. It was like a sword through my heart when I heard of the snakelike underwork that is going on there. Surely this cannot be the spirit of my dear old parishioners.

I will write no more. After a few hours spent in my dear old parish, I returned to Taber with a heavy heart. It does not take many to create trouble in a parish. I am glad I am getting old.

Father L. Van Tighem, O.M.I.

[A flurry of reactions to Leonard's letter to *The Lethbridge Herald* followed. Moore (1915). Transcript:]

Lethbridge, Alberta. November 28, 1915.
Rev. Father Van Tighem
Dear Father, 1731, le t a Northe.

It was with the profoundest regret, that I read your letter in the *Herald*, last night. I fully understand, how you feel on this matter, what a sorrow, and pain it has caused you, and it is with haste I write you, to endeavour if possible to lighten the pain which it must have caused you.

As probably you are aware I along with others went amongst your old Parish[i]oners and friends on the North side of the track, and in every instances I was asked if you were here in Lethbridge to stay, it surprised me that everyone of the Slavonions Houses I called on knew you were in the city, and from the sentiments expressed by all I told Rev. Father Bidault that I was thoroughly convinced, that if you were again to be stationed in Lethbridge that the church as it now stands would be inadequate. This action on the part of one or two will, I am afraid be the means of further division in the already sadly divided Parish. But I have still hopes that his Lordship the bishop will ignore the petition for a secular Priest. I had arranged to present the contra petition to the bishop myself, but Mrs. Deveber volunteered to go as also did the Senator, which goes a long way to show, how the labors of the Holy order of the priesthood has been observed and appreciated at least by two outsiders, they have not returned yet and we hope their mission has been successful, as it ought to be if only as a matter of justices.

Rev. Father let me assure you that you retain the goodwill, and always will do so of all your old parishioners, and on behalf of the old time Slavonians I visited, I convey this message of symp[a]thy. It was with the deepest regret and suppressed emotions I read your justifiable and I may say pathetic letter, to think that after all your years of labor, you should be compelled to do so through the thoughtlessness of one or two individuals. May God in his mercy forgive them. Dear Father, excuse me for taking the liberty of writing you, but I could not refrain from doing so. I sincerely request your remembrance of me in your prayers.

Sincerely yours.
L. Moore.

The Ranch, Taber, Alberta. Dec. 5th, 1915.
Rev. Father Van Tighem
Dear Rev. Father!

I am just answering yours of Sept. 9th with photo enclosed. We are delighted to get your picture, you can bet it will get a place of honor in this house. We will have it at our table on Christmas day so if you cannot be here in person you will be with us on that card. We expect all the Bucxley's and Kate Tennant to feast with us on Christmas. It will be something like old times. I read your very int[e]resting letter in the Herald last week. I can well imagine your feelings. It is no wond[e]r you feel very grieved. If you had been left in Lethbridge these things would not have happ[e]ned the people are still attached to you. Dear Father, do not think I am up holding the people for asking for a change to the secular priest. You pro[ba]bly know as will as I do they asked for the change shortly after you left when the authority's of your order refused to let you stay in Lethbridge and again Father Rosenthal has not taken well with the people. From what I can learn, it is not so much against your order as again those German priests the people w[ere] quar[rel]ling. There would be rejoicing in Lethbridge if the Rev. Father Van Tighem, O.M.I., returned to be the parish priest in that town. Dear Father, ease your wounded feelings by knowing you hold the hearts of all the old timers and they in turn love the order of O.M.I., they know no other. It is very hard to love a German now. I cannot do it; when I think of poor Belgium, it makes my blood boil. The Catholics are getting it from every corner and who are the cause? The Germans. I wish I was great enough to lead an army against the Huns. I feel very sorry for poor Father Bidault. I know he has done nothing against this country. We will not have mass for some time, I guess.

I will remember you to all your old friends here on Christmas day. We all join in wishing you a blessed life in these troublesome times.

Yours in fond remembrance.
Jhos. E. Tennant.

I, after deliberate discussion of this matter with all my consultors at a meeting on December 3rd at my Episcopal residence, have decided to and hereby do, in my quality of Bishop of the Diocese of Calgary . . . inform the said Fathers of my intention to place the said parish and missions in charge of the clergy of the diocese of Calgary, this change to be effected during the week of the 16th of January, 1916 and I require of you, Very Reverend Father, as Provincial Superior of the said Congregation, to hand over to me or before that date the books and property of the said parish and missions.

Permit me to ask you, very Reverend Father, to see that in the meantime no agitation be carried on among the people by your Fathers, and that no more such letters will be made public by your Fathers as that published in *The Lethbridge Herald* by one of them under the date of November 27th last; for all such agitation, whether public of private is of great harm to religion, and those who are guilty of it must bear before God its serious responsibility.

Finally, in renewed proof of my desire to be just and appreciative towards the Oblate Fathers, let me remind you of my offer, unnoticed in your reply, of the excellent parish of Pincher Creek, *titulo perpetuo*, to your Congregation.

[Leonard sent a few letters of support to Father Henri Grandin, who was fighting to keep the Lethbridge parish for the Oblates, as well as the following letter, in English:]
Taber, December 27, 1915.
Reverend Father Grandin,

Most of their letters I have thrown away. I find a couple though, which I enclose. The Father at Lethbridge could perhaps get some copies of the *Herald*. I send you one by this mail. Just came in from Retlaw. I do my best for the abandoned missions here.

Could you believe that they dared to come even to Taber with a petition for chasing the Oblates. The devil's work is really going on.

Excuse me.
Very Busy.
L. Van Tighem, O.M.I.

1916

[Leonard continues:]
War remains the same. The Germans are murdering non-combatants, women and children now with their submarines. They also frequently fly over England with their immense Zeppelins, killing women and babies. (*Kultur* indeed!!!).

But now the Russians are on their legs again. They had no ammunition to fight with, but they have it now and are driving the Huns and Austrians back. All the lines, trenches, remain the same in France and Belgium, no progress on either side.

We are in the summer of '16 now and no peace in view. Romania has cast her lot with our armies. This will help a great deal. There is little change in the long fighting lines, after months of battering at Verdun where very likely about half a million of soldiers were wounded and killed, the Germans seem to have given it up. They are losing ground in France now but nothing on a great scale. It seems that our boys will have to put up a third winter in the trenches. Peace seems to be as far away as ever.

[Around March 1916 Leonard received the following letter, in Dutch, from a Belgian army chaplain]
February 25, '16
Reverend Mr. Van Tighem, pastor.

Here in the battalion of which I am the chaplain I discovered your nephew and because he is a West-Fleming, just as I am, we soon became friends. He told me about you and I thought that maybe pastor Van Tighem could pass on news from Oostende. I cannot write directly to Oostende, but I think you can. I would like to get some news from my mother and sister and brothers who all are in Oostende.

Would you be so kind to write, on my behalf, to Oostende and let them know that I am fine without mentioning that I am at the front. Ask them to write to me in care of you. I ask you a lot, but I pray you, do it. I will be so grateful to you. Your nephew, who gave me your letter, is a nice boy, he is doing fine. He is a good soldier and a good Christian. I feel good about him; he is still always in good health.

I thank you in advance and send you my sincere and well-meant greetings,

Jos. De Visscher.
Army Chaplain for the Belgian Army. A12T, 4th Bon.
The address of my family in Oostende,
Ms. Pierre De Visscher-Allarij
Schipperstraat 46. Oostende. Belgium.

[During 1916 Leonard received letters, in English, from Henry Barnes, a former Lethbridge area farmer and parishioner. In his letter of March 19, 1916, Barnes thanked Leonard for his kind recommendation that helped him to apply for a military college, Trinity College, University of Cambridge, with resulted in Barnes writing, "and here I am." Barnes (July 7, 1916) wrote to his "Dear Friend Leonard," that he passed his exam, got by some lucky chance on the honours list, was now awaiting gazetting and that:]

On receipt of your last letter I went to see the bishop of Cambridge to see what could be done for you. He was very nice and this is the result. You must apply direct to: Right Rev. Mr. Bidell D.D., Archbishop's House, Westminster, London, S.W. He is in charge of the British Army and your name would have to pass though his hand.

And now for a few tips.

1. Tell him who you are, give your family connections and the names of the most influential people you know as references.
2. State your hospital experience.
3. State what languages you can speak. Enlarge on this as interpreters are very scarce.
4. Say as little about age as possible. Drop a few years if you can do safely.

(. . .) You should also write a letter to this address: Secretary, War Office, London. State what you can do and offer your services, that is of course, apply for a commission in the army itself (. . .)

Hoping we will yet be brother officers, and soon, and asking your prayers, I remain,

Your old chum
Henry Barnes.

P.S. have arranged to return to Trinity for my B.A. after the war. Particulars in next letter. HB.

[In August Leonard got another letter, in Dutch, from army chaplain De Visscher:]

19-8-'16.
Very Reverend Sir Pastor Van Tieghem

The news I have to convey is not good. It could be better, it is true, but still it is not very bad. See: I literally write my diary: On last Sunday night July 27 about 10 o'clock one announced that there was a wounded in the front line. We went there, the doctor and I, there we saw Jo Vantieghem laying on a stretcher, his head wrapped. A bullet had hit him, went in under the left eye, the bullet went out from his right eye, right at the upper part of his nose. The boy was full of courage and the first he said to me was: "Mr. Chaplain, would you mind to write to Uncle Pastor." I said yes.

Since he is in the "Belgium Field Hospital" where he is recovering quite well, his right eye is completely gone, but the doctors say that he will see with his left.

The boy is admirable, full of courage, talks about returning to the front. His friends regret that he is wounded, because he was a good companion for them.

I have frequently visited him and see what he charged me with. I had to write to you, that he is wounded on July 28 (the night between 27 and 29 of July 1916) because of assurance – you should write to Mr. Jo Vantieghem, Banker in Canada. He also received a letter from Octaaf, and asks that you would write, because for the moment he cannot write.

Since he is in the Hospital he received a letter from you in which you mention me: causa stamps.

I will send them to you the coming eight days, I had them stamped "Postes militares," as such they have greater value.

Very Reverend Mr. Pastor, this is the sad news. It is sad, it is true, but I might comfort you that Jo was a good soldier and always faithfully fulfilled his duty; that his officer said of him: "En voila encore un de mes meilleurs soldats." It also should comfort you that Jo is courageous and patiently endures everything in honour of God.

Last week he said: "Sir, I have asked to go to mass, but the doctor does not yet allow me."

Very Reverend Sir, accept with the expression of my Christian compassion the assurance that I always will be at your service.

Best Wishes in Xo
Jos De Visscher[212]
Army Chaplain at the Belgian Field Army / B 264/4th B n / E.M.

[Leonard continues:]
On the 28th of July, 1916, Joseph van Tighem, in the front trenches of the Belgian army, got a bullet in the head and may be blind for the rest of his life, he is only a little over twenty years of age and was in Great Falls, Montana, at the outbreak of the war.[213] At his own expense he went to France to go in there with the remnant of the Belgian army. May God help us!! And shorten these terrible days!!!

[About one week later Leonard received another letter from the army chaplain:]

28-8-'16.

Very Reverend Mr. Pastor,

Hereby I send you the requested Belgian stamps. I had them stamped, thinking that it is better; as such they are more valuable.

Jo, your nephew, does very well, I will visit him tomorrow once more; I don't know yet what the outcome of his eyes will be, the doctors did not yet give a statement, they take very good care of him, and say that he will still see with one eye. In any case he is and remains good-humoured; in the sickroom where he is he became the friend of everybody, which is by his good character.

If there is more news, I will keep you posted, God give that he at least will see with one eye!

And now something different! Forgive me my straightforwardness and boldness!

Very Reverend Sir, I plan when our boys have a break, to give them a few agreeable hours in the evenings after their work and exercises. That is why, it is at the order of the day, here as well as in America, that is why, I say, I plan to provide them with cinema shows, so I could apart from religious subjects, also provide them with instructive and fun subjects, to merge the useful with the agreeable, in one word, benefit them.

My soldiers will then stay in their *cantonnementen* and will not wander off to pubs. It is better; don't you think so? But here is the question: for this I would need a projector and this costs around 400 Fr. and (I am straightforward) I don't have it, I do have something, but that is still not much. Say, Very Reverend Sir, do you happen to know a brave soul at your place who could help me with this, it would be such good help for me and it also benefits our poor Belgian boys, to cheer them up a bit, to at least have them forget their misery for a few hours, in one word, benefit them.

I don't have to tell you, that I will be grateful to you and the good people who will help me with this.

Very Reverend Sir, don't blame me that I am asking you this, but speaking straightforwardly, it is out of necessity, and for the good that I am asking you.

Hoping for a small answer from you, I reverently greet you, and thank you a thousand times in advance for what you will do for my good soldiers.

Your Humble Servant
Jos. De Visscher
Army Chaplain at
The Belgian Field Army / B 264/4th B n / E.M.

[P.S.] Hereby two more stamps from Greece, from the 1912–1913 war in Macedonia (they are from one of my soldiers whose parents live in Greece).

[Letter, in French, of Leonard, probably to Father Henri Grandin:]
Sept. 7, '16.
Reverend and Very Dear Father.

I have received your letter and at the same time an other one from the army chaplain De Visscher of the Belgian army, who told me that my nephew got a bullet in his head, and will probably be blind for the remainder of his days.

This happened on the evening of July 27th of last July. The army chaplain gave me the highest praise for his courage and it seems that his officer has said: And here you have another of my best soldiers.

The poor boy has been here for several years, in Great Falls, Montana, near the Rocky Mountains. As soon as he heard that the war broke out, he left for New York on his own expenses. Also paid his ticket across the Atlantic Ocean and went to France in order to join the Belgian army.

What will become of him? He is in a Belgian field hospital, and I am sure, dear Father, that, when you are in Flanders, you will visit and encourage him.

I am going to write to the Chancellor of the Archbishopric of Canterbury, it seems that he is charged with selecting chaplains. But I will not ask for any honours. I will just ask to serve with our wounded in the hospitals.

Tuus in X to J.C & M.Imm.
Father L. Van Tighem, O.M.I., Taber, Alta. Canada.

[Leonard continues:]
The summer of 1916 is past and again we had a magnificent crop in southern Alberta, all is cut now and threshing has began, the average is over 40 bushels per acre and in many places, where the land was well prepared they obtain over 60 bushels per acre. And now the wheat has gone up rapidly. It has been as high as a dollar sixty per bushel. This is really a harvest for our farmers!!! God be blessed and thanked for this!!!

Nothing new in the poor parish of Taber. No improvements whatever at the church. The small debt is not paid as yet and the parish priest has to content himself with the small Sunday collection at High Mass, which amounts from 4 to 7 dollars. Hence he has to do his own cooking and washing and mending. Not much style in this!!!

Happily there is Mr. Hosey, a good neighbor and there is Mr. Reilly at the King George Hotel. The priest won't starve as long as these are here. They are Irish of course.

A letter from the chaplain of the Belgian army in Flanders, dated Oct. 8, '16 (Leonard transcribed this letter in his codex):

"Your nephew Joseph is full of courage. I see him frequently. He underwent a second operation, under the left eye where a swelling appeared, they have extracted several pieces of the bullet (this proves that the Germans used explosive bullets. L.v.T.).[214] We know not how it will all terminate, but there is hope for the left eye.

And now, I am going to tell some extraordinary piece of news: Joseph has been decorated by the King, and he is a Knight of the Order of Leopold II, and moreover he has received the Military Cross of Honour. Proficiat!!! Of course, Joseph is proud now and he deserves all he got.

His Majesty Albert, King of the Belgians, spoke to him, and entertained him in English. His Majesty asked him the particulars of the wounding, how it all happened and Joseph, having answered, added, 'Sire, I am totally blind.' The parting word of the king to him was, 'Courage!'"

So the poor lad is blind for life.

[Barnes wrote again to Leonard:]
Dunkeld, 10-9-1916.
My Dear Friend,

Just a line to tell you that I was gazetted on Aug. 3rd to the Scottish Horse, and have since joined the regiment here. We are right in the Highlands, a very pretty place after flat England. It is quiet, there are three villages close with about 20 homes in the three of them.

We are very short of officers so I have had a busy week. Have been orderly officer twice, and one day commanded a company. The b.o. to-day told me that another officer and myself were to parade the regiments to church tomorrow. I like the life quite well, and like the district greatly (. . .).

I had a very good time while on pass, wandering over a great part of Great Britain. I got in touch with one of the old miner boys, you remember when I farmed, and we had a couple of days at the Shorncliffe, Folkstone and Dover together. He is recommended for the D.B.M.

I wrote you from London with all particulars of what you wanted to know. I am eagerly awaiting your reply, and better still, I am hoping soon to see you as a brother officer.

With very kind wishes and asking your prayers. I need them. I remain,

Your old chum, Henry Barnes. 2nd St. 3/3 Scottish Horse Dunkeld. Perthashire. Scotland.

[Leonard tried to have his poetry published, but received the following response:]

Pro Belgica, the authorized relief work spokesperson for the victims of the war in Belgium.

Rev. M.L. Van Tighem, 32 Sussex Avenue. Montréal.

Taber, Alberta. October 1916.

Dear Sir,

I would have liked to publish the poetry you were so kind to send me, but unfortunately they have returned the manuscript to me because it is not written well enough and I don't know anyone who has sufficient knowledge of the Flemish language who could do the editing.

If you could send it to me written better so the typesetter could set it without errors, I would enjoy publishing it.

As always, I send you my best wishes.

A.J. de Bury.

[Barnes' last 1916 letter is a sad one. Transcript:]

Dunkeld, 3/11/16.

My Dear Friend

I received your letter some days ago and was very, very sorry to hear that you had not been successful at the War Office. I am sure that there has been some mistake; you did not emphasize the fact that you were a British subject. I know there are even Germans and Austrians naturalized, who have commissions in the army. And they want interpreters, for I was asked only last week by the Scottish command if I spoke Portuguese. I have a very limited knowledge of the language. I don't know what will come of it yet. Did you write to the Church people and War Office both? I am going to see some of my senior officers and see what they can do about it.

I am at present at St. Andrews, on a month's musketry course at Madras College. St. Andrews seems principally famed for ruined buildings, Black Friars Chapel, St. Andrew's Cathedral, the first See formed in Scotland, now a ruin but at the time a tremendous building, commenced in 1100 or thereabouts and opened in the presence of the first Robert Bruce (. . .).

Oh, if you had only gotten into smooth water and gotten your commission I could have met you in London, you would probably have a nice War Office job and could get leave, we could have gone to all the familiar places. I know London pretty well, and we might have got over to Ireland, my home, for a little hunting. It would have been my turn to show you around. Fancy, Westminster Cathedral, St. Pauls', Westminster Abbey, the museums, at night the revues, theaters, the Trocadero, restaurants, the Cecil, and I always remember you as a good sport, the nightclub, just to say we had seen it. But there is hope yet, you may be over here a good deal quicker than you think and when you come, the first to meet you in whatever capacity you come, will be he who ask your prayers,

Your old chum.
Henry Barnes.

[On December 13, 1916, Father Lacombe died. "And seated in the sanctuary were the thinning ranks of his comrades who had kept the faith with him ... Legal, Tissier, Merer, Grandin, Blanchet, Therien, Van Tighen [sic], Lemarchand, Jan, Hetu" (Hughes 1920, 460).]

[Blind Joseph, in English, to Leonard, transcript:]
   Ambulance Crois-Rouge de Belgique.
   Calais-Virval, December 14, '16.
   My dear Uncle,

This is to wish you a good New Year, health, chance and all what you wish. I hope it will be a better year than the last one for I know that you got a lot of trouble thinking al the time to us. We shall hope that 1917 brings us the peace.
   I go every Sunday to the mess with my Sister here and every month I go to confession. I am no long in Hoogstaete. Now I am in Calais in the hospital.
   I cannot see but I get accustomed to my fate. I try to be always happy and I do all my best to accept my lot. I think so I deserve much merit for Heaven.
   Now I can get out of bed. I go all about in the barrack and I can find my way and know all the things.
   I can work a little with the Sisters; I like it very much because if I stay too long time in my rocking chair I fall asleep and than I cannot sleep in the nighttime. I take a walk with my Sisters every day when it is nice.
   I have a dog sometimes, which keeps me company and I learn to feel everything with my fingers.
   My Sister is a Belgian one, but she cannot speak flamisch [Flemish]. I speak English with her all the time.
   I got your parcel on the 26th November. Everything was all right inside. I found the rosary in the tabac. Many thanks for all that. But I did not get till now the letter with the stamps in. Maybe it is in Hoogstaete. I gave my new address there, for some times. If you like to collect some French or Belgian stamps I could send you some.
   I hope you are in good health my dear uncle.

Ferdinand writes to me every two weeks and is still in England now. I hope he shall come and see me sometimes. I have no news about Hendriks yet and Gus writes me every month. Everything is all right there.

With all my good wishes and greetings I am yours affectionately.
[In shaky handwriting] Joe Van Tighem.

[Added] He wrote this [signature] himself. Address: My Sister's address (in fear of evacuation): Sister Eva Demortier. Amb + Rouge de Belge. Calais Virval – for Joe Van Tighem.

[The army chaplain, in Dutch, to Leonard:]
December 21, 1916.
Very Reverend Mr.Pastor

I have to thank you for all your efforts for me, I thank you personally, but I also thank you on behalf of my soldiers. The boys deserve so much the night parties with movies and singing, it will do so much good for them.

In my previous letter, I told you about a portrait of Joseph, in my haste I forgot to enclose it. Please find it enclosed this time. On it is his own handwriting. He is as ever well disposed and healthy.

He moved, he is no long in hospital the Hoogstaete. He is now in Calais. Here follows his address:

Amublance de le Croix Rouge Belge. Virval. Calais. Salle Dixmuide. France

Enclosed a letter he sent me at his change of address.

I end wishing you a blissful Christmas and a Blissful New Year and hopefully 1917 will be for us one of victory and peace.

Your wholly dedicated in Xo.
J. De Visscher.
Army Chaplain.

[Nephew Joseph, in Strathmore, to his uncle Leonard, transcript:]
Union Bank of Canada
Strathmore, Alta Jan. 19th 1917
Dear Uncle:

I herewith enclose a letter I received yesterday. I do not know this party. The letter speaks for itself.²¹⁵ As this gives very little information I have immediately asked for further particulars regarding Jan and his family and Elody. Apparantly Father DeVille was able to get to Meulebeke this time. I am very sorry I did not try this time again. From what this party says, starvation is about all these people have in sight.

I presume Father De Ville is likely to take another trip by Spring. Would it not be well for you to get in touch with him. I feel that he will do more [for] you than he would for me. Write him and see if you can get particulars from Meulebeke. If he was been there Jan or Alfonse Desmet must surely have seen him. If it is possible I think we better get Jan's whole family out here. If it can be done I will stand the expenses to get them and Elodie out here.

If you write Father De Ville, c/o Belgian Bureau 431 W. 47th St. New York, this should find him.

All well here. Very cold to day.

Your nephew Joe.

[One more letter, in Dutch, of the Belgian army chaplain:]
Belgian Front
25/1/17.
Very Reverend Sir Pastor,

I gladly received your last letter. I heartily thank you on behalf of my soldiers, these poor boys deserve such pity, in particular right now in the winter. It is not at all pleasant here and taken into account that they are at least another 30 months removed from their beloved family members, this will at least make you think that they are worth our pity. You should see them in the trenches, in mud and water and snow and shelling, yes, they are worth our pity.

But they are brave and patient. Oh, a Belgian is like that, he soon forgets his misery and after suffering he quickly recovers his cheerful disposition.

Now about Joseph, your nephew. Enclosed the card he recently sent me. The news could be better, but the boy is resigned and accepts his fate well disposed. This is what he wrote, I cite:

"Dear Sir Army Chaplain. I have the honor to wish you a happy and blissful New Year and hope that during this year everything for you will be pleasant. I am now in Amiens in a home for the blind. This morning a doctor told me that I am blind. Compliments from Depessinier and the men of the 6th Section. Thanks in advance and I will always remain dedicated to you. (signed) Jos Van Tighem."

The name Depessenier is his friend's as are the men of the 6th Section. The boys still speak about Jos, his pleasant disposition, his composure and his disdain of danger. I do not know yet what will happen to him in Amiens. I think that one will teach him this or that, a trade or something like that.

If I get more news, I will forward it as soon as possible.

In the mean time, with repeated thanks, I urge you to accept the assurance of my best wishes and prayers.

Your Jos De Visscher
Army Chaplain

Nota Bene: G 219/2nd Bon
My address has changed E.M.

[Leonard continues:]
I have received a portrait of our blind knight. It is sad, he is now in a hospital at Calais, France, and all admire his great courage; so now he is Sir Joseph van Tighem. The poor boy stands there in a hospital tunic. He wears a pair of spectacles to hide and, at the same time, protect his lacerated brows.

And the war goes on Germany asks for peace but peace is refused to her, as long no restoration is made of stolen lands and reparation of all the cruelties committed and annihilation of the Prussian devilish *Kultur*.

And now they start over again; their submarines murder at sea and, in our poor Belgium they take all able-bodied men and, shipping them to Germany, reduce them to slavery. How long will the Lord God permit these horrors to go on??? The measure of crimes most surely filled to the brim!!! *Deus in adfutorium nostrum intende!!! Regina Pacis ora pro nobis!!!*

And Taber??

We have made some progress in the parish of late. We have paid off our debts and have about $180 in the reserve. A lady, Mrs. Polinkas has paid for two statues of about 4–6 ft., which will cost about $80.00 delivered. The Sacred Heart of Jesus (pleading) and Maria Immaculata.

March 10, 1917: . . . .

Geloofd zij Jesus-Christus! Amen.

✝

TER ZALIGER GEDACHTENIS

van den Eerweerden Pater

LEONARDUS VAN TIGHEM,

ZOON VAN

BERNARD & ANGELA KUPERS.

Geboren te MEULEBEKE den 14 Juli 1851;
Vertrekt voor Canada, en treedt
in de Congregatie der Oblaten
van Maria Onbevlekt . . . 1874;
Priester gewijd te Sint Albert,
St Joseph's dag 1882;
Als missionnaris in Zuid Alberta
gezonden 1884;
Stichtte er de eerste kerk te Macleod — Pincher Creek — Lethbridge — Coutts — Strathmore
en Langdon;
Overleden te TABER den 3^n Maart
en begraven te SINT ALBERT
den 8^n Maart . . . . . 1917.

Goede Jesus,
geef zijne ziel de eeuwige rust!

▶ *Obituary Leonardus Van
Tighem. Van Tighem
Family Archives*

[LEONARD PLANNED TO continue on "March 10, 1917," but did not live to do this. His death was reported in *The Lethbridge Herald* of March 5, 1917. *The Taber Times* of March 8, 1917, ran the same article under the title: "Father Van Tighem passes away."]

(Special to *The Herald*)

Taber. March 4. – Rev. father Van Tighem, in charge of the parish of Taber, died suddenly of heart failure on Saturday afternoon, while resting in his study at the church. The sudden death came as a shock to the residents of the town, among whom Father Van Tighem had become greatly respected. The revered father had returned early Saturday morning from Burdett, and had held mass as usual Saturday morning.[216] He retired to his study about 10 o'clock, but it was not until three in the afternoon, when a parishioner called to see him, that he was discovered lying dead on his couch in his study. He was known to have been troubled with his heart, and had stated that he had not been feeling well for several days. He was about 67 years of age. It is understood that his remains will be interred at the cathedral grounds at St. Albert, near Edmonton, the headquarters of the Oblate Fathers, of which order Father Van Tighem was a member. Services were held in Taber Sunday by Rev. Cosenet and services will also be held in Lethbridge, where Father Van Tighem was one of the old timers.

Was a pioneer here

With the passing of Father Van Tighem passes another of those conspicuous figures of the northwest, one of those noble pioneers who braved the trials and hardships of early life in the undeveloped west to aid in its spiritual and commercial development. Father Van Tighem was one of the three Roman Catholic pioneers of Southern Alberta. He was a resident of this country even before Father Lacombe, the grand old man who recently passed to his long rest, came here. He and Father Lacombe and Father Legal, now Bishop Legal, of St. Albert, were the three pioneers who covered the south country in the interests of the Roman Catholic church, and became outstanding figures in its history.

Father Van Tighem was particularly identified with the history of Lethbridge and district, and his sudden death, in the midst of apparent good health, was a shock to many of the old timers here today. He came out from Belgium, his native country, in the early eighties, and was first stationed at Macleod in 1884. In 1886 he came to Lethbridge and was accustomed to hold mass in the boarding house at Coalbanks, across the river. After he organized the parish here and built, a great deal of it with his own hands, the old stone church near the station, some years ago vacated. He was parish priest here following that, during all the years of the growth of the community and city, until six years ago, when he went north to take a small parish, and four years ago going to Taber, where he resided till his death.

Was Skilful Carver

Father Van Tighem was noted for his artistic tastes, his love of nature, and his skill as a wood carver. The old R.C. church at Macleod, burned some years ago, bore evidences of his skill in this latter regard, the entire interior decorations and carvings being done with his own hands. His love of nature led him to plant trees and flowers aplenty in his grounds in Lethbridge, and he even experimented to a certain extent successfully with the growing of fruit.

Grew Fruit Trees Successfully

"It is to Father Van Tighem we owed the first successfully-grown trees in Lethbridge," said J.D. Higinbotham this morning, recalling the old days of the late Father's residence here. "He planted trees in his own garden, and he also planted the trees which have made the grounds and residence formerly occupied by Dr. Mewburn so lovely."

The old-timers here all expressed their deep regret this morning on hearing of Father Van Tighem's death, saying that he was a man of great power for good, and one who had always taken a deep interest in the welfare of the community he saw grow to a city. A native of Belgium, he took much to heart, and showed deep grief at the devastation of his native country, and at the loss of relatives and friends in the war.

Jos. Van Tighem, manager of the Union Bank at Strathmore, a nephew of the deceased, is in the city, looking after the funeral arrangements of Father Van Tighem.

[On August 6, 1936, Clyde W. Gilmore wrote an article in The Lethbridge Herald, 'Progress of Roman Catholic Church in City keeps pace with Growth of Lethbridge.' It closely follows Leonard's codex and elaborates on developments following Leonard's departure.]

[Father Frank Van Tighem (1964, 21) about his uncle:]
The funeral was held in Lethbridge in the presence of the entire population and clergy of the district. Bishop McNally, Bishop of Calgary, gave the absolution.

[On October 14th, 1962 a cairn in honour of the memory of the Reverend Leonard van Tighem was erected at St. Patrick's Roman Catholic Church, Lethbridge. Cairns honouring Leonard are also to be found near the R.C. churches in Fort Macleod and Taber.][217]

In Memory of
Rev. Leonard Van Tighem O.M.I.
first pastor of St. Patrick's Parish, Lethbridge
Born in Flanders Belgum, in 1851.
Arrived in St. Albert in 1882 as a lay brother
in the Oblate Congregation.
Ordained a priest by Bishop Vital Grandin O.M.I.
in 1883 sent to Fort Macleod and Pincher Creek
missions. Became first resident priest in Lethbridge
where he built St. Patrick's Church in 1887.
After serving in Lethbridge from 1887 to 1909,
Father Van Tighem served in other Alberta posts,
including Taber, where on March 10, 1917
this pioneer builder and servant of God,
departed his life for his eternal reward.
Lethbridge, Alberta, October 14, 1962.

[*The Lethbridge Herald*, May 2, 1991, mentioned Father Leonard Van Tighem again:]
A pupil from the children of St. Martha Elementary School has come up with the name for a new Catholic elementary junior high school to be built in West Lethbridge. When it opens in September 1991, the school will be called Father Leonard Van Tighem School. Lisa McDonald won first prize in a school-board sponsored contest to name the new school and accepted her award Wednesday at the board meeting.... Ralph Himsl, superintendent of schools, said Fr. Leonard Van Tighem (pronounced teekum) came from Belgium and was one of the first Catholic priests to settle in the Lethbridge area. He started the first Catholic church in the city, St. Patrick's parish, and was instrumental in the formation of the separate school district in the 1800's.

▷ VICTOR'S DIARY • 1886 – 1917

BEFORE 1830, IN spite of their very distinctive objectives the Catholics and liberal bourgeoisie, in the southern part of the Kingdom of the Netherlands, had concluded a *monsterverbond* [monstrous alliance] that united in objecting to the religious and educational politics of the Dutch King, Willem I, who governed as an enlightened despot. Among other things, King Willem I wanted to govern without a parliament, to subject the church to the state, and control the schools. As we saw above, after the split from the Netherlands in 1830, the state of Belgium emerged as an amalgam of a French speaking Wallonia and a Flemish/Dutch speaking Flanders.

When the Dutch took over in 1815 (Napoleon's reign was over; both France and England favoured the formation of The Kingdom of the Netherlands for their own safety concerns and never consulted the Wallonians or the Flemish), most villages had *volks* schools. Here, pious young ladies taught catechism, the alphabet and elementary calculation while most of the timetable was covered with spinning, knitting and lace making. In the summer the schools were empty because the children were busy working the land with their parents. Thus, until 1836, almost all education was in the hands of the clergy. In this chapter we only deal with Flanders, where, after the 1830s, political animosity soon proliferated between the Catholic right and the anti-clerical liberals; "education especially became subject of a bitter ideological battle" (Deschout 1979, 16).

Victor, born in 1845, spent most of his adolescent years in his father's carpenter's shop. In 1871 he entered the Van Dale congregation, established in 1766 by the Flemish priest, Joseph Van Dale (1716–1781), ratified by the bishop and municipal magistrates of Kortrijk and by Empress Maria Theresia (1717–1780), then ruler of the Austrian Netherlands. Just like the Oblate congregation, the Van Dale congregation's goal was teaching (catechism) to poor children. In addition they took it upon themselves to care for the sick and for the orphans.[218] From Brother Lucien's letter (April 5, 2001) to Paul Callens we know that Victor served in the infirmary and that he had been teaching class, "at that time a teacher's certificate was not required."

We also saw above that in May 1874 Leonard was among the recruits who followed bishop Grandin to Canada. Four years later, in 1878, Mgr. Grandin was back in Europe. Among others, he went to Belgium, fulfilling, according to Lepage (1954, 314), the wish of his Belgian novice master Vandenberghe to go there. And to recruit there? That is apparent from the undated letter (cited in Lepage 1954, 319) Bishop Grandin wrote to Bishop P.-L. Goossens of Malines (Mechelen):

I want Belgian missionaries because St. François Xavier appreciated them and so do I. For us they have the advantage that they can speak Flemish and that is why they easily learn English as well.[219]

The bishop of Malines did not bother to reply. On November 18 Bishop Grandin visited, or rather, tried to visit the bishop of Bruges, but was not received by him. Nor did this bishop grant him any cooperation, such as permission to talk/recruit among seminarists. That evening, November 18, Bishop Grandin was the guest of M. de Bethune, benefactor of the Van Dale congregation, who made him forget the "grace" of the Bruges bishop (Lepage 1954, 316).[220]

It must have been around the 18th that Bishop Grandin was the guest of the Van Dale Brothers in Kortrijk as well. He was there to "greet brother Jean Berchmans" (Follens 1983, 42). Bishop Grandin undoubtedly came also to recruit Victor Van Tighem/Van Dale Brother Joannes Berchmans. Mgr. J.J. Faict of Bruges (1864–1895), though did not give the Canadian bishop permission to take Victor along. This changed after Victor got himself into trouble with the law. Follens (1983, 42–3) elaborates about what happened to Victor after Grandin's 1878 visit:

▶ *Reverend Father Van Dale, 1716–1781.*
Collection Paul Callens

After a suspicious court case Jean Berchmans was sentenced to 2 years because of *zedenfeiten* [indecent offences]. Kortrijk's Liberals would have bribed a witness in order to take charge of the elementary school of the Van Dale Brothers. However in 1880 the same Jean Berchmans emerged in Alberta (Canada), where he, at his brother's side, to the end of his life, was active in missioning, dressing and living as a member of the Brothers Van Dale.

In more than one regard we are dealing with a dubious reference. Victor did not "emerge" in Alberta in 1880, but only in 1886. As we will see, Victor did not end up in prison around the years 1878–80 but only around 1884–85. Victor did not work much "at his brother's side," as both brothers generally toiled about one hundred kilometres or more apart from each other. And, Victor did not stay in Alberta to the end of his life. In 1929 he moved back to Kortrijk where he died in 1940. In one regard Follens is right, Victor did dress as a Van Dale Brother, at least as some kind of a Brother, this despite his superior's wish that he would not "pose outwardly" as a member of the Van Dale congregation.

That Victor was not sentenced around 1880 is also apparent from the letter (December 22, 1885) by Bishop Faict of Bruges to the Very Reverend Deacon Roets of Kortrijk. In it he wrote that Brother Johannes [Victor] had communicated his intention to him to move on to the bishopric of St. Albert. Bishop Faict stated that he was completely in accord with Brother Joannes' request, adding:

He also asked me that I would neither dismiss him from his vows, nor lay him off from his congregation. I will certainly not do that and will regard his vows of Purity and Poverty as valid and lasting. However, I would appreciate it if he refrains from posing outwardly as a member of this Congregation. I ask you to communicate this to him at the right moment.[221]

Perhaps Deacon Roets of Kortrijk never communicated the bishop's wish with regard to Brother Joannes' outfit. Maybe he did, but then, how could Victor have lived, at that time, as a pure and poor Brother without being dressed as one? In any case, the impression we got from reading Victor's own account of what had led to his sentence is, see above his letter of January 24, 1886 to Leonard, is that he had turned himself into a target by over-acting as a moral knight.

Follens' text, mentioned above, does raise the question how and why the liberals could have been seizing a school in 1881 by putting one Brother in jail? It was not Victor's imprisonment (c. 1884–85, even if that had taken place earlier) that put the Van Dale school in liberal hands, but the enforcement in 1881 of the much maligned 1879 Van Humbeek Act, which the Flemish referred to as the *Ongelukswet* (Law of Misfortune).

As said, school education in the early days of the State of Belgium was in the hands of the clergy. In the larger, liberal cities, municipalities had taken it upon themselves to free municipal education from its confessional character, but in rural areas education was still entirely of a confessional character (Witte *et al.* 1993, 95). "Spinning" and "poor" schools were turned into elementary schools but their curriculum was geared towards imbuing children with the specifics of the catechism, prayer, and work. "Learning" (meaning calculus or the alphabet) took up only about one hour per day – so many youngsters remained illiterate.

The 1879 Act on Elementary Education, better known as the "Act of Misfortune," overhauled the 1842 Act and changed all this (Mattelaer 2002, 244). From 1879 on, municipal autonomy with regard to education was restricted in favour of the state; each municipality was to have at least one official state school; the state would appoint state-licensed teachers, and municipalities were no longer allowed to subsidize "free" schools led by Catholic clergy. Education was to become neutral; priests could only teach outside curriculum hours and only on the parents' request. Furthermore, subjects such as geography, history, drawing, and sciences became required parts of the curriculum. School inspection was established and school committees were formed (Lermyte 1989, 195).

The 'Act of Misfortune' made Belgian bishops order their pastors to establish 'free' schools. In the churches prayers were offered: "Lord, free us from Godless schools and religiousless teachers" (Delmotte 2001, 386). It meant that parents who continued sending their children to the municipal schools and teachers (who continued teaching there), no longer could be absolved from their sins, or worse, risked being excommunicated. In other words, the Catholics "sabotaged the proper implementation of Van Humbeek's 'Act of Misfortune' by insisting that Catholic parents (under pain of excommunication) should boycott the state system and attend only the Catholic free-school system" (Mallinson 1970, 79).[222]

Ensuing Royal Decrees ordered municipalities to confiscate the buildings of certain foundations, among them the one of the Van Dale congregation. By Royal Decree of April 12, 1880, Kortrijk was ordered to establish one girls' and two boys' schools and transfer the management of the existing free schools to the city. This decree was ignored by the Catholic mayor of Kortrijk, Henri Nolf, who did nothing to enforce it. His attitude counteracted attempts of the liberal provincial governor Heyvaert and made the minister of Justice, Bara, shout during a parliamentary session that Kortrijk had the most appalling administration of the country (Mattelaer 2002, 244).

De Pauw (1953, 76–7) argues that complete secularization, and supreme jurisdiction over the education system by a secular government, had set in and that influence of Freemasons' lodges was behind the policies of the Liberals. Already in 1850, De Pauw argues, the Grand Orient had come out with the slogan "All priests out of the school." De Pauw neither mentions the generally dire educational level of free schools before 1879, nor the attempts of the church from then on to thwart neutral education. De Pauw somehow fails to acknowledge the Freemasons' beneficial influence on Belgian education level.

All in all, after 1879 the mood at the educational stage had soured seriously and that was just the scene Victor found himself in while caring for the sick and teaching at a Van Dale school. A brochure from that time states that the Van Dale school was a Sunday School for adults and youngsters and shows the curriculum of the Day School: 1 or 2 hours education; in the afternoon: weaving.

By the end of August 1881, appeals to the courts were exhausted and the police were ordered to evict the inhabitants of a few convent schools. The Van Dale Brothers were expelled from their premises at the Lange Steenstraat. The *Gazette van Kortrijk* of September 3, 1881 elaborately reported on this sad affair. A handwritten account, in Dutch, of which the last line explains, in French, that it is *"d'après une relation de l'époque chez Baron Joseph de Bethune"* follows below in English translation. It closely corresponds with the 1881 *Gazette* articles on the expulsion of the Brothers and provides a vivid image of the social unrest, the pompous and the pious though defiant ambience of the time.

Expulsion of the Van Dale Brothers 1881[223]

The Holy Sacrament is being transferred away. After the Gent Court of Appeal had decided that the house of the Van Dale Brothers was to be confiscated and belonged to the city, one feared for sudden expulsion. In order to avoid desecration, the Reverend Deacon Mr. Vandeputte will carry the Holy Sacrament to the St. Maarten's Church.

It was by the end of August 1881, about 3 o'clock, that the Reverend Deacon and all of his priests arrived, accompanied by many good people, among other the most notable families of the town: Bethune, Vercruijsse, Goethals, Nolf, Demulié, Debaudt, etc., etc., all accompanying the Holy Sacrament with torches. It was a touching, heartbreaking ceremony: our Dear Lord, who gives life to and conducts everything, who possesses and hands out all goods and riches, being carried out of His house, His residence, out of fear of expulsion. Everyone was subdued and understood the importance of the ceremony. The eyes became wet and tears dripped down the cheeks. The procession passed the big door on the Lange Steenstraat, the Korte Steenstraat, to the church, where Benediction with the Holy [Sacrament] was given. Only crying and sobbing was heard. The Reverend Mr. Deacon, the old grey man, cried in such way that it could be heard throughout the church. There was sadness, love and compassion.

Moving of the school fixtures and furniture. A few youngsters offered to move everything. It happened on Monday, a few days before the expulsion of the Brothers. They worked enthusiastically and courageously. All tried to make the most of it. Some put the stuff outside near the graveyard, others loaded it on wagons and still others brought it to the indicated place. Over one hundred school desks, school fixtures, cupboards, bed linens etc. etc, everything was enthusiastically brought outside and taken away. At noon everything was done. The youngsters really took pleasure in their work.

Expulsion of the Brothers in September 1881. Désiré Deveugele, bailiff, former student of the Van Dale Brothers, came about 7 a.m. with two of the best men of the town (many did not want to go along), Sissen Palto and his friend. The bailiff would have loved to cut it short, because he seemed not to feel at ease. In front of the house already many people had gathered and this crowd kept increasing. The Brothers had not yet finished drinking their coffee and one wanted to take away their table. Brother Modest said, "I will have breakfast first." In the meantime it was pointed out to Deveugele how scandalous his performance was and how he had enjoyed the Brothers' benefactions. One started to carry to the street the few furniture pieces left in the house while the crowd jeered and booed.

Sissen Palto was a bit too quick picking up the stove; he dropped it, screaming that he had burnt his hands. When all the furniture was in the street, it was the Brothers' turn, starting with Br. Director who was the first to be led to the street by the bailiff. Then Br. Modest, carrying the big cross from the lounge, appeared at the door and the crowd jeered, yelled at the bailiff who looked more dead than alive. This scene was repeated every time he appeared in the door opening with a Brother until it was clear that all of the Brothers were on the street and they went in procession, cross in front, to their new residence that was granted them as refuge by the charitable Goethals family. The crowd stayed for a long time in front of the door of the Old Monastery in order to see the bailiff leave. But he did not dare to leave before the police came. A summons was drawn up and a few notable young men were condemned to serve time in prison. Because of the Committee they were treated as the vilest villains.

The house in the Lekkerbeetstraat could not house all of the Brothers. Some had to sleep in Parkel's house near the Bossepoortjes, one of the worst corners of the town, and that is where they had to keep school, too. Judge how they were accommodated: next to the door and right across were two bad inns. Enough said. Once in a while big stones were thrown at their door. A bit further down the street 40 to 50 families lived. They were of the meanest kind. It was there where the Brothers had to keep school and had to eat, in the Lekkerbeetstraat. They had to go to sleep at 9 p.m. in Parkel's house and leave there at 4 a.m. Six Brothers made these walks for over four years, until, in October 1885, when they moved into the Kring House.

There the Brothers have a spacious and healthy residence with nice and big classrooms, a garden and a playground for the pupils. From their house they can go to church, without having to walk through a street. Thank God a thousand times! After this tempest, things calmed down; after the thunder, it is now quiet. God allowed these things to reward the Brothers afterwards. In 1881 the Brothers had only three institutions with 22 Brothers and 600 pupils. In Kortrijk they had about 400 pupils. Now, in 1895, they have nine houses with 50 Brothers and 2,200 pupils. In Kortrijk they now have 1000 pupils.

That the Van Dale Brothers may grow and flourish and extend their branches wide and afar, benefiting the good that God expects them to do.

(Told by a contemporary of that period, Baron J. de Bethune).[224]

[Added at the base of this page:]

"The youngsters that were in prison were Henri Deblock, Victor Moulaert, Edm. Vacquet, Abel Delmotte, L. Raepsaet, Victor Buch, and Jerome Delmotte (I doubt the last one)."

In the following election, in 1884, the Liberals were defeated and subsequently the maligned 1879 Act was amended. Municipalities could subsidize "free" schools again and religious instruction was left intact. Already in 1889 the bishops regulated that the curricula contain more "learning." So, subjects as catechism, reading, language, calculus, some geography

De Grote Kring ca. 1930. In de hoek het klooster van de Broeders Van Dale.

▶ c. 1930: "De Groote Kring:" Mother House Brothers Van Dale.
Courtesy Dr. E. Van Hoonacker (1986, ph. 157)

and French emerged (De Mattelaer 222, 260). After all we may conclude that in hindsight this unfortunate interlude was a blessing to the educational standard for all Catholics.

However, by 1884 Victor found himself in prison. As over the years and during World Wars I and II, Kortrijk's courthouse was bombed and burned time and again, we did not succeed in finding any papers related to his case. The last bombing of Kortrijk occurred on July 21, 1944. "Friendly fire" by the English killed 172 inhabitants of Kortrijk, wounded hundreds of people and hit the east, the west and then the centre of the city.

Fortunately, from letters in the Van Tighem Family Archives we know that from the time Leonard had left, Victor had kept in touch with him. Victor also kept in touch with him during the time he served in prison. In that period he did not write about his whereabouts, just gave vague hints. Only after his release from prison while hiding out in a Trappist Abbey and already having secured and organized his journey to Canada, only then Victor informed Leonard that he was going to join him. In 1886 the passengers' list of the Steam Ship *Belgenland* registered the badly battered Van Dale Brother, Jean Berchmans, as: "Van Tighem V., 40 years. From Kortrijk. Monk."[225]

BY THE TIME Victor arrived in Southern Alberta, its Indian population was fenced in on reserves from 1877 onwards. The Indians were more or less forced to stay there; due to an arbitrary pass system that Indian agents had developed, people could not just leave their reserve. While Leonard had witnessed the hanging of an Indian in Saskatchewan who had resorted to eating his family, an 1879 letter by John Dennis, Deputy of the Minister of the Interior, stated that "the Indians [in Alberta] were starving," adding that rations had to be doled and that arrangements for farm instructors had to be made.[226] Then, in 1883, the railway, whose arrival the bishop had dreaded so much, was completed and settlers, most of them non-Catholic and English-speaking, were pouring in.[227] In their trail a school fight steam-rolled along.

With regard to legislation, the rights of Catholics to separate schools, recognized by Section 93 of the 1867 British North America Act, were recognized as well in the 1875 Northwest Territories Act. An appointed council of five members could pass ordinances, but at that time a taxation system did not yet exist and responsibility for education was still, as it had been in Belgium, entirely in the hands of the clergy.

In 1884 an "Ordinance Providing for the Organization of Schools in the North-West Territories" was passed, ensuring the maintenance of the educational rights of the Roman Catholics. This ordinance also provided for coterminous public and separate school districts and a Board of Education consisting of six Protestants and six Catholics. The ordinance provided for Catholics that books, maps and globes were subject to approval by the competent religious authority. However, ensuing amendments to this ordinance eroded denominational power: for example, religious instruction was moved to the last hour of the afternoon.

From 1887 on, when Victor appeared as an assistant on the educational stage of (the District of) Alberta, the Board of Education consisted of five Protestants and three Catholics; steps were taken to provide for uniform inspection and teachers who failed an exam had to attend a Normal School administered by lay and Protestant teachers.

In 1891 the authority to licence teachers and to appoint inspectors came in the hands of the Lieutenant-Governor in Council and, in Catholic eyes "doubtful ordinances" were passed. Uniform teacher training, certification inspection, textbooks and examination standards were demanded from all schools which received government aid.

In 1892 the Board of Education was abolished and education was placed in the hands of the Lieutenant-Governor-in-Council. Only an Educational Council of four members, two Catholics and two Protestants, was left. Its members could advise but not vote. "Religious instruction might be given during the last half-hour, if the Board of Trustees so directed and the parents or guardians offered no obstruction. English became the compulsory language of instruction. [...]

In 1901 the Council of Public Instruction was abolished and its duties and powers were handed over to a Commissioner who was a member of the government. The final stroke in abolishing denominational schools was dealt" (Hochstein 1953, 31–2).

Victor had left behind the Belgian educational system, which in 1884 recovered from governmental control. Conversely, upon his arrival in southern Alberta, he could witness year after year, ordinance after ordinance, how the government seized the system.[228]

Although said educational and legal struggles in Canada must have come across as familiar to Victor, the specifics of the school fight hardly emerge in his diary. Actually, after having served a number of years as an assistant teacher, he was laid off in that capacity after an Indian agent complained about his teaching skills. Victor never mentioned it in his diary, instead he just grumbled about having to feed his young students, who did not come to school often enough, and about there being so few pupils and so on. Not to mention the fact that they, his pupils, did not convert quickly enough for his liking. In his time, schooling, after all, was in the first place a strategy to convert, not to teach children.

In the late nineteenth century one of the features of schooling was that so many pupils died. They died at his school in Brocket and they died at the Dunbow School for which he recruited students. His own niece, Marie, Joseph's older sister, who was sent to a convent school in Belgium, also died at a young age. Poor Marie once promised her dying father never to leave Rosalie Julie, her stepmother. After the death of the latter, she just lived to learn to write overly polite letters in French. Compared with the letters she wrote in her own language, when still living at home, it is as if her soul had already left before her poor body gave out. Neither Leonard nor Victor mention her death in their diaries or their letters, let alone the untimely death of their numerous other little nieces and nephews. In their old as well as in their new world, the death of (school) children and babies was just a fact of life.

VICTOR STARTS HIS diary with a description of his departure from Belgium in 1886, his journey across the ocean, his arrival in New York, the wonders of that town, his stay in Lachine, Canada, where one still remembered his brother Leonard and where he is shown Leonard's 1874 woodcarvings. He then travelled by train to Winnipeg and notices a pile of buffalo carcasses of about 30 m³. Upon leaving Winnipeg he catches sight of "poor savages," crawling out of their tents. Victor did not connect the two images that indicated how the European expansion had deprived the native inhabitants of their staple livelihood, the buffalo. He just observed and scribbled down what he saw.

From Winnipeg he travelled to Calgary by train. In 1886 the last leg of his trip, from Calgary to Macleod, still had to be covered by horse and wagon, which took him eight days. His account of this trip provides a marvellous description of 1886 Albertan travel and landscape. About his reception at his brother's MacLeod parish Victor notes that Leonard seemed to have forgotten his mother tongue. Whether he perceived that Leonard was erecting some sort of social/emotional barrier by speaking French to him, because of his lowly status of ex-convict/lay-Brother, he does not mention it.²²⁹ Maybe he felt that he deserved it. He may even have felt relieved to be left alone the next day, to be in an environment where nobody knew about him and where he could reinvent himself. Then, after a stay of few months in MacLeod, bishop Grandin decided to assign Victor to the Peigan mission where he was to serve as an assistant-teacher, cook and gardener.

From the diary it appears that Victor in particular enjoyed his employment as gardener and was not very appreciative that others, who were in dire need of the fruits of his gardening, sometimes helped themselves to it uninvited. Victor scribbled a few times "Thieves" between the lines of his diary.

Carter (1990, 209ff.) writes about the time Victor was robbed occasionally of his harvest:

> In 1889 Hayter Reed announced that one of the most potent reasons for insisting that Indians farm their land in severalty was the new "new approved system of farming."

This new system came down to Indians being supposed to farm with hoes, rakes, and sickles, to seed by hand, to harvest with scythes, to raise cows for household purposes. Indians were supposed to form self-contained units and were not supposed to compete on the market. The policy came from Reed's opinion that primitives were not supposed to partake in exchange-economy.

It is hard to understand that Victor did not empathize with the dire situation the "thieves" were in: starvation. As we saw, Witte *et al.* (1993, 70) argue that in Belgium, poverty was seen as "work of nature, so intended by God." Victor will have accepted the effects of poverty – theft, child mortality, disease, alcoholism, starvation and so on – as the normal course of events. In general people don't elaborate on circumstances, occurrences, events or facts of life, that are considered normal.

In Victor's time a certain Oblate, "G." (1897, 399), wrote that due to the disappearance of the buffalo, the government handed out food rations twice a week. "G." notes that he heard several priests complain that this would demoralize the "aboriginals." In Victor's own school biscuits were handed out to the young pupils, to his dismay. Victor profiles himself as a frugal Brother. He will have disliked the idea that his mission was a charge of the diocese and not financially successful, as his brother Leonard's parish was. From his letter of April 7, 1889 to a fellow Brother in Belgium, we get the impression that he shared "G's" view.

Then, in the depth of his loneliness he cursed the Indians, not when they took his vegetables and fruits, but when they did not show up in church and he had to spend Christmas all by himself. Or was he rather cursing his loneliness? Still, over time things changed. Victor no longer referred to the Peigan as "savages," but started to write about "Indians." He even mentioned individuals by their names. Of course he mostly wrote about people who were baptized or made Holy Communion. A number of them were the same people mentioned on an 1897 bill addressed to Bishop Legal: Many Guns worked thirty-three days for $33, Henri Potts, Black Eye and Scott and others were employed as freighters, Ben Big Plume dug potholes for seventy-five cents per day, Jo Manyan delivered five loads of lumber and Joe Smith freighted ½ load of lumber for three dollars.[230] When the Peigan Joe Smith died, Victor eulogized him as "a best friend."

After a good number of years Victor felt at home at the Peigan reserve. Still, in 1912, he was transferred to the Blood reserve. A 1913 photo that emerged from a drawer of Callens' aunt Maria back in Belgium shows that in that year he helped Father Riou build a church on the Sarcee reserve (now called Tsuu T'ina nation) near Calgary. From Oblate codices we know that he worked often as an itinerant carpenter. In 1917, in the year Leonard died, Victor was transferred back and remained with the Peigan until 1929. He then went back to Belgium and lived eleven more years among his fellow Van Dale Brothers, enlivening their evenings by telling "sparkling" tales. He kept in touch with his nephew Joseph and his wife in Strathmore. When he no longer could keep up a correspondence, a fellow Van Dale Brother took over. These letters emerged from the Van Tighem Family Archives in Calgary and are added to the postscript that follows Victor's diary. They render a glorious impression of his last years among a throng of fellow Van Dale Brothers and his extended family.

We will see that here and there is some confusion whether Victor was an Oblate Brother or not. According to an Oblate brochure handed out in Belgium between 1899 to 1910, cited in Follens (1983, 61–2), Brothers (it does not say Oblate or Van Dale) are the ones who "build a hut for the priest, feed him, clothe him, by hunting, fishing or agriculture, they provide him with schools and chapels, they teach the savages all kinds of trades and are teachers and catechists."

As for the diary's style, Victor drily observes on the doings, comings and goings of the many Oblate Fathers using his premises as a stopover. He was supposed to submit to both the will of God and of bishop Grandin and did so, sometimes tongue in cheek. Victor wrote in beautiful Flemish-Dutch with only a few flaws; he often omitted to add a 't' when using a verb in the third person (Dutch language requires that), and often omitted an 'n' where there should be one if a noun was used in plural. He also barely used periods after a sentence, just threaded them together with commas. In the trans-lation of his diary the punctuation and the use of capitals is brought up to current standards. It will be noticed that in the beginning he describes the landscape in his own terminology, writing about meadows instead of prairies. Over time we see that Victor learned about the landscape and also about the people: meadows become prairies and "savages" become Indians and even "best friends." As far as we know there is one exception. On a 1913 postcard to family in Belgium he still wrote "savages;" perhaps in the line of duty – stressing the need for help. After a while Victor's use of his own, Flemish-Dutch language slips somewhat; we see English and French words begin to sneak in – these we left as they occur, in italics.

We only have a few samples of Victor's writing in English, the 1930's letters to the widow of his nephew Joseph. They show that Victor, in the forty-three years he had spent in Alberta, apparently had not really become acquainted with written English language. They also show that he had not integrated nearly as well with the mainstream (immigrant) culture as with the (ab)original people of the area where he spent nearly half of his life.

1▸ Cover of Victor's diary.
Photo Luc Neyt

2▸ Victor's Diary, page 1.
Photo Luc Neyt

③·❹ Victor's diary, "Short description of my journey and adventures in North America"

[ON NOVEMBER 1, 1996, Brother Lucien, Van Dale Brother at Kortrijk, Belgium, sent Paul Callens a copy of Victor Van Tighem/Brother John Berchmans' handwritten diary. Brother Lucien (2001) added the following note about Brother John's departure for Canada:]

At his own request Brother John left for the St. Paul's Macleod Mission on the Peigan Reserve in Alberta to be with the Blackfoot Indians. For him, the mission was not as foreign as his brother who was younger than him by six years, Father Leonard Van Tighem, an Oblate missionary, who had already worked for twelve years in that area. Years earlier, in 1878, Mgr. Grandin, an Oblate and the mission bishop for Alberta, had visited us at our main monastery, De Kring, in Belgium with the idea of involving the Van Dale Brothers in his missionary efforts. As the bishopric did not consent (after all, we are a diocese with just one congregation) this request could not be granted. The bishop, however, did grant the request of Brother John Berchmans to join his brother in Alberta.[231]

Brother Lucien.

G.Z.J.C. + 1886
Short Description of My Journey and Adventures in North America

After tearfully bidding farewell to my Venerable Father Superior and fellow Brothers in Belgium and to my dear family in Meulebeke, I departed full of courage and with joy in my heart.

I left my homeland on the **26th of February** and boarded the steamship *Belgenland* on Saturday, February 27th in Antwerp. The Captain's name was Beynon, (Red Star Line Company).[232]

The large, beautiful steamship has about 230 passengers. In second class there are only about thirty of us, mostly Germans, but I soon find a good Flemish companion, a fellow from Thienen in the Province of Brabant. We stay in the same cabin; we have one clean and warm bed, a good, well-provided table, and a beautiful, well-furnished lounge for entertainment. We walk a lot on the deck in order to observe the miracles of the sea, which I won't describe, as you should see them for yourself and then can exclaim: "How wonderful is God's work!"

For five or six days I suffered, just as the others did, from seasickness; though painful, it is not dangerous. On the fifth day we had to stay inside because of rough weather; waves rolled over the upper deck and at night we nearly rolled out of bed, but I was not afraid and trusted in God and Mary, the Star of the Sea!

After sailing for 13 days we landed safe and sound in New York on Thursday, **March 11th**, at 6 p.m. After the customs officers had checked through our suitcases and travel bags, my travel companion and I went to a hotel where we, after thanking God for our safe journey, rested from our long, tiring journey. The next day I sent the first tidings of my so far safe trip to my dear fellow Brothers in Kortrijk and to my dear family. My dear Flemish companion says goodbye with tears in his eyes and departs for Chicago. Poor fellow, he can hardly speak or understand French.[233]

In a *voiture* I go to the station, which is three miles away. Once underway, we, the *voiture* and the horses included, are ferried by steamboat across a big lake. This first trip cost 6 dollars (30 frs). The train for Montreal only leaves at 6:30 p.m. For the entire day I stroll through New York, the biggest city in America. Everywhere are long, straight and broad streets. The houses, generally of white or red bricks, have six to eight stories and flat roofs. Some of the houses have entranceways with twelve or more beautiful, wide steps with sculptured stone balustrades. There are also many beautiful churches.

The Cathedral is a masterwork of construction, entirely of white stone (Gothic style). I never saw anything more beautiful: the painted windows, altars, white marble pulpits, everything so beautiful. The churches here have no chairs, but beautiful pews for kneeling or sitting. The iron roads here are above the streets and the trains are driven above people's heads. The *voitures*, the *Americains* continue to fill up the streets. You also see all kinds of people here: brown, black, Chinese etc., etc.

I leave for Montreal: how clean and comfortable are the trains in America! Large cars with 40 or 50 seats, beautiful benches painted red, good ventilation, a beautiful dining room, beds, fresh water, etc., etc.

I travel for the entire night and at dawn I see about two or three feet deep snow. I also see many small villages with just one simple, little church.

I arrive in Montreal at **9 a.m.** My suitcases and me are transported by a sleigh to the Reverend Oblate Father's and I am received like a child coming home. In the afternoon I have the pleasure of embracing Mgr. Grandin, receiving his blessings and having a lengthy conversation. His Highness is interested in our family situation, in the adventures on my trip and especially in the establishment of schools of our congregation in his widely extended bishopric of St. Albert. Mgr. reassures me and provides me with a good passport to get to my Reverend brother, who, he says, is already expecting me. I stay here five days and have a good rest. Montreal is quite a big city, but not as beautiful as New York. The Oblate Fathers have a beautiful Gothic church, dedicated to Saint Peter.

On **Sunday** from early morning until the afternoon and also during the evening service, the church was full of believers who very devoutly prayed and many H. Communions were administered as well. All the instructions and the sermon were given in French. The Fathers also manage three Our Lady congregations. In the one for the youngsters, held in the basement of the church, about 400 attended.[234] I find this consoling because I never thought that I would encounter so much religion in Canada! On Sunday I visit the Brothers of Charity of the Gent Institute.[235] They, my fellow country-men, manage a kind of reform school where youngsters of all walks of life are taught a trade. The Brothers already own several homes in America and get many Brothers among the good Canadian youngsters.

Monday in the afternoon I visit with a Father my friend Charles Devriendt from Pittem, in the novitiate of Lachine. The institute, located along the big St. Laurence, is built of blue stone and is very large. They have cows and horses. There are about 50 novices, scholastics and Brothers. On Wednesday two of them confirmed their vows; it was a solemn ceremony. I stayed here for two days. Brother De Vriendt was very happy. We spoke in our beloved mother tongue. I also saw several of my brothers' works here, among others some beautiful Gothic seats in the *capittel*. The Reverend Father Boisramé (superior) still praises him. On Wednesday morning a Brother brings me by sleigh to the station, the snow is about four or five feet deep, but it is not very cold.

In Montreal, back with the Fathers, I was so fortunate to receive bless-ings from and speak with Mgr. Taché, Archbishop of St Boniface and of the Oblate order. At noon we eat together. His Highness is very modest and full of goodness.

Thursday, March 18th. I continue my journey unto Ottawa, the capital of Canada. Just like in Montreal, many houses here are made of wood; how-ever, the Parliament Buildings, the cathedral and the college are beautiful and big. I get on a *voiture* and one takes me to a big college or university, managed by the Reverend Oblate Fathers. I have an evening meal here and after talking a bit with some of the Reverend Fathers a Brother brings me to the scholasticat, 2 miles out of town. Beautiful gardens, woods and mountains surround this beautiful, blue stone institute. Father Van Laar, a Fleming from Limburg, is the first one I meet.[236] While we chat in our mother tongue, Father Naessens, my former student, drops by and happily embraces me. I also find Brother Capelle from Ardoye, here the cook, and Jules Coucke of Kortrijk, gardener for the institute and also my former stu-dent. The last one mentioned is married to a Canadian woman and already has two children. They are all doing very well here and would not like to return to Belgium.

The next day **March 19th,** St. Joseph's Day and patron feast for the Reverend Father-Superior of the institute: big celebration! Solemn Holy Mass, music and big dinner! Then the scholastic students serenade their Reverend Superior. After having toured the institute, my friend Naessens brings me to the college. We tour the most important streets, places and buildings in the city, especially the main church. Then I bid farewell to the Reverend Fathers and we went to the station. My former student Naessens embraced me, clasped my hand and we said farewell and that we hoped to see each other again in the northwest.

After leaving Ottawa, I drive for three days and nights, always passing by woods, rocks, mountains, etc., etc. Every hour we encounter a small railway station and sometimes three or four small wooden houses. They are the only ones seen here during this long journey, apart from a few new cities that have started to grow since the construction of the iron road. In general the woods consist of spruce and leafy trees. There aren't big trees, they grow much too close to each other, many are dried out, splintered or half-burned. I am told that this is caused by thunder. I don't see any special animals or birds, at times just a herd of cows, oxen or horses and buffalo skeletons, sometimes piled up unto 30 square meters. A few years ago these areas were full of buffalo, now there are only a few or none left.[237] For a long while I am in the company of a Reverend Jesuit Father, a missionary from Port Arthur. The good Father gives me some souvenirs; among them

▶ *Father Albert Naessens.*
Van Tighem Family
Archives

some photographs of the most important scenic points and buildings in Montreal and Ottawa.

On **Monday, March 22nd** I arrive in Winnipeg, thank God, safe and sound, though very tired. Four or five years ago this city only numbered 300 inhabitants and now there are already 8 000. Apart from a few special buildings, most houses are constructed of wood. The snow here has nearly melted away; it is already warm but the streets are dirty. Again I will take a break at the Reverend Oblate Fathers, who receive me very well. There are only two and both know my brother Leonard very well. In Lachine they were at the Novitiate at the same time. The church is dedicated to Our Lady, and was only built recently, entirely of yellow stone. The Jesuit Fathers of the St. Boniface College preach at a retreat for the men. I attend the instructions but the sermons and the instructions are all given in English.

On **Friday** I continue on my journey, driving for two days and nights past meadows, where no branches or trees are to be seen. I am in the company of two Grey Nuns who are also on their way to the missions. On Saturday we see the first tents of the savages.[238] They are a few poles put together and covered with linen or hides; what poor dwellings! The savages are crawling out. How grubby and dirty are they. The men cannot be distinguished from the women. They have brown skins, long hairs and are wrapped in a blanket or piece of rug. Unhappy in body and soul! Far away we also see the snow covered Rocky Mountains.

Sunday the 28th I arrive in Calgary. The Sisters and I are brought to the mission. The well-known Father Lacombe is busy preaching in English. After High Mass he embraces me. Mgr. Grandin had advised him of my arrival. After mass two savages are baptized and one pair is married. The Fathers read the marriage mass and serve food. The savages sit flat on the floor, are nice and yet decently dressed; after dinner they smoke a good pipe.[239] Imagine how I must have been watching this. Father Lacombe wants me to take a good rest before I leave for Macleod, to my brother. When the Fathers arrived there about eight years ago, there were nothing than savages and now there are about 800 inhabitants but many of them Protestants. There are three temples. The Fathers have a wooden church. The altar, the tabernacle and Stations of the Cross are made by my brother. I also see a few artifacts that I sent to the mission. Since one year they also have a flourishing school, managed by the Sisters.

On **Wednesday, March 31st,** I continue on my journey, from now on no more iron road! A caravan of seven carts, two wagons and fifteen horses. We travel for eight days, always through meadows, mountain up and mountain down, one after the other.[240] In many places the dry grass is two to three feet high and provides the horses with their necessary food. We have to ford seven or eight rivers, no bridges. Sometimes we have to unload the carts and work half a day to get across. At night we sleep in tents and make a good fire to keep us warm and to cook our food and drinks. We shoot many *canards*, which, when fried, taste very good. On the third day of journey we see a fire in the meadows. In the evening the sight of it is too bad. On the last day it even comes towards us. Fortunately the road provides a firebreak, it is extinguished right in front of our feet, hundreds of miles are now covered in black ash.[241] It is said that such fires occur here often. One match thrown onto the grass is enough to cause such a fire! We see many cows in the meadows, but mainly horses and here and there a farm with some tilled land.

Wednesday, April 7th. I arrive happily though burned completely red by the sun at my brother's in MacLeod. We embrace, shake hands and are hardly able to utter a word. My brother is in good condition and healthy and has not changed much in the twelve years since we last saw one another. We enter the chapel and thank God for my safe trip. After that we ask each other a thousand questions regarding my fellow Brothers, our family and fatherland, my journey, etc., etc. We chat until late into the night, but in French. Leonard has about forgotten his mother tongue. The next day I am pleased for the first time in my life to serve his mass and receive Holy Communion from him. We are both touched. We dedicate mass and Communion to our dear deceased parents.

In the morning Leonard departs by *voiture* for Pincher Creek, 30 miles from Macleod, to administer the holy sacraments to a 106 year-old elder and at the same time have the Catholics of that area observe their Easter duties. Leonard is building a church over there. So for a few days I am alone at the mission. The good Catholics take good care of me and once in a while the good Canadian soldiers keep me company. I am uplifted by these fine policemen; they come and pray in the chapel, go along the Stations of the Cross and sing and play the harmonium at all the religious services. My brother likes them very much. They helped him a lot with painting his chapel and carpet laying.

My suitcases will arrive on Friday and thank God, the ornaments I brought with me from Belgium, which I assumed to be very damaged during the long and difficult journey, are all in good shape. Even the flowers and the glasses of the lamp aren't damaged. I arrange them upstairs in the big living room, the good Catholics come to look at it, praise to a large extent the charity of the Flemish and promise to pray for the benefactors of their mission.

Sunday, Passion Sunday, being alone, we don't have mass. At night we pray the rosary, the litany of Our Lady and sing a few hymns. After that I briefly thank the good Catholics, the soldiers especially, for the help and cooperation shown to my brother. I encourage them, as good Catholics, to fulfill their duties in the midst of this savage and Protestant population, with the assurance that God will generously reward them, even for their temporary interests.

Wednesday, March 14th [This should be April 14]: Return of my brother. How bewildered he is by all the beautiful chasubles, albs, surplices, other linens, the lamp, flowers etc., etc. that he sees. Tears of gratitude flow from his eyes. Very much he would like to especially thank each benefactor individually. These ornaments, he says, will serve him well for the new church at Pincher Creek.

The next day he gets to work, making eight gothic windowsills for the said church. I take care of the kitchen, the chapel and assist my brother in every respect. We make sure that the chapel looks it best for Easter. And I must say that, though it does not contain anything expensive, compared to many churches in the civilized and Catholic areas, it should not stand aside. Leonard constructed and furnished his house himself: Gothic altar with tabernacle, beautiful Stations of the Cross, beautiful curtains and for the rest Belgian ornaments etc., etc. Thanks to the good Canadian soldiers, there is also a beautiful organ. The small but beautiful bell is a gift from Mgr. Taché, the Archbishop of St. Boniface, and he is of from the Oblate Order.

Easter. Solemn High Mass with vespers, lauds, beautiful singing. They prepared a few evenings beforehand, such feasts please the hearts of the missionary and good Catholics.

The Wednesday after Easter Leonard leaves for Lethbridge for a few days, that is thirty miles from here. He will have the Catholics in that area perform their Easter duties. A new town is being established there. Too bad there are no other priests around to perform these godly duties on a regular basis and teach the population (we pray to God that He will send labourers to his vineyard).

It is a May evening. A few Catholics and a few policemen as well asked me to give a few exercises in honour of Our Lady. I am pleased with such a proposal and at 7 p.m. start singing the *Magnificat*, the rosary, the litany of Our Lady and a few hymns.

That Sunday evening, the 2nd of May a great number of Maria's children are present. With a few words I encourage them to persist in attending the services in the month of May and in their devotion to Mary, especially by saying the Angelus prayer, for which the bell rings three times per day to remind them.

Tuesday, May 4th: Return of my brother from Lethbridge, pleased to see so many people attending the services in the month of May. During the month of May he solemnly performs the lauds every evening.

Wednesday, May 12th: Father Foisy arrives at the mission to replace Father Van Tighem, who leaves for a few days to work at his new church in Pincher Creek. During the month of May the meadows and woods on the riverbanks are full of beautiful flowers. Each night I pick them to decorate the chapel.

Monday, May 31st: Closure of the month of May. Mr. Noël of Lethbridge, who the other day sang during the godly service, solemnly leads the singing during lauds.

Between the first and the second of June at 2 a.m., Father Foisy and I notice that the Protestant church is engulfed in flames. There is no wind; the flames go straight up. In less than two hours nothing more than a pile of ash is left. The church with harmonium, pews, books, chandeliers, stoves, etc., etc., everything is destroyed. The general thought is that the fire was set on purpose. That morning Father Foisy and I prayed during mass for God to save us from such disasters.

This week I received several letters from Belgium, from my superior, my Brothers etc., etc. Thank God everything goes well and everyone is very healthy.

Sunday, June 6th: During High Mass I sing a *cantique* for the first time, in honour of the Sacred Heart of Jesus. That night we sing the vespers and laud, some people attend.

Wednesday, June 9th: We are given a splendid rug for the chapel and the big room upstairs. Mr. Girard obtained it for the mission thanks to a small *tombola*. It was purchased in Montreal.

June 12th: Father Foisy leaves again for Calgary.

June 13th: White Sunday. As my brother is still in Pincher Creek, no mass is said and still many Catholics come and pray for a bit in the chapel. For four days the weather is bad: rain, wind, sometimes some hail and thunder too.

Saturday, June 26th: The Reverend Father Leduc, new superior of the district, visits Macleod and surroundings. He is accompanied by Father Legal.

Sunday solemn High Mass. Father Leduc preaches and says that, as per an order from Mgr. Grandin, this mission will from now on be called the Mission of the Holy Cross. He also announces the Jubilee, granted to the Christian world in 1886 by our Holy Father Leo XIII. Father Leduc also talks about the establishment of a Catholic school in Macleod.

July 8, 9 and 10: At night spiritual exercises in preparation for the Jubilee. Father Leduc preaches the sermons.

On **Monday 12th** he leaves Macleod and returns to Calgary through Lethbridge. Father Legal builds a new house with a chapel and school on the *réserve des Peigans*.[242]

August, 1886: Monday, August 2nd, the solemn wedding of Mr. Lebel from Pincher Creek.[243] Once in a while we also have solemn children's baptisms.

Friday the 20th: Father van Tighem leaves for a few days to Lethbridge.

Sunday the 22nd: No mass in Macleod. At night rosary and hymns. During the month of August someone builds a nice wooden fence around a part of the area at our mission. Father van Tighem made the porch himself. Inside the fence I start to layout an English yard. The enormous amount of rocks causes a lot of work, but they come in handy for making borders along the roads and harden them. Father Legal sketches a portrait of the Macleod mission that is very successful.

On **September 15th** I stay with Father Legal for three weeks in order to help him with his new house and school (*réserve des Peigans*). This is a very beautiful area, also along the Oldman River, surrounded by mountains and valleys with a very splendid view of the Rocky Mountains. They seem to be only two or three miles from here, but are about fifty miles from here. There is a great number of savages here, living in small houses and forming kind of villages. They also have some land fenced in so have made some proficiency in growing potatoes. Father Legal baptizes there five or six children. The savages aren't converted, but have their children baptized. Many die young and are angels for heaven.[244]

Saturday, October 9th: We return to Macleod. The weather couldn't be worse: hail, snow, wind and bitter cold. Father van Tighem again spent some days in Lethbridge. He is now quite determined to build a church there as soon as possible. Father Van Tighem had already drawn up a good plan. Tendering started right away. God bless this work!

On Sunday, October 17th at 2:30 p.m. we had the solemn funeral of Sergeant Chassée who died in Lethbridge. The police music and a great number of soldiers form a splendid funeral procession. In such cases the chapel is much too small.

Thursday, December 9th: Mgr. Grandin arrives in Macleod accompanied by Father Doucet, Claude, Foisy and Brother Boone, my oldest and best friend.

On the 10th the annual retreat starts. Mgr. preaches the meditations. I am allowed to attend as many of the instructions as possible. Happy and blissful days! Mgr. leaves with my brother for Lethbridge where the contract for the construction of the church, a stone one, will be awarded. Mgr. has decided that I will remain forever with the Peigan.

On December 22nd I leave Macleod with Father Legal and Mr. Hébert, a Canadian who will teach the savages' children.

December 27th: We open the school. The first day we have 38 students, much more than we bargained for as a starter. The following days, despite the snow and bitter cold, we have an average of 25. That God grants them persistence!

On **January 28th**, 1887, from 9 o'clock in the morning until the afternoon there were wonderful and splendid natural phenomena: three suns and several rainbows fitted out in most beautiful colors.[245] These surpass any artificial fire works. "How wonderful are God's works." Let's keep glorifying His name. Since December 21 we have had constant snow and bitter cold with once in a while some awful blizzards. In this area no one remembers to have ever had such a lengthy and severe season. In the meadows many animals die of starvation and exposure to the cold. I had developed frostbite on my fingers, the mail couldn't be delivered, so not much news.

Snow and cold last until **March 12**.[246] Then a warm wind melts the snow away.

On **March 16th** the temperature is already sixty degrees above zero.[247] The student numbers have declined to about fifteen or twenty. Some, despite their rudeness and inattention, still make good progress with learning.

April 6th: Upon the occasion of Easter coming up, I go with Mr. Héber to Macleod for six days to help my brother and take a break together. On Easter day, solemn High Mass, vespers and lauds. On April 6th [12th?] we return to our savages.[248]

The **18th** we have a visit from Father Lacombe and my brother.

On the **23rd** Mr. Governor pays us a visit. All are content with the progress of our students. On this said date 48 were present. That same day we put up the new bell and for the first time made it ring out its tunes over the mountains and valleys. If only the savages would respond to the invitations and heead the voice of the missionary.

May 12th: Mr. Hébert and I go to Macleod and pick up Father Foisy, who will stay with us to study *Piednoir*.

Sunday **May 15th** at 11 o'clock our house starts to burn; fortunately we notice it in time. Without great effort or damage we were able to master it. We thank God with a *Te Deum*. Father Van Tighem, suffering from arthritis, leaves Macleod for four or five weeks and goes to Banff to take baths for his health.[249] Père Foisy, after having arrived here only ten days ago, leaves for Macleod to replace Father van Tighem. In the month of May we plant a garden in the empty space in front of our house. We surround it with a beautiful yard, which renders me some useful and pleasant pastime. Sowing and planting is my favourite work.

June 15th: The weather is rainy and warm, which is beneficial for our garden; potatoes, peas, etc., etc. look very promising.

Sunday night, **June 12th**: Father Legal baptizes a 30-year-old dying savage who dies the next day. Father Legal gives him a church funeral and also plants a cross on his grave. RIP.

July 12th: My brother has returned to Macleod. I visit him and stay about fourteen days to tidy up his yard and his house. During these days I also receive news from Belgium, from Mgr. Grandin, our holy Bishop, who visited my fellow Brothers as well as our family and served H. Mass. Everyone was very contented with such noble visit.

The 27th I return to the *réserve*.

Sunday the 14th [of August]: Harvest 1887. Solemn consecration of the new church at Lethbridge. Père Lacombe leads the ceremonies, assisted by the Pères Doucet, Legal and Van Tighem: a large crowd is present.

▸ *Cathechism in Piednoir.*
Collection Paul Callens

Wednesday, **17th**: Harvest. The Fathers Lacombe and Doucet come with Père Legal to the reserve and stay a few days in order to transcribe the prayers and catechism into *Piednoir.*

Sunday the **21st**: Solemn High Mass and short sermon by Father Lacombe, after which tea and tobacco are offered. The savages attend in large numbers.

Thursday, **September 1st**: Upon the occasion of Père Lacombe's visit, we treat the savages with a feast. Not necessary to mention that they are present in large numbers.

Friday, **September 2nd**: Departure of Père Lacombe and Doucet.

Saturday, **September 3rd**: For the second time in a few weeks I suffer from a very severe bellyache. I suffer horrible pains. God's Holy Will occurs always!

October 2nd: This last week we took from our yard and put into the cellar: 37 bags of potatoes, that is about 3000 kilograms; five bags of beets; four bags of turnips and five bags of carrots. For the first year, this was beyond all expectation. On a daily basis our school is attended by twenty or thirty. This is a good number, but their attention and progress is worse than the last few months. God forbid!

Tuesday, **October 18th**: Major MacGibbon, accompanied by Mr. Springett, visits the school and looks very satisfied with the progress of our little savages.[250] At present there are 36. Father Légal has been at the Blood *réserve* for a few days. The weather is still good.

Sunday, **October 23rd**: We have the first snow and for three days it is bitterly cold.

November 6th: For the second time we have High Mass. A few students and five or six savages are present. After mass Father Legal instructs in *Piednoir.*

November 9, 10, 11: Bazaar at Macleod: profit for the mission. The result is $750 net. It is beyond all expectations.

From **November 20 to 27**: Annual retreat at Macleod. The Fathers Legal and Foisy will attend. I am alone with Mr. Hébert at the Peigan mission. Everything goes well; about 25 students attend school on a daily basis.

November 29th: Father Legal and Foisy return from the retreat. Father Leduc accompanies them and honours us with his visit. For a few days it snows and it is bitterly cold. This lasts until December 7.

Feast day of **Christmas**: Father Legal replaces Père Van Tighem at Macleod. At 10:30 a.m. Father Foisy sings High Mass. Doctor Girard and Mr. Hébert and most of our students are present, but only a few adult savages. They don't know about God's gift presented to them!!!!

[Victor's efforts for the Peigan mission did not go unnoticed; Father Leduc (1888, 172) noted:]

It must also be mentioned that the Rev. Father Legal, apart from the help he received from his teacher, received astonishingly good assistance from the young and excellent Father Foisy, who was doing his missionary training, and from Father Van Tighem's brother, a religious man from a community of men dedicated to education whose mother house is in Belgium. This good brother Jean Berchmans was sent to our mission on a request from Mgr. Grandin.

January 4th: I go to Macleod to visit my brother with Père Foisy and celebrate the Twelfth Day.

Sunday, January 8th: Père Foisy sings High Mass and preaches and after High Mass he gives the Papal Benediction. During mass at 8 a.m. about twenty people approached the holy Table. How consoling!!!

The 9th we return to the *réserve*. All these days are cold: snow and wind. This severe weather lasts until January 26th. Then there is a genuine meltdown; the following days we enjoy quite summery weather. The good weather lasts nearly the entire month of February.

March: Nearly the whole month it snows and is cold.

At **Easter** I go to visit my brother again for ten days. For the first time in Macleod, someone sings High Mass to music. Good result, many people, $13.30 collected. I tidy up the house and the yard and return on the 11th to the reserve.

April 28th: Mr. Hébert leaves the reserve and will open a Catholic school in Pincher Creek (near Beauvais).[251] I will always remember him; he was a dear friend and my good counsellor.

May 1st: Père Leduc visits us and leaves the next day for Macleod with Père Legal. The river is high; for a few days we are ferried across by boat. Father Foisy and I are left alone for ten days. The school still continues on, in general twenty students these days. This week I sow and plant potatoes. Once in a while it rains.

May 8th: Père Legal returns with Mr. Johnson, an Englishman, who will be in charge of the school from now on.

May 16th: Most savages have left the camp and go to Beaver Creek, where they will hold *Dance du Soleil*.[252] Père Legal and Mr. Johnson will go there and hold classes in a tent. The first few days about thirty to forty students attend. The school at the camp lasts until July 12th. On average thirty-six attend on a daily basis.

July 12th: My brother and Père Gendreau from the Ottawa College, commissioned by the government to visit the reserves in the northwest, pay a visit. In the evening of the same day he leaves again for Macleod. Father Legal accompanies him and Père Van Tighem stays at the reserve until Monday July 14th. Then I accompany him to Macleod and stay until July 24th. I tidy up the house and the yard and return on the 24th to the reserve. You can't burn the candle at both ends.

On July 26th I go with Father Legal and Mr. Johnson on a pleasure trip to Pincher Creek and the Rocky Mountains. We have our first lunch with Mr. Legoan, arrive in Pincher Creek in late afternoon, greet Mr. Lebel and continue on our journey to Beauvais, seven miles from Pincher Creek. There I again meet my dear friend Mr. Hébert. The following day I attend the school inspection. Père Legal pays a visit for the first time as inspector. It is a spacious and well set up classroom, only twelve students, who make wonderful progress in all the courses though school only started three months ago. The next day the school is consecrated and Father Legal reads mass with the students and their parents present. After breakfast we go by wagon for a trip to the lake at the foot of the mountains. This area is a true paradise on earth. After lunch we thank Mr. Beauvais for his generous hospitality. These people are so good and how dearly do they love and honour the priest. We return to Pincher Creek.

Sunday, July 29th: Solemn High Mass and sermon, at night vespers and lauds in the new, beautiful church built by Père Van Tighem in 1886. All the Catholics attend the religious services; the church is full. After lauds, Mr. Cyr's child was baptized.

Monday: In the morning there is the solemn wedding of Mr. Grenier and Ms. LaGrandeur.[253] After having breakfast with Mr. Lebel we leave for our journey to the Rocky Mountains. We arrive in French Flats and have lunch with Mr. Mongeon.[254] Mr. Hébert joins us on horseback and Mr. Mongeon accompanies us unto the waterfalls.[255] It is the first water falls I have seen, what a wonderful sight. We erect our tent and camp there until the following afternoon. We continue on our journey through the hills and valleys: difficult road. I do a lot on foot. Pleasant views. We arrive at the premises of Mr. Lie, and meet up with two bears there; fortunately they are chained up. We wade through the Oldman River; thereafter only high mountains, beautiful parks in the valleys, all kinds of trees, flowers, etc., etc. At 6:30 p.m. we stop between two rocky mountains, (Les Tortues), each about 2,500 feet high.[256] Someone discovered a mineral spring here. The water is full of sulphur; it is the color of dishwater, it smells like sulphur, but it tastes good. Many sick people come here to soak in it. Mr. Lie is constructing a hotel. It is no miracle that the location is famous and attracts many visitors.[257] We stay until Friday, take walks through the woods where hundreds of trees are rotting. We climb the hills; pick flowers and fruit, fish in the river, etc., etc. We return, have lunch at the falls and at night we camp at Mr. Mongeon's. The following Saturday Father Legal reads mass, after which we return to Pincher Creek.

[Nine years later, in June 1897, Father Legal got notice from Archbishop Langevin of St. Boniface that he was appointed coadjutor and would succeed Mgr. Grandin as bishop. This inspired "G" (1897, 395–398) to elaborate on Father Legal's life and his work among the Blood Indians and quote Father Legal's account of his same July 1888 trip. It follows hereunder:]

As I [Legal] was appointed inspector of the Catholic Schools in the district, I went to Pincher Creek to inspect a school located next to the Rocky Mountains. There I united in marriage a good Canadian and a young Canadian woman, our organist. That was the first Catholic wedding in Pincher-Creek; big celebration in the village. At noon, we started our

1▶ *2004: Beauvais Lake.*
Photo Mary E.M.

2▶ *2004: Lundbreck Falls.*
Photo Mary E.M.

3▶ *2004: Turtle Moun-tains.* Photo Mary E.M.

4▶ *2004: Sulphur pond.* Photo Mary E.M.

5▶ *2004: Brick bath above sulphur pond.* Photo Mary E.M.

odyssee toward the mountains.

It was about going to Crowsnest Pass, to the source of a sulphur spring and even to the Crowsnest Lake, about 50 miles from Pincher Creek. First station at the falls of the Middle Fork, the Oldman River. There we camped one night. Pretty falls of 20 à 30 feet, with the Rocky Mountains as background. In the evening and all of the next morning we tried to fish. There was enough fish, we saw them struggle to jump up to the rapids; they scorned our fishing lines and our baits. After dinner, we broke up camp and went on towards the mountains, laid out in front of us, grand and majestically. By 4 o'clock in the afternoon we entered the said pass. To the right and left of us the mountains shoot up. A bit later we arrived at a little log hut, the police post: they told us that we were perfectly on our route to the Sulphur springs, and we moved on in the midst of really grandiose scenes: the river that snakes in million detours, deep below us; the mountains, of which the lower parts are dressed in a black coat of all kinds of pines; the naked peaks tower threatening into the clouds; the deep gorges where the piles of snow was not yet melted by the burning sun rays. The mountains are really beautiful! The perfume of wild strawberries embalms the air and invites us to halt, but we go on. Maybe for the sake of variation the road becomes craggy and rocky, but we reach the sources by wagon. We arrive there quite late in the evening. While we set up camp, night falls and envelops us in its shadows.

The source of the sulphur spring is very abundant; it springs from an excavation at the foot of a mountain, 2,800 feet above the plains where we are; this mountain seems very small among the ones behind it. The water is bluish, has a quite strong sulphur scent and a light taste, one gets quickly used to it; it is very cold and very fit to drink. . . .

[Father Legal goes on with nature descriptions, wonders whether the beavers appreciate the sulphur water as they built a dam to retain it, remarks that the next day the newlyweds arrived at their camp and that he returned on Saturday.]

[Victor continues:]
Sunday, **August 5th**: High Mass, sermon, vespers and lauds. The church is filled with worshippers who are very fortunate to have religious services in their church on two subsequent Sundays.

Monday morning: Requiem Mass for the sister of Madame Lebel, a religious person who recently died in Montreal.[258] There are several confessions and communions, we then continue on our journey, have lunch with Mr. La Grandeur and on Monday, August 6 at 6 p.m. we return safe and sound to the reserve. Such a pleasurable trip benefits the heart and soul.

August 12th: The rain over the last few days is very beneficial for the garden. We have an abundance of all kinds of vegetables and the potatoes and other winter fruits look very promising. Père Legal is in Macleod. He is replacing Père Van Tighem, who is constructing a little house in Lethbridge. Mr. Johnson works for a few days at the agency.

From **August 24th** until September 1st: the annual retreat in Macleod. Father Lacombe does the preaching. I am alone at the Peigan mission.

September 1st: The Fathers return. Father Claude accompanies them.

On the **4th** Father Lacombe joins him. Their goal is to attract some kids for the Industrial School. Mr. Springett also uses all of his influence. They recruit three from the Peigan and one from the Blood reserve. In the month of August we are sent another suitcase with beautiful ornaments, candelabras, flowers, clothes etc., etc., from Belgium. Thanks to my fellow Brothers, family and other benefactors. The Trappist Fathers of West-Vleteren also sent me relics of the Holy Cross, Our Lady, St. Joseph and St. Anne. After the retreat Father Van Tighem went for good to Lethbridge, where he constructs a small house and a sanctuary for the church, which is already too small. Father Lacombe replaces Father van Tighem in MacLeod. A young Brother (he arrived here lately in the Bishopric of Saint Albert with four other Brothers and a Father from France) stays in Macleod.

From the **5th** until the 13th of September I have a retreat in Macleod, it is my first in America and also the first that I do all alone.

[From Macleod, Victor wrote, in Dutch, to Leonard:]
1888 [c Sept 15]
L.S.J.C.
Très chèr frère

Père Legal arrived here this afternoon and we will leave for the reserve at 5 p.m. I was willing to come to Lethbridge, but I see in your letter that you would rather have me postpone it for a few weeks. The Fathers and I also think that it is better, because, I need something to do, or it would soon sadden me. I am glad to have made a retreat, and, having been away from the reserve for ten days already, there will be quite some work for me in my garden and house. Well, if you want me to help you for a few days, let me know; I am sure Père Legal won't mind. Everything here in Macleod is going well. I will decorate the chapel at its best for the feast of the Holy Cross tomorrow.[259] I am also glad that Père Lacombe has a competent Brother with him now (*il est* smart). I have written to Meulebeke. I received word from Kortrijk; everything is going very well. Mr. Plettinck, the Major of Meulebeke, and Mr. Debakker, the Pastor at Blankenbergh, are dead. RIP.[260]

Dear, I will write to you later. I am leaving. Pray for me, take care and don't work too hard, be a bit patient.

Farewell
Your brother, Joannes Berchmans.

[Victor continues:]

The **15th of September** I return to the *réserve*. Our school, which started again on the 3rd, is going slowly, not much openness and even less progress, poor savages! The last week of September I put our potatoes into the cellar, 32 bags 100 kilograms each, beyond expectation: six bags of beets, four and a half of carrots, nine and a halve of turnips, onions and cabbages: a good harvest.

October 7th: A visit from Mr. Lebel and his wife, Mr. Hébert and Joseph of Pincher Creek.

October 8th: I go to Macleod and on the 10th to Lethbridge in order to help out my brother in his new home. He has a nice church with sanctuary and a clean, small house. Lethbridge is growing fast and has a promising future. The Catholics there are very industrious and charitable. Within about a year they provided the priest with a harmonium, furniture etc. and paid for everything.

On **October 23rd** I return to Macleod and on the 24th I return to the reserve. Frère Cunningham will spend the winter with Père Lacombe in Macleod.

December: Father Leduc pays us a visit on the reserve. We also have a visit from Mr. Reade and Mr. MacGibbon and on the 16th from the school inspector. All of them seem to be satisfied with our school and students. Brother Cunningham returns and Father Légal leaves the Peigan for good in order to build a school and a house on the Blood *réserve*.

Christmas 1888: A little snow, good weather. High Mass according to custom. But, not much zeal among the savages. They continuously ask for food and drinks. May God forgive them!!! Yesterday we handed out an amount totalling about 40 or 50 dollars to forty students.

January 1st: Very beautiful weather. During late afternoon there is a nearly full eclipse of the sun. The savages are astonished and some are afraid. A few drop by and we show them the sun through smoked glass. We explain them the eclipse. Hopefully this diminishes their superstition regarding the sun, which they take and honour as their highest god.[261]

January 11th: Père Legal picks up Mr. Johnson to go to the Blood *réserve*. I accompany them for three weeks to organize the new house and the school. In Macleod I get the sad news about the death of my sister-in-law after an illness of 5 months. She is only 29 years old and the mother of 4 small children. Sad and hard for my youngest brother. That the good God give him courage and strength and will protect these small, small children!!!

On the 14th we arrive at the Blood *réserve*: beautiful house and spacious school. Père Legal leaves for ten days to go to Pincher Creek and will organize the inside of the church. He works there with five or six men and in eight days the church and roof loft is a showpiece. The good Catholics of Pincher Creek are very satisfied and proud of it, one collection paid for everything.

Saturday, February 2nd: Père Legal returned yesterday and Mr. Johnson and I take the road to Macleod, stay there until Monday and then return to the Peigan where Père Foisy is waiting impatiently for me. No news on the mission, which, by order of Mgr Grandin, carries the name of St. Paul's mission. The next day Mr. Johnson leaves the Peigan for good. We load his wagon up with eight bags of vegetables. May the Good God bless Père Legal's undertaking and school at the Blood *réserve!* This year there is no winter.

February 17th: In Macleod Brother Cunningham professed his eternal vows in front of Père Lacombe. Père Van Tighem and Père Foisy both attend the ceremony.

March 25th: Père Lacombe leaves Macleod for St. Albert accompanied by Frère Cunningham, where Brother Cunningham will continue his theological studies, while Père Lacombe will instruct missions in the north. Père Blais from Calgary will serve in Macleod and Pincher Creek.[262]

April: A large number of our savages leave the camp for good and settle down in small groups along the river.[263] This leaves our school with very few students. So now Père Foisy will gather and teach the children at one or another savage's tent or house along the river. Poor savages! What can we expect from them!

[Father Foisy (1890, 236 ff) wrote to Father Boisramé:]
Mission Saint-Paul des Piégans,
April 7, 1889.
Reverend and very dear Father,

Since my last letter, dear Father, I have been established 15 miles from Fort Macleod on the Peigan Reserve. For a year now I have been the companion for the Rev. Father Legal, whom I replaced often during his travels to Macleod, Pincher Creek and the Blood Reserve. I could, in a way, little by little get used to managing this small mission by myself and since the 1st of January, I have become the priest for the Peigan, as Father Legal has founded a new mission for the Blood tribe, about 20 to 25 miles from here. He has built there a good boarding school thanks to the help he received from the Department of Indian Affairs, two sponsors and, friends of Reverend Father Lacombe. I am here with the good and dedicated Father Jean Berchmans, the brother of Father van Tighem. The two of us happily manage our small business. I am the actual teacher and he is my assistant. Every three months we receive a small amount from the government to help us maintain our mission. Have you heard much talk about the Peigan? It is a part of the Blackfoot Nation and not even one of them has embraced our sacred religion. The missionaries have had to restrict themselves to baptizing the children and giving the last rites to a few adults. At present, as a last resort, we give all our attention to the school children. That is what the Reverend Father Doucet does with the Blackfoot, the Reverend Legal with the Blood and that is what we, my companion and I, do here for the poor Peigan. There are several reasons for their indifference: children spoiled by the government, food provided by it since the disappearance of the buffalo, which used to be their only means of subsistence, they have not suffered enough and became lazy and took to begging, which takes all of their moral energy. Add to this the bad example from the whites. For the rest of them, they show no hostility towards us; they like us due to their egoism and self-interest because we are charitable, take care of the sick, give them small presents, and encourage them to send their children to school. The school, as I already said, is our last hope and one might hope that this effort is not lost.

[Victor, in Dutch, to Leonard:]
April 20, 1889.
L.Z.J.C.
Peigan Reserve,
Dearest brother,

I wish you a wonderful Easter feast. Père Foisy and I are both doing very well. As I wrote to you recently, not much is left of our school. Our savages took off to live along the river so during the last quarter of the year, we did not even have fourteen pupils per day. The ones who live nearby only come sporadically or not at all to the school. Poor savages, they are too well kept by the government. Père Foisy goes on horseback two or three times per week along the river, gathers the children in one or another savages' house or tent and teaches them something, while I teach the ones that come here and in this way, together we have about ten or twelve altogether. Isn't it sad after all these expenses! It has already been two months since we stopped using the school and I started teaching in the kitchen. Père Foisy will go to Macleod today. Père Blais told us that tomorrow Père Legal will sing a High Mass there. Père Foisy will make a few proposals to Père Legal regarding the schools.

1st) Open a boarding school in our big house for a few savage children.

2nd) Build a log school further along the river where he would teach, while I teach at the school here. What do you think? My opinion is it will all be fruitless as long as the government does not obligate the savages to send their children to school. On the Blood Reserve *tout nouveau, tout beau!* Père Legal promised to hand out nice gifts after one month of school, and when the gifts were handed out, forty or fifty attended, than after that the attendance decreased greatly. The doctor says that when he was there lately, there were only six pupils. No, dear brother, you also know our savages, they are only good at eating, drinking, and smoking pipes. May God improve their fate. But what will Mgr. Grandin say about it? So much the better that your school does well, as well as those at Macleod and Pincher Creek.

I am enclosing another letter from Charles, and also the first letter from his little Marie. I am glad that Charles is showing great courage and he says that he is not short of anything.

Dear brother, when you receive the suitcase from Meulebeke, send me, me as soon as possible, the statue of Our Lady for the May celebrations; about the other things, whatever you don't need yourself. A choir cap would be useful to us here. What are you planning to do with the thurible? Since, because you already have a nice one. The Gothic missal will certainly be a beautiful book. Send me some books and, also, flower seeds.

Recently I received two beautiful, breviaries from Brother Alphonse of Vive-Capelle. He sends his greetings and says that he once sang lauds with you in Vive. All of my fellow Brothers are doing reasonably well. If you were sending something Belgian along with Mr. Paul Watelet to Belgium, perhaps I could send along a few things, too?

The dry weather is not very good for my garden. We are busy making a yard around the garden, bordering the two new roads in which the horse can be kept and in which I will plant trees. Doctor Girard no longer boards here anymore; so much the better. Père Foisy and I would be most happy here if we had a good school and made some progress with the savages! But then again, there is some hope.

Pray for your brother,
Brother Jean Berchmans.

[Victor continues:]
May: The beautiful, but very dry weather is not good for my yard, neither for the fields. For nine months we haven't had more than half an hour of snowfall and only a little snow.

May 12th: Father Blais arrives from Pincher Creek. I accompany him to Macleod to tidy up house and yard. It rains for three days.

On the **19th** we leave together for Lethbridge and visit my brother (Father Van Tighem). He is doing very well.

On the **23rd** we return to Macleod and in the afternoon of the same day, go back to our Peigan mission.

June 17th: Our beloved bishop Mgr. Grandin, accompanied by Father Leduc, honours us with a visit. Nowadays 13 students. The big cross for Father Foisy for the Peigan churchyard on the rise behind the mission is consecrated by Monsignor. Mgr. will visit Pincher Creek and administer the Holy Confirmation just as he did in Macleod last Sunday. Father Foisy accompanies his Highness.

June 29th: Handing out of awards to our students. Today 23 are present. Then we give them a 4-week holiday. The poor savages prepare for the Sun Dance.

July 10th: We install the cross in the churchyard; a Blood Indian and a Peigan help us. During the holidays we paint our house. Though it only costs $10.00, it adds a value of about 200 to 300 piasters.

September 10th: I put our vegetables into the cellar because it freezes every night and more often than not the Indians steal them. Despite the unfavorable and very dry weather, we have 28 bags of potatoes, 2½ bags of carrots, 3 bags of turnips, 1½ bags of beets and one bag of onions. I also stored away all kinds of seeds and many peas. For a few months now I have often been alone at the mission. Once a month Father Foisy gives a religious service in Pincher Creek, [goes] on almost a weekly basis to Macleod, etc., etc. These days almost nobody attends our school. God forbid, it is not our fault!

[Victor wrote to Leonard:]
Peigan *Réserve*, September 24, 1889.
L.S.J.C.
Dearest brother,

Right now I find it impossible to leave the reserve because now is the time to haul all the garden vegetables into the cellar, although Père Legal says that we should make the Indians do it. But the savages only do half the work and you have to pay them dearly and the mission here already has enough expenses; so that is why I prefer to do all that work myself. I have already started digging up the potatoes. It looks like a bumper crop, I think that we will have 25 to 30 bags of one hundred pound sacks each and then the onions, carrots, turnips, beets etc., etc. It takes quite some time. Besides this, preparing meals in the kitchen for five or six persons, helping at the school and my spiritual exercises in accordance with my Rules, I have enough to do right now. Still, dear brother, I would love to come to Lethbridge because I haven't seen that place yet, neither the church nor the house etc. If you want me to help you, fourteen days from now would suit me much better. But you have to arrange it with Père Legal as he will soon start building on the Blood reserve, though he shouldn't count on me because I prefer to stay here with the two of us. I would then have much less work to do than I now have. Père Foisy and I can easily manage things here and we receive $300 from the government. So, some profit for the mission, and except for our small school, the priest does not have anything to do here except study Blackfoot. Poor savages!!! God forbid!!!

Well, dear brother, I will just let you and Père Legal arrange things, I wish you good health: make sure that you eat and dress properly, because I know that sometimes, for no good reason, you don't take good care of yourself. Père Legal doesn't do that! If you have something for me, please send it along with Père Legal. Haven't you received any small candelabras that would suit our chapel?

Brother-Director from Kortrijk is celebrating his 25th anniversary as Superior. Could you write him a few lines? It would certainly please him greatly.

Pray for me.
Your brother,
Brother Jean Berchmans.

[Victor continues:]
October: We design and plant the garden around the churchyard. I go on an outing to Macleod and Lethbridge. Both missions are doing quite well. No special news.

December 3rd: Pères Foisy, Legal and Van Tighem go to Calgary for their annual retreat. I am alone at the mission for about three weeks.

Christmas: As Father Foisy has returned from Calgary this week, we celebrate quite alone. In the afternoon we only had a few children for the prayers. Miserable savages! How stubborn they are!

We have had a persistent winter, however, not too bad. Nothing special at the mission, neither at the *réserve*.

February 9th: Consecration of the new bell at Pincher Creek, a gift from Mr. Lebel. Père Lacombe invited all the Fathers to the ceremony. Beautiful weather, the feast was most successful; a collection of $200 net for the mission.

March 22nd: North Asee, Chief of the Peigan, dies after a lengthy illness.[264] On the 23rd he will be buried with great ceremony on the hill, next to his father and his mother. A few weeks later Crowfoot, Head Chief of the Blackfoot, also dies.[265] Father Doucet is so fortunate to have baptized him before he death. Crowfoot was a brave man and venerated among the whites as well as the savages. He himself had appointed his brother as his successor.[266] Crow Eagle is appointed as Chief of the Peigan.[267]

May: I make a trip to Macleod and Lethbridge. Our benefactors from Belgium again sent us a number of artifacts, among them two splendid chandeliers for the church at Lethbridge. An entire chapel with a cross, 4 candleholders, missal, chalice, ciborium, burettes, clock, Holy Sacrament lamp, etc., etc. And, eight beautiful ornaments, stoles, albs, surplices, etc., etc. and about 200 books for a parish library.

June: Some rain these days; very beneficial for the fields and meadows and especially for my garden. Everything looks good and again very promising. Our school quietly goes on, these days an average of ten or twelve. Again, poor students, stubborn savages!

July: Holiday: Père Foisy goes to Pincher Creek to finish and paint the tower; he will also put up a cross and porch in front of the churchyard and make a yard around the church.[268] He visits the Blood *réserve* and Lethbridge. So I will be here alone for six weeks. No news at the *réserve*. Dry and warm weather. Via Calgary we receive a cross from France. The frame is very damaged. I have a lot of trouble repairing it. It is a quite beautiful one and it decorates our classroom, which is now in use as a chapel because of the small amount of students, who we now teach some place else.[269] Mgr. Grandin also sends me a missionary cross, consecrated by His Highness and privileged with indulgences.

September 21st: As Father Foisy is in Pincher Creek, I do the funeral of the daughter of Omarkopa (Big Weasel), who died yesterday. She has been baptized and received the Holy Extreme Unction.[270] She had been married for a year to a white man called James (Protestant). She leaves him with a one-year-old son. There are already ten buried in the churchyard: eight savages, only two of them not baptized, and two Métis children.

September: Mr. Springett starts to build his house on the elevation straight across from the mission.

September 20–26th: I put the vegetables into the cellar. 25 Bags of potatoes, three bags of turnips, two bags of carrots and half bags of beets, onions, cabbages, etc., etc.

October 5th: Visit from Mr. and Mrs. Lebel. This week they leave Pincher Creek and go to their place of birth (Canada). May the good God bless them. They were great benefactors for the mission.

From the 13th until the **30th of October** I am alone again at the mission. Père Foisy goes to Calgary for the retreat; eight Fathers and two Brothers partake in it. Since a few days Mgr. Grandin is also in Calgary. The bisho-

▶ *Chief Crow Eagle.*
Van Tighem Family Archives

pric of St. Albert will be divided. His High Holiness the Pope established an apostolic Vicariate of the Province of Saskatchewan. My former student from Kortrijk, Père Naessens, will be sent to be the principal at St. Joseph Industrial School in High River.

November 12th: Père Foisy, authorized by Mgr. Grandin, consecrates and erects the Stations of the Cross in our chapel.

November 25th: Père Legal drops by on his way from Pincher Creek. I accompany him to Macleod, Lethbridge and the Blood *réserve*. All goes well in these three missions. Père Van Tighem is building a convent for the Sisters (*Fidèles Compagne de Jésus*) who after New Year will take care of the school.

Christmas: I am alone again for fourteen days. Père Foisy celebrates the religious services in Pincher Creek and then Macleod, as Father Lacombe is sick.

During the night of **November 29 to 30th** I notice thieves in our house. They are two of our students, the theft does not amount to much, but it is sad these students do this after four years at the school. Again, poor school! Poor savages.

Until now we have had a mild winter. We renovate a lot in and outside of the house. No special news at the mission.

March 29th: Easter. Since Friday Père Foisy has been in Pincher Creek. What a poor Easter at this mission. Only one Indian comes for the prayers! For several days it snows, impossible to work in the garden.

April: We place crosses and columns on the graves of the savages with their names carved in them.

May: We erect the last fencing around our house, a beautiful improvement. Our yard looks good and promises to provide a good harvest when we get some rain. Our Lord's Ascension. Visit from the Girard family and Mr. Begin from Macleod. Solemn High Mass.

June: The Indians meet for the Sun Dance.

July: Holiday, no special news. Jaques Toyepie, the best of our students, dies after having received the Holy Extreme Unction.[271]

Aug. 17th: We start school again. Père Foisy starts the school seven miles down the river, not far from LaGrandeur's place.[272] Several Indians have their houses there. Père Foisy buys a house ($20) that will serve as a stable after he has built [his house]. He builds a small but clean log cabin in which he teaches ten to twelve students and here I am teaching five or six or up to eight. It is not encouraging. Poor savages!

September-October: I put the vegetables into the cellar. The many rain showers yielded a double harvest: 52 bags of potatoes and all the other vegetables in abundance. It is unbelievable and now this is the fifth year without any manure. As Père Foisy is nearly always absent, I am always alone and only have mass only three or four times per week. I suffer all this with love. If we could only do something good and make some progress with the savages, but! This summer I received a beautiful woollen cassock, scapular and waistband. All I know is that these come from Belgium, but the giver is unknown to me. May God reward them a thousand times for these.

October 5th: Père Foisy and all the Fathers of this district, except for Father Lacombe, go to the annual retreat, which for the first time is in St. Albert. As the iron road from Calgary to Edmonton is finished, it is now easy to travel to St. Albert. As I am alone here, I do my utmost best with the school and other mission work. Once a week I visit the mission in St. Charles.[273] I go on foot, which is a good stroll (two hours). I baptize a sick child about two months old. A few days later it dies: still, it is one more angel won for heaven. It is the only consolation we have here and the only good we can do for our stubborn savages who decline so many graces.

October 24th: Père Foisy returns from the retreat. Mgr. Grandin is in good health and all the Fathers and Brothers of our bishopric are doing quite well.

November: Father Foisy moves into his new house and starts his school again a few days before Christmas.

Christmas: Père Foisy is in Pincher Creek again. I celebrate the great feast as well as I can with my students. After the prayers I serve them a good feast meal and give them little presents.

New Year's Eve: Big party. Father Foisy comes with the children from the upper reserve, three wagons full, totalling 70. Again a big feast meal and presents. They all show up and are happy as long as they get something. That is the only way with the savages, as well as with the children. That is why we keep the few clothes we have for them and hand them out now and then, to lure them in this way to school.

So far we have had a mild winter, but terrible wind and storm. During the month of January I had fifteen to twenty students on a daily basis and Father Foisy about the same number. If they only would persist, but!

January 12th: Père Comiré, who replaces Father Lacombe in Macleod, pays us a visit on his way from Pincher Creek.

February: We also get a visit from Père Leduc and Père Therien.

March: I go on foot to Macleod and from there with Father Comiré to Lethbridge, Pincher Creek and the Blood reserve. Everywhere I find change and a lot of improvement at the missions.

March 2nd: I receive the sad news that my Rev. Superior Brother Aloysius died the 27th of February at the motherhouse in Kortrijk, after having received the Holy Sacraments of the dying eight days earlier.[274] It is a big loss for our congregation, which he carefully and wisely managed as Superior-General for 29 years. May God give his Soul eternal peace. Upon his death, the Brothers of Love (said Van Dale) congregation consists of five houses in the bishopric of Bruges and have 35 Brothers, four Novices and seven Geniorists. The deceased Brothers number thirty-nine.

April 14th: (White Thursday). Père Foisy returns from Macleod with a small bell that has not yet found its way to Rome. It is another present from Mr. Lebel. Père Lacombe, who returned this week from Montreal, brought it along. It is appropriate for our small, little mission (St. Charles).

April 25–26–27: Horrendous snowstorm. In many places the snow is ten to twelve feet deep. Many horses and horned cattle perish in the snow. Our savages lose at least one hundred of them. Then it snowed for another twelve days. In my yard the snow is at least twelve feet deep. Most of my beautiful trees are shattered.

Since January we have Mr. Pocklington as Agent.[275] Mr. Springett resigned. So far we have not had a bit of trouble with this officer from the department [of Indian Affairs]. Mr. Bourne, the Protestant minister, has also left and since the month of April, a simple schoolteacher replaces him. Just as at ours, they don't have much to do because of the indifference of the savages.[276]

Bourdey School.[277]

May: Brother Alphonsus is elected as Superior-General for the Van Dale Brothers.[278] Good choice. Brother Alphonsus is a very religious and learned Brother. In 23 years he has already done a lot for our congregation and for several years he was Superior at Vive-Capelle and Mont-à-Leux.

June 22nd: Père Foisy leaves for the Industrial School and will remain there for three weeks while Père Naessens has gone to St. Albert for a retreat. Father Lacombe stays here just for this district. He sends me little Wilfried George so he can go to school and learn to serve mass. Père Foisy returns after having been absent for four weeks. All that time I was deprived of mass and Holy Communion.

July 25th: Père Lacombe and Père Legal drop by on their way from Pincher Creek. The following day they leave for Macleod and take little Wilfried along.

July 31st: Our Indians start the Sun Dance near LaGrandeur's place. Everything here is dried out and burnt, the entire summer no rain. No grass in the meadows and even less harvest. Poor area.[279] Père Foisy goes once to visit the Blood reserve and Lethbridge too.

September 11th: Père Foisy, with Père Doucet and Père Lacombe, will attend the retreat at Pincher Creek. A month ago Father Lacombe went to stay in Pincher Creek for good.

[Victor wrote to Leonard:]

St. Paul's Mission, Peigan Reserve September 30, 1892.
G.Z.J.C.
Dearest brother,

I am sending you a few lines to let you know that I am fine, yes, much better than a few weeks ago. It is always the intense heat that makes me sick. I am nearly always alone at this mission. Père Foisy went to Pincher Creek for ten days for the retreat. Last Sunday he filled in for le Père Lacombe who was in Calgary. Yesterday he wrote from Macleod that on Sunday, October 2nd, Père Foisy will replace him at Pincher Creek. On Monday Père Foisy will go to Macleod to take the train to Calgary to meet his sister and other nuns who will be going to Vancouver. Father Lacombe got a pass for him to accompany his sister and the other nuns for a good stretch into the mountains. You can imagine how happy Père Foisy is. Also, the priest has nothing to do here with our sad Indians, the entire summer they do nothing else but beat on drums, dance, sing, smoke and drink tea.

Yesterday Agent Pocklington said that instead of improving, our savages are slowly getting worse. I agree, dear brother, they live like dogs. In four days they will each be paid five dollars and they will spend it partying in Macleod. During that time I will put my potatoes and other vegetables into the cellar. It is even a bigger success than I had expected, and there is something of everything, even though the savages stole a large part, even two sacks of potatoes. One needs to be very patient to spend one's life with such folks! Well, it does not distress me even now I am also deprived of all spiritual and religious celebrations and, even can only attend mass now and then. I think that I am where God wants me to be and that is my entire consolation. Pray for me, dear brother, so I can submit to everything and remain a good religious Brother.

Right now Jean L'Heureux is in Pincher Creek with Père Lacombe.[280] Mr. Birmingham replaces Mr. Hébert at the school in Beauvais place, but I hear that he does not like it and that he will not stay there long. Regretfully I heard about the sad condition of Père Grandin, hopefully everything turns out well, such a young and healthy Father.

I can't remember any other special news. Nothing from Belgium. This week I will write to Brother Scheers.

Your dedicated brother,
Brother Jean Berchmans.

[Victor continues:]
October 4th: Father Foisy leaves for Macleod, Calgary, to meet his sister who goes to Vancouver. So, I am always alone, do my small school, etc., etc.

▶ "*One Spot, Blood; Red Crow, Blood; Jean L'Heureux, interpreter; North Axe, Peigan. Mid-1880s.*" Glenbow Archives, NA−2968-4

October 12th: Payday for the savages and feast in Macleod.[281] In the meantime I put my vegetables into the cellar. Small harvest due to the dry weather and the frost we had this summer.

November 8th: I go to Macleod and the next day I take the train to Calgary. There I meet up with Mgr. Grandin, Mr. Morin, les Pères Leduc, Lestanc, André, Rémas, Comiré and Doucet and the Brothers Bowes and Baraseau. I am so fortunate to serve the mass of Monseignor for three days and on Sunday attend the consecration of the new hospital.

On Monday, **November 14th**, accompanied by the Rev. Père Lestanc, I take the road to St. Joseph Industrial School. Father Naessens, my former student, whom I haven't seen for seven years, meets me. We embrace and talk in our mother tongue. I stay for five days at this institute, which makes great progress. At present there are 46 boys and 25 girls, all savage or half-savage children. A new three-story building for the boys is being constructed. Each night we are honoured with a small concert. The music band under the management of Mr. Scolen, established only one year ago does wonderful.

On **Friday** Père Naessens brings me back to Calgary and the following morning I take the train again to Macleod, and stay there until Monday. Then I return with Père Foisy to my mission, the Peigan reserve, very happy with my outing. It is winter, it snows and for three days it is very cold.

1893

Iron road Macleod-Calgary.[282]

We have a long and hard winter.

February is bitterly cold. Doctor Girard stays with us for fourteen days. We have no students (thieves).

March: The weather improves a bit.

In **April** there are very few nice days, it snows and there is frost.

Only in **May** we [thieves] can work the ground.

In **June** we have all the time a tremendous wind and it is very dry. The agent, Mr. Pocklington, leaves for Regina, very happy to be rid of the Peigan. Mr. Nash replaces him. The savages clamor that they don't want him. These people are not satisfied with anybody. Poor savages, when will they attain better feelings?

In **July** the weather is very good. It rains for several days: good for the meadows and the fields. My garden looks very beautiful and promises a good harvest. Mgr. Grandin, being in Europe, has visited my fellow Brothers in Kortrijk. They were very content with such a noble visit. When he was with my family in Meulebeke, he took my nephew Joseph, who is 11 years old, along and sent him in advance with two Fathers. The boy has already arrived safe and sound in Lethbridge at Leonard's, who, with consent from the Monseignor, adopted him as his child. How happy in body and soul will young Joseph be there. Already he has neither father nor mother.

Harvest – very dry and poor – visit from Père Lacombe and Père Lestanc from Calgary, the Superior of this district. Our savages receive horned cattle from the government in exchange for their small horses. The head-chief also receives a free mower with accessories. Due to the long drought, hay here is still rare – poor area!

September 25th: I put no less than forty bags of vegetables into the cellar. Good harvest!

October 4th: I go to St. Albert for the retreat. I travel for free on the iron road as assistant to the Rev. Père Lacombe. How beautiful a mission the one at St. Albert is! And what an agreeable area: lots of woodlands and tillable land as well. We have fifteen Fathers, four secular priests and eleven Brothers. Everyone is in good health.

November: It is already full-blown winter with snow and frost.

Christmas: This year Father Foisy is here. It is 10 a.m. High Mass, but as usual, the savages couldn't care less.

1894

January, February and March: there is quite a persistent, fierce wind. Mgr. Grandin returns from Europe and is, thank God, in good health. In less than two months no less than 25 children have died from the measles: angels for heaven.

April: My young nephew from Lethbridge will spend 8 days with me. The boy is sturdy and healthy and already speaks English like an Englishman. On the 15th of April *le Père* Van Tighem will pick him up and sing here during High Mass with sermon.

May: It rains a lot. The rivers are very high. Already three men have drowned in the river. Mgr. Grandin, having returned in full health from Europe, is in this district to visit the missions and administer the Holy Confirmations.

June 11th: I look up his Highness in MacLeod and have a long talk with him.

On July 4th Ms. Husiron, the sister-in-law of agent Nash, renounces Protestantism in our chapel, is baptized and makes Holy Communion. The Father has taught her for eight months and she regularly attends mass, which is sung here at 10 a.m. This miss sings with us and plays the organ. She is a real good daughter.

Since July 1st we have been on holiday. Our savages occupy themselves again with the Sun Dance. God forbid! Poor Blackfoot. The weather is very dry and hot.

August: *Le Père* Lacombe leaves for Edmonton. *Le Père* Foisy is in charge of Pincher Creek. He goes there regularly every fourteen days and each time he stays there for five or six days. So I am nearly always alone. My school is very slow. My garden still yields a good harvest. This summer we succeeded in sending ten to twelve children to the Industrial School.

In October I pay a short visit to the Blood reserve. Now they have a hospital with seven Sisters who also teach school.

November 4th: I go to Lethbridge for a visit. *Le Père* Van Tighem and my little nephew are safe and sound. The church at Lethbridge is expanded in size in more than halve by adding on a stone-cross church with sacristy and splendid tower: very beautiful inside and out. Right now *le Père* Van Tighem has a beautiful house with four rooms downstairs and five upstairs. In the convent are 150 children. I am in Macleod. For the midnight mass the church is much too small – someone sang beautifully and about thirty Holy Communions. During High Mass and also during the evening a lot of people showed up. Mr. Gravel, who manages Macleod since April 1893, does a lot of good and is well liked.[283]

[Victor to Brother Stanislas, a fellow Van Dale Brother in Belgium:][284]
St. Paul's Mission, Macleod Peigan Reserve, December 12, 1894.
G.Z.J.C.
Reverend Brother Stanislas,

Thanks for your good New Year's wishes. From the bottom of my heart, I send you too the same blessings and goodness that you bestow upon me. Let's pray, dear Brother that for both of us these wishes come true. You tell me, Brother Stanislas, that you currently are in Marcke, that a good, Christian parish. Happy soul! I did not yet know we had a monastery in Marcke, but, what you did not tell me, is that you are the Director, isn't it! Congratulations, be happy and accept my blessings, that God may grant you grace according to vocation!! I am already extremely happy that our (Van Dale Brothers') congregation is growing so fast. If I am not mistaken, by now we have nine houses. That amounts to something! May God bless the parish more and more!

Brother Stanislas, you tell me that Mr. Pastor Samyn is very sick. I feel so bad! That good man! That holy priest! And he was so happy at Marcke. Tell him that I will pray three Holy Mary's with my savage children in school every day, asking Our Lady to get his health back, if it is a good and sanctifying to him. I also did not forget the de Bethune family, especially the apostate Father who read mass for us in Kortrijk. I did not know that he had fallen so deeply and got married. What a cross to bear for such a Christian family! Also, thank you Brother Stanislas, for all the other news you sent me. Now I will tell you about here.

First of all, I am strong and healthy as always. I have already been here over eight years with the Blackfoot! I feel at home with these people, I love them and they love me, especially when I share something from my kitchen or from my garden. We see that civilization among the savages is increasing without them being aware of it or thinking about it. This summer they put up hundreds of wagonloads full of hay with the machine, which they will sell in Macleod and in other nearby villages to white people. With that money they buy clothes, beds, stoves, chairs, suitcases etc., etc.

I truly think that this is already a lot! Because until 15 to 20 years ago the savages knew nothing else besides wild animals, hides, arrows and bows. It also consoles us to see that we have more baptisms over the years, and we especially see much hope in those that want to be baptized on their deathbeds.

In the bishopric of St. Albert, eight new churches have been built this year (two stone ones), two convents for nuns, one orphanage and six new schools. If our bishop does obtain the means, next summer he will build the first College with a seminary to educate young priests in this bishopric.

It is unfortunate that the Protestants do the same or even more, as they receive much more financial support from England and as many Protestant ministers as they want. Right now Monsignor Grandin is also in good health. My brother missionary, rather the pastor in Lethbridge, is also doing very well as is my young nephew who lives with him. This summer Père Van Tighem expanded the size of his church by more than half and made it into a beautiful cross-church. In his convent there are currently nine Sisters and 150 students.

Père Naessens is also in full health and works hard as the principal of the Industrial School. Concluding, civilization is thriving here and we are following Europe with big steps. Everywhere iron roads, telegraphy, telephony, electricity, fire engines for milling grain, sawing lumber etc., etc.

Farewell Brother Stanislas, write often to me and let's pray for one another.

Your Dear Fellow Brother in J.C.
Brother Joannes-Berchmans.
Missionary / Always the same address.

Paul, your brother also wrote to me. I sent him a few words back. I am glad that he does well in general. He is a big enemy of socialism.

I received a letter from Br. Antonius at the same time as yours. It was six months that the Brothers wrote to me.

[Victor continues:]

January: So far we have had a mild winter and not much snow. School is going slowly and the savages are always the same, eating and drinking, smoking and dancing. After a mild winter we have a cold and dry spring.

June 6–7: Some rain, very beneficial; there is hardly any grass on the prairie. Père Foisy left ten days ago for St. Albert to the retreat. Père Foisy returns after an absence of one month. During all that time I went once in a while to mass and was given Holy Communion by Mr. Gravel from Macleod.

July: It rains and thunders constantly. The savages again hold a Sun Dance. Harvest. Grand celebration in Lethbridge. Mgr. Grandin comes to consecrate the church. The Rev. Pères Lestanc, Doucet, Lecoq, Legal, Fouquet, Cunningham, Van Tighem and I attend the ceremony.

September: I put the vegetables into the cellar: 31 big bags of potatoes, carrots, turnips, cabbages, etc., etc. Good harvest.

October: At the Industrial School it's the 25th anniversary of priesthood for the Rev. Père Doucet.

November: We had a visit from the Rev. Père Legal, Naessens and Brother Morkin. In the weeks thereafter, a visit from the Rev. Père Lacombe and Monsignor Grouard of Athabasca and Mackenzie.

1896

In **March** we will close our day school and start a boarding school for our savage children. The Grey Nuns of Nicolet will come and help us. We adapt our house and prepare to receive the Sisters.

At the end of **May** Sister St. Jean de Dieu, the Superior, Sister St. Julien and Sister St. Anne arrive here. We start the boarding school with three girls. Later we had eight. We cannot house more of them, everything here is too small. The first children give us lots of trouble, as do the parents, because we keep them here.

[Victor to Brother Stanislas:]
    May 6th, 1896.
    G.Z.J.C.
    Macleod, Peigan reserve,
    Very dear Brother Stanislas,

Well, [this letter is] long overdue. But, better late then never. Isn't it, *mon Frère*? Well, the Father and I have been so busy building, painting etc. etc, that I could not find a moment to reply to your very nice letter and thank you for the memorial cards you sent me.

You must know, dear Brother, that Monseignor Grandin sent us three Grey Nuns to help us in our missionary work. The good Sisters will arrive here in eight days. We will give them our house, which, over ten years, we have quietly enlarged and improved. The Father and I now live in a little hut (rather a shack) until we will get the means to build something better. The Sisters will have one decent and quite large house and enough room to accept ten or twelve poor savage girls as boarding school students. They will also cook, bake, sew and do laundry for us. In the meantime I will do school, garden and help the Sisters. The Sisters will also help us to visit and support the sick. Later we will try to build a small hospital and increase the number of Sisters. We trust in Godly Providence.

So, you see, *mon Frère*, as much as we can, we make progress here. I am happily looking forward to the arrival of the Nuns. I have often been alone here for days and weeks, truly alone with my savages, while the good Brother Foisy was travelling for his missionary works. With regard to our savages, *mon Frère*, we enjoy seeing so many changes from their previous way of life and mores. Instead of three, four or even more wives, now the young men only take one wife and some are even married by the priest, after some due preparations. They bring in or have all their children willingly baptized. Still, we have to give them a gift for it – a few yards of flower-printed cotton, a handkerchief or tea or coffee, which the savages like very much. Their sorcery and superstitions have also decreased, but not all at once, my Brother. It takes a long time, because we even find traces of it in the Flemish, isn't it? The superstition, or rather ignorance, of the savages makes us sometimes laugh. Last Sunday we heard the first thunder of the year. When the savages heard it crashing, they all crawled out of their huts and tents and screamed and clapped their hands, saying that *kristekomopie* had arrived and now the summer and warm days will be here for good.[285] For them thunder is a big bird that makes so much noise with its wings and flies through the sky with flaming eyes and sometimes comes down to kill and then eat a horse, cow or even a man.[286] We have explained to them more than once about thunder and lightning, but the savages persist in believing all of those things.

Well, dear Brother Stanislas, thank God I am always safe and sound as are brother Léonard, le Père Naessens etc., etc. But, our good bishop is sick again and according to the doctor His Highness will not see the year's end. Hopefully the doctor is wrong! Let us pray to God that He save this good Father for many more years. His Highness is now 68 years old.

You write that young Brother Henri went to heaven and that both the Brothers Aloyis and Cyriel are ill as well. What difficult times for the Van Dale Brothers! My opinion is that the young Brothers should take more care of their health and stop all the long hours of studying. All these concourses are only idle glory! I am happy that they are abolished, as you write, because it would have put many of our Brothers into the doldrums. I wrote to Brother Director and expect an answer back. I thank you, dear Brother, for all of the news that you communicate. That is so brotherly of you.

My best wishes and a handshake for your good fellow Brothers Gerardus and Paulinus. Let's pray for one another. Please write often and send me all the news about Marcke, Kortrijk etc., etc.

Please send me one of these days a useful book, devotional cards, etc., etc. Each time I receive something from the Brothers, it seems like a visit from them. It has already been sixteen months ago that Brother Antonius wrote to me; from Vyve it is over one year.[287] Brother Victor writes me once in a while and then, lately, I received a letter from Brother Bernardus, the other Brothers never write to me – God forbid![288] I enclose a few flower seeds from the prairie. Do you have a garden in Marcke? Do you have a chapel at your monastery? [I wish you a] good month of May. Think of Brother Joannes.

Farewell.

Your dear fellow Brother in J.C.
Brother Joannes Berchmans,
Missionary / Always my same address.

St. Paul's Mission August 25, 1896.
G.Z.J.C.

Dear Beloved Brother Stanislas,
I received your letter and with it the many beautiful memorial death announcements. Thanks! Thanks! Dear Brother. They are a thousand times welcomed here. My little savages are so happy when they get a card in school as a reward for good behaviour and diligence. They stick them up in their huts and tents because they see statues and paintings hung in this way on our wooden walls. The savages often ask us for a (*Natoyesenaksie*), a little religious statue, in order to have God's blessing for their houses.[289] A good idea for our poor savages, isn't it Brother? Again, thank you Brother Stanislas, for all the news you communicated. Brother Director of Kortrijk has not written to me anymore for over a year. I think that the good man is too busy with the increase in our convents and number of Brothers. It will have been about two years that Brother Antonius has written to me. I don't forgive him as I have written to him lately. Why don't you remind him, give him an earful. If it were not for you, good Brother, and Brother Victor, I would hardly know anything about the affairs at our convents. Please write to me a bit more often, would you mind? It makes me so happy when I receive a letter from my dear fellow Brothers. I thank God!

Always safe and sound with my savage Blackfoot, who slowly give us more consolation. As you know already, we now have three Grey Nuns, who are very helpful to us. They have 10 savage girls as boarding students. They cook, do laundry and sew for us, etc., etc. I work in the school, act as warden, gardener etc., etc. We now have one horse, one cow, one piglet, hens, chickens. The children, who have never seen chickens, look at them with astonishment. When the young cocks start to crow, the boys ask me what they are saying? Simple children! All goes well with brother Léonard, Father Naessens and the other Flemish. Our good bishop is still sick, the doctor has little hope. We trust in God and Our Lady. Please pray a bit for the good Father. Dear Brother Stanislas. I would write more to you, but the stupid mailman is waiting for my letter. Until later. Pray for me and many, many compliments to all the Brothers.

Farewell.
Brother Joannes Berchmans
Always my same address / Write soon / Written in haste.

[Victor continues:]
September: Le Père Foisy leaves the mission and will become a Trappist. I think that he will be better off there than here. He is always too chicken and doesn't dare undertake anything. The Rev. Père Danis is his successor. He is young and very ambitious but not in very good health. We take on

two more students, that makes ten, and, we have a chance to send a few to Dunbow Industrial School.

During the midnight mass at **Christmas** Mr. Eugene Many Guns made his first Holy Communion.[290] He is the first Peigan who makes his Holy Communion here.

1897

We sent a few more children to Dunbow. Now there are 28 Peigan. Excellent number. Our ten children here are doing better all the time.

Feb.: On the Blood reserve Jaco is hung for murder.[291]

February 8: Wedding of Eugene Many Guns to July La Chapelle at the Dunbow School, and in the evening of the same day, the wedding of Mr. Joseph Thomas and Mary Potts.[292] Henri Potts, married for six years, now also comes to church every Sunday, which means now we have three Catholic families.[293] We quietly see some changes among the Peigan, who for such a long time remained deaf to the voices of the missionaries and the grace of God.[294] That is why we urge our Bishop to build a small church.

May: Monsignor allows us to build a small church. And the department [allows us to build] a boarding school for 40 children with a residence for the Sisters.

July: We start to collect the tools for the preparations.

August: The work has begun. We have eight to ten labourers. Spomomanis and his son is hit and killed by thunder.[295] Mgr. Legal, who in June has been anointed as Coadjutor Bishop, visits us and views the construction. Good progress with the construction.

November: The church is almost finished. We have two painters for the hall.

December 12th: We hold the first mass in the church.[296] Lots of people; several young savages now attend church regularly. The number of Catholics quietly grows.

Christmas: Midnight mass with general Communion. What a beautiful and devout feast meal. Christmas tree etc., etc. Big celebration. *Nash fini le chemin de fer.*

1▸ *Dunbow or St. Joseph's Industrial School, De Winton.* Courtesy Provincial Archives of Alberta. Neg. no. A 4703

2&3▸ *2003: Barns Dunbow Industrial School.* Photo Mary E.M.

4▸ *2003: Dunbow School Cemetery.* Photo Mary E.M.

5▶ 2003: Offerings at original grave side
6▶ High River bank

7▶ 2003: Remains of St. Paul's Church at Peigan Nation. Photo Mary E.M.

8▶ 2003: 1/16th Replica of St. Paul's Church, Brocket, Peigan Nation. Photo Mary E.M.

January: Every Sunday lots of people attend the godly services. [297]

March: Right now the Sisters are in their new, big building. The number of boarding school students increases. Monsignor comes to consecrate the church and the school and to establish Stations of the Cross. Solemn ceremony and lots of people.

April: Père Danis leaves the mission and trades with Père Doucet. May God's will come to pass! Sister St. Jean de Dieu trades with Sister George of the Blood reserve. There also arrived another Sister. Right now there are four Sisters and twenty boarding school students.

October: We have twenty-six children and everything goes well.

December: Christmas, nineteen Confessions from Peigans, fourteen Holy Communions at the midnight mass. Christmas tree and concert. Grand celebration. Wilson Agent.[298]

1899

January: Retreat and visit to Dunbow School. There are twenty-six Peigan children.

February 26th: Visit from Mgr. Legal. Grand celebration. Baptism and wedding of Chief Black Eye.[299] Seven First Communions, fourteen Confirmations. Status.

May: Visit from the Rev. Mother of the Sisters of Nicolet. Celebration. She takes Sister St. Anne along with her, despite everything we did to keep her here. The choir and the organ will miss out much!

June–July: Lots of rain, good for the garden. Harvest.

[Victor to Brother Stanislas:]
 Macleod, Peigan reserve, June 4, 1899.
 Just to Brother Stanislas!
 Dear fellow Brother,

Yes, we have not written to each other for a long time. Sometimes there are somber days and thunder that is feared by all men and which silences them. But, when gust calms down, the weather gets so much more beautiful. Well, I hope that thunderstorms cleared up the air at the Van Dale Brothers too! So that rest, love and unity, the building blocks of monastic life, may rule again and the Superior revered by all; so that our Holy Rule will be adhered to as punctually as possible. That is what I hope for, wish for and ask for on a daily basis from God. It is true that even though I am far from you all, but I remain dedicated to the Van Dale Brothers in body and soul. My greatest consolation in the midst of my manyfold missionary activities is to now and then receive some good news from those I love as my true Brothers; to hear that all goes well, that the number of the Brothers increases more and more, and that new foundations are being accepted. See, that is the consolation that I long for, for all of you. That once in a while one of the Brothers goes to heaven to receive his reward for his sacrifices and good works, that is how it goes in the world and soon it will be our turn as well. Therefore, dear Brothers, let us carry our crosses with complete submission and love and our reward will be even bigger. When we all live as true religious men, when we only do good, we can win souls for heaven and that should be our only goal. Saint Theresa exclaimed: Suffer and Die; and my motto is: Suffer and Work and don't die yet!

I heartily thank Brother Emilianus for his long letter. I would love to send a letter just to him, but as I have to send one to Paul, it would be too much work. That is why I send some news for all of you jointly now. First of all, thank God, I am still safe and sound, as stout and strong as I have been for twenty years, although I am now 54 and getting bald headed. I am finding more and more consolation with my savage Blackfoot. They get more civilized and convert more than the first ten years when I was here with them. Many of my first students are already married and are good examples. They love me a lot and I too, I love them as my own children. In March our bishop came here. We had a big celebration: fifteen Confirmations were administered and seven First Communions and [we had] the baptism and wedding of a chief (Black Eye) who had been preparing for it for two years. There was also a big dinner with speeches in French, English and *Piednoir*. In the evening our savage students held a beautiful concert, everything was very successful. Monsignor and a few white men, among them two Protestants, were amazed with the progress of our students. These celebrations are enjoyed by the children's parents and that is how we attract them more and more to us and to their conversion. This year we have already had fourteen first Communions. Others are still preparing, among them the aforementioned chief. Without a doubt it has changed since my arrival. A few more years and with God's grace the Peigans are civilized and converted. Pray for them dear Brothers and pray for the one who hasn't forgotten you and who always calls himself

Your dedicated fellow Brother in J.C.
Brother Joannes Berchmans / Missionary.

[Victor continues:]
September, October: Nothing special. Sun Dance, funeral. We hold a beautiful celebration for all our Catholics.

November: Sister St. George also leaves for Nicolet. Sister St. Patrick replaces her as superior.

November, December: Illness and death and funeral of Joseph Thomas, the first and best Catholic at this reserve. He was my adopted son. What a loss for our mission. He was a good example in everything and he died a saint! RIP.

Christmas: 27 Confessions. Midnight Mass: fourteen Communions by Indians. No celebration. We are all in mourning because of the loss of our best friend J. Thomas.

February 7th: Visit from Mgr. Legal and the Rev. Père Naessens. Wedding of Peter Bob, Leo Smith and Henry White Dog.[300] First Communion for J. Black Eye and wife of Peter Bob, Johnny Sutten and six Confirmations. Big celebration.

March 9th: The fierce wind tears apart our little church. Everything is damaged and our beautiful statutes are in a thousand pieces. God's will comes to pass!

April: Our church is re-erected and strongly enforced at a cost of $200 and our beautiful statutes!

24: Easter celebration: twenty Communions and wedding of Leo Ketopie and Jimmy English.[301]

May 29th: Brief visit from Mgr. Legal. Departure for Pincher Creek. We have a ferry on the river. The south side of the reserve is surrounded by a garden. The Peigan do all of the work. The sawmill, partly paid for by the Peigan, is also in operation. Many improvements in the Agency and all over the *réserve*. Civilization marches on. Now we have about one hundred Catholics among the 500 Peigan.

June: During the summer for several weeks the school children suffer from an eye ailment. There are 27 students.

Christmas. Ten adult baptisms, six weddings, 46 confessions and 28 Communions by savages.

1901

January: Big changes. Père Doucet goes to the Blood and the Rev. Father Danis comes back here. We, and all the Peigan are very satisfied with it. We are dealing with a certain dangerous disease here among the students. Three have already been sent back to their parents, another one is to the Blood hospital and still others are dangerously ill. A terrible ordeal. Only a few weeks ago Rosa Crow Eagle died from consumption.[302] Many sick people all over the reserve.[303]

February: Six of our children die and there are about 25 dead all over the reserve.

February 12th: Ben Big Plume married Mary Morning Robe, both our students.[304] Bishop Legal comes here with Pères Lestanc, Naessens and Blanchet. Fifteen First Communions and 23 Confirmations. Big celebrations!

14: Banks [illegible] *Eglise payé et le frais de transport* 25 *piastres.*

Father Naessens brings along another three children for the Dunbow School. Crow Eagle, the Head Chief, dies well prepared.[305] We give him a solemn funeral service and burial.

[Victor to Leonard:]
Peigan Reserve, March 25, 1901.
Dear brother,

Your Palm branches are almost ready to be shipped by train. Well, I am glad that you will have them. After Easter I will try to visit you. I will bring you the money from the bank. Do you want me to send it to you, or can you pay the $100 using your own money or wait until Père Danis and I come. Tell me what is the best. But I think that it would be better that you send the money than that we do because everything is in your name. Send me news about Joseph as soon as you have any. As always, many children are still dying here, but no small pox any more. Thank you and farewell,

Brother Joannes Berchmans.

[Victor continues:]
July: Right now we have 24 pupils. Sister St. George is again Superior. Few sick people, still deaths. Good weather, high water, beautiful garden.

Sister Louise of the Blood [Reserve] arrived here as Superior. Always changes. In one year we have all new Sisters; that is how they want to kill the mission school. Poor Sisters! This year the savages produced about 2,000 tons of hay. Twenty-one mowers: more and more progress in civilization and also in converting. In general our Catholics do well, nearly every week confessions and communions of the savage. God bless him!

Sept: Mr. Butcher appointed chief.[306]

1902

January: Father Danis moves to Macleod to assist Père Lebret. Father Doucet will return back here. Always changes! And no improvements! Sam Potts dies a saintly death, as does Johnny Smith.[307] RIP. Solemn funeral service. Lots of people.

March 23rd: Joe Potts marries Sam's widow with dispensation from Mgr. Legal.

June 6th: Joe Smith of the Protestant School in Calgary makes his first Communion and marries Kate, from our school.[308] We have two horrible floods; everything is flooded.

October: Visit from our Bishop. Seven First Communions and nine Confirmations.

Christmas: Midnight Mass, High Mass, Christmas tree, concert etc., etc.

[Father Riou (1902, 163) about the course of affairs:]

It was in 1888 ... [that] Father P. Foisy, who was since two years in the district and who was charged with MacLeod since 1886, took care of the Peigan Reserve with Brother J. Berchmans, the brother of the Rev. Father Van Tighem. Brother J. Berchmans is a Brother of Charity from Kortrijk (Belgium). Up April 8, 1886 he arrived at MacLeod.

1903

January: Father Naessens has returned from Belgium.[309] I will visit him at Dunbow. He gives six ornaments etc., etc. from Belgian friends and benefactors. Since December Father Salaün is here to study the language. His health is quite frail.

April: Visit from Father Naessens. We give him three more children for his school. At present 21 children from here are in Dunbow and here in the boarding school we have nineteen.

July: Visit from Bishop Legal. One first Communion and two Confirmations. The mission is not doing very well. Many of our Catholics are dying. The other savages clamor about it and prevent new conversions. Not many people show up on Sundays. God help us! This summer the weather is good, lots of rain, beautiful garden. The Sisters paint the fence around their house. Everything there looks beautiful.

September: Lots of vegetables. The Indians produce lots of hay. This summer they planted a garden on the other side of the reserve.

Christmas: Midnight Mass, general administering of Communion and wedding of Mr. Joseph Prairie Chicken.[310] Christmas tree and concert.

Father Lepine replaces Father School. Salaün, who moves to the Blood reserve.

1904

January: Visit to the Dunbow All goes well, about 90 children, 23 Peigan.
Jan.: Good weather.
February and March: Cold and snow.

[Victor to Brother Stanislas:]
Macleod, Peigan reserve, March 22, 1904.
G.Z.J.C.
Beloved Brother Stanislas,

Your honoured [letter] just arrived here on February 5th, the day before yesterday, due to the heavy snow that stopped the trains. Since the beginning of February we have continuously had snow and continuous bitter cold and until today it has not improved much. It goes without saying that your letter was very agreeable and welcome. News from the Fatherland, news from friends and fellow Brothers will always be utmost welcome. And I trust that you will write to me again by Easter and communicate the result of the elections. Just like all of the Brothers I am very interested in this election.

Well, dear Brother Stanislas, thank God I can tell you that my health is still very good. Even though on April 9 I will be 59 years old. You have known all along that I am happy here. I have been here for 18 years and I never regretted it nor did I ever, for one day, think of returning to Belgium. You, dear Brother, as an old friend, know better than anyone, that a missionary's life has always been my goal. On our walks we often, didn't we, talked about nothing else than about the missionary life. About Mgr. Grandin (holy remembrance), savages, mountains, valleys etc., etc. Yes, you know it. My first call was for the missionary life. Although I was happy the first 15 years with the Van Dale Brothers, the core idea about the savages of North America was never far from my thoughts. How often we discussed it, how welcome were the letters from my brother missionary who has been here for 30 years now. The letters from Mgr. Grandin and especially his visit to us in Kortrijk. Yes! God wanted me to be a missionary. But before that he wanted to put me through a hard tribulation.''' Yes! A tribulation I would not wish on anyone, but still it was the means for me to get to my first calling. Considering all of this, we must agree with the Prophet David: "How wonderful is God in all of his works."

Understand me well, fellow Brother, these 18 years seem like it has been only one year since I first arrived here. But, what changes since my first arrival! The area does not look the same any more! Towns and villages everywhere. Our savages themselves have changed into white people with regard to their mores, manners and way of dressing. Their tents and huts have been changed into neat and comfortable houses. They have stables and sheds for their horses, cows and other animals. To sum it up, the savages are now civilized people. Yes! Even better than many of the foreigners who arrive here by the thousands from all counties, nations and languages. What consoles us even more is that a good number of our savages are now good Christians. For twenty years they did not know of nor pray to any other God than the sun, for whom they danced about the entire day and night and to whom they made sacrifices! Yes dear Brother, it gives us much solace to see our church on every Sunday full of savages who pray and sing with us and partake in the Holy Sacraments. Thinking about it causes tears of affection and joy to well from my eyes and I say thanks to God, who sent me here, to contribute a bit to the conversion and change in the Blackfoot's life style. Yes Brother, I love my savages like my own children and they love me too.

Well, dear Brother, we do our best under the conditions God has presented us. Let us try to be good religious men. Let us adhere as much as possible to the Holy Rule, only then will we be happy here on earth, despite what people think or say about us. Being despised and even persecuted, is the lot of the true friends and disciples of Jesus Christ. What didn't he put up with? Is the servant any better than the master?

Well, I wish you, dear Brother Stanislas and all your good fellow Brothers a good and glorious Easter – and, if it is possible, try to send me an Easter egg. I would say, some francs. I would like so much to make an altar for our little church, so far there are only a few spokes with cover of cotton fabric stretched over them. Please try to find a good soul in Meenen who will send me alms. Do your best to get something and send it in a money order! Thank you in advance.

My brother le Père Van Tighem is still well and healthy. At the beginning of this year I spent a few days with Father Naessens. He told me about his visit to you in Meenen. He is very happy here. He was very much needed here for our Industrial School. Father Devriendt (cousin of Brother Dominicus) is in Belgium again at the Basilica of the Holy Heart near Brussels.[112] I think that our bishop wants to go to Rome this summer and maybe to Belgium too. Farewell dear Brother, many compliments to everyone and all the Brothers there. Don't forget my Easter.

Your dedicated Brother in X[te] Mass.
Brother van Tighem

[Victor continues:]
Easter: Ice on the river breaks up. Nobody can cross the river. Few people at mass and at lauds. Our agent Wilson moves to the Blood reserve. May God save him. He was not good for the mission. He behaved like the king of the reserve and had no friends.[113] He is replaced by Mr. Gooderham. He is a very friendly man.

Father Lepine replaces Father Salaün who will go to the Blood reserve. Peter Bob dies a very devout and saintly death on May 22nd. RIP.[314]

December 8th: Splendid feast here.

1905

Joe Smith makes an altar at our church.

March: The altar is beautiful and it is a big improvement for the church. I have paid all the expenses for the altar with money from family and friends in Belgium. Andrew Butcher, son of the Head Chief, marries Sophie Cross Chief from our school where she has spent over 8 years.[315] Andrew, a former student from the Calgary Industrial School, is now a good Catholic and took his First Communion that very day. The mission is doing quite well. Every Sunday there are a sufficient number of Catholics at mass.

May: Right now we have 30 children at our school and 19 at Dunbow.

August: I have a chance to go to Belgium for free, to accompany Brother Scheers, who is almost blind and deaf. He has spent 33 years in the far north. I have Father Doucet take this opportunity.

[Victor (1905) to his nephew Henri Van Tighem in the seminary in St. Albert near Edmonton:]

Peigan Reserve, September 1, 1905.

Dear nephew

Today Brother Scheers and Father Doucet left from here for Montreal. They will arrive in a few days in Belgium. Cousin stayed for 10 days with me. We chatted a lot, in Flemish and in French. Brother [Scheers] is still doing well, but his eyes. Mail me the *Gazette* with the description of the Meulebeke church. Cousin gave it to you. Compliments of Monsignor. I am happy that he sent Father Doucet. Here everything is well. My new cassock from Kortrijk has not yet arrived.

Farewell, write to me and let us pray for one another.

Your uncle,
Brother Joannes Berchmans.

[Victor continues:]

Christmas: Grand celebration. Midnight Mass. All our Catholics take the Holy Sacraments. Two First Communions. Mild winter.

On treaty day only 492 Indians.

New harmonium, 25 dollars.

1906

March: Father Doucet returns again from Europe very satisfied with his trip. Many cows and calves die. *There is not grass in the prairie.*

May 20th: Visit from our Bishop. Lots of people. Confessions and Holy Communion, four Confirmations. Lots of rain. Good for the prairie and the fields. Father Lepine moves to the Blackfoot reserve. Father Doucet and I are alone again at the mission. There is not enough work for two Fathers.

Father Naessens leaves Dunbow in May and moves to Edmonton. Father Riou will go to Dunbow. Annual visit to Dunbow: all goes well.

Long and hard winter, cows die by the hundreds. Mr. Gooderham moves to the Blackfoot reserve.[316] He is replaced by Mr. Jougmans.[317]

May: Visit from Mgr. Legal. The Agency wants to haul grain to the Brocket station.

[Victor to Brother Stanislas:]
Peigan reserve, June 16, 1907.
G.Z.J.C. M. and J.
Very beloved Brother Stanislas, Macleod

I received your letter. Thank you! And congratulations on your great celebration, which circumstances you communicated to me! Such celebrations and especially such noble visits are rare in your area. The bishop an entire day with the Brothers; that does not happen every year. I am greatly pleased that you have several new Bothers and happy that Brother Alphons is elected again as Superior-General. I knew him to be a good-hearted and holy man. May God safeguard him for many years!

Don't think, Brother, that we don't have celebrations here! On the same day, May 22nd, our Bishop Mgr. Legal honoured us with a visit and not for just one day, but for three days! Days of happiness and sweet joy. We had solemn celebrations: First Communions, Confirmations, etc., etc. Speeches, a concert and beautiful decorations in the church, school and convent. You see, dear Brother, God sometimes does send us a bit of consolation and also some encouragement, because in his Omniscience [he knows] that everyone needs it once in a while. It excites us and provides new encouragement to go on with the troublesome task we have taken on.

Well, Brother Stanislas, tell all the Brothers that Brother Joannes is doing well like always and is happy with his dear Blackfoot. I am still strong and healthy and can still work just like 20 years ago. The area here is very good for the health, with lots of wind that sweeps away all the angry and bad moods. Last winter was very hard and long, but now the weather is very good and there is lots of rain, good for the prairie and for the fields. My garden looks very well. My fellow companion, Father Doucet is doing well, as are our good Sisters (six in all). The school is going well. The savages work nearly year round. Father Naessens is now pastor in Edmonton, the capital of the Province of Alberta. It is a loss for

▸ *St. Jean Berchmans. Stained glass window in St. Joachim's church, Edmonton.* Photo Mary E.M.

our school, but obedience comes first. Yes, Brother Victor replied right away on the letter sent to you. My compliments to your brother Paul. I pray for him and for all of you. My compliments to all of the Brothers and old friends, especially to Paul and his family. How are Henri Ryckaert and his brother doing?

As always with affection,

Brother Joannes Berchmans.

[P.S.] There are six of us Van Tighems here now – My brother and four nephews, all from Meulebeke. All are doing very well.

[Victor continues:]
August: Wife of Mannean dies. Henri, his eight-year-old son was missing for four days. He sleeps in the bushes for 4 days, without food – Miraculous![318]
October: Mannean shot himself in his house after having killed his son Henri and a half-blood and Cropy near Raymond.[319]

1908

We renovated our house since it was very old, built in 1886. Mild winter.
March 20th: Julia Many Guns dies in the Blood hospital.[320] She was a very good Christian woman. Her three children attended school here. We have 33 children here and 16 in Dunbow.
April 7th: For the first time someone hands out rations in Brocket.[321] Long winter. Lots of rain.
June: Flooding everywhere. For over two months the river is high. Nobody can cross.
July 2nd: Visit from our bishop. Seven of our students receive the Holy Confirmation.
October: Visit from Mgr. Brunauld from Nicolet, Mgr. Legal and Father Lacombe and Father Blanchet.
Christmas: Over 40 Communions during the midnight Mass. Visit to Dunbow, very cold.

1909[322]

From Dunbow I go to Calgary, now a big and beautiful city.

February 4th: I go to Lethbridge for the wedding of my nephew Gustaf to Sidonie Lecluyse, living in Great Falls.[323]

May: Again to Lethbridge. Père Van Tighem leaves for good to go to Edmonton. At the reserve and the mission everything is going well. We have 38 children at the school and once in a while we send a few to Dunbow.

July 12th: Visit from Mgr. Legal and Père Blanchet. 6 Confirmations. Charlie Greer is one of them.[324] Lots of rain this summer. The prairie and the fields look very beautiful.

November 24th: The westside of the reserve is sold at $17 per acre to Pincher Creek.[325]

Christmas: Grand celebration. 42 Indians make Communion.

Death of Victor Mannean and Thomas Pretty Face.

1910

Mild winter, very dry. The Indians lay out the fields. They work with a *steam plower*. They also bought very big horses with the money from the land they sold.

June: We paint our house and church, a beautiful improvement.

June 24th: Visit from our Bishop. Seven Confirmations. Wedding of Charlie Provost, etc., etc.[326] Long drought, no grass, no harvest, in the last year not even half a foot of rain has fallen.

July 20th: Chief Running Wolf dies, only sick for two days.[327] He was over 80 years old. He is buried on the hill, near his son's place.

October: Father Doucet leaves the mission again and moves to the Blood. Father Salaün comes back again here.[328]

Christmas: According to custom, grand celebration. Lots of people, lots of Communions etc., etc.

1911

January, very cold, lots of snow and a fierce wind. Many cows die, and horses too – much sickness and death on the reserve.

February: I visit Dunbow, Calgary, Edmonton and St. Albert. Was welcomed everywhere and much change in the entire area. No sick people in the school here. Only 25 students.

June 18th: Smith dies as good as suddenly. He had a bad accident with his horse two [days?] ago, which caused his sudden death.[329] It is a big loss for his wife and three children. Joe was the best carpenter and worker on the reserve and a good Catholic and best friend. RIP. The altar in our little church is a souvenir from Joe, as are many other works.

July 12th: Visit from Mgr. Legal, big celebration: nine Confirmations. The summer is very good: lots of grass, good harvest and beautiful garden.

November 7th: For eight days it snows and is very cold. We have no coal and are forced to chop the fence around the garden for firewood. The Indians have made good money with their grain and oats. Many die, among others Henri Potts, Henri Side Hills, both die suddenly.

Christmas: Big celebration as usual, a lot of people. I leave for Great Falls, Montana. Visit my family – beautiful city. I stay there for one month. Every day I serve mass for Mgr. Lanighum, the bishop of Great Falls.[330] I return and visit Browning, Holy Family Mission, Joe Potts etc., etc.[331] I return and again a change at the mission. I leave the Peigan with which I have been for over 25 years. Mgr. sends me to the Blood. I arrive there on February 7, 1912. I return to the Peigan on April 12, 1917.

▶ *Brother Joannes Berchmans, Grey Nuns and Indian Students.* Collection Paul Callens

▶ *Brother Joannes Berchmans and Indian students.* Collection Paul Callens

②·❺ Postscript: "Sparkling tales: fire out of cow dung"

1912: "An obedience for Brother Jean, he will go to the Blood. Father Salaün will stay alone in Brocket" (*Codex Historicus de la Mission St. Paul des Peiganes*).[332]

1913 [from a few photos and from a conversation with Leonard C. Van Tighem in Okotoks in February 2005 we know that Victor helped Father J. Riou to build a chapel at the Sarcee Reserve][333]

March 1914: "Brother Van Tighem arrived here with another Brother to build a house that will serve as a church in Chokis. Will then go to Cluny" (*Codex Historicus Blood Reserve*).[334]

Winter 1914–15: "Brother Van Tighem makes a beautiful altar and confession stool for the new church" (*Codex Historicus Blood Reserve*).

April 12 [1917]: "Father Riaux and Jean Berchmans back in Brocket. The Brother has to renovate his room that has stood empty during his absence" (*Codex Historicus St. Paul des Peiganes*).

1923: "Fifty-year anniversary of Brother Jean, little séance and ad hoc feast at the school" (*Codex Historicus St. Paul des Peiganes*).

April 14–25: "Jean to Great Falls to visit one of his nephews" (*Codex Historicus St. Paul des Peiganes*).

October 27: "Father Le Vern, Jean and four boys repair the bridge over Beaver Creek" (*Codex Historicus St. Paul des Peiganes*).

[Smith and English, n.d., about Brother Jean and the Peigan mission:][335]
1921: Brother Jean Berchmans, oblate, bragged to the children that he collected $85.00 at Christmas Midnight Mass.[336]

1923: 29 Catholic Families. Total Catholic population 195. Total Population Peigan Reserve 385

1926: Sacred Heart School built with one small and one large classroom in 1926 (by the grotto). Moves mission from north of river to new site by wagons, between Christmas and New Year 1926–1927.

1▸ "*Het kerkske dat ik
geboudt hebt bij de wilde
Sarcee genaamd* (The
church that I built
at the savages called
Sarcee)." Courtesy
Maria Desseyn-de Witte

2▸ "*Eenigen van onze
wilde katholieken, Sarcee
genaamd* (A few of our
savage Catholics called
Sarcee)". Courtesy
Maria Desseyn-de Witte

3▸ *2005: Steeple of 1913
Our Lady of Peace Church
at Sarcee (now Tsuu T'ina
Nation).*
Photo Mary E.M.

1927: Approximately 20 Catholic Families in Brocket.

[Brother Lucien (2001), to Paul Callens, in his accompanying note to the diary:]

Brother John returned [to Belgium] at the end of 1929. As an anecdote: the Brother who received him at the [Groote] Kring (Kortrijk) did not know him. He notified the superior: "There is a foreign gentleman in clergy outfit in the waiting room." That young Brother had never met with him.

It was a cordial reception: he was kindly received and could rejoin the Brothers without any problems. He was then 84 years old. At the age of 84! He retired in our monastery in rural Viven-Kapelle (St. Kruis)."[337]

I often met with Brother John at our study house in Torhout (1937–1941).[338] Once in a while he came to tell stories to the students. What beautiful moments! He could never stop telling us about his "Blackfoot." In a large circle we would listen to him, to the man with the eternal cigar in his mouth and we looked up to him with admiration, a man who had experienced such unusual events and who could recount, brimming with English words, such sparkling tales.

[Brother Lucien's kind words are still not the last we hear of and from Victor/Brother John. Letters to and from the family and a handwritten report (Van Dale Archives) that gives a splendid account of Brother John's "diamant" anniversary follow.]

[Elodie, in Dutch, to her brother Joseph Van Tighem and his wife Jane in Strathmore:]

12-1-30.

Dear brother and sister,

I visited Uncle Victor and asked him that. He rather had it at once. He said that the superior was very good for him and, he said, that they also need him in the monastery. He does get there tobacco and snuff. Uncle looks very well and is very happy there, they are with four Brothers.

Uncle Victor told me that he would go to Meulebeke and that he hoped to see me there. Uncle Pastor went along and I saw uncle Victor alone. Uncle Jean and aunt Mathilde also look well.

Much is being built in Meulebeke; straight across the police office there are now new houses.

Best wishes from uncle Pastor and in particular from your loving sister, Elodie.

Uncle Victor also told me that he received a long letter from you. Jo, tell Janie that the women's folk here also cut their hair. I don't cut it, even if I were the only one.

Adiel wrote to Maria that he postpones his visit to Belgium. I learned

1▶ 1930: Victor/Brother Joannes Berchmans at the 50th wedding anniversary of his brother Jean and wife Mathilde Linclau. Van Tighem Family Archives

2▶ Brother Joannes' 60th anniversary as Van Dale Brother. Van Tighem Family Archives

3▶ Brother Joannes. Van Tighem Family Archives

at Uncle Jean's that Adiel's wife would come in the year '30. When are you coming? And Janie and all of your dear children? And Uncle Joseph and Aunt Irma? I don't here about it anymore.

Again, best wishes for you, Janie and all of your dear children.

Elodie.

1932, May 16

2nd Ascension Day. Jubilee (diamond) of Brother Joannes Berchmans.

1. Jubilee Mass with sermon by the Rev. Administrator, Marcel Dejonghe.
2. Celebration in St. Maartenskring (Jubilarian, Family and Brothers). Singing, presentations, sketches. Presentation of portrait.
3. Feast meal in the Brother's refectory: the Rev. Deacon Camerlynck, Family, Brothers (Menu and feast songs at the other side).
4. Toasts by the Rev. Administrator, the Rev. Deacon and Brother Director

Here follows the speech by Brother Firminius (Director) but mainly written by Brother Romanus:

Dear Brother Jubilarian, Reverend Sirs, Dear Family Members, Dear Fellow-Brothers,

Brother Joannes has already been celebrated and praised in feast letters, poems, songs, in annual reports and toasts. Now I take it upon me to acquaint you with Brother Joannes in his daily life that he lives over and over again in Viven-Capelle. Viven-Capelle, where he lives, and which should not stay behind in all of this partying and jubilating. Viven always is the first. I will reveal something to you. In Viven (I am allowed to say so, as I was there) we celebrated Br. J. on the real day of his 60-year convent life. It was very pleasant and well-meant and we looked forward to what was meant to be, today's solemn Jubilee celebration. We offered the jubilarian a single flower. Now he gets the entire bouquet.

All of you know Br. Joannes, isn't it? But do you know Brother John from Viven? No, I don't think so. That is one hundred percent Br. J., that is John, seen in all his nooks and crannies, not of his face, but of his soul, of his daily occupations and his coming and going. Whether he now grumbles or not, he will have to enter the stage and it will honour him!

Br. J. is 88 years old, but that is only what counts in the books of the civil registry of the City of Meulebeke. In his heart he actually stayed eternally young. And in order to show that, I only have to point to what he does in Viven-Capelle. And I tell you, in the first place, he narrates. Did you hear John narrate? No? Then you should join him around the stove on a Sunday afternoon and listen, just listen and look. He lit a cigarette, puffs with short puffs, so pleasantly blowing the smoke to the front of him and then digs from his rich life experience such treasure of stories and anecdotes, that it never bores to listen to and to look at. In general it deals with his mission in Canada, and then he has a smile around his mouth, and then the words come out by them selves, and then one story pulls out the next one, and then his cigarette extinguishes!

Oh! Pupils and poultry! Oh! Crown-Eagle and Blackfeet! How many sweet hours you have given us!

Oh! Canada! Belle patrie!

Du Canada sont mes amours! (bis)

Second: Brother Joannes works. And I will never think of him without him wearing an 'apron' while he buzzes and buzzes as a bee, and shuffles, working, through house and garden. He peels the potatoes and chops wood, takes care of the rabbits and feeds the hens; he plants, sows, and weeds and rakes, sprays and fertilizes, digs and labours, harvests and enjoys and buzzes, buzzes. Buzzing is always going on. All in

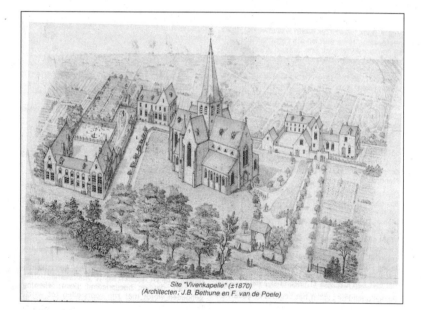

Site "Vivenkapelle" (±1870)
(Architecten: J.B. Bethune en F. van de Poele)

▶ *c. 1870: Vivenkapelle.* Courtesy John Goodderis (2001, 85) and Baron E. de Bethune all one truly witnesses: "Brother John still looks quick for his age!" And when you do not believe this? Well, you better look at him: clean-shaven as a gentleman, thoroughly washed and groomed, a cigarette between his lips and reading his newspaper. Brother Joannes is the man of the *News of the Day* and he reads solemnly and correctly, he reads with his glasses on top of his nose, he reads forgetting everything and anyone and then, forgetting to read, he dozes off! And truly, he deserves it after work done!

Finally, Brother Joannes prays. He prays a lot, he prays piously. It is uplifting to watch him when his Pater Noster slides through his old fingers and he mumbles his Hail Mary's. How often he prayed Mary's rosary he himself will not know, but the one who knows it and the one who looks down upon the old Brother as if upon her dear child, that will be his Heavenly Mother herself.

See, dear Brother Jubilarian, whenever you will lay down your old head, you will have left all of us such a beautiful testament: your magnificent example of diligence and prayer, of cosiness and Brotherly companionship and you yourself will celebrate your eternal Jubilee for long with God and your Mother!

First this, Brother John, you might give the congregation a centenarian, and you can do it because you look still quick for your age! And you only have to fulfill what you promised two years ago to Dr. Tybergheim of St. Kruis: "You allow me ten more years, I'll then will add another four and then I am 100."

Dear Brother Joannes, I, Superior, I thank you for your faithfulness to your congregation, for your uplifting example, it should once more be repeated, of extraordinary diligence and well-meant piety. How wonderful does your life style contrast those of many weak-hearted ones of nowadays, who always shout at work: "It is too much!" and at recreation: "It is not enough!" May your example teach them that diligence and a virtuous life is the best guarantee for a long and happy life on earth and for a splendid reward in Heaven!

[Menu of the banquet at the occasion of the Diamond Jubilee of the Rev. Brother Joannes Berchmans in the monastery of the Van Dale Brothers:]
God's blessing over the meal.
   Oxtail Soup
   Cow tongue in turtle sauce and Fatherlanders [potatoes]
   Beef in Godart sauce and vegetables
   Grain chickens and salad
   Ice cream and whipped cream – Fruit basket
The Lord be praised for his gifts
Kortrijk, May 16, 1932.

[Feast Song for the Rev. Br. J. Berchmans, at this diamond Jubilee, April 16, 1932:]

1. Opgeruimd van geeste,
   Vieren wij dit feeste;
   en geen feestgetij
   zonder lied erbij!
   Hij is d'oudste van ons allen,
   Broeders, laat ons zangen schallen:
   Vivat, vivat! Hij leve, leve lang! (2 x)

2. Sedert zoveel jaren
   toont hij onze scharen
   't voorbeeld van de deugd
   en de ware vreugd.
   Drager van "Van Dale's" vane
   Gaat hij voor op d'hemelbane
   Vivat, vivat! Hij —

3. Hoeveel Canadeezen
   heeft hij onderwezen,
   en geleid tot God,
   tot hun zalig lot,
   maar wier duurgekochte zielen
   anders in de helgloed vielen
   Vivat, vivat!

4. Hoeveel deugden gaven,
   zorgen, bidden, slaven,
   heffen hem zo hoog
   in des Heeren oog.
   En hoe glansrijk prijkt de krone
   die hem wacht in d'eew'ge wone!

5. Dat de hemelzegen
   op hem nederregen!
   Mocht hij op zijn baan
   heil steeds tegengaan!
   Mochten wij hierna te gader
   jub'len met hem rond ons "Vader,"
   Vivat, vivat! Hij leve, leve lang (2 x).

[Translation of this song by Mary E.M.:]

1. Joyful of spirit
   we are celebrating
   and without a song
   no celebration.
   He is the oldest of us all,
   Brothers, let our singing sound
   Vivat, Vivat! That he may live, live long! (2x)

2. Since so very many years
   he showed our flock
   examples of virtues
   and genuine joy.
   Bearer of "Van Dale's" banner
   He will preceed us on heaven's lane
   Vivat, vivat! He —

3. How many Canadians
   will he have been teaching,
   and led to God,
   and their blissful fate,
   but whose souls, that were bought the hard way,
   otherwise would fall in hellish glow
   Vivat, vivat!

4. How many virtuous gifts,
   cares, prayers, slaving,
   in the Lord's own eye
   lift him up that high.
   And how splendid shines the crown
   that waits for him at his eternal home

5. That heavenly blessings may
   bestowed upon him!
   That he on his trail
   may just meet with acclaim!
   Hereafter we will together
   celebrate with him around our "Father,"
   Vivat, vivat! He live, live long (2x).

▷

Vyven-Kapelle, 9 Dec.'34.

My dear cousine,

I was glad to have a word from you this summer, and I hope that you are over the loss of your dear husband.[339] We cannot say other than it was the will of God. Always I pray for him, and for your family. I hope they are all in good health. Is Leonard back in the Seminary, and when you thing he shall be ordained priest.[340]

I read your letter to the sister of Joseph. The poor girl was also very sorry of the loss of her brother, which she loved so much. She is altimes living by her oncle the priest, and her health is very good.

Now for me, I am near 90 years of age, and God thank my health is excellent, and I can yet work and wolf as a young man. All the other members of the family are all in good state, and now I wish you a very happy Christmass and a Good New-Year, and also at all the children, especially at Leonard.

Your devoted uncle

Brother John / Brothers Van Dale / Vyve-Kapelle / Ste. Kruis / West-Vlaanderen / Belgium

N.B. I hope to get a word from you.

[Victor to Jane Anne Van Tighem-Kelly in Strathmore. Transcript:]
March 22nd, 1937.

My dear niece, Viven-Kapelle,

I wish you a joyful and happy Eastern-feast. I was gladd to have a good news from you last Christmass, and to see that you are in the best of health. I am gladd to tell you, that I am still allways in a good health. On the 29 of April, I will be 92 years. My brother John has 88 years, and his Misstress, 84. Mathilde, you will remember her, and they are all yet in the best of health.

Your sister Elody, in Anseghem is also in a good health as is her uncle the priest, they are happy together.

I hope to have now and then, news from you, and your family. I remember you all in my prayers.

We have got a very soft winter, but very much rain, more than I have known in long years ago. It is a hard time for everyone, but we hope it will change soon.

The perspective that Leonard will be priest in a short time fills my hart with pleasure, and I would love yet a bitt to keep that happy news from you. I pray that he may persevere in his vocation.

I wish the best for you, and the whole family.

Brother John Berchmans
Brother Van Dale / Vive-Kapelle / St. Kruis / West-Flanders / Belgium.

[Brother Firmin to Jane Anne Van Tighem-Kelly in Strathmore. Transcript:]
Courtray, 30 December 1938.
My Dear Lady

Brother John Berchmans thanks very much his lovely niece for her amiable attention to send him Chris[t]mas and New Year-wishes. He wishes you reciprocally all what can be agreeable to you. He gives you the tiding that he must keep the bed, having attained the age of 94 ye[a]rs and his lorces decreasing slowly.

Please, excuse me for my bad letter and receive my very sincere respects and the thanks of Brother John.

His superior
Brother Firmin.

[Brother Firmin to Jane Anne Van Tighem-Kelly:]
[Stamp of the Van Dale congregation]
[illegible]

Kortrijk, 17th January 1940.
Dear Family

Brother John Berchmans thanks you very much for the letter and the good wishes. He prays for you all. He is always in bed and says: "I will die this winter!" That is possible, but I do not believe it. I hope he will recover his health by the good weather of spring.

Meantime we have a very hard winter with snow and freezing weather. Till now we are spared from war. Would to God it were so for ever.

Thousand respects from us all, and especially from your uncle Brother John, and from

Brother Firmin, Superior.

[Brother Firmin to Jane Van Tighem-Kelly. Transcript:]
  Kortrijk, Belgium, April 13, 1940.
  Mrs. Janie van Tighem and children,

What your uncle, Brother John Berchmans, predicted since several months has arrived; he died the 4th of April at mid-day. Till the last moment, he kept his presence of mind and his death was very sweet. He has been buried on April 8th with very fine ceremonies of the Church and in the presence of several members of the family from Meulebeke. Please find enclosed a "rouwgedachtenis [death memorial card]" of your uncle.

  Yours respectfully,
  Superior Van Dale Brothers.

The April 13, 1940, letter is not the last we heard about Victor / Brother Jean or John. On January 17, 2004, Paul Callens and I visited the Van Dale congregation in Kortrijk and were cordially received by the Brothers Geert, George, Rudolph and Walter (superior). They all had known him while being novices in the congregation in the 1930s. What they remembered and told us about Victor was the following: "He had a big wart on his hand – he was very cheerful – he was a very nice guy – when he was telling something, he moved his hands and feet a lot – he was old and, slimly built." Brother Walter even remembered a lecture Brother John held in 1939 in Torhout. "Do you remember anything of that lecture?" Brother Walter closed his eyes, went about 65 years back in his memory, opened his eyes, and said, "Yes, over there they made fire out of cow dung."

(M = Meulebeke)
(RQB = Rivière-Qui-Barre)
(×× = second marriage)

Damiaan Van Tighem (1772 M–1840 M) × Maria Anne Scheers (1780 M–1806 M)

Bernard van Tighem (1807 M–1884 M) × Angela Ghislena Kupers (1810 Ingelmunster–1872 M)

| Jean Marie (1849 M–1940 M) × Marie Mathilde Linclau (1854 M–1937 M) | Victor Octaaf (1845 M–1940 Kortrijk) *Went to Canada in 1886* | Gustave (1842 M–1904 M) × Nathalie Van Hollebeke (1854 Ingelmunster–1882 M) *One child.* ×× Maria Ludovica Catteeuw (1846–1919 M) | Van Tieghem, *stillborn* (1848 M) | Gislena Virgina (1839 M–1849 M) | Leonard (1851 M–1917 Taber) *Went to Canada in 1874.* |

Marie Rosalie (1881 M–1969 M) × Silvanus Arthur Désiderius Dewitte (1888–1959 M)

Gustave Alphonse (1883 M–1952 Great Falls) × Sidonie Lecluyse (1909 M–1961 Great Falls)

Henri Ludovicus (1885 M–1964 RQB, Alberta) × Marie Rose Juneau (1882 Juneau Farm, AB–1990)

Karel Lodewijk Bernard (1887 M–) × Marie Vansteenkiste (1885–1919)

Angelina Ghislena Francisa (1888 M–1923 M)

Joseph (blinded) (1889 M–1974 Kortrijk) × Maria Helsocht (1894–1919) *Five children* ×× Adriana Helena Velghe (1889 M–1981 Kortrijk), *widow of Aloïs Louvaert*

Margarita Irma (1890 M–1948 Kalispell) × Adolf Lippens *Two children*

Ludovica Bertha (1891 M–1891 M)

Leonard (1893 M–1894 M)

Ferdinand Joseph Antonius (1894 M–1995 l.a.) × Edna A. Wokurka (1895 Santa Barbara–1993 L.A.) *One child*

Clara Philomena (1896 M)

Alphonse Antonius (1897 M) × Agnes Hertele *Four children*

Maria Julia Mathilda (1923 M) × Isidoor André Desseyn (1920 Pittem–1979 Kortrijk)

Charles Louis Jules
(1856 M–1892 M) ×
Alida Amelia
Desmet
(1860 M–1888 M)

| Maria Josephina (1881 M–1895 M) | Joseph Leon (1882 M–1933 Strathmore) × Jane Anne Kelly (1888 Ontario–1947 Calgary) | Clodie Marie Therese (1883 M–1971 Tielt) Lived with a priest uncle, A.K.L. Desmet (1876 M–1938 Anzegem) | Emillie Demetria (1886 M–1886 M) | Camillie (1887 M–1888 M) | Euphrasia Ghislene (1888 M–1889 M) ×× Rosalie Van Hecke (1865 Ardooie), ×× Arthur Henri Van Fleteren |

Demetria Margarita (1890 M)

Adile Adolph (1892 M–1975 Strathmore) × Maria Caenepeel (1902 M–1993 Calgary)
Nine children

| Leonard Charles (1911 Strathmore) × Delma Thompson (1923 High River) Two children | Patricia Geraldine (1914 Strathmore–2004 Calgary) | John Victor (1917 Strathmore–1991 Calgary) × Eileen F.C. McParland (1925–) Ten children | Clarence Joseph (1921 Strathmore–2003 Ottawa) × Noelle Mary Waters (1920–) Three children | Francis Patrick (1925 Calgary–) |

American Letters I (August 18, 1875)

By Jules Boone
Translated by Mary Eggermont-Molenaar

May 26, 1874.[341]
Montreal (Canada),
My very dear parents, brothers and sister!

In keeping with my promise, I will try to relate to you about my journey across the ocean and also about the peculiar things I encountered. I first have to report that I am in good health and I hope that the Lord has kept you in good health as well.

On Wednesday, May 6, at 11 p.m., three brothers, a Rev. Father and I left Paris and on Thursday, May 7 in the afternoon, we arrived in Le Havre, where we boarded and started sailing on the endless big pond.

When I was about to board, I understood more than ever before, what a sacrifice it is to leave all one loves on earth, to cross into the center of all that is unwholesome and dangerous. But, it is for heaven, for the glory of God and for the salvation of our own souls, and it is this thought that chases out other melancholic thoughts, that consoles, invokes and strengthens me.

The journey along France's coasts had been as good as it could be and Friday at 8 a.m. we anchored at a distance of 2 miles from Brest. That is when we could speak freely about what had already happened and about what lay ahead of us.

We experienced joy and consolation, that is, we were lucky to be on the first journey of the steamship *Satellite* and in the company of Monsignor Grandin, another three priests and three Brothers. To our unspeakable joy we were also told that the Rev. Father Bonalde, who accompanied us, could celebrate H. Mass at the Sisters of Good Hope and that I and my fellow Brothers could approach the Holy Table.[342]

On Friday morning at 9:30 a.m. we gracefully enjoyed receiving Our Lord Jesus Christ. My very dear parents, brothers and sister, it would be futile to tell you how zealously I committed myself and my Brothers to His Holy

Heart and how trustingly I put my entire journey into His Heart. And thanks to his help, my situation could not be better.

On **Saturday, May 9** we boarded again in Brest and for a long time we said goodbye to the French coast that slowly disappeared from our sight. The weather was beautiful and everything went just fine. By Sunday morning it was becoming impossible to discern the French or English coasts any longer. In the afternoon we saw many ships.

Monday 11: the weather is still favourable and the sea is calm. Three quarters of the passengers are already seasick and it is seldom that even half of the people sit down at the dinner table.

Also, in the dining room nobody can stand being there for more than a quarter of an hour; everyone wants to go back to bed, hoping to find some peace and quiet there. But even on the top floor of the ship, anyone who ate anything suffers from an upset stomach. Moreover, it is even insalubrious to stay inside the ship for long; there is no ventilation and the air is terrible. As far as I am concerned, I am a happy exception to the general rule. I am doing fine and am feeling no sickness or discomfort. I make use of my fortunate condition to entertain our company for a while.

We had barely finished our lunch when the passengers who went upstairs for some fresh air stormed downstairs again and announced that a frightful thunderstorm was approaching on the horizon. And yes, before nightfall we found ourselves in a situation that provoked thoughts about the last hours of one's life. The sea became a raging turbulence, the furious waves filled up the ship incessantly and the ship was being battered and slung about so that one had to hold onto the bed railings with both hands. Outside the sea could be heard howling and roaring, inside things were falling and breaking because the ship was nearly tossed upside down.

Those of us about to die from suffocation and others from seasickness, tried to find the bishop. And true to form, he reassured us; he encouraged us to pray and then to sing. His orders were immediately executed and our entire company is and remains full of courage and trust, and yes, even feeling humorous and entertaining.

The thunderstorm continued on this way for three days and then on **Thursday**, Ascension Day, the sea quieted down a bit. On the occasion of this beautiful feast day, in the morning on top of the bridge we sang the *Kyrie Eleïson*, the *Gloria*, the *Credo*, the *Sanctus* and *Agnus* at the top of our lungs. In the afternoon several times we started to sing the *Magnificat*. Each evening we sang the *Ave Maris Stella* together, the litany of Our Good Lady and several other odes.

On **Friday the 15th** the sky remains overcast, but the sea does not look too great. We also experienced the pleasure of seeing several sailing boats around, which had not happened over the last four days. Once in a while one notices miraculously big sea monsters. Around noon the sea is very calm and the temperature very pleasant. Everyone wants to enjoy this beautiful weather and nearly all the passengers are upstairs on the bridge.

However as dusk falls, things get angry. Indeed, whatever force, that can disturb a sea journey, is displayed for us, and then we arrive at the fearful and dangerous place called *Trou du Diable* where, according to the sailors, not a day passes by without a thunderstorm.

On **Saturday** we are in the center of this dangerous spot in the sea, however, as we have had bad weather from the start, we are getting used to it. And, we did not come to improve our own situation, but to expose ourselves to suffering and hardship, to declare war on the devil, to jerk souls away from him and to make courageous Christians out of them and, in the meantime, work on our own salvation.

Because of these reasons we bear our fates with ease and even in the center of this entirely sad and dangerous situation, it enables us to savour a genuine inward and outward joy. Monsignor is also most entertaining.

On the afternoon of **May 16** the entire population of the ship watches many tall and miraculous icebergs, when a number of them float by on both sides of our sailing route. So far we already count 17 and several of them are three or four times as tall as the church in Meulebeke.

It is now **May 17th**, Sunday again. I can't describe how much it hurts to be deprived, for the third time on a holy day, to miss mass and vespers, or to visit some congregation or religious society. But there is nothing to be done about it and the bishop and the priest are as "happy" about it as I am.

With regard to the weather, this morning it is great, the sea is calm, the wind is almost favourable, but the temperature is biting cold.

Around noon and partly during the afternoon we are enveloped in a thick fog, so that the ship has to divert course on a regular basis in order to avoid colliding with other invisible ships. After having prayed diligently to our Lord and our good Mother Mary, we end the day singing hymns and vespers and for recreation we watch in wonder at the fish in the sea that are as big as horses and that are fighting and playing about.

Monday the 18th: the sea is generally calm and the weather has warmed up a bit but the rain, time and again, drives the passengers into their cabins. About 7 p.m. we discern a steamship and right away both vessels greet one another by raising their flags. We also start to notice that the days shorten as we approach America. And also that while it is 12 o'clock in Meulebeke, it is only 7:30 here.

Tuesday, May the 19th: the weather remains dark and foggy. It is impossible to see ahead in order to discern the route the ship will take, so around noon we appear to have been drifting a bit away from it. Also, we are now in the middle of the sandbanks of Terre Neuve, and only a distance of 100 hours from the American coast. We are in danger of hitting spots here and there where the sea is too shallow to keep our vessel afloat. This is why the ship stops from time to time, to probe the depth of this immense water puddle, but so far they still sound a depth of 155 meters. During the afternoon the weather is very beautiful.

Wednesday at dawn everybody is up and about and dressed in his best. The weather is exceptionally beautiful and from the top of the ship we see more than one hundred ships and vessels of all kinds, so we must be very close to the harbour. And indeed, about 7 o'clock around us we see American soil. Another three hours later, and we are in the New York harbour. The Frenchmen, Germans, Italians, Spaniards, English, Swiss, to sum it up, all of the passengers sing, and I, a Belgian, the only one from my country, I sing also! Yes, everybody sings and also admires the really beautiful view in one of the most beautiful harbours of the world.

Here in New York the winter is barely over and nature is still asleep, but the mountains and small isles are covered and busy with their green shrubbery and small houses. The valleys are crammed with lakes whose quiet waters mirror the sky. There are hundreds of different kinds of buildings such as high church steeples – unfortunately most of them protestant churches! – and monuments that are a miracle of architecture. All this provokes a longing for spring to make it splendid in all its beauty.

A canon announces our arrival and not much later we see a curious crowd of white and black Americans who greet us on the wharves. As far as we are concerned, we have the exceptional luck to meet the Rev. Father Lacombe in the crowd. From now on he will serve as our interpreter and guide. After only a 5-hour wait we have collected our luggage and it is carried at once to the train station. At 5 a.m. we depart from New York.

It is impossible for me to describe to you the beauty of this station; it is a miraculous sight. As we arrive at the station, there are agents who ask us in English whether our company would like to take a whole coach. The Rev. Father Lacombe happens not to be around at that moment and because my comrades don't understand English, I have to be the spokesperson. I tell the servant that we will likely take a sleeping coach. As soon as Monsignor and Father Lacombe are back, I advise them of this and by 10:30 p.m. we are in the coach in our beds.

I would love to tell you how beautiful these sleeping coaches are designed and manufactured, but it is impossible for me to explain it in writing. These coaches are twice as long as the ones used in Europe. Each one has a stove and a water basin on both sides. It has a room for men and one for women and as one travels along, a servant goes around with food and drinks.

The train engines are also of a different make than ours, but much better. The iron roads are poorly taken care of and should yield much more profit than ours in Europe. They are not wide and because only two tracks lie beside each other, one drives over and through everything that is out there: through cities and villages, over paved and dirt roads. I think that on a daily basis many accidents would have to occur. It seems also that travel goes much faster than in Europe, because the distance from New York to Montreal is 200 miles and it takes the train only 19 hours.

Thursday, the 21st at 7 a.m. we arrived at the Albany station. We had to wait there half an hour so we had breakfast. It is our first meal in America and it consisted of a lovely, tasty bun with cheese. Our drink was pure clear water, a cup of coffee was out of the question. From now on we might as well say goodbye to beer and wine, as well as to other things and seriously start to feel the sacrifice we made for the love of our fellow human beings, for God and to earn heaven.

Only when we depart from Albany can we look freely at the part of the world that we volunteered for. Nature is miraculously beautiful. The soil is muddy because this area has barely woken from its winter sleep. The population here is far less dense than in Europe. In winter and summer three quarters of the country is not ploughed and once in a while one encounters marshes that stretch for hours.

Timber appears not to be highly regarded and undervalued since many woods and trees are also being burned down. On all sides one sees thousands of stumps sticking up that look like cabbages. One also comes across many trees that have fallen down because of their age and are lying to rot in the marshes.

Most houses are made out of wood and built in a peculiar way. When looking at a few at the same time, they look like a beautiful painting.

There is very beautiful shrubbery here, also gorgeous meadows that are watered by streams and rivers from all directions, rimmed on all sides by high mountains with their peaks sticking out of the clouds. And then there are steep rocks, with peaks like gigantic high towers, and many soft gurgling creeks that stream along all kinds of rock walls, water foaming and dazzlingly hurtling down from heights of 8 or 10 meters into a stream or a lake. Oh! all this strikes and affects the traveller so gently that he forgets about the fatigues of the journey and reflects in graceful wonder on the might of He who created all this beauty.

Around noon we had to wait another 3 hours in the Tritland station. We took advantage of this occasion to have lunch. Our food consisted of a bit of meat and a potato and coffee for drinks. The coffee here tastes bad and according to the Europeans, who have been here a long time already, there is no better coffee to be found. The rest of the time we hurried to find a Catholic Church in the city so we could, after 13 days, kneel down once more before our Lord Jesus Christ in his H. Sacrament.

At 3 we flee again in our American devil. At 9 p.m. we drive over the famous bridge Victoria, the worlds biggest and longest bridge. This bridge is over the St. Laurence River and is between three and four kilometres long, taking about 3 quarters of an hour to cross.

At 10:30 we arrive in Montreal and at 11 we find ourselves, by the grace of God, in our congregation. True, in a monastery in America, but still, among our Brothers. We all experience a most sweet contentment and embrace one another. In a few moments the table is set and it seems like we are in our father's house. At 12 everyone is directed to their bedrooms and we go to bed. In the morning we are happy to resume our religious exercises with ease. By noon another great happiness was awaiting us: Monsignor Taché, Archbishop of St. Boniface, who belongs to our congregation, honours us with a visit, so two bishops partake in our lunch. They are Monsignor Grandin, accompanied by Monsignor Taché! Our joy was boundless – a long journey well done, a brotherly reception among Brothers in the presence of two princes of the church and all Brothers still together! Thanks to God, thanks to Mary!

That very day twelve of our companions left for the Chinese monastery, which is the novitiate three miles from here. With regard to myself, I leave right away for the Grey Nuns, whose profession is, like ours, to serve at the mission.

Saturday at 6 o'clock Monsignor will read mass here and then will stay with me for three days, He suffers from an ailing eye, probably a lingering fatigue from that miserable sea journey. As for myself, I have an abscess in my mouth, so we can worry together. We are treated like emperors and by Sunday I am completely recovered. As Monsignor is not yet recovered, I occupy myself with reading books and letters to him.

We are at an institute where about 500 people live: Sisters, old men and women, children and orphans. The piety and devotion in the church is so edifying, of such a soul-touching nature, one does not come across this in Belgium nor in France. The solemnity of the month of May has been celebrated without parallel and the singing so compellingly beautiful, that each time I heard it, it gave me the impression of being in heaven..

Today, **Sunday**, I had the unspeakable joy of speaking Flemish with the Flemish. The Brothers of Love and their superior came to ask Monsignor for his blessings. Among these monastic priests are several Flemish from the Bruges diocese and I spoke for a long time with them.

Monday in the afternoon, after having bid farewell and thanked the good nuns for all their care, we left their institute to join the other Brothers and continue on our journey. It will perhaps take another three months.

Assuring you that I am doing fine, I bid you to pray for me and I will always remain your faithful son and brother:

JULES BOONE.

American Letters II (August 21, 1875)

[Note of *The Gazette of Thielt* editor:]

Before continuing the peculiar travel account in our "American Letters," we introduce a funny letter from Brest that should have been published at the start and could have served as an introduction.

Brest, May 11, 1874.
Dear parents, brothers and sister!

At this moment I am in Brest, a mile from the harbour where our ship is moored. From Le Havre to here we have already enjoyed a stretch of sea. We are about to board again, head out to sea, up to far away America.

Thank God, my health is good and instead of making me ill, the sea makes me stronger. I am in the company here of my friend, Rev. Father Bonalde, and another three Brothers. The food provided to us here is plentiful and good, but few are able to enjoy it, and my four Brothers are doing poorly! One hears incessant moaning and complaining and many insist that they are about to die! Yesterday evening I carried one of our Brothers from the bridge, he was lying there in bad shape and lamenting bitterly.

You would laugh your head off if you could see how poorly people are acting here. They moan and groan so much that I nearly explode from laughing. It is so funny, but not for the people who are so sick, but I cannot help myself and it is not dangerous. It is seasickness, as they say, and whoever is not used to being at sea and wants to get acquainted, has to experience it for a while.

Yes, that big pond is full of dirty tricks!

It is strange that I am doing so well, my stomach feels fine and if it continues on like this, I might put on some weight before this journey is over! Well, dear parents, brothers and sister, there is no very sad news to relate, isn't there, and I think that there is a good chance I will not have to communicate any bad news either, a good start is like half the work is being done.

Friday at 11 I will greet Monsignor and seven other priests and accompany them to the ship. Our ship is called *La Ville de Paris*, and it is the most beautiful and biggest to be found on the ocean. We are travelling second class and are doing fine.

Dear parents, I want to relate to you many more details, but time is short, I am very busy. Later, after our journey has ended or if we have a stop here or there, I will write more extensively about what happens to me and about what I hear and see. In the meantime, let us pray for one another. This happens to be the continuous bond that cannot be broken by seas or by distance. Our fate is in God's hands and, standing in front of the endless ocean with its abysses and shallow spots, with its cliffs and rocks, its pools of danger and doom, this is what I feel most of all.

Please bless me dear parents and accept my best wishes, your submissive and dedicated son:

JULES BOONE.

[Note by *The Gazette of Thielt* editor:]
Now we continue with the peculiar journey to deep America, as told by the brave Fleming, the brave monastic Brother.

St. Albert (date missing), 1874.
Dear parents brothers and sister!

We stop here for a while. One of the first things I do is continue to write in order to relate the details of my journey. First of all it must be mentioned that, thank God, my health is fine. I hope to repeat this often, which is better for me and more pleasant for you.

Before we left the good Christian population of Montreal (Canada), a ceremony took place, so to speak, in our honour. It was so solemn and touching, I have never attended anything like it.

The celebration was held in the public church of St. Peter, which belongs to our monastery. It was announced from the pulpit a day earlier and the following day, at the start of the ceremony, the church was filled with people, about four to five thousand were present.

Monsignor gave a long, though beautiful and fascinating sermon. We were on the steps of the beautifully decorated altar and the Bishop spoke so touchingly that most of the audience started to weep. Benediction followed and then a choir of sweet angelic voices started singing soul-stirring songs about separation and departure.

On **June** 1 at 9 a.m. we left Montreal. Our company consisted of two bishops, 18 missionaries or Brothers, five nuns and two female servants. In the afternoon of that Monday Peter Lucifer must have tried to stop the army that was about to fight his supporters. The stations here are sometimes 20 to 30 miles apart, the population is sparse and on both sides the iron road is trimmed with gorgeous shrubbery and high mountains.

Well, between Prescott and Brockville, the chains on our train broke three times. The engine and the coaches with the other travellers continued full speed ahead while the coaches with our company, time and again stood still. Each time they came back for us and connected us up again.

Next we drove past beautiful cities such as Kingston and Toronto, and we also passed beautiful Lake Ontario.

On June 2 we reached the outer border of Canada. A broad river separates this land from the United States. We had to cross this river, but the bold American inventors cut it short: our train, consisting of the engine and twelve big coaches full of travellers, was simply guided onto a gigantic steamship on rails that connected the soil and the ship and that is how we crossed the stream. Then, once across the river, we arrived ashore in the same way.

Once we arrived in Sarnia, we waited for the steamship *Manitoba*, on which we had to sail 4 to 5 days along streams, rivers and lakes. At 4 p.m. we boarded this beautiful vessel and travelling on it was much easier and nicer than on the train.

You should know, dear parents, brothers and sister, that we passed by St. Boniface, where there is a monastery of our congregation. It is about 900 miles from Montreal. The journey can be done by train or by ship. By ship it takes longer, but trains are more expensive and less comfortable. Our two bishops journeyed by train to arrive before we did.

At 11 p.m. we left Sarnia, our vessel lifted its anchor and steamed up the waters of the St. Claire River.

In the morning of June 3 we were at the beautiful and extensive Lake Huron. At 9:30 we had four hours near the city of Goderich and our priests, who had not had any food, used the occasion to read mass. The pastor of the Catholic parish was very happy to see us and immediately left his altar for our priests. I served mass in the Sisters' convent. Goderich is a village of 5000 souls and there are only 100 Catholics among them.

Thursday, June 4. We are in the most beautiful part of this area. We sail and twist around numerous isles, but the thick fog prevents us from admiring all the beauty. The entire day we see the shore, sometimes nearby, sometimes far off. The area is sparsely inhabited and it is useless to look for ploughed and seeded land. We are surrounded by the mountains.

Next to the most beautiful woods or at the foot of the mountains and rocks sometimes one can see little villages, however the groupings of these very few villages are only comprised of log barracks and huts. Sailing around one of the many isles, we saw a bunch of savages come out of the wood. They went fishing in their boats along the shore of the lake. By evening the steamship had sailed upstream to Ste. Marie and on the 6th we were in beautiful Lake Superior, the largest lake in the world, a true sea.

On Sunday the 7th we moor near the silver mines. About 40 passengers get off here in order to seek their fortunes in the famous mines. The silver mines are on two small isles. On the main rock is a large opening in which the silver explorers have worked and drilled so deep that they are already beneath the bottom of the lake.

At 10 we moor again in the harbour of Prince Arthur. The ship will be docked there for the day. In the evening we had to sit through listening to how the Protestants sing their religious exercises aboard the ship.

On the **8th** our journey in this beautiful lake is ended and we dock near the city of Duluth. From there we have to take the train and travel another 16 hours.

To be continued.

American Letters III (August 25, 1875)

After transferring our luggage to the station, we rent a barracks where we can await the train and have lunch. Two of us hurry to look for bread while I saw and chop wood and light a fire. Our brave and industrious Sisters are cooking. They warm the food left over from eight days ago, pour tea and we get a full bucket of milk from a charitable Catholic man from the country.

By 11:30 we are all sitting at the table, this means that we are eating. God must bless our food because it tastes excellent and we keep eating as if there is a fair in town. We are so fortunate to meet up with an Oblate missionary, yes, a Brother in Christ. I can't describe how happy he is upon meeting so many fellow Brothers in the middle of the wilderness. He is the sole Catholic priest here and has to convert about 15000 savages at his mission. He has already won over around 3000 for God and the church. At 1 o'clock we continue on.

It is absolutely impossible for me to describe how wonderful the nature is that we encounter along the railway tracks. During this season the meadows and woods are dressed in their best and thus we travel a distance of 190 miles without seeing anything else than the landscape as created by the Almighty. The hand of man has never touched it here. The mountains are covered with all kinds of strange green and miraculously thick trees. Red and blue rocks are seen, sometimes emerging beside valleys, hovering over ravines of incalculable depth. The St. Louis River can be seen streaming along, it is not navigable because sometimes the water flows into rapids, rushing between gorges where there are rocks, dens and caves in which bears, deer and wolves live. It is nature in its twisted fierceness and its utmost splendour. And all of these wonders enthral the heart and mind, lift the soul and cause one to reflect on the endless greatness and charity of He who created it all. For the Christian heart these wonders are mute and at the same time eloquent preachers evoking even more love for the Creator, even more ardent longing for Him and a desire to serve Him even more industriously.

The morning of June 9 we dismount to board a steamship again. We steam up the Red River, the course of which you can see on the map. Once again the life of the missionary is tested. Our vessel is small and it still carries many passengers. There are no beds available and when night arrives many men stretch out next to each other on top of the bridge and start to snore under the open sky. Whoever gets a cabin calls himself a lucky man. From now on seeing people is no longer rare, from all sides they come out of the woods and they are still a bit more civilized than the ones we will encounter later. After having spent four days on this river we arrive in St. Boniface.

Our wonder is indescribable. We have travelled a road about 200 miles long through the wilderness, through all that is rugged and rough and here we find a beautiful city, a beautiful area, well populated and civilized! This is the work of Monsignor the Archbishop and the missionaries of our congregation.

Monsignor Taché and Monsignor Grandin, who were already there, met us moments after the steamship had signalled its arrival. They were accompanied by several Fathers from our congregation and students from the college, among whom about twenty musicians who immediately filled the air with joyful tunes. In a procession we were led to the Archbishop's house. The entire population received us with joy and reverence and in the orphanage, the Sister's pension and the college; they performed several theater productions in our honour. We stayed here ten full days in order to rest and prepare for the next difficult journey.

We left St. Boniface on **June 22nd**. Our caravan consisted of 21 persons. Monsignor is always with us and on horseback. The Sisters have a coach for themselves. We, the priests and Brothers, each have our own cart that is so loaded down that we often have to go on foot in order to lighten the burden for the horses. We have 14 carts, which are nice and not badly built, and there is not one piece of iron on them, not even one nail. In front of this are 19 horses, all of them very skinny. We march about 6 to 8 miles daily, thereafter find a place suitable to set up camp, kitchen and stay overnight.

As soon as we have found a good place, we halt; the horses are unharnessed and, with a whip, chased to the woods and the meadows. We have four tents, just big enough to accommodate us all. They are immediately set up and in a few moments the whole parish is in their dwelling. Each has its own curtains, everybody wraps him or herself up and falls into a sound sleep lying flat on the flour.

We perform our religious exercises in common. Each day H. Mass is read between four and five p.m. and is attended by everyone. We can confess, approach the Holy Table, each according to his or her own devotion, as often as one wants. Four beams and a plank form the altar on which the necessary decorations are placed. Sometimes we meet with other caravans of savages that want to attend mass, so in this case Monsignor preaches.

Our dining table, in other words, the table to eat on, is very easy to find and also very wide. It is nothing other than the ground itself and Monsignor and the others don't have anything better. So far we still have the bread that we brought along from St. Boniface. However, it is starting to mould because it is about 12 to 14 days old. For meat we have fat pork dishes and also the famous *pemmican*, a mix of all kinds of meat that is years and years old. It has a disagreeable, kind of dirty smell and tastes like cherries.

We drink tea, but sometimes it has a weird taste. Water is difficult to find, which often causes us to keep moving for 2 to 3 hours longer than we had intended. Still, sometimes it is brown, and other times green and muddy. Well, it is better not to be too fussy about it and each time we eat, we enjoy it.

Mosquitoes torture us incessantly, day and night. They ascend down on us in gangs like clouds and they bite so severely that it makes one sick from being so swollen. Only when it rains we have a break from the mosquitoes, but the rain itself is also like a pest to us because then we have to camp in the slippery mud.

Before leaving in the morning, it is no small business to retrieve our horses that sometime wander off one to two miles from our camp. For this we employ two *Métis*, people from Monsignor's diocese, who are very adept at catching horses. They mount the few horses that we keep around, ride full speed after the others, and as soon as they see them, the horses cannot escape. They carry along a rope with a noose and throw it at the horses from a distance of 10 to 15 meters away. The noose holds them and whether or not they want to walk or if they walk slowly, they are forced to walk and are held by the ropes.

How miraculous that we also cross the rivers, sometimes through deep water, sometimes full of slippery mud, in our loaded carts. But, we have to go over and through everything here because there are no roads and bridges.

The 2nd of July we halt the entire day to wait for the caravan that follows us with Monsignor's luggage. Finally the guides arrive with the other eight loaded carts and we hurry to continue on together.

So far the area has been a vast, expansive plain, but now it changes into a hilly and very beautiful area. There are exceptionally high mountains with firs and other plants that give off a nice smell in the middle of this wilderness. Adjacent to the mountains there are sometimes vast expansive stretches of land that are entirely covered with wild red roses and the most beautiful valleys which are, so to speak, covered with lakes that, when the sun shines, are mirrors likes pearls in the sky. And despite all these wonders and all this beauty, 9 full days go by before we meet one person, encounter one barrack or one hut.

It takes a lot of effort to climb the hills with our luggage and so far we have been able to continue on without any accidents.

On July 7 we crossed the Assiniboine River. Fortunately, the water was not high and its river bottom was of solid soil.

On the 10th we have to cross the Saskatchewan River that you can see on the map. Past the river we met up with three different caravans that consisted mostly of savages. They were loaded with skins and they were taking them to St. Boniface to sell them there. It is touching to see the high regard people have for Monsignor. They dismount their horses and fall to their knees to receive his blessing.

At dusk we camp on a high mountain between two lakes. From the top of the mountain we see wild chickens swimming in flocks in the very beautiful waters. I also shoot a few of the birds with my gun. You should know, dear parents, I have become a very good hunter and when I have something in my sights, it has little chance to escape. That is why Monsignor trusts me with the gun, to shoot the animals that can be of service to us. Many strange birds have experienced my good aim. Each time we have a good chance to shoot some wildlife, it is like a fair day. Despite our lack of butter or fat to fry our catch in, the meat is so much better than that awful *pemmican*.

We are through the bread we bought in St. Bonifacius and we have to use the little flour we have with us. I took upon myself to make something with the flour. I made dough out of water and flour, put it near the fire until it turned colour a bit and then passed it off as bread. To really bake the dough properly is impossible and we also don't have enough time for that. But we don't make a fuss and everyone would still rather have the biggest piece.

On **July 9th** we are on an endless plain. Nearly daily we experience severe thunderstorms accompanied by lighting and dreadful thunder. It is so scary. In Belgium or in France no one has ever seen anything like it.

Currently we can see a comet, it is an incredible miracle to see its aura in the sky. In the evening and at night it lights the entire plain with its glow.

This week we were in the company of two other caravans. The first one had been frightened by an encounter with a horrendous large bear. The men had killed the monster and gave us part of its meat. We all like the bear meat very much and we will get no better from now on.

On **July 24** we arrive at the diocese of Monsignor Grandin. We recognize the poles that are placed like a big cross on top of a high mountain.

Dear heaven, what an agreeable area! Entire fields are planted with mulberries, gooseberries and all kinds of lovely flowers that release a lovely perfume. We soon find out that the temperature here fluctuates a lot. Sometimes it is sweltering, sometimes icy cold.

On the **28th** we meet a gang of savages requesting flour, tea and tobacco and then they hand us a letter. The following explains why. The caravan that preceded Monsignor, Brother Henri Scheers was among them, had been attacked by the savages. There were only seven men, so they had been forced to give the savages a part of their provisions. The savages also used force and killed one of their oxen. Then one of the Fathers gave them a letter and made them believe that they had to await our caravan in order to get a larger supply of everything. They had to hand the letter to the bishop who was in the next caravan, as he was the Superior, and everything would be fine.

The letter was written in Latin and served to inform us about the activities of this gang. As far as we are concerned, we did not have any trouble with these savages. We gave them about one kilogram of flour, half a kilogram of tea and some tobacco, for which they paid us 18 wild chickens.

To be continued.

American Letters IV and End (August 28, 1875)

On the 30th of July we were very lucky to visit the first missionary on this side of the diocese, the Rev. Father Andreus. He received us in his hut. Monsignor drove three days ahead in order to settle some business and not lose too much time.

Two Fathers and one Brother from another mission of the diocese, Ile de la Crosse, about 100 miles from here, also met with his Highness, their bishop, so we could embrace several of our new neighbours and fellow-Brothers. We were all so happy and, it even kept us quiet for half a day.

As soon as we had travelled a little distance away, we came to a broad river, had to cross it and on the 1st of August we arrived in Fort Carlton.

After more than a month of not having encountered either hut nor barrack in our path; it was really something new and even consoling to be able to look at a dwelling. The headman of the \English, though a Protestant, was very accommodating with us. He hosted Monsignor for a day and a night during which time the prelate looked at the news and the letters that had arrived for him at the house from Europe or from the northern part of America.

On Sunday, August 2, this gentleman and his wife came to visit our camp, had lunch and spent the main part of the day with us. He was also present during the singing of our edifying hymns.

On the 3rd we continued on our journey to the area we wanted to reach. Three other caravans joined us. Now the caravans also watch out for companies of other civilized people in the hope they can protect against the savages who we expect to encounter time and time again and who will be out to steal our horses and provisions. The people from the caravans also attend our H. Mass and other religious exercises.

Our entire train is comprised of 69 carts and about 90 horses. We are in an endless prairie. We travel two and a half days without being able to find a single piece of wood. As we knew this beforehand, we all carried a load of wood on our carts.

On the 7th we travel the entire day up and down over mountains and rocks. In the afternoon about a half-hour after leaving camp we were descending from a high mountain when a miraculous scene came into view. The plains in front of us were covered with buffalo. A moment later four hunters on horseback (*Métis*) from the other caravans went by and sped out of sight. Buffalo can actually run very fast and only the best horses in America can catch them. Ten minutes later we heard five shots. I was already underway to catch up and when I arrived I saw that the hunters had one of the largest buffaloes.

The buffalo that was hit was an animal with chocolate coloured fur on and around its head, the hair there was very long and everywhere else it was short, just like a lion's and its size was similar to most oxen in your area.

It was enjoyable to see the hunters process that buffalo. How skilful and experienced they are! In less than one hour the buffalo was skinned, its meat cut into pieces, then tied together with strips of the skin, loaded onto the horses' backs and brought to the camp. The meat was handed out to everyone. We got a generous share, among it the finest pieces. Everyone was very happy to be able to eat fresh meat because we were very bored with the dried meat and the pemmican.

On **Sunday, August 8th**, we met a band of savages that stayed the entire day and night at the camp that we had set up. From all sides they try to get something from our carts. One leans against a cart, another creeps underneath, the third pulls at something and despite a tremendous rainfall that pours down the entire day and night, we are forced to meticulously stand guard.

On the **9th** we hurry to leave the place and get away from the band as quickly as possible. From then on we are in an area that is fully populated by savages. Each caravan has to take turns standing guard at night. In the evening the carts are driven into a circle, the tents are set up around it and the horses are driven into the circle in order to better protect against being robbed by the savages who are hiding in the woods all around.

The rest of the week we also see many wild goats and a herd of buffalo of which we kill five. For nine days this provides us with fresh meat.

The **10th, 11th, 12th and 13th** we are again without wood. Yes, four days in a stretch we don't see a piece of wood, either nearby or in the distance. It is true, we had prepared ourselves as well as possible for it, but still there is a shortage. So we look for the dried bones of animals that have been killed or have died and we gather the dried dung of buffalo. With this little fuel we can light a fire and cook our food in order to take away the nauseating taste of raw meat and other food. We are also out of bread, vegetables and salt so often when our table is set it is a miracle. Well, God also blesses the little we have to eat and it keeps us alive and healthy. So far we still have flour and make a kind of pie from it as I explained before. When we encounter savages, we take care to hide the flour because they like it very much.

The **14th** we had to pass through a camp of 50 families, altogether 300 persons. Despite their appalling living conditions it was still a wonderful scene. They have such nice manners, and it is difficult to describe them. Their clothing is also so wonderful, there are people wrapped in skins, others wear a kind of cloth around their shoulders, some are decorated with pearls, pieces of flowered earthenware, with feathers or coloured frayed fringes. They bought all these items from fortune hunters who risked their lives in order to exchange skins for any kind of article. There are also clothes that are painted in either black, red or yellow, which gives them a strange and ghostly appearance.

Their chief is recognized by his feathers and a big load of rings dangling from his ears. He and his wife are the only Christians. This chief is a good elder, he deems himself very lucky to find a priest because he had not met a missionary in over three years. One of our fathers, who travels in this area and knows the savage language, Father Doucet, gives him a painting, just like the one I left at home. The Rev. Father explained the painting to him, wishing him much courage and diligence and then bids him farewell.

One thing about trading things with these people, for two or three franks it is very easy to get dried meat or skins from them that are worth about 30 or 40 franks.

The 15th was Ascension Day. Monsignor was consoled by bringing all the *Métis* from the other caravans and from ours for confession and to the altar. On the top of a high mountain High Mass was sung with all the solemnity that we had to offer and that night the sky reverberated with the singing far and wide. As a way of bidding farewell we also sang humorous songs. Monsignor's caravan, though, was pressed for time to get to its destination and the next day it had to go ahead somewhat hastier and leave behind those who were less pressured.

It is the 17th. We are in full march. However, the ox that pulls my cart is a big lazy one and I can't keep up with the horses that walk much faster. So I am behind and find myself with Monsignor who is always on horseback and at the end. Then suddenly our other Brothers walk toward me and say that there is a wild beast in their way that does not want to step aside. You must know, dear parents, that the gun has its home in my cart. Immediately I am on foot and looking for the wild beast. Oh, it is a wild goat. I shoot it in the head and also shoot another one. They are two beautiful animals, brown and yellow fur on the back and white on the underside. They have very long legs and can move like flashes of lightning.

In the meantime the caravan continues on. Monsignor had wanted to load the goats on his horse in order to catch up with the carts. But that was not possible and someone from the caravan had to go back in order to bring the animals along. At noon, as soon as we had unharnessed, the slaughter started and everybody was happy with another meal of fresh meat.

On the 18th we arrive at the La Bataille River. This stream of water is not much wider than the Leye River, but is very deep and the shores so full of quicksand that one could be sucked down in it. We have no barge, and still we have to cross it. Everyone is reserved and fearful. In the evening people occupy themselves with chopping wood in order to make a sturdy boardwalk over the quicksand to get the carts over it to the shore of the river. That night we have no rest and the next day, already in the early morning all masses are dedicated to the almighty God for the purpose of crossing the river without mishap. After the holy masses and breakfast we immediately start to work.

The honourable letter writer had to stop writing because his letter might become too heavy. The next letter is dated from St. Albert and is also very curious. We summarized the first part and then left the remainder untouched for the author to continue writing about his other dangerous encounters during his travels.

We are so far apart from each other, wrote the writer to his family, but that does not prevent me from thinking about you daily. On the contrary, the distance brings us closer, it makes love stronger, it makes it glow, and for you, dear parents, brothers and sister, who live among your children, your brothers, your friends, it is impossible to understand how warm parental and brotherly love can burn in the heart of the one who is thousands of miles removed from those he loves most on earth. Yes, in such moments one also thinks of the sacrifices one makes when leaving one's homeland, home and hearth for a life in a faraway country, in wild areas, with savage people. But heaven suffers from violence. So it is for the salvation of my soul, for the glory of God and also for you, dear parents, that I make this sacrifice. Yes, for you, that the Lord may bless you in this life and the next life. This thought strengthens, encourages and changes the few moments of nostalgia into pure joy. Everything is for God and for heaven, where we will find each other, to be separated never again!

It puzzles me greatly, dear parents, to not have received a single letter from you. Nine months have passed by since, at the Brest harbour, I sent you my address. By now, other monastic priests have already received several newsletters from their families and I am the only one who is missing this consolation. I also ask you again to indicate which letter you last received from me. Don't be puzzled when there is a long time between my letters, after all, only twice per year do we have the opportunity to hand letters to a merchant who is passing by.

I don't mean to say, dear parents, that you should write only twice per year. Please write often, short or long, but often! Sometimes it happens that we receive our letters from Europe through the savages or others. With regard to myself, dear parents, thank God I enjoy good health and the coldness seems to benefit me. Currently I am in the fourth month of the novitiate and dress like a member of the congregation. The mission where I will stay during my novitiate year does quite well. The church, albeit a wooden one, is reasonably good. It has a harmonium and during the feast days we also celebrate the solemn ceremonies.

The population is often integrated with Canadians and is becoming more and more civilized. The savages are only a few hours away, in the plains and the woods that we passed by, in the midst of the wild beasts, in order to have their food close at hand.

While I speak of savages, I hasten to assure you that I have absolutely nothing to fear from them. They honour the religious man and look upon him as a supernatural being. From the start of our mission, no one has ever heard that one of ours has been caused grief. Moreover, a Brother faces less danger than a Father does, as the Brother just doesn't go about with the savages on his own.

Our slave labour also consists of working the soil to sow barley so once in a while we can eat some barley bread. I also started to work the land with a team of horses or oxen. The first day I had great trouble to get the drag-harrow moving and to get the animals started, but after a few days it went better, just as if I had been the world's best farmer.

Currently I am busy diligently learning how to work with wood so I can help with building churches, monasteries and schools; all of this is lacking here. Here in St. Albert to travel from one mission to another we have perhaps about fifty horses and sixty horned animals. Among the horned cattle are also a few cows that give us some milk and some butter. These animals walk about freely in the prairies and the woods, sometimes about seven to eight hours from our house. If a few are needed for travelling, strangely, one has to look for them.

Our food consists mostly of dried meat from the wild animals, mainly buffalo meat bought from the savages. In general, the savage makes his *pemmican* from the buffalo meat. The animal is caught, killed, skinned and than hacked into pieces. The hacked pieces are wrapped in the skin, the skin is then sewn together and then the clumps of meat are tossed onto piles. That is how the meat that has been lying there for months gets such a strange and horrid taste.

The population living around the mission, that is, around the church, is mainly Christian and civilized, but still not inclined to work. They live from the hunt, just like the savages and the inhabitants of the dioceses' other missions. Around our house a few other little huts have been built, but the rest of the people have their skin tents that are stretched out on sticks. With these skin tents they travel and hunt around all over the place.

According to the inhabitants of this area, the temperature has been quite moderate. But don't believe that winter here is like winter in Belgium. We already had frost from 26 to 30 degrees, which is enough to freeze anything bare: hands, nose or jaws. And they say, I am assured, we may well expect 40 to 50 degrees below zero! It is also curious that for the entire winter we shouldn't touch metal with our hands. I have already tested it, as one learns by experience. One day I thought that it was not too cold and, without my thick gloves, I went to fetch a barrel from outside, one fitted with iron bands. I was barely holding the barrel with my hands but my fingers burnt and glowed like fire. And that was not all. As you may imagine, I hurried to let go, but it was impossible, my fingers were glued to it. By pulling on them with all my might I left my skin behind, attached to the barrel.[343] We have to be careful not to get frozen stiff, so we wrap our hands and feet in skins and protect them from the cold.

Right now, dear parents, brothers and sister, I can't write any longer about the mores and customs of the people here, civilized or savage. Next time I hope to receive some news from you very soon. I ask for your benediction and I remain always your dedicated son and brother:

JULES BOONE.

P.S.: My letter was just about to be mailed when, to my great joy, I received news from you. As I stated above, this is still the first news from you. So your previous letters got lost. Please pay strict attention to the address and repeat any previous news. Would you mind to, on my behalf, thank the courageous souls who pray for me because without their prayers I don't think that I could be so happy in my Spartan situation.

Would you mind also giving my compliments to M. the Mayor and tell him that the region, Monsignor included, is very happy because I brought tobacco seeds along. Now we all expect to be able to fill a pipe with it. Parbleu! If the tobacco does well, it could be a true fortune for our mission. The savages also smoke a kind of tobacco, it is peeled from a certain kind of wood but it does not resemble our tobacco in the slightest.

After having said a few words to friends and family, the honourable writer sends them all his most respectful and hearty compliments and signs himself:

JULES BOONE.

Abbreviations

Glenbow Archives, Calgary	▶ GAC
Missionary Oblates / Grandin Archives, Provincial Archives Alberta	▶ MOGAPAA
Missions de la Congrégation des missionnaires oblats de Marie Immaculée	▶ *Missions*
Van Dale Archives, Kortrijk	▶ VDAK
Van Tighem Family Archives, Calgary	▶ VFAC

❖

ALFONS (VAN DEN BROUCKE), BROEDER. 2003. To Paul Callens. November 17. [In it quotes from: Faict, J. J. 1885. To the Rev. Mr. Roets, Deacon of Kortrijk. December 22. Acta 1885, and a note of November 11, 1893 about Mgr. Grandin consecrating three altars in the St. Elooi church in Bruges. fol. 422 bis]. Trans. Broeder Alfons. Westvleteren: Archives Abbey Sint Sixtus.

ALLOSSERY, P. 1925. *Onze West-Vlaamsche Zendelingen [Our West-Flemish Missionaries]*. Boekdeel [Part] I. Brugge: Drukkerij Verbeke-Loys.

BAERT. G. 1987. "*Van aubergine, lantsherberghskens en brandewijnhuysen te Meulebeke van 1600 tot nu [About inns, rural inns and brandy houses in Meulebeke from 1600 until now]*." *De Roede van Tielt*, 18, no 3, 1-112.

BARNES, HENRY. 1916a. To Leonard. July 31. VFAC.

———. 1916b. To Leonard. September 10. VFAC.

———. 1916c. To Leonard. November 3. VFAC.

BARNETT, MARY ET AL. 1986 *Strathmore, the Village that Moved*. Strathmore: The Strathmore History Book Committee.

BERNAD, MARCEL, O.M.I. 1927. "Massacre des Pères Fafard et Marchand." *Missions*, 753–62.

BETHUNE, EMM. DE, 1981. Preface. Jozef Van Dale. "Katalogus van de tentoonstelling georganiseerd door de Kongregatie van de Broèders

Vandale in samenwerking met de Stedelijke Kultuurdienst en de Stedelijke Openbare Bibliotheek van Kortrijk naar aanleiding van de 200e verjaring van het overlijden van Jozef Vandale." [Catalogue of the Exhibition organised by the Van Dale Brothers in honour of the 200th anniversary of Jozef Vandale's decease in 1781]. Ed. Hans Vandekerckhove and Rieta Swyngedouw. Kortrijk.

BETHUNE, BARON JOSEPH DE. N.D. "Uitdrijving der Broeders Van Dale 1881." [Expulsion of the Van Dale Brothers 1881]. Handwritten essay. Kortrijk: Municipal Library, file JHB 152.b.

BOONE, J. 1874. "Amerikaensche Brieven (American Letters)." *De Gazette van Thielt*. Feuilleton, I-IV: 18-8-1875/28-8-1875. FOO1-F027.

——. 1885. To Leonard Van Tighem. August 19. VFAC.

——. 1888. To Leonard Van Tighem. July 26. VFAC.

BOTTING, GARY. 2005 *Chief Smallboy: In Search of Freedom*. Calgary: Fifth House Ltd.

BRETON, PAUL EMILE. O.M.I. 1955. The Big Chief of the Prairies.The Life of Father Lacombe. Trans. Hugh Dempsey. Palm Publishers.

CALLENS, PAUL. 1995. Interview with Ferdinand Van Tighem quoted in letter to "Greg," July 31.

——. 2000a. *Amerikaanse Zantingen. Een persoonlijke blik van Pittem naar Amerika. (American Gleanings. A Personal View from Pittem to America)*. Tielt: Vlaamse Vereniging voor Familiekunde.

——. 2000b. *Vriendenboek Valère Arickx: Enkele Plaatsnamen in de Verenigde Staten en Canada. (Valère Arickx: Some Names of Places in the United States of America and Canada)* Roeselare: Vlaamse Vereniging voor Familiekunde.

——. 2002. *Death Memorial Cards. Part I-VII*. Tielt: Vlaamse Vereniging voor Familiekunde (Flemish Association for Genealogy), Afdeling Tielt and Genealogical Society of Flemish Americans. Roseville, Michigan, USA.

CARRIÈRE, GASTON, O.M.I. 1967. *L'Apôtre des Prairies. Joseph Hugonnard, o.m.i. 1848–1917*. Rayonnement 2585, Montréal 4.

——. 1976. *Dictionnaire biographique des Oblats de Marie-Immaculée au Canada*. Ottawa: Éditions de l'Université d'Ottawa.

——. 1977. *Dictionnaire biographique des Oblats de Marie-Immaculée au Canada*. Ottawa: Éditions de l'Université d'Ottawa.

——. 1979. *Dictionnaire biographique des Oblats de Marie-Immaculée au Canada*. Ottawa: Éditions de l'Université d'Ottawa.

CARTER, S. 1990. *Lost Harvests*. Montreal & Kingston: McGill-Queens's University Press.

CHOQUETTE, ROBERT. 1995. *The Oblate Assault on Canada's Northwest*. Ottawa: University of Ottawa Press.

CLAERHOUT, FLOR, PASTOOR. 1995. *Deken L. de Bo (1826-1885) en het "Westvlaamsch Idioticon" gesitueerd in het kader van het Westvlaams Taalparticularisme*. Roeselare: Uitgeverij Familia et Patria.

CLAES, JO, ALFONS CLAES AND KATHY VINCKE. 2002. *Sanctus. Meer dan 500 heiligen herkennen. [Recognizing over 500 saints].* Leuven: Davidsfonds en Uitgeverij Kok.

COCCOLA, NICOLAS. 1988. *They Call Me Father. Memoirs of Father Coccola.* Ed. By Margaret Whitehead. Vancouver: University of British Columbia Press.

Codex Historicus Blood Reserve, MOGAPAA: 71.220, 2002, BOX 48.

Codex Historicus St. Paul des Peiganes, MOGAPAA: 71.220, 2002, BOX 48.

CROWSHOE, REG AND SYBILLE MANNESCHMIDT. 1997. *Akak'stiman: A Blackfoot Framework for Decision-Making and Mediation Processes.* Calgary: University of Calgary Press.

DANFORD, RUBY. 2003. *1905-2005 Taber.* Taber and District Museum Society.

DEANE, R. BURTON. 1999. *Tales of a Mounted Police officer: Superintendent R. Burton Deane of the Lethbridge N.W.M.P. division, 1888-1902.* Selected and edited by William (Bill) M. Baker. Lethbridge: Lethbridge Historical Society.

DE BURY. A.J. 1916. To Leonard Van Tighem. October. VFAC.

DE CLERK, KAREL, BIE DE GRAVE AND FRANK SIMON. 1984. "*Retrospectief. Dag Meester Goedemorgen zuster, goedemiddag juffrouw. Facetten van het Volksonderwijs in Vlaanderen (1830-1940)."* [*In Retrospect. Hello Master, Good Morning Sister, Good Afternoon Miss. Facets of Volk Education in Flanders (1830-1940)*]. Tielt: Lannoo.

DELMOTTE, M. 2001. "*Honger en armoede te Waregem (1815-1855) en het gemeentelijk onderwijs ten tijde van Pieter Poma (1849-1877) en Henriette Vandenbulcke (1857-1878)."* [*Hunger and Poverty in Waregem (1815-1855) and municipal eductation at Pieter Poma's era (1849-1877) and Henriette Vanden Bulcke (1857-1878)*]. *De Gaverstreke*, 29th Annual Report, 287-393.

DEMPSEY, HUGH A. 1972. *Crowfoot. Chief among the Blackfeet.* Edmonton: Hurtig.

———. 1984. *Big Bear: the End of Freedom.* Vancouver: Douglas & McIntyre.

———. c. 1991. *Treasures of the Glenbow Museum.* Calgary: The Museum.

DE PAUW, COMMAR A. REV. 1953. *The Educational Rights of the Church and Elementary Schools in Belgium.* A Dissertation submitted to the Faculty of the School of Canon Law of the Catholic University of America in partial Fulfillment of the Requirements for the Degree of Doctor in Canon Law. Washington D.C.: The Catholic University of America Press.

DESCHOUT, THÉRÈSE. 1979. *De Congregatie van de Zusters van Maria van Pittem. Ontstaan en uitbreiding to na de tweede wereld oorlog. Verhandeling voor het verkrijgen van het Licentiaat in de Godsdienstwetenschappen.* [*The Congregation of de Sisters of Maria van Pittem. Establishment and Expansion up to the Second World War. Tractate for obtaining the licentiate degree in Religious Studies*]

DE VISSCHER, JOS. 1916a. To Leonard Van Tighem. February 25. VFAC.

———. 1916b. To Leonard Van Tighem. August 19. VFAC.

———. 1916c. To Leonard Van Tighem. December 21. VFAC.

———. 1917. To Leonard Van Tighem. January 25. VFAC.

"DIAMOND JUBILEE OF THE AMERICAN COLLEGE OF THE IMMACULATE CONCEPTION. 'ARCHBISHOPS. MOST REV. CHARLES JOHN SEGHERS. ARCHBISHOP OF OREGON CITY.'" 1932. American College Bulletin XXV: 105–07. Leuven: University of Louvain.

DENNIS, J. S. 1879. Letter to Edgar Dewdney, Ottawa. May 31. GAC: Edgar Dewdney fonds. Series 5, M-320. P. 180–89.

DE VOCHT, JOSEPH. CSSR. *Eternal Memory. Father Delaere & Canada's Ukrainian Catholic Church.* Ed. Paul Laverdure. Canada: Gravelbooks.

DONAT, F., O.M.I. 1890. "Lettre (7.4.1889) à Rev. Father Boisramé, Maître des Novices en N.D. des Anges." *Missions*, 238.

DROUIN, EMERIC, O.M.I. 1981. *The Beginnings and Development of the Catholic Church in the Edmonton Area and the Contributions of Oblate Fathers and Brothers.* Edmonton.

EGGERMONT-MOLENAAR, MARY. 2000. Ed. "Fidler's Journal. Encounters with the Inhabitants of 'Alberta' in 1792–1793." Edited first by Bruce Haig, Lethbridge. *Yumtzilob*, 7–56.

FALTER, ROLF. 2005. *1830: De scheiding van Nederland, België en Luxemburg (1830: The Separation of the Netherlands, Belgium and Luxemburg).* Tielt: Lannoo.

FAURE, A., O.M.I., 1922. "'Semaine Religieuse', Quebec." *Missions*, 919–25.

FITZGERALD, WALTER P. (REV.). c. 1978. *The Wheels of Time: a History of Riviere Qui Barre.* [s.i., .s.n.].

FIRMIN, BROTHER. 1938. To Jane Van Tighem-Kelly. December 30. VFAC.

———. 1940. To Jane Van Tighem-Kelly. January 17. VFAC.

———. 1941. To Jane Van Tighem-Kelly. April 13. VFAC.

FLAHERTY, C.M. 1984. *Go With Haste Into The Mountains. A History of the Diocese of Helena.* Montana: Catholic Diocese of Helena.

FOISY, D., O.M.I., 1890. "Lettre du R.P. Donat Foisy O.M.I. à R.P. Boisramé, Maître de Novices à N.D. des Anges." *Missions*, 236–38.

FOLLENS, N. 1983. "De Paters in Waregem en Nieuwenhove (2). Les Oblates 1901–1926." *De Gaverstreke*, 11th Annual Report, 11–83.

———. 1984. "De Paters in Waregem en Nieuwenhove (3)." *De Gaverstreke*, 12th Annual Report, 23–96.

———. 1985. "De Paters in Waregem en Nieuwenhove (4). Les Oblates 1901–1914." *De Gaverstreke*, 13th Annual Report, 160–217.

FORT MACLEOD. HISTORY BOOK COMMITTEE. 1977. *Fort Macleod, a Colorful Past.* Fort Macleod. Alberta.

FREEBAIRN, A.J. 2001. *60 Years in an Old Cow Town.* Pincher Creek: John Freebairn, Agnes Freebairn Mitchell and Linde Freebairn Farley.

"G", 1897. "Mgr. Émile Legal, O.M.I., 'Une excursion aux montagnes rocheuses.'" *Missions*, 395–98.

GIBBON STOCKEN, H.W. 1976/1987. *Among the Blackfoot and Sarcee.* Calgary: Glenbow Museum.

GILMOUR, W., 1936. "Progress of Roman Catholic Church In City Keeps Pace With Growth of Lethbridge.'" *Lethbridge Herald.* August 6. P.8.

GLADU, LOUIS, O.M.I. 1914. "L'Oeuvre des Oblats dans L'Ouest Canadien. III. 'Les Oblats apôtres du Nord-Ouest.'" *Missions,* 469–482.

GODDEERIS, JOHN. 2001. *De Neogotiek in West-Vlaanderen. Een Herkerstening in Steen [Neogothics in Flanders. A Rechristianization in Stone].* With cooperation of Willy Detailleur, Gidsenkring Oostende and Vincent Deflou, Gidsenkring Oostende.

GOLDEN JUBILEE 1905–1955. 1955. Commemorating Fifty years of Picture History of Taber, Alberta. (n.p.)

GRANDIN, HENRY. 1909. "Alberta et Saskatchewan." *Missions,* 133–41.

GRANDIN, V., O.M.I. 1874. "VOYAGES DE MGR. GRANDIN EN FRANCE." *Missions,* 129–51.

———. 1881. "Missions Étrangères. Saint-Albert. 'Journal de Voyage de Mgr. Grandin. A la rivière aux Castors, en canot d'écorce, me rendant au lac Vert et à l'ile à la Crosse. 20 mai, 1880.'" *Missions,* 185–222.

———. 1886. "Rapport de Mgr. Grandin au T.R.P. Supérieur Général, Ottawa, 2 novembre 1885." *Missions,* 5–46.

———. 1889. To Leonard Van Tighem. St. Albert. February 20. VFAC.

———. 1901. To Joseph Van Tighem. Saint Albert. November 28. VFAC.

———. 1989. *The Diaries of Bishop Vital Grandin. 1875–1877.* Vol. I. Translated by Aland D. Ridge. Ed. By Brian M. Owens and Claude M. Robert: Edmonton, The Historical Society of Alberta. Amisk Waskahegan Chapter Edmonton.

GRAY, HAROLD E. (LONG STANDING BEAR CHIEF) AND LENORE MCKELVEY PUHEK. 1992. *Ni-kso-Ko-Wa. Blackfoot Spirituality, Traditions, Values and Belief.* Browning, Montana: Spirit Talk Press.

GRINNELL G.B. 1972. *Blackfoot Lodge Tales. The Story of a Prairie People.* Williamstown: Corner House Publishers.

HALL, D.J., 1977. "The Half-Breed Claims Commission." *Alberta History.* Vol. 5:2, 1–8.

HERMANT, LEON, O.M.I. 1948. *Thy Cross My Stay. The life of the Servant of God. Vital Justin Grandin. Oblate of Mary Immaculate and First Bishop of St. Alberta.* Canada. Toronto: The Mission Press.

HIGH RIVER PIONEER'S AND OLD TIMERS ASSOCIATION. 1960. *Leaves from the Medicine Tree.* Published by the Lethbridge Herald.

HOCHSTEIN, L.A. (SISTER F.C.J.C.). 1954. *Roman Catholic Separate and Public Schools in Alberta.* M.Ed. Thesis. GAC: M1395.

HOFMAN, BARBARA. 1995. "Women of God. The Faithful Companions of Jesus." *Alberta History.* 43:4, 2–12.

HUGHES, KATERINE. 1914. *Father Lacombe. The Black-Robe Voyageur.* Toronto: William Briggs.

———. 1920. *Father Lacombe. The Black-Robe Voyageur.* Toronto: McLelland & Stewart.

JAENEN, C.J. 1968. "French Public Education in Manitoba." *Revue de l'Université d'Ottawa*. 19–34.

JONQUET, EMILE, O.M.I. 1903. *Mgr Grandin: Oblat de Marie Immaculee, premier eveque de Saint-Albert*. Montreal.

JOHNSTON ALEX AND ANDY A. DEN OTTER. 1985. *Lethbridge, A Centennial History*. Lethbridge: The City of Lethbridge and The Whoop-Up Country Chapter, Historical Society of Alberta.

JOURNÉE, MARC. 2006. Go West. *Een Verhaal van Vlaamse Emigranten naar Canada (A Story of Flemish Emigrants to Canada)*. Antwerpen: Snoeck.

KIRSCHBAUM, J.M. 1966. "Slovaks in Canada." Proceedings of the First National Conference on Canadian Slavs. Edmonton: Inter-University Committee on Canadian Slaves.

———. 1967. *Slovaks in Canada*. Ontario: Canadian Ethnic Press Association of Ontario.

KNOWLES, N. 2004. *Winds of Change: A History of the Roman Catholic Diocese of Calgary since 1968*. Calgary: Roman Catholic Dioces of Calgary and St. Mary's College.

KOSSMAN, E.H. 1978. *The Low Countries 1780–1940*. Oxford: Clarendon Press.

LAMMERANT, YOLANDE. 1997. *Van Meulebeke naar Amerika en Canada [From Meulebeke to America and Canada]*. Brussels: Studie (No 2951) based on Archives of Ministry of Foreign Affairs.

LAMPARD J. ROBERT. 2005. "Early Alberta doctors tough, inventive." *Calgary Herald*. August 14, B5.

———. 2006. "Frank Hamilton Mewburn, M.D., FACS, OBE 1858–1929." *History Now*. No. 1. April. Historical Society of Alberta.

LAVALLÉE, PAUL, O.M.I., 1923. "Nouvelles. XXI. 'L'ouest Canadien et les Évêques Oblats.'" *Missions*, 795–803.

LECLUYSE, PHARAILDE. 1892. To Joannes [Victor Vantieghem]. October 10. VFAC.

LEDUC, H., O.M.I., 1873. "Lettre du R.P. Leduc, au T.-R P. Supérieur Général. Saint-Albert. 22 Décembre 1870." *Missions*, 194–206.

———. 1880. "Condamnation, conversion et exécution du sauvage Kakisikutchin (Jean-Baptiste), le 20 décembre 1879, au fort Saskatchewan, territoire du Nord-Quest. – Canada." *Missions*, 157–66.

———. 1886. "De opstand der Mestiezen in Canada. [The Metis Rebellion in Canada]." *Gazette van Thielt*. January 6. Earlier published in the *Parisian Univers*.

———. June 1888. "Missions Étrangères. District of Calgary. 'Lettre du R.P. Leduc à R.P. L'Hermite. 31 Décembre 1887.'" *Missions*, 151–73.

———. 1901. To Joseph Van Tighem. November 28. MOGAPAA: 72.61.

———. 1903. To Joseph Van Tighem. September 25. VFAC.

LEPAGE, F., O.M.I. 1954. "Aux Origines de la Province Belge. 'L'action de Mgr. Grandin en Belgique.'" *Missions*, 294–340.

LERMYTE, J.M. 1989. "Het hoogepunt in het clerico liberaal conflict: de schoolstrijd in de 19e eeuw." [The climax in the clerial-liberal conflict: the school fight of the 19th century]. *Ons Heem*, vol. 43, No 6, P 194-202.

LESTANC, J.J., O.M.I. 1888. To Senator Richard Hardisty. July 21. GAC: M 5908/1738.

———. 1890. "Paroles, June 1st." *Missions*, 385–90.

———. 1894a. "A l'Ecole industrielle de Saint-Joseph." *Missions*, 386–88.

———. 1894b. "Chez les Gens du Sang." *Missions*, 388–90.

———. 1896. "Not in Jeopardy." *Lethbridge News*. June 29.

Lethbridge Herald, 1935. "Cordial Relations Between Early Church Leaders in Lethbridge," July 11, 96.

Lethbridge News, 1901. "Convent Concert." June 27.

LEVASSEUR-QUIMET, FRANCE. 1999. *1899–1999, Saint-Joachim, la première paroisse catholique d'Edmonton*. Edmonton: Édition Levasseur-Quimet.

LIBEERT, K. 1977. "Dokter Prudent Plettinck, burgemeester van Meulebeke (1819–1888). [Doctor Prudent Plettinck, mayor of Meulebeke (1819–1888)]." *De Roede van Tielt*, 42–76.

L'HEUREUX, JEAN. 1871. "Description of a portion of the North-West and the Indians." GAC, M675.

LUCIEN, BROEDER. 2001. To Paul Callens. March 5. Collection Paul Callens.

MACDONALD, GRAHAM. 2004 (1837). Transl. and Ed. *Frederic Baraga's History of the North American Indians*. Calgary: University of Calgary Press.

MACGREGOR. J.G. 1975. *Father Lacombe*. Edmonton: Hurtig.

———. 1978. *Life of Richard Hardisty, Senator Hardisty's Prairies, 1849–1889*. Saskatoon: Western Producer Prairie Books.

MAJEAU, SHIRLEY. (SISTER, FCJ.). ED. 1983. *Journeying through a Century, Sister Pioneers 1883 1983*. Edmonton: Sisters, Faithful Companions of Jesus.

MALLINSON, VERNON. 1970. *Belgium*. New York: Preager Publishers.

MANITOBA JOURNAL. 1884. July 30, "Deux Sermons." Quoted in *Missions*. No author, 1884, 401–03.

MATTELAER, PIERRE. 2002. "De Fundatie en Congregatie Verrue in Kortrijk" [The Foundation and Congregation Verrue in Kortrijk]. *De Leiegouw* 44: 2, 227–80.

MCCLINTOCK. 1923/1992. *Old Indian Trails*. New York: Houghton Miffin.

MCGREGOR, JAMES. 1972. *A History of Alberta*. Edmonton: Hurtig.

MOORE, L. 1915. To Leonard Van Tighem. Taber. November 28. MOGAPAA: 72.61.

MISSIEALBUM. 1950. "Tot Vroom en Stichtend Aandenken aan de overleden priesters-missionarissen, missiebroeders en missiezusters. Tot Hulde en Roem aan de nog levende gezanten in alle werelddelen. [A Pious and Edifying Memento to the Missionary Brothers and

Sisters. To the Honour and Glory of the still living representatives].”
Dekenij Tielt. Bisdom Brugge.

MUSSCHOOT, DIRK. 2002. *Wij Gaan Naar Amerika. Vlaamse Landverhuizers naar de Nieuwe Wereld: 1850–1930. (We are going to America. Flemish emigrants to the New World: 1850–1930)*. Tielt: Lannoo.

O.M.I. 1910. “Rapport sur ‘Ecole industrielle Saint-Joseph à Dunbow.” *Missions* 1910, 25–38.

PAREL, ROLANDE. 1986. *St. Mary. The First Hundred Years*. Calgary: Calgary Roman Catholic Separate School District.

PARKAP-OTOKAN (BAD-HEAD). n.d. *19th Century Chronology*. Trans. by Dr. H.A. Dempsey. GAC: Levern Collections, M 8521 File 4.

PINCHER CREEK HISTORICAL SOCIETY. c1974. *Prairie Grass to Mountain Pass: History of the Pioneers of Pincher Creek and District.*

PHILLIPPOT, A, O.M.I. 1930. “Rapports. Province d’Alberta-Saskatchewan. ‘L’oeuvre des Oblats polonais parmi les Polonais de l’Alberta.’” *Missions*, 334–361.

RAPPORT DU VICARIAT DE SAINT-ALBERT. 1898. “District de Calgary.” *Missions*, 193–245.

REPORT OF THE ROYAL NORTHWEST MOUNTED POLICE. 1907. “Annual report of Superintendent J.O. Wilson, Commanding ‘K’ Division, Royal Northwest Mounted Police. October 31, 1907,” 76–77. Calgary: Glenbow Museum Library.

RIOU, J., O.M.I. 1902. “‘Aperçu historique sur les Missions des Pieds-Noirs.’ Lettre du R.P. Riou au T.R. Père Général.” *Missions*, 153–72.

ROELSTRAETE, JOHAN 1998. *Handleiding voor Genealogisch Onderzoek in Vlaanderen*. Roeselare: Vlaamse Vereniging voor Familiekunde.

RONAGHAN, A. 1994. “The 9th.” *Alberta History*. Spring, 10–13.

ROSS, HAZEL. 1985. “Awatoyakew – White Tailed Deer Woman. Also known as Mary Brown.” In: *100 Women in 100 Years*. Edmonton: Mathesis Club. Book Committee; Sheila Petherbridge, Dorothy Pragnell, Hazel Ross, Ethel Dunn.

SANDERS, HARRY M. 2003. *The Story Behind Alberta Names. How Cities, Town, Villages and Hamlets Got their Names*. Calgary: Red Deer Press.

SISTERS, FAITHFUL COMPANIONS OF JESUS. 1890. Annual Report Lethbridge. CAG: M1395, file 7a2.

———. 1895. Annual Report Lethbridge. GAC: M1395, file 9.

———. 1898. Annual Report Lethbridge. GAC: M1395, file 13.

———. 1900. Annual Report Lethbridge. GAC: M1395, file 15.

———. 1901. Annual Report Lethbridge. GAC: M1395, file 17.

SMITH, PAUL AND LOUISE ENGLISH. n.d. St. Paul’s Parish. Brocket, Alberta. Pamphlet. Brocket, Peigan Nation.

SMITS, A. 1983. 1830. *Scheuring in de Nederlanden [Split in the Netherlands], Volume I and II*: Heule: (Series: Standen en Landen nr. LXXXIII).

STOCKEN, H.W. GIBBON. 1976/1987. *Among the Blackfoot and Sarcee*. Calgary: Glenbow Museum Library.

STONECHILD, BLAIR AND BILL WAISER. 1997. *Loyal till Death. Indians and the another North-West Rebellion*. Canada: Fifth House Ltd.

STRATHMORE HISTORY BOOK COMMITTEE, 1986. Strathmore: the Village that Moved. 1986. Alberta.

STREISEL, LUKE. 2004. "'The Miners Strike Out. The Lethbridge Coal Miners' Strike of 1906." *Alberta History*. Vol. 52:4, 2–6.

TABER HISTORICAL COMMITTEE. 1977. *From Tank 77 to Taber Today. A History of Taber, its district and its people*.

TASSAERT, FEBRONIE. 1892. To Victor Vantieghem. Meulebeke, December 12. VFAC.

———. 1893. To Leonard Van Tighem. February 10. VFAC.

TENNANT. JHOS. E. 1915. To Leonard Van Tighem. December 5. MOGAPAA: 72.61.

TRUYERS, GHISLAIN AND RAYMOND RUTTEN. n.d. "Dagkalender van Alle Heiligen." BMP. Book & Media Publishing.

TUCKER, E.G. ET AL. n.d. *Pincher Creek 1878–1958*. Pincher Creek: Old Timers Association.

UHLENBECK, C.C. AND R.H. VAN GULIK. 1930. *An English-Blackfoot Vocabulary, based on material from the Southern Peigans*. Verhandelingen der Koninklijke Akademie van Wetenschappen te Amsterdam. Afdeeling Letterkunde. Nieuwe reeks, Deel XXIX, 4. Amsterdam: N.V. Noord-Hollandsche Uitgevers-Maatschappij.

UHLENBECK, C.C. AND R.H. VAN GULIK. 1934. *A Blackfoot-English Vocabulary, based on material from the Southern Peigans*. Verhandelingen der Koninklijke Akademie van Wetenschappen te Amsterdam. Afdeeling Letterkunde. Nieuwe reeks, Deel XXXIII, 2. Amsterdam: N.V. Noord-Hollandsche Uitgevers-Maatschappij.

'UN TEMOIN:' 1899. Vicariat de Saint-Alberty. "Cinçuante Années de Sacerdoce. Les Noces d'Or du R.P. Lacombe, O.M.I.," *Missions* 376–92.

UNE SOEUR DE LA PROVIDENCE. 1916. *Le Père Lacombe, "L'homme au bon Coeur," in Blackfoot "Arsous-kitsi-parpi"* Montreal: Imprimé Au Davoir.

VALKEN, M. EDITOR. 1985. Kroniek van de 20ste eeuw. "Lusitania getorpedeerd." Amsterdam/Brussel: *Elsevier*. P 177.

VANDEKERCKHOVE, HANS AND RIETA SWIJNGEDOUW. 1981. "Herdenkingstentoonstelling Jozef Van Dale 1716–1781." [Memorial Exhibition Jozef Van Dale 1716–1781]. Kortrijk: Stadsbestuur.

VAN DE VIJVER, SOFIE. 1977. *"De Vlaamse Emigratie naar Noord-Amerika en de Gazette van Detroit."* Antwerp: Unpublished Paper.

VANHECKE, ROSALIE JULIE. 1893a. To Leonard Van Tighem. January 27. VFAC.

———. 1893b. To Leonard Van Tighem. December 20. VFAC.

VAN HERK, ARITHA. 2001. *Mavericks. An Incorrigible History of Alberta*. Toronto: Penquin/Viking.

VAN HOONACKER, E. 1986. *Duizend Kortrijkse Straten [One Thousand Kortrijk Streets]*. Self-published.

VANLANDSCHOOT, ROMAIN. 1996. "Het Eerste Lustrum van de Davidsfondsafdeling in de streek van Tielt. 1875–1880." [Fifth Anniversary of the Davids Foundation in the Tielt area], 92–3.

VAN TIGHEM, ELODIE. 1893. To Leonard Van Tighem. December 13. VFAC.

———. 1930. To Joseph and Jane Van Tighem, January 21. VFAC.

VAN TIGHEM, F.P. n.d. "Reverend Leonard van Tighem, O.M.I." (1851–1917). Lethbridge: Archives Sir Alexander Galt Museum, File 19770016000.

———. 1964. "Father Leonard Van Tighem. O.M.I." *Alberta History*, 17–21.

VAN TIGHEM, KAREL (CHARLES). Early 1889. To Victor Van Tighem. Not dated. VFAC.

———. 1889. To Leonard Van Tighem. April 14. VFAC.

VAN TIGHEM, (NEPHEW) JOSEPH. 1901. To Mgr. V. Grandin. November 5. VFAC.

———. 1917. To Leonard. January 17. VFAC.

VAN TIGHEM, (BLIND) JOSEPH. 1916. To Leonard. December 14. VFAC.

VAN TIGHEM, LEONARD, O.M.I. 1875. First Codex (1875-1909). VFAC.

———. 1884. "LETTRE DU R.P. VAN TIGHEM AU R.P. LEDUC. MACLEOD, LE 11 NOVEMBRE 1883." *Missions*, 198–200.

———. 1894. To Leonard Van Tighem. Nouvel An. VFAC.

———. 1900. "Letter (Sept. 29) to his Worship the Mayor and the Gentlemen of the council." Lethbridge: Sir Alexander Galt Museum, P 1977 00 16000.

———. 1901a. To Mrg. Legal. Lethbridge, November 20. VFAC.

———. 1901b. To Joseph Van Tighem. June 4. VFAC.

———. 1901c. To Mr. Boeckard. Lethbridge, September 26. VFAC.

———. 1901d. To Mgr. Legal. Lethbridge, November 14. VFAC.

———. 1902. To Father Lacombe. January 1. MOGAPAA: 72.61.

———. 1903. To Father Lacombe. December 8. MOGAPAA: 72.61.

———. 1904a. To Joseph Van Tighem. October 2. VFAC.

———. 1904b. To Joseph Van Tighem. August 16. VFAC.

———. 1904c. Account of meeting with Pope X. VFAC.

———. 1908. "Family Van Tighem." Unpublished Paper. VFAC.

———. 1909a. To Willie English. September 20. VFAC.

———. 1909b. To Willie English. June 23. VFAC.

———. 1909c. Second Codex (1909-1917). Fonds Leonard van Tighem. Ottawa: Archives Deschâtelet, HEF 3282. L573.

———. 1910. To Father Lacombe. April 11. MOGAPAA: 72.61.

———. 1915a. To the Editor of *the Lethbridge Herald*.

———. 1915b. To Father Henri Grandin. Dec. 27. MOGAPAA: 72.61.

VAN TIGHEM, MARIE. 1905. To Leonard Van Tighem. March 16. VFAC.

VANTIEGHEM, VICTOR (MONASTIC NAME JOANNES BERCHMANS). n.d. *Korte beschrijving mijner reis en lotgevallen in Noord Amerika (1886–1917)*. *[Short Description of my Journey and Adventures in North America (1886–1917)]*. Trans. Mary Eggermont-Molenaar. Unpublished Paper. VDAK

———. 1894–1907. Brieven aan Broeder Stanislas: St. Paul's Missie Macleod Peigan Reserve, 12 december 1894–6 mei 1896 –25 augustus 1896 –4 juni 1899 –22 maart 1904 – 16 juni 1907 [Letters to Brother Stanislas, St. Paul's Mission, Macleod, Peigan Reserve, December 12, 1894, etc.]. Unpublished Papers. VDAK

———. 1884a. To Leonard Van Tighem. March 25. VFAC.

———. 1884b. To Leonard Van Tighem. June 12. VFAC.

———. 1885a. To Leonard Van Tighem. April 26. VFAC.

———. 1885b. To Leonard Van Tighem. October 17. VFAC.

———. 1886a. To Leonard Van Tighem. March 15. VFAC.

———. 1886b. To Leonard Van Tighem. March, 28. VFAC.

———. 1888. To Leonard Van Tighem. December 16. VFAC.

———. 1889. To Leonard Van Tighem. February 21. VFAC.

———. 1893. To Leonard Van Tighem. January 4. VFAC.

———. 1894. To Brother Stanislas. December 12. VDAK

———. 1896a. To Brother Stanislas. August 25. VDAK

———. 1896b. To Brother Stanislas. May 6. VDAK

———. 1899. To Brother Stanislas. June 4. VDAK

———. 1901. To Leonard Van Tighem, March 25. VFAC.

———. 1904. To Brother Stanislas. March 22. VDAK

———. 1905. To Henri Van Tighem. September 1. MOGAPAA: 71.220, Mi. 14. Box 5272.

———. 1907. To Brother Stanislas. June 16. VDAK

———. 1934. To Jane Van Tighem-Kelly. December 9. VFAC.

———. 1937. To Jane Van Tighem-Kelly. March 22. VFAC.

VARIÉTÉS. 1874. "Voyages de Mgr. Grandin en France" *Missions*, 129–52.

———. 1895. Première consecration d'église dans le diocese de Saint-Albert. *Missions*, 506 08.

———. 1905. "La Fête Mariale." *Missions*, 82–94.

VAUGHAN, W. 1920. *The Life and Work of Sir William van Horne*. New York: The Century Co.

VENINI BYRNE. M.B. 1973. *From the Buffalo to the Cross. A History of the Roman Catholic Diocese of Calgary*. Calgary: Calgary Archives and Historical Publishers.

VERSCHUERE, ANTONELLUS O.F.M, 1941. *De Zusters van 't Geloove [The Sisters of the Geloove]*. Tielt: Lanno.

WAUGH, EARLE. 1996. *Dissonant Worlds. Roger Vandersteene Among the Cree*. Wilfrid Laurier University Press.

———. 2005. *Een wereld van verschil. Roger Vandersteene bij de Cree-Indianen. Met een inleiding van Ulrich Libbrecht*. Leuven: Davidsfonds.

WILSON, J.O. 1907. "Report of the Royal Northwest Mounted Police." Calgary: Glenbow Library, 78–80 Edward VII. Sessional Paper No. 28. A. 1908.

WILSON PAPERS 1958. Edited and annotated By Philip H. Godsell. "Dances, Societies, Legends etc., etc." F.R.G.S., F.R.E.S. Calgary: Glenbow Foundation, M4422.

WITTE, ELS. With contributions of Jan Craeybecks and Alain Meynen. 1993. Politieke Geschiedenis van België van 1830 tot heden [Political History of Belgium From 1830 Until Now]. Antwerpen: Standaard Uitgeverij.

Abbreviations

Glenbow Archives, Calgary	▶ GAC
Missionary Oblates/Grandin Archives, Provincial Archives Alberta	▶ MOGAPAA
Liber Animarum. Mission St. Paul des Pieganes, Brocket	▶ LAB
Missions de la Congrégation des missionnaires oblats de Marie Immaculée	▶ *Missions*
Van Dale Archives, Kortrijk	▶ VDAK
Van Tighem Family Archives, Calgary	▶ VFAC

❖

1 The others were: *Death Memorial Cards.* Part I, II, III. Complied by Paul Callens.
2 Because of the differences in vocabulary and accent, we should refer to the language of these and other people from Flanders as Flemish-Dutch. However, in this volume we have mostly cut it short to Dutch. See Kossman (1978, 1).
3 "The Peigan belong to the Blackfoot Confederacy, which consists of four different member nations ... [they are] the Blood (Kanai), North Peigan (Aputosi Piikani), and Blackfoot (Siksika), all located in Alberta, Canada; and the South Peigan" (Amaskapi Piikani, Blackfeet, or Peigan) in Montana, U.S.A" (Crowshoe and Manneschmidt 1997, 2). Both Victor and Leonard write "Piegan" when they refer to the Canadian branch of this tribe, currently known as Peigan Nation. Only by the end of Victor's diary he changed his spelling to "Peigan." We have changed all references to "Piegan" into "Peigan."
4 The Congregation of the Oblates of Mary Immaculate was founded in 1817 by Eugène de Mazenod (1782–1861), who, in 1837, was consecrated bishop of Marseilles. Motto of this congregation is: Bring the Gospel to the poorest.

5   Edmonton, 297 km north of Calgary, is Alberta's capital. The city started out as a Hudson's Bay post in 1795, was incorporated as a town in 1897 and as a city in 1904. Edmonton is possibly named Edmonton to honour Hudson's Bay Deputy Governor James Winter Lake, a native of Edmonton, Middlesex, which village now lies within the boundaries of London, England (Sanders 2003, 124–25). Alberta was from 1882 on a North West Territories district and from 1905 on a province.

6   Strathmore, about 45 km west of Calgary, was incorporated as a village in 1908, as a town in 1911 and is named after Claude Bowes-Lyon, 13th Earl of Strathmore (1824–1904) (Sanders 2003, 283).

7   Bishop Vital-Justin Grandin was born in France in 1829 and died in St. Albert, Alberta in 1902. In 1854 he was ordained priest by Mgr. Charles-Joseph de Mazenod. In that same year Father Grandin went to Canada and served in Saskatchewan. In 1857 he became coadjutor of Mgr. Taché, bishop of St. Boniface, and from 1869 on he served in the North-West Territories/Alberta (Carrière 1977, 106–07).

8   The original handwritten version is located in the Missionary Oblate, Grandin Archives (Provincial Archives of Alberta [MOGAPAA] Accession 71.220, Box 104, File 4394). Father Camille Piché, O.M.I., Edmonton, kindly gave permission for publication. "The Blackfoot word *okotok*, 'rock,' is the source of this town's name and refers to the massive glacial erratic located eight kilometres west of town." At first the name was used for the post office, it was changed a short while into Dewdney (1835–1916), Indian Commissioner from 1879 to 1888 and Northwest Territories Lieutenant-Governor from 1881 to 1888). In 1897 the name Okotoks resurfaced (Sanders 2003, 234). Okotoks is about 40 km south of downtown Calgary.

9   The Flemish-Dutch letters from Belgian family members are translated by Mary E.M. with great help of Paul Callens for the purely Flemish expressions. The letters and articles in French are translated into English by Mary E.M., in a few instances with the help of Hayo Westra *et al.*

10 *Poorterschap* (burghership) was an ancient institution. Already in 1340 its *keure* (statute) stated that a burgher had to live at least three periods of forty days annually in the city. Advantages of having the status of "burgher from outside the gates" in the County of Flanders [now part of Belgium] among others included freedom from having to give up a piece of inherited land; one could avoid local courts and entrust one's cases to the well-provided *schepenbanken* (sheriff's courtrooms). Poorters also were free from paying capital gains tax when selling a house (Roelstraete1998, 337). About the name Vantieghem (which here and there and over time has different spellings), the first recorded is Arnoldus van Tiegem, patron saint of millers, innkeepers and beer brewers, born about 1040 in Tiegem. He served, as knight for Boudewijn of Flanders, later became a Benedictine monk and bishop of Soissons. He died in 1087 in Oudenburg (Claes *et al.* 2002, 113–4). 1 £= 1 lb = 1 pond = 20 schelling (http://home.pi.be/~ldeprost/gilistranslation.htm).

11 The original handwritten text is in a red velvet booklet in VFAC.

12 Lethbridge, about 180 km southeast of Calgary, is named after William Lethbridge of London, a partner in a company that invested in the North Western Coal and Navigation Company. After the coal mining settlement became known as Coal Banks, in 1885 the official name became Lethbridge (Sanders 2003, 192–93).

13 St. Albert is 14 km northwest of Edmonton and named after Father Lacombe's patron saint. During a walk in 1861 with Mgr. Taché, Father Lacombe determined the location for this new mission. St. Albert was incorporated as a village in 1899, as a town in 1904 and as a city in 1977 (Sanders 2003, 266–67).

14 This novitiate was established for Belgian Oblate novices. Of the first eight students, seven were born in Belgium.

15 In 1875 the *Gazette van Thielt* published "Amerikaensche Brieven (American Letters)", four travel accounts which Brother Jules Boone sent to his family. Boone's travel accounts are reproduced in English translation, by Mary E.M., as Appendix B to this volume.

16 Chokitapix is also spelled as *Saukitapix*, meaning *Prairie People*. "This manuscript was written in French by Jean L'Heureux.... The translation was made by the Glenbow Foundation in 1960." (Hugh A. Dempsey in his foreword to L'Heureux 1871).

17 In *Dissonant Worlds, Roger Vandersteene Among the Cree,* author Earle Waugh (1996) discusses the good, the bad and the ugly of the efforts to convert the Indians.

18 "The colonizers were successful. By the end of the 19th century, the Blackfoot civilization had largely been overrun by American savagery. This savagery included military repression, the whiskey trade, residential schools and cattle ranching" (Harold E. Gray / Long Standing Bear Chief, cited in http://www.columbia.edu/~lnp3/mydocs/indian/blackfoot.htm). The situation in Canada did not differ much from the one in America. Father Leduc had already come along with Mgr. Grandin in 1859. "At the Seminary of Mayenne, the Superior presented the students in Philosophy to the Bishop [Grandin] and said: 'My Lord, take your choice!' Placing his hands on the two nearest him, he replied: 'These two will I take.... They were the young Leduc and Légeard' (Hermant 1948, 31). Father Hyppolyte Leduc was born in France in 1842 and died in Edmonton in 1918. From 1867 to 1874 he was in St. Albert where he built the cathedral in 1870. He served in Fort Pitt, Fort Edmonton, Lac St. Anne, Lac La Biche, St. Albert, Calgary, St. Albert, and Edmonton, where he built the St. Joachim's church. In 1897 he established a hospital and in 1900 a convent (Carrière 1977, 288–89). Father Légeard was born in Mayenne in 1843 and died in Saskatchewan in 1879. In 1867 he came to western Canada and served in Pembina, North Dakota, Lac-Canot and Green Lake (Carrière 1977, 300–01).

19 Father Alexandre-Marie Blanchet was born in Mans in 1846 and died in St. Albert in 1929. He studied Cree, went along on hunting expeditions,

founded the Pélican Lake mission, served for one or two years in numerous missions and parishes; among others, from 1897 to 1906 he was the first resident priest in Pincher Creek. He served at Fort Macleod from 1906 to 1916 and then went on to Lethbridge (1918 to 1921), Calgary (1921) and St. Albert (1921 to 1929) (Carriére 1976, 101).

20 "A scholasticate is a 'study house for philosophy and theology.' After the fifth year one was ordained a priest and one year later the young Fathers left for their work areas, indicated by the superiors (obediences)" (Follens 1983, 39n3). Also: a novitiate is one year, one has to enter between the age of 16 to 40 years. After a one-year novitiate one can make eternal vows and one is already a member of the congregation. Otherwise one can make a vow for one year and thereafter. In order to become a priest, one has to study two years of philosophy and four years of theology. One then can be ordained a priest, Follens (1983, 60, 61) citing an Oblate brochure.

21 Brother Louis Dauphin was born in France in 1857 and died there in 1930. He left for Canada in 1874 and became a priest in 1882. He mainly worked in Saskatchewan and northern Alberta (Carrière 1976, 255). Father Michel Mérer was born in France in 1851 and died in Edmonton in 1920. He became a priest in 1878 and came to western Canada in 1878. He worked mainly in St. Albert and at missions in Saskatchewan (Carrière 1977, 384).

22 In a 1922 historical overview it is confirmed that retention and evangelisation of the European settlers had priority above those of the Indians (Faure 1922, 922).

23 Fort Macleod, 40 km west of Lethbridge, is named after James Farquharson Macleod (1836–1894), who became assistant-commissioner in the North-West Mounted Police. He founded Fort Macleod, which in 1892 was incorporated as Macleod. The original name, Fort Macleod, was restored in 1952 (Sanders 2002, 142–43).

24 Gros Ventres split in the late 1600s from the Arapaho; in the late 1700s they allied with the Blackfeet, in the 1800's they were decimated by small-pox, in 1861 they became hostile to the Blackfeet and in 1878 they settled on the Fort Belknap Reservation in Montana (http://www.native-languages.org/gros.htm and http://www.mnsu.edu/emuseum/cultural/northamerica/gros_ventre.html).

25 In 1874 Nicholas Sheran came to Lethbridge and became the first commercial exporter of coals (Ross 1985, 6).

26 Nicholas Sheran drowned on May 20, 1882 (Ross 1985, 6). At the time he was living with a full-blooded Peigan Indian woman, Awatoyaken (White Tailed Deer Woman), also named Mary Brown. Her name was Brown because she lived with her sister who was married with a Brown. Sheran had two sons with Mary, Charles, and William who was born three months after Sheran's death. The Sheran estate went to Nicolas sister Ellen Sheran, who lived in New York, as the judge decided that Nicolas and Mary were married 'per verba de presenti,' and neither were married according to Catholic or local Indian rites (http://library.usask.ca:9003/native/cnlc/

volo3/636.html). As Mary Brown could not afford to raise her children, she enthrusted them to Mrs. Marcella MacFarland, who handed them over to the orphanage of the Sisters of Charity at St. Albert and "arranged first for the two youngsters to be baptized in the Roman Catholic Church and, on 18 May 1884, brought Father Leonard Van Tighem from Fort Macleod to Lethbridge to perform the ceremony. These were the first recorded baptisms on the Lethbridge townsite" (Johnston and Den Otter 1985, 38). Kipp is a hamlet on Highway 3, about seven kilometres northwest of Lethbridge. A few kilometres from Kipp, the American Joseph Kipp (1847–1913) and Charlie Thomas built a trading post in 1870 (Sanders 2003, 182).

27 Sir Alexander Tilloch Galt (1817–1893) "was Canada's high commissioner to Britain in the 1880s . . . one of his responsibilities was to promote the development of the NWT and its resources. . . . His public and private endeavors converged in the North Western Coal and Navigation Company" (Sanders 2003, 193). William Stafford (and captain Bryant) was sent to Alberta to choose a mining site. Their choice for Coalbanks "determined the location of the City of Lethbridge" (Johnston and Den Otter 1985, 38).

28 Blackfoot Crossing is the location, currently Siksika Nation, 90 km east of Calgary, where in 1877 Treaty 7 was signed. Medicine Hat, about 150 km east, northeast of Lethbridge, was incorporated as a village in 1894 and as a town in 1898 (Sanders 2003, 213). Blackfoot Crossing is also the location of a story about a son of Charles Dickens (http://folklore.library.ualberta.ca/dspImage.cfm?ID=183&Current-3).

29 "Fur traders, gold seekers, and homesteaders came via steamboats to Fort Benton, the 'Head of Navigation' on the Missouri River. A fur and buffalo robe trading post at first, it became the hub for trade and travel for all of Montana and Western Canada. Lewis and Clark, Jim Bridger, Kit Carson and John Colter all explored the area. During the gold rush, fifty steamboats a season docked along the Fort Benton levee, unloading equipment and supplies, and loading tons of gold for the trip back to St. Louis. Whiskey followed gold, and infamous trails were forged into Canada, including the Whoop-up Trail into Alberta and the Fort Walsh Trail into Saskatchewan. Gradually law and order replaced lawlessness and ranchers and farmers occupied the plains and Fort Benton became the hub for one of the largest wheat producing areas in the state" (http://www.fortbenton.com/about.htm).

30 Dunmore, 5 km southeast of Medicine Hat, is named after one of the shareholders of the NW Coal and Navigation Company, Charles Adolphus Murray, 7th Earl of Dunmore (1841–1907) (Sanders 2003, 121).

31 The 1885 Half-breed Rebellion is currently known as the Riel Rebellion.

32 Saint Jean Berchmans, Jesuit, was born in Diest, Belgium, in 1599, was sent for further studies to Rome, where he died in 1621 (Claes, Claes, Vinke 2002, 220-21).

33 Jean is their brother, born in 1849.

34 Father Albert Naessens, born in 1864 in Courtrai (Kortrijk), Belgium, died in 1942 in Edmonton (Carrière 1979, 10). Having been Victor's "former student," Father Naessens must have attended the Van Dale School in Kortrijk. Throughout Leonard and Victor's writings, we will hear from Albert Naessens, who had a very successful career in the Oblate congregation. He became the third director of the Dunbow Industrial School (1890–1901 and 1902–1907), pastor in Calgary (1911–1914) and later Provincial of the Oblate congregation (1936–1942). Brother Charles Devriendt, born in 1860 in Pittem, died in 1933 in Oostende, Belgium. He studied in Tielt and at the juniorate in Ottawa (1884–1885), entered the novitiate of Lachine in 1885 and "fit le profession" in 1886. In August 1887 he made his eternal vows. In 1890 he was sent to British Columbia were he was ordained priest, subsequently he served as priest in Cranbrook (1891–1894), Williams Lake (1894–1898), New Westminster (1893–1903). Back in Belgium he served in Brussels (1903–1910) and La Panne (1910–1933) where he is buried (Carrière 1976, 285).

35 The municipal registry of Meulebeke registered one Emile Verbrugghe, born in Roeselare on December 15, 1859, living at Ledestraat 183.

36 Brother Jules Boone, born in Meulebeke in 1852, travelled in 1874 to St. Albert together with Leonard and his cousin Henri Scheers, Bishop Grandin and his nephew Henri Grandin and a number of other recruits. Apart from what we learn about him from his own letters, a brochure (Smith and English, n.d.) notes: "1881: Bishop Grandin visits the [Peigan] Reserve. Brothers Alexandre and Boon built a log house." After a few years Boone returned to Belgium and left the congregation (Missiealbum 1950). Back in Belgium he married to a widow with children. Henri Scheers was born in Meulebeke in 1840 and died in France in 1917. He was the first Belgian Brother to persevere in the Oblate congregation. He entered the novitiate in Nancy in 1867 and arrived in Canada in 1874; he worked in Lac-La-Biche, Fort Resolution, Fort Providence, the N.W. Territories and at Fort Chipewyan in Alberta (1878–1904). Back in Belgium in 1905 he dedicated himself to the minor seminary in Waregem. During the First World War he went to France, where he died in 1938 (Carrière 1979, 168 and Missiealbum 1950). Henri was related to the Van Tighem brothers by their paternal grandmother, Maria Anne Scheers.

37 Jean Goethals, born in Tielt in 1811, became alderman of Meulebeke in 1854 and member of the Catholic Council for the Tielt district in 1870 (Libeert 1977, 67n102).

38 "The word 'geuzen' was used for the first time on April 5, 1566. On that day in Brussels about 300 'lower' noblemen and citizens offered a petition to Margaretha of Parma, Governess of the Netherlands: they petitioned for absolution of anti-protestants law and congregation of the Staten-Generaal. During this public audience Charles, Comte de Berlaymont, saw that Margaretha got nervous. He said to her, in French, 'Have no fear, they are only gueux [beggars].' Since then the people who opposed [whatever] in the

Netherlands took over this label, Guru, or Gauze. In the nineteenth century freethinkers in Belgium, that in 1830 was separated from the Netherlands, took this label and it is also the motto of the Free University of Brussels which was established in 1835" (April 2003 e-mail from Prof. Dr. Hugo de Schepper, Nijmegen).

39 On September 2, 1881 the fourteen Brothers, living at the Lange Steenstraat in Kortrijk, were evicted from their home by the Gauze and had to seek shelter here and there. Their house, built for them by Father Jozef Van Dale, became a state school and still is. In 1885 the Brothers bought another building, "De Kring," and moved into it (Vandekerckhove 1981, 7–26).

40 Mgr. Charles John Seghers, born in Gent, 1839, was curate of the Cathedral at Victoria, B.C. and consecrated bishop of Vancouver Island in 1873. In 1878 he became coadjutor to the archbishop of Oregon City, archbishop in 1880. In 1884 he resigned and was transferred to Vancouver Island. In 1886 he was murdered in Alaska by his servant Francis Fuller who "from the journey [to Alaska] had become deranged and turned against the man whom previously he had learned to love and admire" (Diamond Jubilee of the American College of the Immaculate Conception 1932, 105–7).

41 Of the 220 men of the 9th Voltigeurs that left Quebec City in April 1885 to help suppress the 1885 North-West Rebellion, "the companies 1, 2 and 8 were sent to Fort Macleod to watch over the large Blood Reserve and the nearby Peigan Reserve" (Ronaghan 1994, 10, 11).

42 Alida De Smet was his brother Charles' wife.

43 Leonard and Victor's father, Bernard Vantighem, died October 11th, 1884.

44 Gustaf Vantighem, born in 1842, was the oldest Van Tighem brother. He was a widower at the time, because his wife, Nathalie Vanhollebeke, had died in 1882.

45 Jean Marie Van Tighem, born in 1849, was Leonard's and Victor's brother. Mathilde Linclau is Jean's wife.

46 This Gustaf is Father Gustaf D'Hertoghe, the son of Ivo Leonard D'Hertoghe and Anna Kupers, Leonard and Victor's aunt on mother's side.

47 Uncle Ivo, a brother of Bernard Van Tighem, married to Sophie Vande Ghinste, who died in 1900 in Meulebeke. They had five children. Uncle Ivo then married Maria Theresia Vansteenkiste and had two children with her, Maria Gislena, and Prudentia.

48 "Flemish Lourdes came into being because of a private initiative of a noble woman, Marques de Courteboune. She built a grotto in her yard out of devotion for Our Lady of Lourdes. After the blessing of the grotto in 1873 local residents asked permission to pray at the grotto. A stunning miracle enforced this wish. On April 7, 1875, Peter De Rudder was cured from an open leg ulcer" (Wilma Helmet, *Het Volk*, May 8 and 9, 2004).

49 Father Émile Legal was born in France in 1849 and died in Edmonton in 1920. Upon his arrival on the American continent he practised his English in New York, came to St. Albert in 1881, resided in Calgary until 1886 from where he visited Fort MacLeod (1882–1884), founded the Peigan Mission

(1883–1889) while visiting Pincher Creek in the period 1845–1889. He then founded a school and a hospital on the Blood Reserve (1889–1897), became bishop of Poglia and coadjutor of St. Albert in 1897, bishop of St. Albert in 1902 and archbishop of Edmonton in 1912 (Carrière 1977, 296–97).

50 In 1880's Mr. Frank Levasseur of MacLeod came from Madawaska, New Brunswick, joined his brother George who had been working in mines and as a freighter. His brother George had built a residence opposite the Catholic Church in Macleod. Later both brothers settled in Pincher Creek (Historical Society Pincher Creek 1974, 93–4).

51 Under a letter of Father Lacombe to Father Legal, March 22, 1888 is "a little note for all the priests in the delicate handwriting of Bishop Grandin ('I am truly desolate because of the illness of our dear Father Van Tighen [sic]. . . . Your affectionate brother, Vital, O.M.I." (Hughes 1920, 317). In 1888 this illness is not mentioned by Leonard nor by his brother Victor. Perhaps the bishop still had Leonard's 1886 illness in mind.

52 Pincher Creek, about 85 km west-southwest of Lethbridge, named after lost and later found "pinchers," became a village in 1898 and a town in 1906 (Sanders 2003, 243–44).

53 By "pear tree" is possibly meant the Cleen Peirboom or Het Peireboome, a pub on the road from Tielt to Kortrijk, that was closed in the 19th century, and/or was renamed Au Petit Paris (Baert 1987, 70).

54 The Sisters of Love (Liefde) was a congregation founded by Joseph Van Dale in 1768. Its goal was to educate poor girls and teach them lace-making. "E.H. Jozef, Ignatius Van Dale (1716–1781)," n.d., no author, 4, Collection Paul Callens.

55 This notebook could not be located.

56 According to a letter (November 17, 2003) by Brother Alfons, archivist of the Sint Sixtus Abbey, one of the Brothers of the Sint Sixtus Abbey was Henricus, Carolus Ludovicus Van Tychem who was born in Ichtegem in 1846 and died in 1915 in West-Vleteren. Having possibly a relative or acquaintance in this monastery might explain Victor's hiding out in this location.

57 Father Albert Lacombe was born in Quebec in 1827 and died in Midnapore, Alberta in 1916. He was the great-grandson of a Saulteaux Indian. He founded St. Albert, became a parish priest at Fort Macleod, was the first principal of the Dunbow Industrial School near Calgary, wrote dictionaries and grammars of the Indian languages, was involved in conducting Treaty Seven and Eight, was pastor along the construction of the railway in Alberta on Indian lands. He retired in 1897 and went back to, as he claimed, to be "a hermit on a hill near Pincher Creek." Father Lacombe died in the Lacombe Home, established by himself, in Midnapore, Alberta (Une Soeur de la Providence 1916, passim).

58 Father Léon Doucet was born in France in 1847 where he started his priest studies, which he finished in Lac St. Anne, Alberta. In 1870 he became the first priest ordained in Alberta. He worked in Brosseau, Ile de la Crosse,

Green Lake, and St. Albert, over-wintered with hunters and was the first to set up a tent in Calgary. Six months later this spot became Fort Brisebois and later Fort Calgary. He visited Fort Macleod between 1876 and 1878 and resided in Brocket (Piegan Reserve) from 1878 to 1883. He then visited posts along the railway, Blackfoot Crossing, Swift Current, Maple Creek, Lethbridge, Canmore, Cochrane, Banff, Medicine Hat, Dunmore, stayed with the Blood, the Sarcee, again the Blood, was back in Brocket from 1902 to 1910, then Midnapore, Cluny, Dunbow School, Cardston, Cluny, Blood Hospital, Cluny, St. Albert, Cardston and back to St. Albert where he died in 1942 (Carrière 1976, 295–96). Father Doucet's Blackfoot name was "Inuk-a-to-i-apeekun" (Gibbon Stocken 1976, 53). Father Doucet came to Canada with Mgr. Grandin in 1868 (Hermant 1848, 74). Father Charles Claude, born in France in 1856, died in France in 1920. He studied in Nancy, came to Canada in 1880, to St. Albert in 1881 where he was ordained priest, worked in Calgary, along the construction of the railway (1882) and in Cochrane. From 1884 to 1890 he was principal of the Dunbow School, he visited Banff, Canmore and Okotoks, left the Oblate congregation in 1890 and became a secular pastor in France (Carrière 1976, 207).

59 Marialoop is a parish, partly in Meulebeke, Oostrozebeke and Tielt, Belgium.

60 Joseph Lestanc was born in France in 1830, worked in Manitoba (1855–1860), Alberta and Saskatchewan. He was director of the Dunbow School from 1901–1903 [during Father Naoooeno' absence] and died in Calgary in 1912 (Carrière 1977, 321). Lestanc was one of Leonard's teachers when he studied for the priesthood. In 1909 Lestanc took over Leonard's parish in Edmonton.

61 Jules Boone stayed in Belgium; on June 4, 1889, he married Irma Valerie Octavie Debrabandere, widow of a brewer. Boone died in Kortrijk on October 24, 1928.

62 During a lecture on the Peigan Reservation in Browning, Montana, on August 20, 2004, Narcisse Blood, member of the Blood tribe in Alberta, commented on Father Lacombe: "They say that he was fluent in our language. If he had been, he would not have tried to convert us, he would have understood that we did not worship the devil."

63 Brother Edward Cunningham, son of Métis parents, was born in 1862 in Edmonton and died there in 1920. From 1888 to 1890 he completed his theology studies and was ordained priest in 1889. He served at the missions of Fort MacLeod and Brocket (Peigan) in 1888, Saint Albert and Lac-La-Biche, 1889, Onion Lake, Saskatchewan 1892–1897, Alberta 1895, 1897. He visited a number of missions in Alberta and Saskatchewan and served from 1917 to 1920 in Lac-Ste.-Anne, Alberta (Carrière 1976, 242).

64 Mgr. Isidore Clut was born in France 1832 and died in Alberta in 1903. He served mainly in north-Alberta, helped several missionaries with their studies of Indian languages and is co-author of a polyglot dictionary with Father Emile Petitot (Carrière 1976, 210–11).

65 Leonard transcribed this letter in his codex.

66 In a following letter (March 9, 1889) Karel announced the death of his ten-month-old daughter, Euphrasia.

67 Brother Scheers served from 1878 to 1904 in Fort Chipewyan, Alberta (Carrière 1979, 168).

68 The Geloove convent started out in 1833 as a school, financed by the Bal sisters. In 1840 the congregation's Rule was accepted by Bruge's bishop, Mgr. Bousen; from then on the pious, teaching women were entitled to call themselves Sisters. In 1844 it developed into a lace-making school where children worked and were educated about one to one and a halve hour per day. After 1845, after contagious diseases had broken out, the Sisters expanded into caring for the sick (Verschuere, Antonellus O.F.M., 1941, 7, 14, 36, 39, 40).

69 This was Euphrasia (May 1888–February 1889). A year earlier there was a Camile in the family who only lived from May 1887 to January 1888.

70 "The first large Slovak colony, known as such, was established in Lethbridge, Alberta, by Slovak miners who came to Canada in 1885 from the coal mines of Shelby, Montana." (Kirschbaum 1967, 49). "In 1887 a new group of 130 persons came from the United States. They intended to settle in Esterhazy [around Whitewood, Manitoba], but a fire destroyed so many houses that it was impossible for this group to settle there. Paul Esterhazy made an agreement with Moore and Hunter Company (mining) that all of the men in the group would work in Medicine Hat. The working conditions, however, very soon forced all of them to leave their jobs" (Kirschbaum 1966, 26). "Even if they belong to Rome, Slovaks of the Slavonic Byzantine rite prefer to be called Slovak 'Greek Catholics,' in contrast to those of the Latin Rite who are Roman Catholics. . . . Greek Catholics differ from the Roman only so far as they use the old Slavonic language and the Greek Rite in their Liturgy" (Kirschbaum 1967, 249–50).

71 Cf. De Vocht, 2005, passim.

72 The correct spelling of the translation of "every day" and "every Sunday" in this sentence is respectively: *Každýdeň and 'každúnedel'u* (Fax message from Andrej Kral, May 5, 2005).

73 "I've seen different explanations for the change. The entry on the 'Sign of Cross' in the Catholic Encyclopedia (which you can see online at http://www.newadvent.org/cathen/13785a.htm) says that medieval mystic envisioned the gesture as chasing the devil away, and thus 'pushing' him from left to right. Orthodox authors have a different idea, claiming that Western congregations were so ignorant that they simply repeated what they saw the priests in front of them doing, and therefore did it backwards!" (March 8, 2004 e-mail from Dr. Ayse Tuzlak to Charles Willemen, Calgary, which Willemen kindly passed on).

74 From 1526 to 1918 the Slavonians or Slovaks were ruled by the Austro-Hungarian Habsburgs. "After the Austro-Hungarian Ausgleich (Compromis) of 1867, the Hungarian government resumed their control over Slovaki and

pursued a policy of Magyyarization there, which stimulated many Slovaks to emigrate, particularly to the U.S." (Encyclopaedia Britannica IX, 275–76).

75 In 1888 the Canadian Pacific Railway Company acquired the Minneapolis, St. Paul & Sault Ste. Marie line and the Duluth South Shore & Atlantic. These two companies went on under the phonetically spelled name, Soo (Sault) line (http://www.willisville.ca/Rail%20Line%20History.htm and http://www.crowsnest-highway.ca/timeline.pl?page=7).

76 The Sisters, Fidèles Compagnes de Jésus, form the Society of Faithful Companions of Jesus on the American continent. In 1820 this society of apostolic women was founded in Amiens, France, by Madeleine de Bonneult d'Hoët. They take their inspiration from Mary and the Holy women of the Gospel (http://www.fcjsisters.org/fcj-french/index.html).

77 Mr. William van Horne was born in 1843 in Chelsea, Illinois and died in 1915 in Montreal. He was a descendant of Jan Cornelissen van Horne who in 1635 settled in New Amsterdam. In 1881 Van Horne came to Winnipeg as general manager to build the Canadian Pacific Railway System (Vaughan 1920, passim).

78 Father Walter Comiré was born in 1865 in Quebec and died in 1945 in Edmonton. From 1891 to 1892 he resided at the Dunbow School. He travelled to Pincher Creek in 1891 and served in Fort Macleod from 1891 to 1892. From 1892 to 1896 he was in charge of the missions along the railway track at Midnapore, Cochrane, Canmore and Banff. Thereafter he served in Saskatchewan (Carrière 1976, 215–16).

79 This is the first time Leonard refers to his brother Victor, who went in Canada by his monastic name, Jean or John Berchmans.

80 Brother Jean Baptiste Brochard was born in Germany in 1856. In 1885 he pronounced his eternal vows in St. Albert; he served there from 1879 to 1893 and in Calgary and in Banff from 1893 to 1894. In 1893 he built the church in Canmore. In 1894 he went back to Europe. In 1895 he received dispensation of his vows (Carrière 1976, 139).

81 Brother Janvier Danis, son of Jean-Baptiste Danis and Martine Lacombe, was born in Quebec in 1865 and died in Alberta in 1946. He quit his priest studies because of poor health. He was invited by Father Lacombe to come to the west and was ordained priest in 1894 in Calgary. Between 1892 and 1906 he served with the Blood, at the Dunbow School, Calgary, St. Albert, the Dunbow School, the Peigan, Blackfoot Crossing, again the Peigan, worked along the railways, Blackfoot Crossing, Fort Macleod and Strathcona (Edmonton) (Carrière 1976, 251).

82 Father Louis Royer was born in France in 1862 and died in Edmonton in 1934. In 1894 he came to western Canada, served in Edmonton, St. Albert, Calgary, St. Albert, Blackfoot Crossing (1905–1908), Edmonton (1908–1910) and Pincher Creek (1910–1917) and back in Edmonton until his death (Carrière 1979, 148–49).

83 Bishop Brondel was born in Bruges in 1842 and became a priest in 1864. In 1866 he arrived in America; in 1879 he became bishop of Vancouver Island, in 1883 Apostolic Vicar of Montana and in 1884 the first bishop of Helena, Montana, where he died in 1903 (Allossery 1925, 1–3).

84 Father Dols from Holland was ordained in 1874 and died in 1898. Father Dols was pastor at St. Patrick's church in Butte about 1883. However, as he had said some unkindly things about the Irish, he was forced to leave Butte. The struggle between "Americanism" (a liberal movement in the church at this time) and more conservative elements may have been behind this. Father Dols was pastor at St. Ann's church in Great Falls, which became the cathedral of the Great Falls diocese when it was created in 1904. Father Dols died May 31, 1898 (September 2, 2003, e-mail from Sister Dolores Brinkel, Helena Montana).

85 Somehow Leonard must have retrieved his mother tongue, which Victor, upon his arrival in Lethbridge in 1886 noted as "lost."

86 During the 1302 war with the French, Vlaanderen den Leeuw was a battle cry. The song Vlaanderen den Leeuw was written by Hippoliet Van Peene, music by Karel Miry, in 1847. Around 1900, it was seen as Flanders' national song, and in 1973 the first two verses officially became Flanders' national song (http://www.vlaanderendeleeuw.be).

87 Archbishop Alexandre Taché was born in Quebec in 1823 and died in Manitoba, 1894. In 1850 he became coadjutor of Mgr. Provencher, after his death in 1853 bishop and in 1857 archbishop of St. Boniface (Carrière 1979, 210). "Mgr. Alexandre Taché, Archbishop of St. Boniface, had come from a long line of statesmen, explorers and military men. Among his ancestors were Joliet, Boucher de Boucherville and Varennes de la Verendrye" (Breton 1955, 16).

88 Gleichen is a hamlet about 65 km northeast of Calgary. It is said that the hamlet is named after Count Albert Gleichen (1863–1937), an investor in the CPR Gleichen became a village in 1899, "but has since reverted to hamlet status." (Sanders 2003, 149).

89 The Congregation of Sisters of Charity at the Hôpital Général of Montreal, commonly called Grey Nuns because of the colour of their attire, was founded in 1738 by the Venerable Marie-Marguerite Dufrost de Lajemmerais (Madame d'Youville) and the Rev. Louis M. Normand du Faradon, at that time Superior at the seminary of St. Sulpice of Ville Marie (now Montreal). Nicolet was a branch of St. Hyacinth. In 1844 a colony of Grey Nuns left their convent in Canada to devote their lives to providing relief for the Indian tribes and educating the youth in the far Northwest (http://www.newadvent.org/cathen/07031a.htm). She founded the Congregation after she was widowed from François Madeline d'Youville (http://www.sgm.ca/english/marguerite.html).

90 Because the words of the missionaries had failed to soften "the by vice hardened hearts" of the "most fierce and attached to their superstitions" Blood Indians, the establishment of the hospital on the Blood reserve,

around 1900, was to serve as a means to convince them of the sincerity and truthfulness of the missionaries' religion by the dedication of the Sisters of Charity (Gladu 1914, 481).

91 In 1896 Father J. Adéot Thérien (1862–1936) was recruited by Father Lacombe to administer the St. Paul des Métis settlement, 28 km north of St. Paul, but the community dispersed (Sanders 2003, 290).

92 Lauwe is a village near Kortrijk.

93 After the death of his wife Alida, Charles married Rosalie Julie Van Hecke.

94 Pharailde Lecluyse was a daughter of Leonard's uncle, Charles Louis Vantyghem, baker, who was married to Lucie Lecluyse (Meulebeke, Civil Registry 1881–1890, Section H, 210).

95 The Holy Cross Hospital in Calgary was founded in 1891 by four Sisters of Charity (Grey Nuns of Montreal) and closed in 1979.

96 Father Alexis André was born in France in 1833, and died in Calgary 1893. He served in the missions of the Red River, North Dakota, from 1865 to 1871 St. Albert. In 1876 he read his first mass in Prince Albert, Saskatchewan. He then served in Duck Lake and Carlton in 1877. He assisted Louis Riel at the scaffold in 1885 and back in Calgary, from 1886 to 1893, he established a church (Carrière 1976, 26–7).

97 Febronie Tassaert was the third child of Jean Francies Tassaert and Francisca Gislena Kupers, a sister of Angela Kupers, Leonard and Victor's mother (Bevolking [Population] Meulebeke 1881–1890, 777).

98 The *greffier* is Leopold Constantin Pieter Sacrez, Febronie's husband, a registrar at the courthouse.

99 A Chinook "blows from the direction of the country occupied by the Chinook Indians. . . . It is a 'descending wind' that flows over the Rocky Mountains, following the low pressure on the eastern side, which draws it down the mountains to the plains" (McClintock 1923/1992, 52).

100 These children were Marie (1881–1895), Joseph (1882–1933) and Elody Marie Therese (1883–1971), which he had with Alida, and Margarita (1892–?) and Adile (1892–1975) which he had with his second wife, Rosalie Vanhecke.

101 Father Victor Bourgine was born in France in 1841 and died in St. Albert in 1893. He pronounced his eternal vows in 1878, served in Edmonton, accompanied hunters during their buffalo chases and served mainly at Lac St. Anne, St. Albert, Slave Lake and Fort Pitt (Carrière 1976, 124–25).

102 Bishop Grandin went to Belgium in September 1893. Before he went he asked Cardinal Ledochowski, Prefect for the Propaganda, for a letter of recommendation in which he set three goals for his visit: (1) steer emigration to his area to counter balance the protestant immigration, (2) an appeal to young clergy to join him, as Oblates or as secular priests and (3) financial aid (Lepage 1954, 317–18). "On November 11, 1893, Mgr. Grandin consecrated three altars in the St. Elooi parish in this city [Brugge]." (Acta 1893, fo 422 bis, Archives Diocese Bruges). Translation of this letter, from Latin to Dutch, is kindly provided by Brother Alfons of the Sint Sixtus

Abbey, Westvleteren, Belgium and Father Karel Denys, CICM, Arlington, Virginia. Text cited by Brother Alfons 2003.

103 This brother (-in-law) was Febronie's husband, the *greffier*.

104 Adile Desmet was probably a brother of Alida Van Tighem-Desmet.

105 Brother Patrick Bowes was born in Ontario in 1830 and died in St. Albert in 1908. He served at many missions. He built the ones in MacLeod in 1881, Hobbema in 1881 and 1884 and Dunbow in 1882. He worked in Edmonton where he helped build the cathedral and mill on the Sturgeon River (1869–1871). From 1889 to 1890 he served with the Blackfoot in Calgary, thereafter in St. Albert, Calgary, Lethbridge, Canmore, Banff, Cochrane, Lac-la-Biche again, Lac-La-Selle and in Calgary. "The Brother became the big builder of missions" (Carrière 1976, 129).

106 This school was also known as the Dunbow or St. Joseph's Industrial School. "St. Joseph's Industrial School, commonly known as Dunbow, operated from 1884 to 1924. It was built by the Canadian government, east of High River, Alberta and was operated by the Oblates of Mary Immaculate as a Catholic residential school for Blackfoot children. It was one of the first three Indian residential schools in western Canada. The principals of the school were Father Albert Lacombe (1884–1885), Father E. Claude (1885–1890), Father A. Naessens (1890–1907), Father J. Riou (1907–1912) and Father J.A. Demers (1919–1922). The Commissioner of Indian Affairs in Regina and the Superintendent of Indian Affairs in Ottawa supervised the operations of the school" (http://ww2.glenbow.org/search/archivesMainResults.aspx. St. Joseph's Industrial School fonds). "When Father Lacombe served as principal, two lay brothers and two Sisters of Charity staffed the new school, with a curriculum including academics and a music program for half of each day. The other half-day consisted of stock raising, blacksmithing, carpentry and crop raising" (http:// www.wcr.ab.ca/news/2000/0605/ fralbertlacombe060500.shtml). "Due to poor health care and increased exposure to diseases such as tuberculosis, as many as 73 First Nation and Métis students may have died at Dunbow School" (Aboriginal Framework News 2002:I, 1). "Traditional and Christian ceremonies commemorated the reburial of 34 human remains from the St. Joseph's Industrial Residential School (Dunbow School) cemetery, located approximately 40 to 30 km southeast of Calgary, to a new location at the St. Joseph's Industrial Residential School Provincial Historic Site. The graves were relocated as a result of the Bow Highwood River eroding the riverbank, causing human remains to be exposed. Removal of the human remains began March 22, 2001 after consultation with, and at the express wishes of First Nations and Métis representatives" (Government of Alberta News Release, May 5, 2001). Father Charles Lefebvre was born in Quebec in 1863 and died there in 1900. In 1893 he left for western Canada and served at the Dunbow School from 1893 to 1894. Because of his father's health he had to go back east (Carrière 1977, 291). Cf: http://www.albertasource.ca/methodist/The_Missionary/ Pre_1870_Oblates.htm

107 Thomas Morkin was born in Ontario in 1871, entered the Lachine novitiate on October 7, 1893. He pronounced his eternal vows in Lethbridge in 1900 and died in St. Albert in 1955. He served in St. Albert in 1894, in Calgary in 1894, at the Dunbow School from 1894 to 1922, in Cardston from 1922 to 1938 and at the Indian school of Stand Off from 1945 to 1952. He then retired to the Foyer Youville in St. Albert (Carrière 1979, 407). Laurence (?) Carrière just mentions one other Morkin, John, who was born in Ontario in 1867 and died in Duck Lake, Saskatchewan in November 1925. He entered the Lachine novitiate on May 23, 1896 (so not in 1893). He professed his eternal vows in the Dunbow School in 1904, worked there from 1894 to 1922 and then went on to the Indian school at Duck Lake (Carrière 1979, 407).

108 Grassy Lake is about 80 km east of Lethbridge. "The name comes from the Blackfoot moyi-kimi, 'grassy waters,' but refers to the grassy prairies, and not to a body of water" (Sanders 2003, 152). From a conversation with local residents in the bar of the Grassy Water Hotel, July 2004, I learned that the Catholic Church was sold to the Mennonites. As Grassy Waters is along the railway, we guess that Leonard went there by train. Danford (2003, 175) states that in 1893 the Canadian Pacific took over the narrow gauge line that was completed in 1885 by the Northwest Coal & Navigation Co. and that John J. Devine, from Ireland, then from Nova Scotia, "spent one whole year as section foreman of a gang of men tearing up and putting down rails and ties to change the narrow gauge line."

109 "The First Catholic Slovak Union (IKSJ) was the largest Slovak fraternal organization in the United States and he second largest in Canada from the time of its foundation in 1890 in Cleveland, Ohio, by Rev. Stefan Furdek." This union was meant to "support the sick and crippled brethren, to help widows and orphans in their predicament and to take care of the education of orphans in order for them to become good members of human society, to maintain and strengthen the faith inherited from ancestors; to keep alive Slovak national consciousness and traditions and to educate the members of the Union to become good citizens of the United States." (Kirschbaum 1967, 182–83).

110 In 1921 the Slovaks in Lethbridge, who originated from the villages Slovinky, Poráč, Závadka in the county of Spičs, established the Peter and Paul parish (Kirschbaum 1967, 250).

111 Father Léon Fouquet was born in France in 1831 and died in British Columbia in 1912. In 1854 he was ordained priest by Mgr. Charles-Joseph-Eugène de Mazenod. In 1859 he was sent to British Columbia. In 1860 he was the first priest to read mass in Vancouver. Due to indifference of the Indians to his mission (St. Michel, Fort Rupert) he was sent in 1871 to the Saint-Eugène des Kootenays (Cranbrook) where he stayed until 1888. From 1888 to 1890 he served in St. Albert, was pastor of the St. Joachim Church in Edmonton from 1890 to 1894, pastor of the Saint Mary church in Calgary from 1894 to 1899, and was then charged with the missions at Cochrane, Banff and

Canmore. From 1899 to 1912 he was back at Mission City's mission, where he died (Carrière 1977, 42–3).

112 Father Adélard Langevin was born in Quebec in 1855 and died in Montreal in 1915. In 1895 he became archbishop of St. Boniface, Manitoba (Carrière 1977, 245).

113 In 1890 a common public non-sectarian school system was introduced in Manitoba, which in 1892 led to the lawsuit City of Winnipeg v. Barret whereby the Manitoba court held "that Catholics had not lost their right to their own schools (they had only lost public tax support for them)." In 1895 the Privy Council in Brophy v. Attorney-General for Manitoba commented that the duty of the court is "to interpret, not enact," . . . and that "the public Schools Act of 1890 did affect rights or privileges of the Roman Catholic minority in relation to education and that appeal to the Governor in Council (federal cabinet) and federal intervention by remedial action were in order'" (Jaenen 1968, 27–28).

114 "Pend d'Oreilles, 'ear pendants,' an important tribe of Salishan stock originally residing about Pend d' Oreille lake and river, in northern Idaho and northeast Washington, and now gathered chiefly upon Flathead reservation, Montana, and Colville reservation, Washington" (http://www.newadvent.org/cathen/08594a.htm).

115 Father Pierre Lecoq was born in France in 1850 and died in Rochester, Minnesota in 1926. After his priest studies he was sent to Canada, served at Duck Lake, Cumberland House, Pelican Narrows, Grand Rapids, and passed through St. Albert from 1885 to 1887. Later on he served in Manitoba and also made a tour to France and Belgium to recruit colonists (Carrière 1977, 283–84).

116 Leonard transcribed the following report in his codex; between dashes, in a different handwriting, he added the names of the other churches.

117 A new church has to be constructed out of stone and be free of debt, otherwise it cannot be consecrated.

118 The College of the Sulpiciens was founded in 1767 by Jean-Baptiste Curatteau de la Blaiserie and was replaced and rebuilt a few times [from 1803 on it is located on the Rue Sherbrooke] (http://recit-us.cspi.qc.ca/histoire/1997-1998/sulpiciens/curatt.htm).

119 Cf.: "Van Tighem did not enjoy the friendship and admiration of Lethbridge's social leaders, who belittled his work among the 'foreign element.' Nevertheless, Van Tighem continued his endeavours. . . . He fought hard to secure for his school a fair share of the district's taxes" (Johnston and Den Otter 1985, 72).

120 In Montana these "Cris" or Cree-Indians had been reviled and rejected and "forced to wander from the garbage dumps of Helena [capital of Montana] to the unfriendly confines of the Blackfeet Reservation" (Dempsey 1984, 199).

121 Actually, Big Bear is said to have done everything to prevent murders and uprisings. After the first blows and shoutings were exchanged, "Big Bear

realized that the combination of excitement and alcohol was producing a dangerous situation ... he sent a young girl to Kehiwin's reserve to urge the Woods Cree to come to Frog lake to help keep the peace. Eventually, the entire band came, but by then it was too late" (Dempsey 1984, 156). "The Crees, who had fled to Montana after the Riel Rebellion, had been rounded up and send back to Canada. Among a band of 71 Indians who owned 340 horses Lucky Man and Little Bear were found" (Deane 1999, 24). The Indian prisoner was Imasees, born in 1851. His second name was Apistakuos or Little Bear (Dempsey 1984, 25).

122 Father Fafard knelt beside someone who was shot, prayed, and was moments later shot himself and "then finished off with a single shot in the head" (Dempsey 1984, 159). Another account of the two Fathers' massacre (Bernad 1927, 753–63) states that an old chief, La Victoire, had begged Father Fafard to flee before the violence broke out and that he refused. During the fighting La Victoire lost his own son too. "Father Marchand, who had been looking at the scene in terror ... and raised his eyes to heaven, just as an Indian shot him in the neck ... a seventeen year old Wood Cree named Mesunekwepan, who came upon the dying Marchand ... recalled.... He was still alive, breathing slowly. I said to him: 'I am very sorry but it must be God's will'" (Dempsey 1984, 159). In November 1885, Round the Sky was hung for "having finished off the already dying Father Fafard." (Stonechild and Waiser, 1997, 224). Father Félix-Adélard-Léon Fafard was born in Quebec in 1858 and died in Alberta, at Frog Lake, on April 2, 1885. He founded and was superior of the Frog Lake mission (Carrière 1977, 13).

123 As said, the other prisoner was Lucky Man, "a prominent man in Big Bear's camp. Both he and Imasees were arrested for their part in the Frog Lake affair but were released for lack of evidence.... Imasees and his followers [Ed.: who, in the end went back to Montana] were given the Rocky Boy Reservation in eastern Montana in 1916 after more than thirty years of wandering." (Dempsey 1984, 199). "It was found that at this late date, 11 years after the commission of the crime, it was impossible to obtain evidence to justify their committal for trial, and they were accordingly discharged" (Deane 1999, 25) (cf. Stonechild and Waiser 1997, 221–24).

124 Little Bear's wife was a daughter of Lucky Man and Lucky Man was locked up with him. Big Bear was sentenced to three years at the Stoney Mountain Penitentiary. After his release he lived with his daughter Earth Woman (daughter by his third wife) in Saskatchewan, and died on January 17, 1888 (Dempsey 1984, 192–98). It is not clear who are meant by "parents." With regard to the 1896 deportation, Botting (2005, 42) sums up the oral (grandchildren and great-grandchildren and friends of Big Bear, Little Bear, Bobtail, Coyote and Rocky Boy) and the written tradition by historians such as Dempsey and Dusenberry. Leonard Van Tighem's account seems to fit both oral and written tradition, quoting Little Bear as he did.

125 Carrière does not mention any Biagoutte. Father Louis Lebret was born in France in 1829 and died in Calgary in 1903. Since his arrival in Canada he

served in Ottawa, Témiscamingue, Massachusetts, Montreal, Lachine, St. Paul, Minnesota, Ottawa, New York, Winnipeg, Prince Albert. From 1895 to1903 he was superior of Fort Macleod from where he served Pincher Creek (Carrière 1977, 276–77).

126 "The Manitoba Schools Question was 'settled' by the Laurier-Greenway Compromise in 1897" (Jaenen 1968, 29). For the terms of the agreement on the Manitoba school question, see: http://victoria.tc.ca/history/etext/manitoba.school.html.

127 Bishop Paul Durieu was born in France in 1830 and died in British Columbia in 1899. In 1854 he was ordained priest by Mgr. de Mazenod, founder of the Oblate congregation. In 1890 Durieu became the first bishop of New Westminster (Carrière 1976, 326–27).

128 Father René Rémas was born in France in 1823 and died in St. Albert in 1901. He worked in numerous places, from 1883–1884 among the railroad workers around Calgary. In 1897 he went to Montreal for treatment (Carrière 1979, 119).

129 This young Blackfoot would have been Eugene Many Guns, the first Peigan to make his First Communion, Christmas 1896. Cf. the last lines of 1896 of Victor's diary.

130 Red Deer is named after the glacier-fed Red Deer River, which flows into the South Saskatchewan River. In 1894 Red Deer was incorporated as a village, in 1901 as a town and in 1913 as a city (Sanders 2003, 251–52).

131 Mother Mary Greene was a member of the Society of the Sisters, Faithful Companions of Jesus. In 1883 she and four fellow Sisters had travelled from France to what is now Saskatchewan. There they ended up in the Riel Rebellion and were for one month prisoners of Big Bear (who had been safe-keeping them). In 1885 these five sisters arrived in Calgary and laid the foundations of "what was to become the first, publicly supported, separate school district in the Northwest Territories, under the Ordinance of 1884" (Parel 1986, 3–5).

132 Father Zépirin Lizée was born in Quebec in 1856 and died in Edmonton in 1928. He served from 1885 on in St. Albert, Lac St. Anne, at the Hobbema Indian school, at Stony Plain and Winterburn and Lac St. Anne again. In 1900 he founded a Cree journal, La Croix de Sainte-Anne, and in 1905, together with Father Léon Balter, a journal, Kitcitwa miteh Atchimomasinakigamissa. From 1912 to 1928 he served at Rivière-Qui-Barre, his last post (Carrière 1979, 330).

133 The feast of the Immaculate Conception is on December 8.

134 Father Jean-Louis Le Vern was born in France in 1871 and died in 1960 in Lethbridge. He was sent to western Canada in 1900 and spent his life there at the service of the Peigan and Blood (Carrière 1977, 325–26). Father Jean-Louis Le Vern translated many religious texts in Blackfoot and was the author of a Blackfoot-French grammar, translated into English by Sister Cléophée Beaudoin, s.g.m. Cardston, Alberta, February 28, 1973 (GAC M 8521/4357). Brother Alphonse-Joseph Barreau was born in France in 1867

and died in Alberta in 1933. After having arrived in Alberta he stayed in Calgary in 1888 and Macleod "en qualité de fac-totum." He then served at the Indian school at the Blood Reserve and subsequently fifteen years at the Indian school at Blackfoot Crossing. From 1922 to 1926 he was in St. Albert and from 1926 to 1933 at the Peigan mission (Carrière 1976, 4).

135 "Father Honoré B. Allaeys was born in 1857 in Woesten, Belgium, and was ordained a priest there in 1882. He died in Butte, in 1903, after surgery for a hernia. Several years earlier he had been thrown by his horse and injured as he hurried on a sick call one night. More about him in Indian and White in the Northwest by Lawrence B. Palladino, SJ, 1894, 327" (E-mail of September 2, 2003 from Sister Dolores Brinkel, Helena, Montana).

136 "To deal with the claims in the organized Territories to the south . . . in March 1900 two new commissions were established. J.A.J. McKenna, an official of the Indian Affairs Department and a Treaty Commissioner in 1899, and Major Walker of the Half-Breed Commission of 1899, were appointed to deal with claims in Assiniboia and Alberta." (Hall 1977, 5).

137 Cf. Hall 1977, 7.

138 Carrière mentions three Fathers Perreault, Camille (1881–1962), Siméon (1867–1949) and Wilbrod (1886–1918). None of them died about 1900.

139 Thanks to Arnaud Morena, Marina Siponin and Hayo Westra for helping to decipher and translate this letter.

140 After Father Danis became ill, he went to California; he was pastor in the Plaza Church in Los Angeles (1906–1907), served at an Indian school in Fort Yna, Arizona (1907–1908), in Santa Fé where he lost an eye because of his illness, subsequently became pastor in an Albuquerque hospital, in Bacubiri in Mexico (1909–1911), in Concordia (1911–1912) and in Villa Union, Mexico (1912). After his return in Canada he served in Saskatoon, Saint-Louis, Prince Albert, Star City, Saint-Albert, North Battleford, Fish Creek, Batoche, Cold Lake, Cluny. He retired in Saint-Albert (Carrière 1976, 251).

141 "Mr. Jim Gilruth had worked on the railroad, herded sheep and taken possession of a hill north of Chief Mountain, where his parents joined him. 'Old' Dave [Gilruth] persuaded Jim to donate the bells for the catholic church in Pincher Creek when it was built. . . . The Oblate Missionaries were always welcome at this homestead; at times Mass was said in the tiny log shack." (Pincher Creek Historical Society 1974, 854).

142 Father Victor LeGoff was born in France in 1874 and died in Alberta in 1960. After his arrival in western Canada he started to study Cree from 1900–1901 in St. Albert. He taught at the minor seminary in St. Albert from 1901 to 1902. In 1902 he was in Macleod, in 1903 in Edmonton and from 1903 to 1927 he served in Lac-La-Biche. After that he worked intermittently in Saskatchewan and Alberta (Carrière 1977, 302–03).

143 Chief Johny Black Eye (or Takes the Gun in the Water or It-soyenamarkaw) married three times: with Apaxis-tor-kikniw or Maltsistaesinnie, the former wife of Bull Pen, with Kotorxpi-etapi-akew and, and with Kate Napi-akew, the widow of Jos. Smith. He had eleven children, of which

seven died in infancy (LAB, 26). John Black Eye worked as a freighter when the Catholic Boarding School in Pincher Creek was being built (GAC M1832 file 1).

144 Dr. Frank H. Mewburn graduated in Montreal and was the first surgeon in the west. He acted as assistant surgeon of the Mounted Police and was medical officer of the mining establishment (Deane 1999, 9). Dr. Mewburn M.D. FACS, OBE (1858–1929) performed the first appendectomy on the Prairies in Lethbridge in 1893, operated on the first ectopic pregnancy in 1892 and performed the first caesarean in 1903 (Lampard 2005, *Calgary Herald*, August 14, B5 and *History Now*, 2006, no. 1, 10–4).

145 Brother Victor Lalican was born in France in 1831 and died in 1902 in St. Albert. He pronounced his perpetual vows in Paris in 1864, was then sent to the Red River missions and spent, from 1870 on, 25 years in Alberta. In between he served at the missions of St. Paul des Cree, Lac la Biche, Lac St. Anne, and Hobbema (Carriére 1977, 237).

146 Father Jean-Marie Salaün was born in France in 1876 and died in Lethbridge in 1942. In 1901 he came to western Canada where he served among the Blackfoot in Gleichen from 1901 to 1902, among the Peigan from 1902 to 1904, the Blood from 1904 to 1914 and in Macleod from 1905 to 1906. During WWI he served in Europe; thereafter he came back to Alberta (Carrière 1979, 158).

147 Father Jaques Riou was born in France in 1869 and died in Calgary in 1949. He was sent to the west in 1896 and served among the Blackfoot in Cluny in 1896, among the Blood in Cardston from 1896 to 1901, at Blackfoot Crossing from 1901 to 1907 during which time he also served in Beadry, Medicine Hat and Fort MacLeod. From 1907 to 1912 he was the principal of the St. Joseph School in De Winton, lived there one more year in which he built a chapel for the Sarcee (now called Tsuu T'ina, located west of Calgary). From a photo that emerged in Belgium we know that Victor helped building this church in 1913. While serving among the Peigan he was called to arms and became an army chaplain in Montreal. The French government put him on a list of deserters, which caused him to go to Bordeaux, where he served in a military hospital. Later he came back and served again among the Blackfeet, who called him Natoye-Poharsin, "la sainte parole." The bad ones called him Imoyestoyew ("La bouche pointue") (Carrière 1979, 129–30). Father Georges Jeannotte was born in Quebec in 1885 and died in Saskatchewan in 1951 (Carriére 1977, 172).

148 Chin, 25 km west of Lethbridge, hamlet. The name refers to a butte nearby that looks like a chin (Sanders 2003, 84).

149 From 1903 to 1914 Father J.A. Fitzpatrick from Ireland was parish priest in Calgary. He succeeded Father Lacombe who had "his farewell service at Calgary's St. Mary's church on May 3, 1903" (MacGregor 1975, 324).

150 Father Lacombe had built himself a little shack which he called "Ermitage de Saint-Michel." He spent there some time in the years 1892–94 and

1903 (MacGregor 1975, 292). Letters he sent from there had as letterhead "Ermitage de Saint-Michel" (Un Soeur 1916, 399).

151 On September 24, 1900, Father Lacombe visited the Austrian emperor Franz Joseph and asked him for funds "to build chapels and priests to minister in them and to retain these people in their Ancient Faith. But the splendor, the coldness and formality of the interview numbed the man of the Plains." (Hughes 1914, 404). In 1904 Father Lacombe would visit the Emperor again, now in the company of the Archbishop of St. Boniface, "but the failed to get the monetary support they requested" (De Vocht, 2005, 62–3).

152 Father Emile Jonquet would become author of *Mgr Grandin: Oblat de Marie Immaculée, Premier Eveque de Saint-Albert*. Jonquet (1903, 439) argues that Mgr. Grandin's visit to the southwest must have been consoling to him because he could see the flourishing missions there, consecrate the first stone church in Lethbridge, that the generosity of the Belgians, Irish, Hungarians, Flemish, Scottish, Polish and Canadians was apparent and that the missionary Father Vantighem, woodworker, sculptor easily working with marble and designer, had not spared any effort. Jonquet adds that the bishop had written in his journal that twenty-seven years ago he had not thought that mass ever could have been said in the Calgary district and that he was now convinced that God had wanted him to extend and establish his Rule. Jonquet goes on to describe the Macleod and Pincher Creek missions. Actually, by the time Father Jonquet preached this retreat, his manuscript must have been about finished as it counts 323 pages and was published in the same year, in 1903, he interviewed Leonard.

153 Brother Patrick Ryan was born in Ireland in 1844 and died in Alberta in 1919. He started to work in British Columbia in 1869. In 1894 he moved to Alberta where he served at the Dunbow School, subsequently in Calgary, Macleod, and Pincher Creek and, after 1911 in Edmonton and St. Albert (Carrière 1979, 151).

154 Stirling, 30 km southeast of Lethbridge, became a village in 1901 and is "the best remaining example of the Mormon agricultural village pattern transplanted to southern Alberta from the United States" (Sanders 2003, 282).

155 Father Nicolas Coccola was born in Corsica, France, in 1854 and died in British Columbia in 1943. He served in the missions in B.C. from 1880 on and from 1881 to 1887 in Kamloops. During his time in Cranbrook he helped the Indians to secure a reserve and founded two Indian schools (Carrière 1976, 209–10). Father Coccola was also author of *They Call me Father. Memoirs of Father Nicolas Coccola*.

156 Father Wilhelm Schulte was born in Germany in 1872 and died in Alberta in 1945. In 1902 he came to western Canada, where he served in Alberta from 1902 to 1903, in Medicine Hat from 1903 to 1904, then in Saskatchewan, again in Alberta, the U.S.A and back again in Canada. He is buried in Battleford (Carrière 1979, 174–75).

157 Leonard C. Van Tighem, oldest son of adopted nephew Joseph, upon hearing this story, commented: "Father Leonard was a firebrand!" (Personal communication in May 2004).

158 The two Belgians were Léon van Haverbeke, 24 years old, farmer. He brought 200 fr. and spoke Flemish. The other one was Alphonse Vanden Berghe, 44 years old, smith. He also brought 200 fr. and spoke Flemish (Lammerant 1997, 27).

159 Father Jean-Baptiste Frigon was born in Quebec in 1871 and died in an accident in Florida in 1930. He started to serve in 1893 in Buffalo, New York, then in Texas, Brownsville, Massachusetts, New York, Montreal, Winnipeg, Minnesota and Texas. He is buried in St. Antonio, Texas (Carrière 1977, 51).

160 Brother Henri Van Tighem, born in 1885 in Meulebeke, left for western Canada in 1905, served at the Holy Family Seminary at St. Albert from 1905 to 1911, then served in Edmonton. Later he went into the Canadian army; he did not return to his congregation (Carrière 1979, 260). After the war Henri came back to Canada and married Marie-Rose Juneau, the daughter of the oldest white settler in the Rivière qui Barre area (near St. Albert). Henri built the open air Basilica and the Stations of the Cross at Lac St. Anne; also the church and missions at the Alexander Reserve (Fitzgerald 1978, 348). Henri Van Tighem was a son of Leonard's and Victor's brother Jean Marie.

161 "Hof" refers to the house and garden where Joseph once lived with his parents.

162 Father Paul Kulawy was born in Poland in 1877 and died in Auschwitz in 1941. He and his brothers Albert and Jean Kulawy studied at the minor seminary in Valkenburg, Holland. Father Kulawy came to western Canada in 1903, served in Edmonton, in Calgary from 1904 to 1906, and in numerous other places (Carrière 1977, 323–24). Father Kulawy went the last months of 1903 to Lethbridge, "a small mining town, in the south of the diocese, where R.P. Van Tighem had founded a flourishing mission." (Phillippot 1930, 344).

163 Father Joseph Dozois was born in Quebec in 1863 and died there in 1941. He served mainly in Quebec (Carrière 1976, 297).

164 Henri Grandin was born in France in 1853 and died in Paris in 1923. In 1874 he traveled to Canada with Bishop Grandin, who ordained him priest in November 1875. Father Henri became superior of the Holy Family seminary from 1875 to 1880, director of the mission at Lac St. Anne from 1880 to 1883 where he became a private professor in theology. He then became resident priest in Edmonton and pastor of the St. Joachim's church from 1883 to 1889, from where he visited Lamoureux (Lourdes, Fort Saskatchewan) in 1887. He became superior of Lac-La-Biche (1889–1897), then in Saddle Lake (1897–1903) with an interruption (1901–1902) in St. Paul. From 1905 to 1921 he was vicar of the missions and then to 1923 provincial of Alberta-Saskatchewan, residing at the St. Joachim's parish or the provincial house

in Edmonton. In 1908 he founded a juniorat in Pincher Creek that was transferred in 1910 to Edmonton and in 1917 the scholasticat in Edmonton. He is buried in Montmartre, Paris (Carrière 1977, 105–06).

165 Father Alphonse Jan was born in France in 1874 and died in Saskatchewan in 1934. In 1898 he came to western Canada, served in Calgary, Edmonton (Strathcona), British Columbia, back in Strathcona, back in B.C. and was pastor in Calgary before the Oblates were forced to abandon their posts. He ended his career as pastor of the cathedral of Prince-Albert (Carrière 1977, 169).

166 Mr. E. de Wilde was expelled from France in 1903 by the (anti-clerical) Combe law and appointed by Bishop Legal. Father De Wilde served all the towns in the Crow's Nest Pass, Blairmore, Bellevue, Hillcrest, Frank and Lille (Venini Byrne 1973, 222).

167 Ferdinand was a son of Jean Vantighem and Mathilde Linclau. "He was a clever young boy . . . his parents did not have the money to give him a good education in Belgium. . . . He finished school at 15 years and got working at the Union Bank of Canada. . . . He was a soldier in the Canadian Army from 1915–1918. . . . He came for his job to California in 1923. The Bank of America later took over. . . . He build a house in L.A." (Callens 1995).

168 Father Louis LeJeune was born in France in 1857 and died in Ontario in 1935. When in Canada, he became a professor at the University of Ottawa, founded the *Revue littéraire de l'Université d'Ottawa* (1900–1906) and published, among other, the *Dictionnaire général du Canada* (Carrière 1977, 306–07).

169 Prémontré Fathers belong to the "Order of canons founded by Saint Norbert at Prémontré [France] at the beginning of the Twelfth Century. Saint Norbert devoted his life to the revival of authentic Christianity among the people of his time. At the heart of Norbert's vision for the reform of medieval Catholicism were local churches served by religious priests striving to live together according to the 'Apostolic life' of common ideals, property, worship, and service. He envisaged a way of life that mixed elements of the monastic tradition with active priestly ministry, and so he chose the Rule of St. Augustine as the basis for community life at Prémontré" (http://www.catholicvocation.org.au/OPraem.htm).

170 The name of this village, incorporated in 1905, was spelled Tabor after the biblical Mount Tabor. In 1907 the village became incorporated as a town and was from then on spelled as Taber (Sanders 2003, 287).

171 Staffordville was in 1913 annexed to Lethbridge (http://www.ourheritage.net/index_page_stuff/Local_History_Links/sa_grid/SA_13_Mar29-Apr4.html).

172 The minimum wage was increased to $3 per day. "The mines may have begun to operate again in December of 1906 but miners had few of the protections that they had sought" (Streisel 2004, 6).

173 Father Jules Le Chevallier was born in France in 1876 and died in Saskatchewan in 1952. In 1902 he came to western Canada, served at the Blood reserve, in Gleichen from 1902 to 1906, at the Dunbow School from

1906 to 1907, again at the Blood Reserve from 1907 to 1909, at Dunbow from 1909 to 1911, in Macleod 1911 to 1912, Midnapore, St. Paul des Métis, Cold Lake. During WWI he served as a soldier in France. After his return he served again in Alberta. During his last years he was archivist of the Provincial House in Edmonton (Carriére 1977, 277).

174 Warner, 60 km southeast of Lethbridge, "originally known as Brunton Siding, when a narrow gauge railway – known as the Turkey Track Trail because of its meandering route – was constructed. It was renamed in 1906 for Alfred L. Warner, a Minneapolis land agent who encouraged Dakota farmers to resettle here.... Warner became a village in 1908" (Sanders 2002, 310).

175 Father Hercule Emard was born in 1862 in Quebec and died in 1924 in Saskatchewan. In the west he served Kenoro Saskatchewan, Winnipeg, Calgary in 1907, in Edmonton from 1907 to 1908, in Fort Macleod from 1908 to 1909, in Winnipeg from 1909 to 1911, rested with his brother and served from 1919 on in Duluth, Kenora, Lestock and Crooked Lake (Carrière 1977, 336).

176 Earlier that year, on July 21, the newly built church in Taber was blessed by Bishop Legal and dedicated to St. Augustine. In: *From Tank 77 to Taber Today* 1977, 535. Bow Island, 54 km south of Medicine Hat, became a village in 1910 and a town in 1912 (Sanders 2003, 58). These new posts are all located along the railway.

177 Mgr. Augustin Dontenwill was born in France in 1857 and died in Rome in 1931. He left his fatherland after the 1870–71 French-German war. He served in the U.S. and Canada and on September 20, 1908 he was elected superior-general of the Oblate congregation (Carrière 1976, 291–92).

178 Father Aloysius Rosenthal was born in Germany in 1878 and died in South Dakota, U.S.A. in 1955. He came to western Canada in 1905; he served in Edmonton from 1905 to 1909, was pastor of the St. Patrick Church in Lethbridge from 1909 to 1912. Until 1916 he lived in Lethbridge and from that year on he served in the U.S.A.; he is buried in Illinois (Carrière 1979, 137-38). Rosenthal's resignation as pastor in Lethbridge had to do with the troubles Leonard refers to in his letter of November 27, 1915 to the editor of the *Lethbridge Herald*. Father Conrad Meyer was born in France in 1881 and died in Saskatchewan in 1962. In 1908 he came to western Canada, served in St. Mary's in Calgary from 1908 to 1909, in Lethbridge from 1909 to 1914, from then on in Warner, Allerton, Taber, Vauxhall, Formost, Edmonton, Grosserder, Regina, Fox Vally, Revenu, de Salvador, Kerobert, Denzil, Unity and Battleford (Carrière 1979, 389).

179 Father André Dubois, Keeper of the Archives of Deschatelets, Ottawa, kindly gave permission to publish this codex (HEF 3282. L57C 3).

180 Willie English was born in 1889 in Bruges and died in 1986 in Winnipeg. In 1907 he came to Canada where he joined the Union Bank in Lethbridge. In 1914 he married Stella Burns, sister of Pat Burns, the millionaire meat-

packer (Communication with Rev. Frank Van Tighem, 2005). Willie was a brother of the famous Flemish artist Joe English who died during WWI.

181 The Reverend Father Guillaume Charlebois was born in 1864 in Quebec and died there in 1939. Father Charlebois worked at the University of Montreal; he was professor in Moral Theology from 1905 to 1906 and superior from 1906 to 1913 (Carrière 1976, 185).

182 In 1989 the Historical Society of Alberta published the *Diaries of Bishop Vital Grandin, 1875–1877*, Volume I.

183 "At once" means that Leonard started in 1892 with a flashback.

184 Leonard refers here to his first diary. So far we have not been able to locate this publication. Leonard mentioned in his first codex that he could not keep his diary for a while because he lent it to the Sisters.

185 Notre Dame des Anges was established by the Jesuits in 1625 in the St. Lawrence Valley. On a portion of the land ceded to them by the viceroy of New France, the newcomers built a modest habitation of about thirteen by seven metres, which housed a chapel dedicated to Notre-Dame-des-Anges (http://parkscanada.pch.gc.ca/lhn-nhs/qc/cartierbrebeuf/natcul/nat-cul3_E.asp).

186 Fort L'Auguste was built in 1794 by the Northwest Fur Company, next to the Hudson's Bay Company's Fort Edmonton. In 1807 the Blood Indians burned down both forts. They were rebuilt in 1808. In 1819 Fort Edmonton was re-established (http://www.gov.edmonton.ab.ca/corp_services/city_clerk/Election&Census/History/timeline.html).

187 In 1672 the Hudson's Bay Company obtained a charter from King Charles II, granting them and their successors, under the name of "The governor and Company of Adventurers trading into Hudson's Bay" the sole right of trading in all the country watered by rivers flowing into the Hudson's Bay. The charter also authorized them to build and fit out forts and to prevent any other Company from carrying on trade with the Natives in their territories, and required that they should do all in their power to promote discovery.

188 "Richard Hardisty, Chief Factor of the Hudson's Bay Company, whose wife was a sister of the Methodist Reverend John McDougall, requested Bishop Grandin to remove St. Joachim Chapel from within the Fort Enclosure" (Levasseur-Quimet 1999, 37, citing Drouin 1981, 21). MacGregor (1978, 136, 137) elaborates upon the removal of St. Joachim's and its possible connection with the zealous Methodism of the Hardistys.

189 "Malcolm Groat (1836–1912) came from Scotland to the Hudson's Bay Company's Fort Edmonton to take charge of the gardens and livestock, being a farmer by birth and inclination. When the Hudson's Bay Company sold their lands in the North West to the Canadian Government in 1867 Malcolm Groat was one of the first to take up a homestead, River Lot 2, just west of the HBC Reserve land around the Fort. He married the Chief Factor's daughter, Margaret Christie, but remained with the company until 1878 when he bought another large parcel of land to the west of his homestead giving him over 1000 acres" (present-day 121st Street to 149th

Street between the river and 111th Avenue) (http://www.edmonton.ca/comm_services/rec_facilities/ cemeteries/virtual_tour/malcolm_groat.html).

190 "Lac La Nonne (La Nun) trading post is established by the Hudson's Bay Company [1870] on Lake La Nonne at the outlet to the Athabasca River. This post is abandoned before 1894. It is noteworthy that the Metis occupied the Lac La Nonne area, fishing and raising horses, for at least twenty years before this date" (http://www.telusplanet.net/public/dgarneau/alberta4.htm).

191 "Two years later, in 1883, Macleod had a priest and a small, gratuitous school. Father L. Van Tighem, the missionary of the south, daily assumed the role of schoolmaster for about twelve children" (Hochstein 1954, 13).

192 Mr. F.X. Girard appears on a list of advertisers in *The Gazette* and other newspapers between 1882 and 1890. "Girard, F.X. M.D. Surgeon to Indians of Treaty Number Seven. Will attend to private practice" (Fort Macleod History Book Committee. 1977, 97).

193 Father Lacombe was the first principal of the Dunbow School.

194 Mr. Cyr's hotel was the property of the "Dolphus Cyr [who] managed the Alberta Hotel in Pincher Creek. Mrs. Dolphus Cyr was the granddaughter of Sir Adoplhe Basile Routhier (1838–1920), Judge and author of Canada's national song, Oh Canada. Her father was Jean Charles Routhier who came to the west during the Riel Rebellion in 1885" (Pincher Creek Historical Society 1974, 93 ff.). Mr. Remi Beauvais from Union, Oregon, travelled three months with a covered wagon up north and homesteaded near a lake that was later named after him, Beauvais Lake (ibid., 219).

195 "Mr. Timothe [Thimothée] Lebel [owner of T. Lebel & Co. Limited. General Merchants], was born in 1857 in Cacouna, Quebec . . . in 1884 loaded a cargo of goods on the old Red River carts and set out for Fort Macleod . . . opened up a small store in Pincher Creek . . . was [the] Licence Commissioner from 1904 to 1907. . . member of the town council and school trustee in 1907–1907 [and] member of the Lethbridge Lodge No 1590 of the Knights of Columbus. He and his wife both died in 1935" (Pincher Creek Historical Society 1974, 90–1, 197). Before the Lebels built the mansion they lived in a house across from their store in Main Street. Since 1983 the Allied Arts Council of Pincher Creek owns and is major tenant of the Lebel Mansion (Undated brochure, The Lebel Mansion – a Pincher Creek Landmark. A Brief History and Self-Guided Tour).

196 Father Gustave Simonin was born in France in 1869 and died in Hobbema, Alberta in 1941. In 1894 he came to western Canada and served in several places in northern Alberta; from 1908 to 1921 in Gleichen, from then on he served one or two years in Lac-La-Biche, Cut Knife and Aldina, Saskatchewan, Pincher Creek, Cold Lace, Lac St. Anne and from 1940 to 1941 again in Hobbema (Carrière 1979, 191).

197 Langdon is a hamlet 18 km east of Calgary. John or Jim Langdon (1826–1895) had a long career in building bridges, canals, flourmills and railways (Sanders 2003, 189).

198 Shepard, a hamlet one kilometre west of Calgary, is as Langdon is, named after one of the contractors of the railway (Sanders 2002, 273). Currently Aakenstad is a separate Roman Catholic School district. Aakenstad used to be known as the Aakenstadt area, a Dutch colony northeast of Strathmore under the guidance of Fr. Van Aaken who arrived there in 1908 (Barnett *et al.* 1986, 114). Cheadle, a hamlet 40 km west of Calgary, is named after Dr. Cheadle, a medical student who explored the western Canadian prairies and published *Cheadle's Journal of a Trip Across Canada, 1862–1863* (Sanders 2003, 83).

199 "In 1908 the Duff Block was built for Mr. Duff from Brooks . . . It contained a grocery store, a bake shop, a drug store and T.E. Wright Men's Wear, and all of the second floor was apartment rooms. After the prohibition years of 1916–1924 it gradually changed into a hotel with bar and café. . . . At this time [1986] it is a highly rated, first class hotel" (Barnett *et al.*, 1986, 75).

200 "The first active agitation for a church extension or home mission society for the Catholic Church in North America was begun in 1904 by an article of the present writer, published in the *American Ecclesiastical Review* (Philadelphia)" (http://www.newadvent.org/cathen/14078a.htm).

201 Newspaper clipping, n.d., no name, in VFAC.

202 Father Damase Dubois was born in Quebec in 1863 and died in St. Albert, Manitoba in 1949. He came to western Canada in 1896. He served in De Winton, in Calgary, at the Hobbema reserve, in Calgary again and from 1905 to 1916 in Okotoks (where nephew Joseph lived before he married). After 1916, replaced by a secular priest, he served in Strathcona, Dunbow, Saint-Paul, Cold Lake, Leduc, etc. (Carriére 1977, 304). The newspaper misspelled the name; there was a Father Rioux, O.M.I., but he served all his life in Saskatchewan and Manitoba; however, it was Father J. Riou who assisted with the wedding.

203 Acme, 63 km northeast of Calgary, became a village in 1910. Acme is a Greek word, meaning "highest point" (Sanders 2003, 26). Irricana, 42 km northeast of Calgary, became a village in 1911. The name is an amalgam of "irrigation" and "canal" (Sanders 2003, 174).

204 Bassano, about 125 km east-southeast of Calgary, is named after one of the shareholders of the Canadian Pacific Railway, Napoléon Maret, Marques de Bassano (Sanders 2003, 41).

205 On November 12, 1912, Pope Pius X separated the diocese of St. Albert from the ecclesiastical province of St. Boniface by Apostolic Constitutium "Aeternam Humani generis," and formed the new ecclesiastical province of Edmonton. This caused the Oblates to be replaced, over time, by secular priests.... On 1 June, 1913, Right Rev. John Thomas MacNally, D.D., ordained on 4 April, 1896, parish priest of Almonte, Lanark, Ontario, in the

Diocese of Ottawa, was consecrated at Rome, first Bishop of Calgary (www. newadvent.org/cathen/16034a.htm).

206 Father Camille Deman was born in Belgium in 1875 and died in Quebec in 1952. After he was ordained priest in 1903 he served in Belgium and came in 1911 to western Canada, to Strathmore, from where he also visited Rockyford and Carbon. During the WWI he tried to set up an asylum for Belgians along the Peace River, but did not succeed (Carrière 1976, 268–09).

207 Currently Retlaw is a ghost town, about 100 km northwest of Taber. The place was named after an official of the CPR named Walter Baker, but spelled backwards (http://www.ghosttowns.com/canada/alberta/retlaw).

208 "In 1913 Bishop Legal recorded in Taber a Catholic population of only sixty. The mines had already failed and most of the population had gone" (Rev. Father L. Van Tighem, Documentation of Fort Museum, MacLeod).

209 In 1910, John Ell, in whose hotel visiting priests had read mass, donated "corners of their adjoining properties for a formal place of worship. . . . Not surprisingly, the little building dedicated to Our Lady of the Assumption was known colloquially called by the local community as 'John Ells' church'." (Knowles 2004, 296). Coal City must have existed but somehow disappeared. Coaldale, 10 km east of Lethbridge, derives its name from the house of Elliot Torrance Galt (1850–1928), an assistant Indian commissioner for the North-West Territories and son of Sir Alexander Tilloch Galt (1817–1893) (Sanders 2002, 90). Purple Springs, 25 km. east of Taber, was around 1900 a hamlet and now, in 2004, there are only a few houses along the railway tracks. A local resident, Anne Jonkers, showing the foundation of the once one-room classroom, explained: "The area was too dry and that is why the community dwindled away. There are springs in this area and around it grow purple flowers, hence the name."

210 "On May 7th, 1915, the Lusitania, a British passenger ship on its way to New York, was torpedoed near by a German U-20 and 1198 people died, among other Alfred G. Vanderbilt" (Valken, 1985, 177).

211 The 14-year old son of Albert the Great was Leopold III (1901–1983). He was Prince of the Belgians, Count of Brabant and King of the Belgians from 1934 to 1940. During World War II he stayed in Belgium, what caused him to have to step down in 1950.

212 Joseph Desiderius De Visscher (1879–1953) served around October 8, 1916 as Adjunct Army Chaplain at the front line (Letter of June 25, 2003, by Director-General L. Vanneste, on behalf of the Minister of Home Affairs, Belgium, to Paul Callens).

213 This Joseph Van Tighem (1899–1974) was a son of Leonard's brother Jean Marie Van Tighem and Marie Mathilde Linclau.

214 Leonard transcribed this letter in his diary and added his own comment between brackets.

215 Enclosed in the envelope is a newspaper clipping that summarizes, in Dutch, the efforts of Father DeVille, who in 1916 was travelling in Belgium contacting family members from Belgians in America and Canada and who was at that time about to emigrate 300 Belgians from their war-torn country. The summary is from articles in the *Gazette van Moline*, Thursday, 12 (illegible), 1916 (VFAC).

216 Burdett is a village about 63 km west southwest of Medicine Hat. "Angela Burdett-Coutts was fabulously wealthy and generously philanthropical.... Charles Dickens dedicated a novel, Martin Chuzzlewit, to her.... The Baroness invested in North Western Coal and Navigation Company which developed coal resources in southern Alberta and in the Alberta Railway and Irrigation Company ... and [she] donated £50·to each of four Lethbridge churches" (Sanders 2003, 64–5).

217 Text on cairn in VFAC.

218 Brochure Herdenkingstentoonstelling Joseph Van Dale [Memorial Exhibition Joseph Van Dale]. Page 8–12.

219 Lepage (319) added a footnote, 92, to Bishop Grandin's letter: "At that date we had the Fathers Van Tighem and Naessens in the St. Albert Vicariaat."

220 The Bethune family had a long record of sponsoring the Van Dale schools. In 1747 Josef Van Dale's sister, Joanna, married Jan-Baptist Bethune, who, after Van Dale had established a Sunday school and started his studies, became 'inspector' (Vandekerckhove and Swijngedouw 1981, 11–2).

221 Quote from bundle C381, Acta 1885 fol. 562 Archives Diocese Bruges. Translation of this letter, from Latin to Dutch, is kindly provided by Brother Alfons of the Sint Sixtus Abbey, Westvleteren, Belgium and Father Karel Denys, CICM, Arlington, Virginia. As far as we know, while in Canada, Victor or Brother Joannes, Jan, John or Jean Berchmans always dressed as a member of the Van Dale Congregation. From the bishop's letter it is not clear whether he believed in Victor's innocence and perhaps was embarrassed or angry about the events surrounding the court case.

222 Cf: Vanlandschoot 1976, 88ff. Witte *et al.* 1993, 95 ff. Mattelaer 2002, 243ff. De Clerck et at. 1984, 16.

223 Municipal Library Kortrijk, Fonds Joseph de Bethune, Handschriften (Handwritten documents) 152.

224 This is Baron Joseph-Felix-Marie-Ghislain Bethune (1859–1920).

225 *Belgian Laces*, November 28, 1983 (Working Group Emigrations, Vlaamse Vereniging voor Familiekunde, Afdeling Antwerpen (Flemish Association for Genealogy, Antwerp), 1992).

226 Letter of May 31, 1879 by John Dennis, Deputy of the Minister of the Interior from November 14, 1878 to December 31, 1881. Cf. Carter 1993, 81–2.

227 For an overview about the railway's history see http://www.cprheritage.com/history/display1.htm.

228 This is not to argue that a more or less uniform school system would not benefit all, but to show that Belgium and the Alberta area were both strug-

gling to come up with an acceptable school system and that a school fight was just another feature that the Kingdom of Belgium and Alberta had in common.

229 "By speaking French, social barriers [in Flanders] were maintained and enforced" (Witte *et al.* 1993, 75).

230 1897 Bill of Peigan Agency to Bishop Legal for "Labor and freighting for Roman Catholic Boarding School. Peigan Reserve" (M 1832, file 1, GAC).

231 As we saw, that was not in 1878, but in 1885.

232 In 1873, the Philadelphia International Navigation Company, founded in 1871, and the Antwerp Société Anomyme de Navigation Belgo-Américaine, founded in 1872, started to operate a line under the name of Red Star Line (http://belgium.rootsweb.com/migr/ships/redstarline.html). More about the specifics of Flemish people journeying across the ocean with this company and their arriving in Canada (Journée 2006, passim).

233 Question remains whether knowledge of French would have been of any use for "the poor fellow" in Chicago.

234 The Congregation of the Sisters of Our Lady of Mercy was founded in Warsaw, Poland by Mother Teresa Eva Potocka on November 1, 1862 (http://www.sisterfaustina.org).

235 In order to rebuilt the charity system in the aftermath of the French revolution, "the Catholic priest Canon Peter Joseph Triest reorganized the charitable works in the city of Gent (Flemish-Belgium) and founded four congregations. The Brothers of Charity was one of them, founded in 1807" (http://caritas4.tripod.com/thebrothersofcharity/id7.html).

236 Father Van Laar was born in 1841 in Maastricht, the Netherlands, and died in 1909 in Klerksdorp, South Africa. In 1876 he went to the novitiate in Lachine, worked in Massachusetts, became director of the minor seminary of the University of Ottawa and ended his career as Economist-Provincial in Pretoria and Klerksdorp (Carrière 1979, 260).

237 At the end of the 19th century buffaloes all over North America were killed – their hides were in high demand for leather conveyer belts in factories. Killing of the buffaloes forced the Indians into dependency on rations provided by the government. This and a pass system, that required people to ask the Indian Agent for permission to leave, enabled the government to keep the Indians confined to their reserves and open the country for settlers.

238 Brother John's use of the Dutch word "wilden," which word is translated as "savages," was commonplace at his time. One explanation is that terminology such as "poor" and "savage" served to justify the white people's quest for the "savages" soul and soil.

239 In 1837 Frederic Baraga noted that when Indians are offered a chair, "they will accept it and sit down, but soon afterwards they give it up in order to sit on the floor" (MacDonald 2004, 88).

240 At this time, Victor did not yet know the word prairie and must have experienced every elevation of the road as a mountain.

241 The Indians often set these fires because later grass would grow abundantly in the burned area, making it attractive for wildlife, subsequently making the area attractive for the hunt. A certain Scalp Roller told Agent R.N. Wilson: "I was told they [the Blackfoot] got the name from walking on the ground [after] a prairie fire" (Wilson Papers, Vol. II, 336, M 4421, GAC). Cf. a very different explanation by Father Lacombe in Une Soeur (1916, 405–06).

242 "Between 1883 and 1887 Bishop Emil Legal was school inspector for the area from a base at Stand Off" (Fort Macleod 1977, 12).

243 "In 1886 Miss Marie Hortense Chasse of Cacouna, Quebec, ('Mr. Lebel's sweetheart') came west. Mr. Lebel met her in Lethbridge and they were married in Fort Macleod" (Pincher Creek Historical Society 1974, 91).

244 Cf. Riou (1900, 11) in a letter about the Blood Reserve, "and, the majority of the children die before the age of two or three years. What consoles us is that most of them are baptized, they are angels for heaven."

245 Two of the suns must have been reflections in ice crystals.

246 "The winter of 1886–87 was a terrible one with a heavy loss of cattle" (Fort Macleod 1977, 341).

247 Victor means 60 Fahrenheit, which is about 16 Celsius.

248 Victor must have meant that he returned on April 12.

249 Father Vantighem will have taken baths in the Banff sulphur hot springs.

250 From 1888 to 1892 Mr. A.R. Springett was Indian Agent at the Peigan Reserve.

251 "The first Beauvais school was a small log affair ... the new Beauvais school ... was built in 1910" (Pincher Creek Historical Society 1974, 223).

252 Freebairn (2001, 212) gives a splendid eyewitness account of a Peigan Sun Dance and the performances at that occasion of members of societies such as the Crazy Dogs, the Ravens, the Kit-Foxes and the Warriors.

253 Mose De Motlette LaGrandeur was born in Montreal of old aristocratic Quebec stock. His wife was Julia Livermore; they married in Grand Valley, Oregon in 1874. They had six children, including two girls. Philomene married Alfred Pelletier and Emma married Walter Cridland (Pincher Creek Historical Society 1974, 88–9). So who married to Mr. Grenier?

254 The French Flats is an area named after its first settlers, who were French and who moved north from Oregon. Among them was the LaGrandeur family, the Mongeons, and the Beauvais. At present this is the hamlet of Cowley in southern Alberta (Tucker et al., n.d., passim).

255 These falls are now known as the Lundbreck Falls. In 1902 Breckenbridge established the Crows Nest's Pass Lumber Companie with partner Peter Lund. In 1903 they formed the Breckenbridge and Lund Companie and not long later a coal mine near Cowley. The water falls nearby shares this (Lundbreck) manufactured name (Sanders 2003, 202–03).

256 It appears that the party arrived at Turtle Mountain, the mountain that crumbled partly away in a landslide in 1903, killing and burying ninety-three people; the mountainside is now known as Frank Slide.

257 This location was probably at the 10th Siding, presently the village of Blairmore. According to McGregor (1972, 150) Mr. Lee, spelled "Lie" by Victor, built a hotel at the siding.

258 The husband of Mrs. Lebel's sister died in 1889 and the sister became afterwards seriously ill. After her death the Lebels from Pincher Creek adopted the "wee baby," Marie Blanche (Pincher Creek Historical Society 1974, 91).

259 The feast of the Triumphant of the Cross is on September 14. Conversation with the Reverend Frank Van Tighem, April 8, 2005.

260 Meulebeke's major, Prudent Plettinck, was born in Tielt on April 4, 1819 and died in Meulebeke August 11, 1888. He started his career as a physician and became mayor in 1855 (Libeert 1977, passim).

261 "The Blackfoot Indians did not believe in a personal God. They looked to the sun as the source of all power, believing it was everywhere – in the mountains, lakes and rivers, birds and wild animals. They believed that Sun Power could be transferred to man" (McClintock 1923, 241).

262 Father Moîse Blais from Calgary was born in 1853 in Quebec and died there in 1917 (Carrière 1976, 99).

263 These small groups were the so-called bands or clans of extended families who used to hunt and live together.

264 "North Asee" was North Axe, also known as Apatortse-kaxakin or Stoyemistuw, who died on March 22, 1890. His wives were Awakws-akew and Akka-piks-akew. Children: Joseph, Mary, William and Louis (LAB, 17). North Axe was the son of chief (Sitting on) Eagle Tail (Dempsey 1972, 201).

265 Crowfoot, one of the signatories of Treaty Seven, not only lost all of his children and his foster son, but had been sick for a long time, and suffered from erysipelas. Father Lacombe was not the only one around at the time of Crowfoot's death. "During Crowfoot's final illness, Mr. Haynes had his tent next to the Chief's teepee, so that he could help the ailing man" (Fort Macleod 1977, 281). The funeral of Chief Crowfoot was a mix of Catholic and tribal rites. He received the last Sacraments, his merry was shot at his grave, part of his coffin was below the surface and part of it was above and a small log house was built over it for protection (Dempsey 1972, 209, 214).

266 Crowfoot's head chieftainship was taken over by his foster brother Three Bulls, who proved to be incapable of handling the responsibilities of the high office (Dempsey 1972, 215).

267 "In July 1873 – 18 Children were Baptized by Father Scollen at Peigan Mission (Crow Eagle Camp)" (Smith and English, n.d.).

268 "Upon hearing that a new parish priest had painted his church, Father Lacombe, often away on mendicant trips, said: 'What a foolish expense of money so painstakingly collected'" (Breton 1955, 129).

269 "He [Bishop Legal] established a classroom at the Peigan reserve in 1890, which was run by Father Foisy and Brother Jean, a teacher" (Fort Macleod 1977, 12).

270 Big-Weasel was Omark-apau, Joseph, who was baptized on January 28, 1899. The daughter that died might have been Mary Ann or Mary Akkaenikkiw (LAB, 61).

271 According to Eddie Big Plume, South Peigan, Browning, Montana, the name is Tokiipis, meaning Earrings (Communication on August 15, 2003).

272 LaGrandeur's place is "at the junction of the Pincher Creek and the Old Man River" (Pincher Creek Historical Society, 88).

273 The St. Charles Mission was located on the terrain north of the Oldman River that was ceded in 1909.

274 Brother Aloysius was Bruno Dejonghe, born in 1826 in Izegem, Belgium. He died in Kortrijk on February 27, 1892. From 1863 to 1892 he was general-superior of the Van Dale Congregation (Death memorial card, VFAC).

275 The agents were, respectively: Norman Thomas Macleod (1880–1881), C.E. Denny (1882–1883), W. Pocklington (1884), A.R. Springett (1888–1892), H.H. Nash (1893–1897). However, according to Victor's diary, Pocklington came back until June 1893. See Victor's remark in June 1893.

276 This was the Rev. Mr. H. Bourne who from 1884 assisted the Reverend Samuel Trivett with his work on the Blood Reserve (http://www.telus-planet.net/public/mtoll/revtriv.htm).

277 With Bourdey school, Victor must have meant to write "Boarding school." Cf.: "1890: The Residential school connected with the bqE [?] on the Peigan Reserve was first opened on this 10th day of April, 1890. It was designated the Peigan Mission Home. The boarding school was opened by Rev. T.H. Bourne, and his wife in connection with the day school for which they were receiving a grant of 300.00 per annum" (Parish History, Anglican Church Calgary Diocese Records, Special Collections Archives, University of Calgary Library, 1/15/4).

278 Brother Alphonsus was Piet Van Besien. He was born in Lapscheure in 1847 and died in Kortrijk in 1908 (VDAK).

279 "The Peigans started out in the early 1880's planting crops ... and were quite successful until a drought in 1886 started about 15 years of crop failures" (Fort Macleod 1977, 11).

280 "Jean L'Heureux was born near St. Hyacinthe, Quebec, in about 1825 and studied for the priesthood. Before completing his studies he was involved in some criminal activities and was expelled. He went west to the Montana gold fields in about 1859, and after a short period there he made a cassock and passed himself off as a priest at the Jesuit mission on Sun River. When the truth was discovered and he was caught in homosexual activities, he already had gained the friendship of many Blackfeet. He moved to their camps and drifted northward into Alberta, where he went to the

St. Albert mission. He succeeded in convincing the Oblates that he was a priest and, by the time news of his true identity came from Montana, he had been seen so often with the priests that the Indians never could be convinced he was an imposter. L'Heureux then moved to Crowfoot's camp and remained with the Indians until they settled on their reserve. During this time he performed marriages, baptized children, and performed all the rites of a priest. He also acted as interpreter and scribe for the chiefs. In about 1880 L'Heureux became interpreter for the Indian Department but was dismissed in 1891 for his continued religious work. Throughout his life he was a controversial figure, despised and distrusted by many fur traders, an asset and embarrassment to the Oblates, and received by the Blackfeet with the mixed emotions they had for crazy people. After his dismissal from his interpreter's position, he became a recluse near Pincher Creek and finally died in Lacombe Home near Calgary on March 19, 1919" (Dempsey 1972, 83n8). A report on the Dunbow School about the Fathers who served at the missions reads: "we have to add two names, the one of M. Jean L'Heureux, the great recruiter of children in the first days, and of Brother Jean Berchmans, Brother of Love, who at present seems to want to be his imitator." On page 27 this report notes about L'Heureux's recruitment method, "Jean L'Heureux entertained them [the parents] as good as he could with his songs and stories until everyone, giving in to their fatigue, wrapped themselves in blankets and fell asleep. The guide did not close his night eyes and at dawn one left the camp as quickly as possible" (O.M.I. 1910, 37). At that time, 1884, Father Lacombe was superior of the Dunbow School. In 1871 L'Heureux wrote the report, which we partly cited above, arguing the need for a police force in Blackfoot land and in 1878 he wrote, in beautiful handwriting, an English-Blackfoot dictionary.

281 Probably it was Treaty Day. By Treaty 7 the Indians ceded most of their land. Beside free education and medical care, the Blackfoot, Stoneys and Sarcee were promised $5 annually per person. These terms are still adhered to; it was $5 then and at present the descendants still get $5 annually.

282 Iron road = railroad.

283 Rev. E. Gravel, O.M.I., 1888 (Fort Macleod 1977, 61).

284 Brother Stanislas was Ernest Van Haverbeke. He was born in Kortrijk in 1858 and died there in 1931.

285 Cf.: "Ksistsikúma an. thunder, pl. ksistisikúmaiks (by the side of –ksistsikùmiks, v. paÐtsíksistsikùm)" (Uhlenbeck and Van Gulik 1934, 205).

286 "Blackfoot religion, philosophy, literature and ethics were all combined in their stories, just as was the case in Greek civilization during the time of Homer. Like the bards of Homeric Greece, the Blackfoot story-tellers relied on their memory to transmit the tales from one generation to the next. We are fortunate that the ethnologist George Bird Grinnell recorded the Blackfoot lodge tales back in 1892" (Harold E. Gray (=Long Standing Bear Chief) cited in http://www.columbia.edu/~lnp3/mydocs/indian/

blackfoot.htm). Cf.: Grinnell (1972, xii). Macdonald (2004, 172) describes how the Ojibway-Indians managed to retain oral history.

287 Brother Antonius was Charles Debosschere. He was born in Kortrijk in 1858 and died there in 1903 (VDAK).

288 This Brother Victor, according to his death memorial card, was Théophiel Van Kerschaver (1858–1926), a Van Dale Brother from 1882 on (VDAK).

289 Cf.: "Natoápsinaksin in. Bible (lit. Holy Writ) pl. natoápsinaksists" (Uhlenbeck and Van Gulik 1934, 244).

290 Eugene Many Guns or Akkaenamarkaw or Apatortse-kaxakin married Julia Lachapelle (Dunbow pupil) on February 8, 1897 (LAB, 116). Father Naessens in a letter of January 2, 1897, to the Indian Commissioner: "Many Guns wishes to marry one of the girls of our institution. The girl, nr. 039, Julia Lachapelle, half-breed and orphan, belonging to the Blood reserve.... Should not the girl be presented with a sewing machine?" (GAC M 2019, Vol. 3–4 (278)). Julia died on March 20, 1908.

291 "Jaco" was Charcoal, "whose name among the Blood Indians was Bad Young Man and Dried Meat." He had killed Medicine Pipe Stem in October 1896, "for the unsavory behavior of the latter with Charcoal's wife." A month-long manhunt followed. In November during the chase, Charcoal killed Sergeant Wilde. He was acquitted for the murder of Medicine Pipe Stem and hanged for killing Sergeant Wilde (Fort Macleod 1977, 31). "1897: Its-estap-istarpi "Parkap-anikapiw (Charcoal). The year the Blood was hanged at Macleod (buried in the Stand-off cemetery, the 16th of March, 189/ by M. Legal U.M.I. who had instructed and baptized him and was present at the hanging)" (Parkap-otokan (Bad Head) n.d. Page 11).

292 Mary Esther Potts, daughter of Jerry Potts and Kayetsipi-inikiw, married Thomas Saeskokiw (LAB, 100). According to the C.H, de la Mission St. Paul des Peiganes. Mr. Thomas' name is Joseph Thomas Under Badger.

293 Henri Potts or Emots-enaw, half-breed, Jerry Potts' son, married on May 4, 1890, with Mary Spearson. Of their nine children, seven died in infancy, childhood or just young (LAB, 119).

294 In 1897 Indian Agent Nash reported: "Indians are not at all susceptible to religious influences ... but it wasn't for lack of effort on the part of the missionaries" (Fort Macleod 1977, 12).

295 Otter Above or Spom-ammonis or Ottark-oskistkisom or Attorkan and his little son Patrick "are killed by thunder in 1897." Patrick was born March 20, 1894 (LAB, 88). According to the C.H. de St. Paul des Peiganes, Flying Above was killed by thunder.

296 "1897. A new church is built, the cost $507.50 in material, $190.75 for labor. TOTAL: $697.95. Deficit: $6.95" (Smith and English n.d.).

297 "1898: Total population Peigan Reserve 536" (Smith and English n.d.).

298 Mr. R.N. Wilson was Indian Agent from 1898 to 1903.

299 Joseph Black Eyes or Sik-apiniw or Ipisey-atsinaw or Ksixistaki-ortsim, was baptized and married Mary Akka-ikiskim-akew on February 28, 1899. He

died on May 1, 1929 (LAB, 84). Black Eyes was employed as freighter when the boarding school in Pincher Creek was built (M 1832, file 1, GAC).

300 Peter Bob, or Bob Yellow Robe, a son of Big Weasel or Omark-apaus, was baptized, one year old, in 1879 and would die in 1904 (LAB, 61). Leo Smith or Mikkirtsenaw or Onistaepoka' first wife, Api-ksixistaiak (illegible) died in 1898. Leo then married Rosa Api-ksixistaki-akew, Big-Weasel's daughter, Peter Bob's sister (LAB, 128). Henry White Dog or Side Hill (Kaestoe etsînnayiw), later married Mary Ann Aka-ess-itsitkakew in 1910 (LAB, 135). Peter Bob's wife was Rosalie Pann-orkomiakew, (Running Wolf's daughter) (LAB, 68).

301 Jimmy or Johnny English or Natos-onistaw, ex pupil Dunbow, married Emma Fox, or Natoye senopa-akew, Blood, Dunbow pupil, on July 8, 1900 (LAB, 111).

302 Rosa is not mentioned in the list of Crow Eagle children. LAB (37) lists Louisa, John, Joseph, John, Julius, Mary, Edward, James and Louis to continue with: "etc., etc."

303 Tuberculosis was raging at the time; however, according to the Bull Plume Winter Count, the children died of measles (M 4364, GAB).

304 Ben Big Plume or White Bull, ex-pupil of Dunbow, died on February 3, 1912, at the age of 28. His wife, Mary Many Robes, ex-pupil of Dunbow, died on August 11, 1908 at the age of 22 (LAB, 104). An 1897 Bill of Peigan Agency to Bishop Legal for "Labor and freighting for Roman Catholic Boarding School. Peigan Reserve." (GAC M 1832, file 1).

305 Crow Eagle, or Mahestoe-pita of Ninnapiw (Joseph Edward, 66 years, bapt. 16, buried March 26, 1901). Wives: (1) Akka etsipim. (2) Kata-asapapistato-akew. (3) Ssokk-akew" (LAB, 37).

306 Mr. Paul Butcher was Astark-ennotaw or Ninna-Saskikiniw. He died in 1930. His wives were: Akkaesscipiw, Istsitsaw, Api-ksiscistakiw and Ma-tsé-namarkaw (LAB 11).

307 Sam Potts or Natospìstow, brother of Henry and Joe Potts, married Pauline in 1898. Sam and Pauline had a son, called John Berchmans, who was baptized on August 12, 1901 and died in 1903 in the U.S. After Sam died, Pauline married Sam's brother Joe (LAB, 120). In 1903 Johnnie Smith and Commodore were arrested for assisting at a Woman's Dance. Their sentence was suspended. Jim Rides Ahead was sentenced to three years in the Manitoba Penitentiary for holding the dance (M 1832, GAB).

308 Joe Smith (Mesam-iniki-ort-Joe), prot[estant]. ex-pupil, married Kate Run among Buffalo's on June 6, 1902. After he died in 1911, Kate married Black Eyes (LAB 127).

309 From August 1901 to September 1902 Father Naessens was Director of the Oblate Junoriat [high school preparing for priesthood] in Waregem, Belgium, also called Le petit séminaire du Transvaal, but was thanked for his services by French Oblates who, escaping the anti-clerical climate of the French government, had taken over the school (Follens 1984, 28, resp.

1985, 162–63). Follens (1983, 67, 71) notes that the new director, Naessens, had told Father Mazure that he had to teach literature and that Father Peskens had to teach math and sciences. When Father Mazure asked what Naessens meant with "literature," Naessens answer had been: "Well, that is Latin, Greek, French, Flemish, History and Geography." The school's timetable was intermittently one hour recreation and one hour teaching. Both teachers rejected this timetable saying that maybe in a mission school such as Dunbow, this would do, but that in a civilized country it was done in another way. After changing the timetable three times, Naessens was "pushed aside" and eager to return back to the Dunbow School. From the spring of 1902 on education of the Waregem juniorat was in French Oblat hands, "Director Naessens was thanked for his services rendered" (Follens 1985, 163).

310 Joseph Prairie Chicken was the son of chief Big Swan. He married Marie, the daughter of chief North Axe (C. H. des St Paul des Peiganes).

311 Victor seems to hint at his trial and to the tribulations he went through before coming to Canada.

312 Brother Dominicus (1853–1911), according to his death memorial announcement "in the secular world Henri Defour," was a Van Dale Brother from 1876 on.

313 Wilson had not only been acting as an "agent"; he also volunteered as an ethnographer and was friends with George Bird Grinnell, author of Blackfoot Lodge Tales. The difference/clash between Brother John's/ Victor's objectives, saving souls and weeding out Peigan culture, and Wilson's interest in Peigan culture might have contributed to his opinion (Wilson Papers, M 4422, GAC). According to a note in the C.H. de St. Paul des Peiganes, "Wilson complained. Jean no longer does class. [Wilson] was an atheist of the 33rd degree, was rude and had no manners." The animosity between Wilson and Brother Jean (and his superiors) might have been mutual.

314 According to LAB (68) Peter Bob (Yellow Robe) died on May 23, 1904.

315 Andrew Butcher or Sarko-otsin or (illegible), Protestant ex pupil, married Sophie Cross Chief on February 15, 1905. Andrew would die on February 12, 1917 (LAB, 107).

316 J. H. Gooderham was Indian Agent from 1904 to 1907.

317 Mr. "Jougmans" was E.H. Yeomans, Indian Agent from 1908 to 1912.

318 This action of young Henri might have been a vision quest, that is being alone for a few days in an uncomfortable place without anything to eat or drink, hoping to get some strength from the spirit of an animal that would come to him in a vision and/or attempt to contact his mother.

319 In the 1907 "Report of the Royal Northwest Mounted Police," Superintendent J.O. Wilson reported: "The most serious crime occurred at the close of our year, when a half-breed named Harry Victor White, a squaw named Croppie and an indian boy name Henry Manyon were found dead . . . on October

29, 1907, near the Fifteen Mile Lake, 6 miles north of Raymond. . . . Scout Manyon identified the body of 'Croppie' [identified as Ame Tusta] and that of his brothers and also the horses, wagon and the property as that of his father. . . . The murder evidently took place on October 21" (Wilson 1907, 76–7).

320 After Julia's death Eugène Many Guns married Rosa Sesin-akwe (Grassy Water's daughter) (LAB, 116). Of the twelve children out of this marriage, number five, born in 1905, was named John Berchmans Many Guns (LAB, 111, 138).

321 A new rations house was built and one had to send the Peigan there to pick up the meat and that in this way the costs for a quarter of meat are increased (C. H. de St. Paul des Peiganes).

322 "1909: Total population of the Peigans is 471" (Smith and English, n.d.).

323 Gustaf Vantighem and Sidonie Lecluyse later had four children, Joannes, Maria, Alphonse and Joseph.

324 Charly Greer will have been James, son of Grier, Pane or Spitaw and Natsikapoy-enikiw. He was born on December 25, 1886. Charly married Julia Provost on January 2, 1911 (LAB, 99, 113).

325 According to Van Herk (2001, 85) 28,496 acres were sold. According to the C.H. de St. Paul des Peiganes, 36 half-sections north of the river were ceded and the St. Charles Mission was on this terrain. Earlier that month, on November 9, the Lacombe Home in Midnapore, where Father Lacombe was to spend his final years, was opened with a solemn "Bénédiction solon-nelle" (Une Soeur 1916, 520). The meatpacker Mr. Burns paid for the home. Apparently Victor was not invited or he did not mention it in his diary.

326 Charles Provost or Pitsistow, son of Pete Provost, married Sally Moustach on June 24, 1910 (LAB, 121).

327 Chief Running Wolf, also known as Brings-down-the-Sun, was also in-formant for McClintock's The Old North Trail. According to the C.H. de St. Paul des Peiganes, around 1878 Running Wolf helped the Fathers Scollen and Doucet with their Blackfoot-language studies.

328 On October 5, nephew Joseph, raised by Leonard, married Jane Kelly – some-how neither Leonard nor Victor mention it.

329 Joe Smith died on June 17 at the age of 30 (LAB, 127).

330 "Bishop Lanighum" was Bishop Mathias C. Lenihan, the first bishop at the Great Falls diocese from 1904 to 1930 (2003 E-mail from Sister Dolores Brinkel, Archives of Catholic diocese, Helena, Montana).

331 Browning is the administrative centre of the Blackfeet Reservation in Montana. The Holy Family Mission, located at Two Medicine River, was built on land donated by White Calf, a friend of Father Prando S.J. who established this mission school in 1890. The final construction of this school was made possible by a gift of $14,000 from the Drexel Sisters of Philadelphia (Flaherty 1984, 41).

332 (Mi. 71: 220. 2002. Box 48. Grandin Archives in Provincial Archives, Edmonton. Translated from French by Mary E.M.).

333 On May 27, 1913, Thomas J. Fleetham, Indian Agent on the Sarcee Reserve from 1912 to 1918 wrote in his Daily Journal: "Ration day to all hands. Meeting at request of Department to have a vote on Roman Catholic Church. Indians started work this afternoon" (GAC M 379).

334 Cluny is a hamlet about 75 km east of Calgary. Trader "Cluny" McPherson Stades operated an early trading post at Cluny, "a station established and named by the Canadian Pacific Railway in 1884" (Sanders 2003, 89). "In 1914 the church and the priest's house were moved at the beginning of the year to the new school site about a mile from Cluny" (Venini Byrne 1973, 50). "Church" probably refers to the church at Ouelletteville in the district of Crowfoot Creek, built in 1902 by Father Salaün (Ibid.).

335 Thanks to Brother Leon Jansen, Brocket, who kindly provided us with this brochure.

336 According to Brother Leon Jansen, Brother John Berchmans was an Oblate; anyway "Brother John signed sometimes birth certificates adding O.M.I. behind his name" (Personal communication, May 2004).

337 Viven-Kapelle was part of Sint-Kruis and it is presently part of the larger town of Bruges.

338 Brother Lucien resided in Torhout from 1937 to 1941.

339 "Joseph Van Tighem, long a resident of Strathmore, Alberta, and a member of Calgary Council, Knights of Columbus, since 1907, passed away at Holy Cross Hospital on Thursday last, May 4, 1933, after a few days' illness. Brother Van Tighem was a pioneer banker in Strathmore and was well and favorably known in banking circles throughout the west. He was the first manager of the Union Bank at this point, which he opened in 1908, retiring in 1929 to go into business for himself.

"Joe, as he was familiarly called, was a nephew of Father [Leonard] Van Tighem, one of the pioneer priests in the Lethbridge district, with whom as a youth he and William English, now manager of the Royal Bank at St. Boniface, Manitoba, came to Canada many years ago," (Newspaper clipping, no name, n.d. VTAC) "A very forceful and impressive funeral sermon was preached to a crowded church . . . there were many spiritual and floral offerings from numerous friend." (The Western Catholic Vol. 14, Nr. 19. p. 5, May 17, 1933).

340 The oldest son, Leonard C. Van Tighem, "attended Campion College in Regina and graduated in 1930 with a B.A. from the University of Manitoba. He carried on the Van Tighem Agencies after the death of his father" and was Secretary-Treasurer of Bow Valley and Highwood, enlisted in the Army in 1941 and was discharged with the rank of Mayor (Barnett et al. 1986, 554). Leonard C. was also the one who kindly provided us with his uncle's first codex (C. H. de Lethbridge).

341 Gazette van Thielt, FOO1, 18/8/1875.

342 Étienne Bonnald was born in Le Rienfort de Raudon, La Roche (France) in (?) and died in Saint-Laurent (Manitoba) in 1928. After he became a priest he served from 1872 to 1874 as teacher at the juniorat of Notre-Dame de Lumières. In 1874 he travelled to the Calgary, Blackfoot region (1874 to 1875), at the same time in Edmonton, founded the missions of Fort Cumberland, de Pukatawagan, and served in a number of places in Manitoba and Saskatchewan (Carrière 1976, 116).

343 Grandin (1989, 1) noted in his diary on January 11, 1875: "Departure of Father Dupin and Lambert. It is very cold. Brother Boone has a frozen hand, we manage to thaw it but he will suffer for some time." And, on January 13: "Brother Boone is very much better."

Blackfeet 76, 112, 322, 369, 372, 384, 388, 401–402, 406
Blackfoot 371, 402
Blackfoot Crossing 22, 129, 131, 148, 373, 377, 379, 387–388
Blackfoot missionary 102
Black Eye(s), Joseph 300, 403–404
Black Friars Chapel 221
bladder stone 99
Blairmore 154, 164, 391, 400
Blais, Father 273, 275, 276, 400
Blanchet, Father 11, 23, 129, 151–152, 154, 164, 166, 222, 302, 311–312, 371
Blanchet, Sister 23
Blankenbergh 271
Blood 76, 112, 322, 369, 372, 384, 388, 401–402, 406
Blood Reserve 12, 81, 89, 91, 100, 153, 158, 169, 274, 275, 317, 375, 376, 387, 392, 399, 401
Blood Reserve Hospital 77, 87, 89, 91, 92, 288, 302, 311, 377
boarding school 7, 86, 274–275, 292, 295, 298, 304, 388, 398, 401, 403–404. See also Dunbow School; See also St. Joseph's Industrial School
Bob, Peter 301, 307, 403–405. See also Yellow Robe, Bob
Boeckard, Mr. 138
Bonalde (Bonnald), Father 333, 339, 407
Bonini, Frank 115
Boone, Brother Jules 7, 23, 27, 31, 35, 40, 42, 50–51, 64, 79, 261, 333, 338, 340, 352, 371, 374, 377, 407, 408. later Boone, Mr.
Boone, Léon 79
Boone, mother & father 34
Bossuit, Mr. Jos 94
Bossuit, Robert 94
Boundary Line 86, 89
Bourgine 84, 381
Bourne, Mr. 283, 401
Bourveau, Father 98
bowel hemorrhaging 145
bowel inflammation 75
Bowes 89, 91–92, 286, 370, 382
Bowman, Mr. 162
Bow Island 172, 392
Bow River 21
Brandon 57, 98, 140

Brest 7, 333–334, 339, 350
British Columbia 73–74, 99, 110, 116, 374, 383, 386, 389, 391. See also B.C.
British North America Act 245
Brochard, Brother 23, 72, 89, 91–92, 379
Brocket 246, 297, 309, 311, 317, 319, 369, 377, 407
Brockville 340
bronchitis 68
Brondel, Bishop 73–74, 103, 380
Brother Cunningham 54, 272–273
Brussels 3, 28, 122, 306, 374–375
Buch, Victor 241
Bucxley's 213
buffalo(es) 10, 274, 373, 381, 398
buitenpoorter(s) 3
Bulgary 210
Burdett 229, 397
Burns, Mr. Pat 77, 392, 406
Burns, Ms. Stella 187, 392
Butcher, Andrew 307, 405
Butcher, Paul, Chief 302, 404
Butte City 85

C

Calais 222–223, 225
Callaghan, Mr. 116
Camerlynck, Rev. Deacon 321
Canadian Pacific Railway Company 379. See also CPR
Canmore 377, 379, 382, 384
Capelle, Brother 255
Cardston 377, 383, 386, 388
Carr, Jos. 194
Carufel, Mr. 193
Catholics
    Austrian Catholics 132
    Greek Catholics 96, 378
    Irish Catholics 27, 47, 64, 72, 126, 187
    Italian Catholics 64, 111, 114, 126, 187
    Slavonic Catholics 64, 65, 87, 96, 158
Champness, Mr. Fr. 145
Charlebois, Father 178, 393
Cheadle 190, 199, 395
Chicago 254, 398

France 3–4, 7, 30–31, 34, 61, 78, 81, 84, 88, 97, 121, 123–124, 127, 146, 151, 153, 160, 163, 171, 181, 205, 210, 215, 217, 219, 223, 225, 235, 271, 278, 333, 338, 346, 370–372, 374–377, 379, 381, 383–394, 407
Frank (town) 166, 391
Frank coalmines 154
Frank Slide 149, 399
Freemason(s) 6, 16, 238–239
freethinkers 4–5, 375
French Flats 267, 399
Frigon, Father Jean-Baptiste 158, 390
Frog Lake 24, 111, 385
Furne 159

G

Gabillon, Father 23
Gagnon, Father 75–76
Galt, Sir 22, 42–43, 92, 396
Galt railroad 86
Garrick, George 150
Garrick, Joe 150
Garrick, Mrs. 150
Gateau, Miss 135
Gay, Mr. 55
Gazette van Thielt, De 24, 371, 407
Geloove (Geloof) convent 59, 378
Gendreau, Père 266
General Chapter 88, 123–124, 158–159, 162, 185, 201, 210
General Council 188
Gent 29, 31, 34–35, 160, 239, 255, 375, 390
George, Brother 328
George, Wilfried 283
German(s) 64, 73, 89, 126, 187, 201–202, 210, 211, 213, 215, 220, 221, 253, 336
Germany 104, 147, 153, 202, 225, 379, 389, 392
Geuzen 28, 30, 374
Gibbons, Card. 153
Gibbs, Mr. 42
Gilmore, Clyde W. 230
Gilruth, Mr. Jim 146, 387
Gilruth bells 147
Gilruth Family 147

Girard, Doctor F.X. 182, 260, 264, 275, 287, 394
Girard family 32, 281
Gleichen 75, 189–190, 380, 388, 391, 394
Goethals 239
Goethals, Jean 27, 374
Goethals family 240
Goethals ladies 80
Gooderham, Mr. J.H. 306, 309, 405
Gorman, Bishop 136
Grandin, Bishop 7, 10–12, 24, 29–34, 37–39, 41, 48, 52, 61–62, 64, 98, 104–105, 107, 118–119, 123, 125–126, 128–129, 131, 140–141, 145, 153, 178–181, 185, 211, 235–236, 253–254, 257, 260, 261, 263, 265, 267, 273, 275–276, 278–281, 286–288, 291, 305, 371, 374, 376, 377, 381, 389–390, 393, 397
Grandin, Father 165, 169, 179, 180, 191, 213–214, 219, 364, 374, 390
Grand Orient, the 238
Grassy Lake 92, 172, 199, 201, 383
Gravel, Bishop 87
Gravel, Father 87, 102, 288, 291, 402
graveyard 62, 109, 115, 240. *See also* churchyard
Great Falls 66, 72–74, 103, 110, 113, 115, 129, 153, 171–172, 217, 219, 312–313, 317, 380, 406
Greece 219, 402
Greek priest 120, 129
Greek Rite 16, 378
Greek United Church 64
Green, Mother 120, 153
Greer, Charlie 312, 406
Grenier, Mr. 267, 399
Gretna 75
Grey Nuns 75, 87, 89, 92, 104, 122, 146, 257, 292, 294, 314, 338, 380–381. *See also* Sisters of Charity (Grey Nuns)
Grimbergen 159
Groat, Mr. Malcolm 180, 393
Gros Ventres 21, 372
Grouard, Bishop 74, 291

M

Macedonia 219
MacFarland, Mr. 117
MacFarland, Mrs. 21, 116–117, 373
MacGibbon, Major 264, 272
MacGrath, Mr. 165
Mackenzie 291
Mackenzie River 91
Mangin, Mr. & Mrs. 170
Manitoba 10, 71, 102, 106, 125, 130,
    341, 377–378, 380, 384, 386,
    395, 404, 407
  Schools Question 111, 386
Manitoba Journal, The 183
Manitoba Provincial Government
    102
Mannean, Henri 311
Mannean, Mr. 311
Many Guns 250, 295, 311, 386, 403,
    405, 406
Maple Creek 116, 377
Marchand, Father 111
Marcke 289, 293
Marialoop 51, 377
Mazenod, Bishop 7, 181, 369, 370,
    383, 386
McAdams, Mr. 116
McCormack, Mother 145
McDonald, Lisa 231
McDonald, Mr. 125
McDonald, Mrs. 125
McDonnel, Bishop 74
McKillop, Mr. 137
McLean, Archie 117
McNally, Bishop 199, 201, 213, 231
McRae, Mr. 165, 193
McRae, Mr. (Teacher) 55
measles 92–93, 108, 115, 288, 404
Medicine Hat 22, 67, 73–75, 77, 92,
    102, 107–108, 123, 127, 129,
    137, 147, 152–153, 157–158,
    167–169, 171–172, 191, 373,
    377–378, 388–389, 392, 397
Mérer, Father 12, 123–124, 165,
    180–181, 372
Methodist 116–117, 393
Métis 7, 16, 24, 126, 278, 345, 347,
    349, 377, 381–382

Meulebeke 3, 5, 7, 27, 38, 40, 51,
    53, 60–64, 79–80, 84–85, 87,
    93–94, 96, 138, 141, 158–160,
    162–163, 167, 179, 224, 253, 271,
    275, 287, 307, 311, 319, 321,
    328, 335, 355, 374–375, 377, 381,
    390, 400
Mewburn 148, 169, 230, 388
Mexican 187
Meyers, Father 199
Middle Fork 270
Midnapore 376, 377, 379, 392, 406
Milk River 89, 115, 154, 158, 174
mine 20, 22, 63, 141, 196, 399
miner's strike 96, 120, 167, 168
miners 16, 27–28, 48, 71, 85, 96–97,
    109, 120, 126, 127, 151, 168,
    378, 391
Miron 147
Missionary(s) 7, 10–11, 13, 23, 25, 29,
    31–32, 34, 36, 37, 41–43, 47,
    56, 76–77, 89, 97, 102, 104,
    106, 117, 122–123, 152, 154, 159,
    177–179, 182–183, 186, 210–211,
    236, 253, 256, 259, 262, 265,
    274, 278, 290, 292–293, 295,
    299–300, 305, 340, 343–344,
    347, 349, 369, 370, 377,
    380–382, 389, 394, 403
Miss Carman 125–126
Modest, Brother 240
monastery 28, 30, 33, 37, 199, 253,
    289, 293, 319, 323, 337–338,
    340–341, 376
Mongeon, Mr. 267
Mont-à-Leux 283
Montreal 7, 39, 48, 66, 71–73, 87, 92,
    97, 107, 115–116, 118, 122, 131,
    133–134, 146, 164, 179, 183,
    254–255, 257, 260, 270, 283,
    307, 333, 336–337, 340–341,
    379–381, 384, 386, 388, 390,
    393, 399
Morkin, Brother(s) 92, 107, 124, 132,
    148, 291, 383
Moulaert 241
Moulaert, Victor 241
Mulatto 64
Murray, John 93, 373

S

W

Y

Legacies Shared Series

Janice Dickin, series editor
ISSN 1498-2358

THE LEGACIES SHARED series preserves the many personal histories and experiences of pioneer and immigrant life that may have disappeared or have been overlooked. The purpose of this series is to create, save, and publish voices from the heartland of the continent that might otherwise be lost to the public discourse. The manuscripts may take the form of memoirs, letters, photographs, art work, recipes or maps, works of fiction or poetry, archival documents, even oral history.

❖

❖